THE WORLD'S GREAT CLASSICS

LIBRARY COMMITTEE

TIMOTHY DWIGHT, D.D. LL.D.
RICHARD HENRY STODDARD
ARTHUR RICHMOND MARSH, A.B.
PAUL VAN DYKE, D.D.
JULIAN HAWTHORNE

ILLUSTRATED WITH NEARLY TWO HUNDRED PHOTOGRAVURES ETCHINGS COLORED PLATES AND FULL PAGE PORTRAITS OF GREAT AUTHORS

CLARENCE COOK · ART EDITOR

THE · COLONIAL · PRESS ·
· NEW · YORK · MDCCCXCIX ·

MICHEL EYQUEM DE MONTAIGNE.
Photogravure from the original painting in the Louvre at Paris.

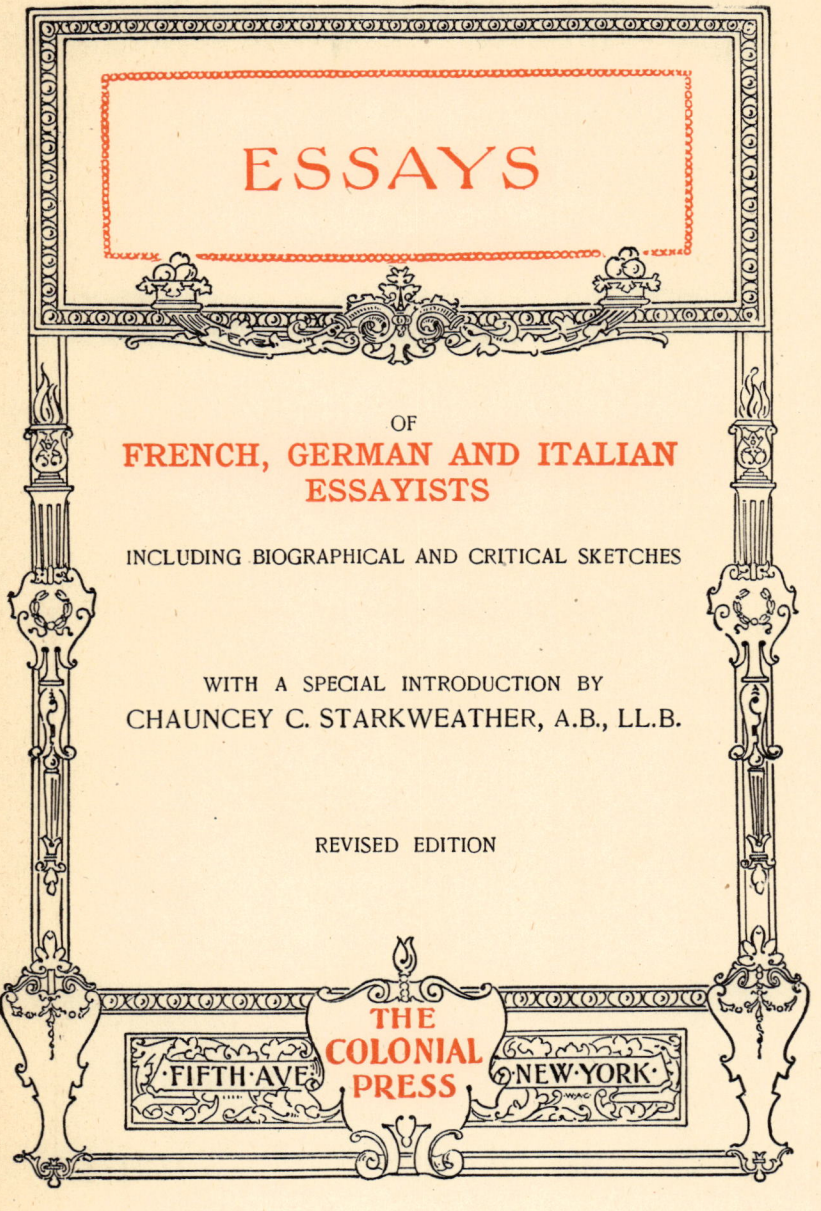

ESSAYS

OF
FRENCH, GERMAN AND ITALIAN ESSAYISTS

INCLUDING BIOGRAPHICAL AND CRITICAL SKETCHES

WITH A SPECIAL INTRODUCTION BY
CHAUNCEY C. STARKWEATHER, A.B., LL.B.

REVISED EDITION

THE COLONIAL PRESS
·FIFTH·AVE· ·NEW·YORK·

Copyright, 1900,
By THE COLONIAL PRESS.

SPECIAL INTRODUCTION

THE spirit of the French race and language lends itself naturally to the essay. Ever appreciative of style and form, ever alert with raillery and badinage, ever keen with critical acumen, there is no people with whom the essay should rather flourish. In fact, whatever kind of prose composition the Frenchman may try, it may be said that he cannot keep from essay-writing. Into the novel, the treatise, the history, the essay is interjected. The Frenchman lives in an art atmosphere; if he be not an artist he must perforce be a critic. Oftentimes he is both, for it is not disputed that one may be an artist in criticism. The plastic sense, the poetry of color and tone, is in the very air the Frenchman breathes from birth. If not creative, he must be appreciative. And does not the whole nation pride itself on its logic? If not logical, the Frenchman is nothing. And this sense of close and accurate argument and inevitable inference is the basic quality of his caustic irony, his withering sarcasm, his matchless innuendo, his smiling but inexorable *reductio ad absurdum*. It is quite natural, then, that the father of the modern essay should have been a Frenchman. To speak of the great Montaigne with any degree of adequacy a volume would be required. We can only note a few of his characteristics, and briefly hint at his influence on the world of letters. The unity of his desultoriness lies in the spirit and treatment, and, again, in that he is always concerned in the portrayal or discussion of the nature of man. He will always remain popular because he is so human. Theoretically a radical, he was satisfied to let things rest pretty much as they were. He did not preach a great reform, but inculcated a cheerful and grateful resignation to the asperites of life and the irresistibleness of death. He taught the dignity of good-sense. In his grand confessional the loquacious egotist talks about himself, and the world has not yet tired of listening. What a revelation was his good-natured gossip, what a charm of carefully concealed art, lightly facile, playful, amiable, learned and well-bred. " What do I know? " was his motto. Posterity has answered: You knew how to be interesting. For that we have made you immortal.

To the writers of the French language his value is incalculable. In the history of the development of style his works are of the highest importance, ranging, with complete mastery, from the quizzically trivial to the height of sustained eloquence. He is easily at the head of all the French writers of his century.

When enjoying his " great picture gallery " we may exclaim with Madame de Sévigné: " Oh, what an amiable man! What good company he is! He is my old friend, but he is always new."

While we may well have an affection for Montaigne we can have only an admiration for Voltaire. Harsh have been the epithets applied to him by his own countrymen. One French critic has called him an " ape of genius, sent as the devil's missionary to man." Another, with equal politeness, describes him as " a unique man to whom hell has given all its powers." In him we miss the sweet serenity of Montaigne, and the genial amiability of character and tone. Voltaire was a " lord of irony," bitter and caustic. His imprisonment in the Bastile and his exile did not sweeten his temper, nor did the burning of some of his books by the public executioner. And yet he was the most complete representative of the French mind of his time. His scope was universal—a model of simplicity in his letters, and just as a literary critic, indefatigable in every field, and the acknowledged leader of public opinion. His activity was ceaseless. He was orthodox, he even built a church, but was an enemy of intolerance. He believed in God, but fought against certain abuses of the Church. In affairs of the State, and also as a literary critic, Voltaire was a conservative. His mind was a microcosm of the eighteenth century.

To French literature Rousseau brought a love of nature and a hatred of society. Quarrelling with all his friends, he quarrelled with society too. He led the great revolt of the individual. He was the " emancipator of the ego." As an attorney for the individual he framed an indictment of civilization. He was the great idealist, brooding and dreaming over the wrongs of the people. The Revolutionists were his disciples. The skins of those who ridiculed his works "went to bind the second edition." His hope was to regenerate humanity; he was the seer and prophet of popular emancipation. His "Émile" overturned the educational ideas of France. Education became less artificial and more natural. He preached the gospel of reform. Voltaire sneered at him, but the Revolution obeyed him, going too far in its frenzied zeal. But the resultant of modern reform was suggested by Rousseau, and his soul " goes marching on."

In the one hundred works of fiction written by Honoré de Balzac he showed himself to be the Shakespeare of the French novelists. Humanity is his topic, and he is an "anatomist of passion," looking upon life as a gigantic comedy. From the darkness of his novels come refulgent lessons of virtue. His satire was somewhat heavy, as he took himself too seriously to rely upon the lighter graces of wit and sprightliness. The two thousand personages in his works portray the conflict of classes between the old and the new régimes.

Victor Hugo's work illumines half a century. He was the leader of the Romantic school, a writer of limitless imagination and great will power. Were this the place in which to speak of his verse we might demonstrate that he was the greatest lyrical poet of France. His great novels were prose epics. Into these he introduced chapters which were really essays on a variety of subjects. He was one of the founders of the "Conservateur Littéraire." How interesting must have been those literary "reunions" at which he met De Vigny, Sainte-Beuve, the two Deschamps, de Musset, and Dumas, where the new ideas of the leader were promulgated.

Sainte-Beuve was the first scientific and universal critic. Year after year, in the columns of the "Constitutionnel" and the "Moniteur," he continued to attract the attention of the whole literary world. His theories of criticism were broad and sound, founded on a wide study of literature, taking account of the object which the author had in mind, and studying the writer both personally and in relation with his other works. His taste was well-nigh flawless.

The German mind has always loved cloudland. It has loved to soar in the lofty realms of philosophical and psychological speculation. Philosophers with "theories of vigor and rigor" have risen and flourished. Accurate scholarship and wide research have marked German thinkers and teachers. In poetry Goethe and Schiller attained the highest rank of creative genius, and Germany has never lacked songsters. Her novelists have had a vast influence. In science and medicine she is well at the fore. It has been said that the form of the essay was not congenial to German thought, that in German hands the essay turned out to be a treatise, rock-ribbed with scholarship and heavy with pedagogic didacticism. But while we may miss some of the more engaging characteristics of the English essay, in its best examples, we find in the German a compensating depth of feeling and sympathetic human interest and sincerity. Let us look for a moment at some of the traits of the essayists whom we here introduce. As the Thirty Years' War had retarded the growth of culture for more than a century, so the Seven Years' War gave the German literature ideas of unity and nationalization.

Western Europe was far ahead when Lessing and Wieland stepped into the breach. After Luther, Lessing was Germany's first great individuality. He taught Germany that she might have a literature of her own apart from slavish imitation and all-pervading foreign influence. He helped to create the golden age of German literature. What great names are those of three generations of German culture which must be bracketed with his! And by them all was Lessing's influence felt. From Anacreontics and war-songs and prose fables Lessing turned to criticism, amusing and instructing Berlin by conversational and witty attacks on the bad taste then prevalent. He redeemed the drama by a play constructed according to his new theories of the stage. In his famous Laocoön, opposing Winckelmann, he taught the proper limitation of the several arts of poetry, painting and sculpture. His dramatic criticisms, continued during two years at Hamburg, were of great value. He deemed the drama the highest form of poetry, attacking the false methods of the French school of tragedy and praising Sophocles and Shakespeare. He broke the bonds of the pseudo-classical. Although brilliant, caustic and destructive, he was also positive and constructive. If he attacked false theories he supplied new and true ones, in their place. He was a revolutionary force in art and criticism.

Wieland did not reject the airs and graces of the French school, but proved that they could be quite at home in good German. Intent upon amusing, he sought to attract by urbanity and a happy and polished style. He displayed a remarkable versatility. One field was not enough for him; he cultivated many. And in them all he reaped a smiling harvest. From grave to gay and back again he wandered, expounding, reviewing, creating. Although coquetting with the French influence in letters, he was mindful of the English too. His translation of Shakespeare gave great impetus to the growth of the purer and simpler English tendencies. As a critic Wieland was virtually a dictator and his opinion had all the weight of a decree. The matchless "Oberon" won all hearts, and by this epic he established his supremacy forever. In his forty-two volumes one may cull the flowers of rhetoric, one may learn of the evolution of true criticism and may gain visions of the mountain-tops of art.

Herder taught the unity of all mankind. He set forth in persuading argument the correlation of human forces, and the organic growth in literature, science and art. He emphasized the value of popular song and the worth of the poet as reflecting the life of humanity. He followed at first in the revolutionary path of the great Rousseau. He sang and preached the brotherhood of a man. He not only influenced to a great degree his famous contemporaries, but also he has left his impress on the literature and thought of succeeding generations.

Herder had two pupils, Goethe and Schiller. These names are household words. Prolific as each of these immortals was, more has been written about them than they ever wrote about anything. Wiseacres have "peeped and botanized," pedants have oracularly analyzed, critics have viewed and reviewed. It is as if one should try to put the Andes or the Himalayas under a microscope, as if one should try to catch the roar of Niagara in a phonograph. Goethe and Schiller: they stand side by side, great beacon-lights of German poesy. And not German poesy alone. They are Titans of world-genius, crowned kings of universal literature, known to every schoolboy and poet and philosopher of two continents. Safe in the heart of humanity, the ages will be their heirs. They are on the heights with **Homer** and Sophocles, Milton and Shakespeare, " like gods together," treasured by mankind.

Richter was an idyllic sentimentalist in sixty-five volumes! He was enlivened with satirical humor and had great warmth of heart, paving the way in his writing for the Romantic school.

August Wilhelm Von Schlegel was remarkable for his studies in foreign literature, for his translation of Shakespeare, and for his eminence as a critic. He appreciated the value and advocated the spread of the Greek and English influence in letters.

The great pessimist Arthur Schopenhauer was the exponent of a gloomy Buddhism. His sombre philosophy reacted upon his own life and was a part of it. How lonely and dismal he became!—viewing everybody with suspicion, the very embodiment and apostle of discouragement and despair.

The laughing, suffering, jeering, amiable, witty, caustic Heine is always a captivating study. Fond of travel, yet condemned to years upon a mattress grave, his mind was ever alert. If you are a German you will find German humor in his works; if a Frenchman, you will discover the flashes of French wit. However local his reference may be he is at the same time universal, a true cosmopolitan, a citizen of the world. It is this spirit of genuineness and universality about him which makes him appreciated in translations, always fatal to the mediocre and the banal. His haunting lyrics linger in the memory and are popular wherever German song is known.

Chauncey C. Starkweather

CHOICE EXAMPLES OF BOOK ILLUMINATION.

Fac-similes from Illuminated Manuscripts and Illustrated Books of Early Date.

THE ALMIGHTY ORDAINING THE CREATION.

Miniature from the Clermont Bible, written about 1370.

The art of miniature-painting, or illuminating manuscripts, reached its fullest perfection in the fourteenth and fifteenth centuries, in France and Italy. The French style, with its Gothic *motif*, is well illustrated in this medallion from the Clermont Bible. It possesses all the fine symmetry, rich yet sober color, and animation of the fourteenth-century Gothic artist, while it is not only strictly ecclesiastical, but devotional and theological in design. It embodies the idea that the Creator ordained the Church before the foundation of the world. The orb of the world held by the Divine figure is surmounted by a cross, and contains the outline of a church building. The four evangelists are figured in the corners of the square. The freedom of the drawing, and the arrangement of the draperies show a great advance beyond the hieratic stiffness of the Byzantine artist. The use of the two tints in the dividing lines of the picture points to the French character of the work, while the delicate insertions of gold-leaf and the elaborate tracery of the two backgrounds exhibit a perfection of skill which belongs only to the best age of illuminative art. Nothing can be more exquisitely harmonious than the color arrangement of the whole panel—one of the choicest examples of pictorial art in this department.

CONTENTS

	PAGE
MICHEL EYQUEM DE MONTAIGNE	1
Of Cruelty	3
Of Repentance	19
Of the Inconvenience of Greatness	35
Of Managing the Will	41
VOLTAIRE (FRANÇOIS-MARIE AROUET)	65
Of Ceremonies	67
On Cromwell	69
JEAN JACQUES ROUSSEAU	75
The People	77
GOTTHOLD EPHRAIM LESSING	85
Aristotle and Tragedy	87
CHRISTOPHER MARTIN WIELAND	119
Philosophy Considered as the Art of Life and Healing Art of the Soul	121
JOHANN KASPAR LAVATER	127
On the Nature of Man	129
Of the Truth of Physiognomy	135
JOHANN GOTTFRIED VON HERDER	143
Tithon and Aurora	145
JOHANN WOLFGANG VON GOETHE	161
The Vicar of Wakefield	163
FRIEDRICH VON SCHILLER	185
Upon Naïve and Sentimental Poetry	187
JEAN PAUL FRIEDRICH RICHTER	211
On Consolation	213
ARTHUR SCHOPENHAUER	217
On Authorship and Style	219
GIACOMO LEOPARDI	239
The Academy of Syllographs	241
HONORÉ DE BALZAC	245
About Catherine De Medici	247
HEINRICH HEINE	281
Don Quixote	283

CONTENTS

	PAGE
VICTOR HUGO	303
Funeral of Napoleon	305
CHARLES AUGUSTIN SAINTE-BEUVE	327
Alfred de Musset	329
Rabelais	341
Balzac	355
Montaigne	371
GIUSEPPE MAZZINI	387
Byron and Goethe	389
JOSEPH ERNEST RENAN	409
The Poetry of the Celtic Races	411
CAMILLE FLAMMARION	457
The Plurality of Inhabited Worlds	459

ILLUSTRATIONS

                                                                FACING PAGE

MICHEL EYQUEM DE MONTAIGNE . . . *Frontispiece*
    Photogravure from the original painting

THE ALMIGHTY ORDAINING THE CREATION . . . viii
    Fac-simile Illumination of the Fourteenth Century

EARLY VENETIAN PRINTING 74
    Fac-simile of a page from Appian's Roman History

THE BOEC DES GULDEN THROENS 216
    Fac-simile example of Printing and Engraving in the Fifteenth Century

EARLY VENETIAN PRINTING 280
    Fac-simile of a Page from Jenson's Bible

OF CRUELTY

OF REPENTANCE

OF THE INCONVENIENCE OF GREATNESS

OF MANAGING THE WILL

BY

MICHEL EYQUEM DE MONTAIGNE

MICHEL EYQUEM DE MONTAIGNE

1533—1592

Michel Eyquem de Montaigne was born at his paternal home of Montaigne, in Perigord, France, in 1533. His father, a somewhat eccentric nobleman, had his son instructed in Latin as the language of his every-day life and conversation, and it was no doubt partly owing to this circumstance that he subsequently developed that rare taste for the Latin poets and deep appreciation of Latin thought and culture which mark his essays, and which led Sainte-Beuve to call him the French Horace. Educated at the Collège de Guienne, at Bordeaux, under some of the most famous scholars of his time, and trained in the study of the law, Montaigne's youth and early manhood were passed in the court, the camp, and the council chamber, in a life of pleasure and adventure similar to that of most young noblemen of his day. It was during this period that Montaigne acquired that wide experience with life and deep insight into human nature that give to his essays much of their enduring value and charm.

In 1571, when thirty-eight years of age, Montaigne abruptly quitted these scenes and retired to his estates, devoting the remainder of his lift to study and literature. The death of his friend, Etienne de la Boëtie, an ardent young nobleman of his own age and similar tastes, to whom he was devotedly attached, was one of the leading reasons for this retirement, and his first care was to edit the works of his deceased friend. In the midst of the terrible scenes that followed the massacre of St. Bartholomew, Montaigne lived quietly at home in his château, having, as he himself said, "no other guard or sentinel than the stars." In 1580 he published the first two books of his "Essays." From 1581 to 1585 Montaigne held the important position of mayor of Bordeaux, and during this period he frequently acted as mediator between the contending factions. In 1588 a fifth edition of the "Essays" was published, to which Montaigne added a third book containing a smaller number of essays than the two earlier books, but of a higher order and displaying greater care. His essays entitled "Of Repentance," "Of Managing the Will," "Of the Inconvenience of Greatness," first appeared in that volume. His death occurred in 1592.

Montaigne's style reflects the Gascon origin of the man. It is fresh, racy, discursive, at times garrulous, but withal simple, direct, manly, genuine. Egotistic to a degree paralleled by no other writer in literature, Montaigne's essays give us the man himself. When the King of France met Montaigne after the publication of the first two books he told the author that he liked his essays. "Then, sire," he replied, "you will like me; I am my essays." Though Montaigne's style was influential in the development of French prose, it was his method and manner of thinking that constitute his chief contribution to literature. Prior to Montaigne the essay had no recognized place in literature, and to him more than any other writer must be given the credit of creating this most charming, useful form of literary expression. Few writers have enjoyed a greater or more distinguished following than Montaigne. Emerson said: "This book of Montaigne the world has endorsed by translating it into all tongues, and printing seventy-five editions of it in Europe; and that, too, a circulation somewhat chosen, namely among courtiers, soldiers, princes, men of the world, and men of wit and generosity."

OF CRUELTY

I FANCY virtue to be something else, and something more noble, than good nature, and the mere propension to goodness, that we are born into the world withal. Well-disposed and well-descended souls pursue, indeed, the same methods, and represent in their actions the same face that virtue itself does: but the word virtue imports something more great and active than merely for a man to suffer himself by a happy disposition, to be gently and quietly drawn to the rule of reason. He who, by a natural sweetness and facility, should despise injuries received, would, doubtless, do a very fine and laudable thing; but he who, provoked and nettled to the quick by an offence, should fortify himself with the arms of reason against the furious appetite of revenge, and, after a great conflict, master his own passion, would certainly do a great deal more. The first would do well; the latter virtuously: one action might be called goodness, and the other virtue; for, methinks, the very name of virtue presupposes difficulty and contention, and cannot be exercised without an opponent. 'Tis for this reason, perhaps, that we call God good, mighty, liberal, and just; but we do not call him virtuous, being that all His operations are natural and without endeavor.[1] It has been the opinion of many philosophers, not only Stoics, but Epicureans—(and this addition I borrow from the vulgar opinion, which is false, notwithstanding the witty conceit of Arcesilaus in answer to one, who, being reproached that many scholars went from his school to the Epicurean, but never any from thence to his school, said in answer, " I believe it indeed; numbers of capons being made out of cocks, but never any cocks out of capons." [2] For, in truth, the Epicurean sect is not at all inferior to the Stoic in steadiness, and the

---

[1] Rousseau, in his " Emile," book v., adopts this passage, almost in the same words.

[2] Diogenes Laertius, " Life of Arcesilaus," lib. iv. § 43.

rigor of opinions and precepts. And a certain Stoic, showing more honesty than those disputants, who, in order to quarrel with Epicurus, and to throw the game into their hands, make him say what he never thought, putting a wrong construction upon his words, clothing his sentences, by the strict rules of grammar, with another meaning, and a different opinion from that which they knew he entertained in his mind, and in his morals, the Stoic, I say, declared that he abandoned the Epicurean sect, upon this, among other considerations, that he thought their road too lofty and inaccessible; *Et ii qui φιληδονοι vocanturs unt φιλοκαλοι et φιλοδίκαιοι omnesque virtutes et colunt et retinent"* [3])—these philosophers say that it is not enough to have the soul seated in a good place, of a good temper, and well disposed to virtue; it is not enough to have our resolutions and our reasoning fixed above all the power of fortune, but that we are, moreover, to seek occasions wherein to put them to the proof: they would seek pain, necessity, and contempt, to contend with them and to keep the soul in breath: "*Multum sibi adjicit virtus lacessita.*" [4] 'Tis one of the reasons why Epaminondas, who was yet of a third sect,[5] refused the riches fortune presented to him by very lawful means; because, said he, "I am to contend with poverty," in which extreme he maintained himself to the last. Socrates put himself, methinks, upon a ruder trial, keeping for his exercise a confounded scolding wife; which was fighting at sharps. Metellus having, of all the Roman senators alone attempted, by the power of virtue, to withstand the violence of Saturninus, tribune of the people at Rome, who would, by all means, cause an unjust law to pass in favor of the commons, and by so doing, having incurred the capital penalties that Saturninus had established against the dissentient, entertained those who, in this extremity, led him to execution with words to this effect: That it was a thing too easy and too base to do ill; and that to do well where there was no danger was a common thing; but that to do well where there was danger was the proper office of a man of virtue.[6] These words of Metellus very clearly repre-

---

[3] "And those whom we call lovers of pleasure, being, in effect, lovers of honor and justice, cultivate and practise all the virtues."—Cicero, "Ep. Fam.," xv. 1, 19.

[4] "Virtue is much strengthened by combats."—Seneca, "Epistolæ ad Lucilium," 15.
[5] The Pythagorean.
[6] Plutarch, "Life of Marius," c. 10.

sent to us what I would make out, viz., that virtue refuses facility for a companion; and that the easy, smooth, and descending way by which the regular steps of a sweet disposition of nature are conducted is not that of a true virtue; she requires a rough and stormy passage; she will have either exotic difficulties to wrestle with, like that of Metellus, by means whereof fortune delights to interrupt the speed of her career, or internal difficulties, that the inordinate appetites and imperfections of our condition introduce to disturb her.

I am come thus far at my ease; but here it comes into my head that the soul of Socrates, the most perfect that ever came to my knowledge, should, by this rule, be of very little recommendation; for I cannot conceive in that person any the least motion of a vicious inclination: I cannot imagine there could be any difficulty or constraint in the course of his virtue: I know his reason to be so powerful and sovereign over him that she would never have suffered a vicious appetite so much as to spring in him. To a virtue so elevated as his, I have nothing to oppose. Methinks I see him march, with a victorious and triumphant pace, in pomp and at his ease, without opposition or disturbance. If virtue cannot shine bright but by the conflict of contrary appetites, shall we then say that she cannot subsist without the assistance of vice, and that it is from her that she derives her reputation and honor? What then, also, would become of that brave and generous Epicurean pleasure, which makes account that it nourishes virtue tenderly in her lap, and there makes it play and wanton, giving it for toys to play withal, shame, fevers, poverty, death, and torments? If I presuppose that a perfect virtue manifests itself in contending, in patient enduring of pain, and undergoing the uttermost extremity of the gout, without being moved in her seat; if I give her troubles and difficulty for her necessary objects: what will become of a virtue elevated to such a degree, as not only to despise pain, but, moreover, to rejoice in it, and to be tickled with the daggers of a sharp gout, such as the Epicureans have established, and of which many of them, by their actions, have given most manifest proofs? As have several others, who I find to have surpassed in effects even the very rules of their discipline; witness the younger Cato: when I see him die, and tearing out his own bowels, I am not satisfied simply to believe that he had then his soul totally exempt from all trouble and horror: I cannot think that he only maintained himself in the steadiness that the Stoical rules prescribed him; temperate, without emotion and imperturbed. There was, methinks, something in the virtue of this man too sprightly and fresh to stop there; I believe that, without doubt, he felt a pleasure and delight in so noble an action, and was more pleased in it than in any other of his life: "*Sic abiit e vita, ut causam moriendi nactum se esse gauderet.*" [7] I believe it so thoroughly that I question whether he would have been content to have been deprived of the occasion of so brave an execution; and if the goodness that made him embrace the public concern more than his own, withheld me not, I should easily fall into an opinion that he thought himself obliged to fortune for having put his virtue upon so brave a trial, and for having favored that thief [8] in treading underfoot the ancient liberty of his country. Methinks I read in this action I know not what exaltation in his soul, and an extraordinary and manly emotion of pleasure when he looked upon the generosity and height of his enterprise:

"*Deliberata morte ferocior.*" [9]

not stimulated with any hope of glory, as the popular and effeminate judgments of some have concluded (for that consideration was too mean and low to possess so generous, so haughty, and so determined a heart as his), but for the very beauty of the thing in itself, which he who had the handling of the springs discerned more clearly and in its perfection than we are able to do. Philosophy has obliged me in determining that so brave an action had been indecently placed in any other life than that of Cato; and that it only appertained to his to end so; notwithstanding, and according to reason, he commanded his son and the senators who accompanied him to take another course in their affairs: "*Catoni, quum incredibilem natura tribuisset gravitatem, eamque ipse perpetua constantia roboravisset, semperque in proposito consilio permansisset, moriendum potius, quam tyranni vultus aspiciendus, erat.*" [10] Every death

---

[7] "He quitted life, rejoicing that a reason for dying had arisen."—Cicero, "Tusc. Quæs.," i. 30.
[8] Cæsar.
[9] "Bolder because he had determined to die."—Horace, "Odes," i. 37, 29.
[10] "Nature having endued Cato with an incredible gravity, which he had also

ought to hold proportion with the life before it; we do not become others for dying. I always interpret the death by the life preceding; and if anyone tell me of a death strong and constant in appearance, annexed to a feeble life, I conclude it produced by some feeble cause, and suitable to the life before. The easiness then of this death and the facility of dying he had acquired by the vigor of his soul; shall we say that it ought to abate anything of the lustre of his virtue? And who, that has his brain never so little tinctured with the true philosophy, can be content to imagine Socrates only free from fear and passion in the accident of his prison, fetters, and condemnation? and that will not discover in him not only firmness and constancy (which was his ordinary condition), but, moreover, I know not what new satisfaction, and a frolic cheerfulness in his last words and actions? In the start he gave with the pleasure of scratching his leg when his irons were taken off, does he not discover an equal serenity and joy in his soul for being freed from past inconveniences, and at the same time to enter into the knowledge of things to come? Cato shall pardon me, if he please; his death indeed is more tragical and more lingering; but yet this is, I know not how, methinks, finer. Aristippus, to one that was lamenting this death: "The gods grant me such a one," said he.[11] A man discerns in the soul of these two great men and their imitators (for I very much doubt whether there were ever their equals) so perfect a habitude to virtue, that it was turned to a complexion. It is no longer a laborious virtue nor the precepts of reason, to maintain which the soul is so racked, but the very essence of their soul, its natural and ordinary habit; they have rendered it such by a long practice of philosophical precepts having lit upon a rich and fine nature; the vicious passions that spring in us can find no entrance into them: the force and vigor of their soul stifle and extinguish irregular desires, so soon as they begin to move.

Now, that it is not more noble, by a high and divine resolution, to hinder the birth of temptations, and to be so formed to virtue, that the very seeds of vice are rooted out, than to hinder by main force their progress; and, having suffered our-

---

fortified with a perpetual constancy, without ever flagging in his resolution, he must of necessity rather die than see the face of the tyrant."—Cicero, "De Offic.," i. 31.
[11] Diogenes Laertius, ii. 76.

selves to be surprised with the first motions of the passions, to arm ourselves and to stand firm to oppose their progress, and overcome them; and that this second effect is not also much more generous than to be simply endowed with a facile and affable nature, of itself disaffected to debauchery and vice, I do not think can be doubted; for this third and last sort of virtue seems to render a man innocent, but not virtuous; free from doing ill, but not apt enough to do well: considering also, that this condition is so near neighbor to imperfection and cowardice, that I know not very well how to separate the confines and distinguish them; the very names of goodness and innocence are, for this reason, in some sort grown into contempt. I very well know that several virtues, as chastity, sobriety, and temperance, may come to a man through personal defects. Constancy in danger, if it must be so called, the contempt of death, and patience in misfortunes, may ofttimes be found in men for want of well judging of such accidents, and not apprehending them for such as they are. Want of apprehension and stupidity sometimes counterfeit virtuous effects: as I have often seen it happen, that men have been commended for what really merited blame. An Italian lord once said this, in my presence, to the disadvantage of his own nation: that the subtlety of the Italians, and the vivacity of their conceptions were so great, and they foresaw the dangers and accidents that might befall them so far off, that it was not to be thought strange, if they were often in war, observed to provide for their safety, even before they had discovered the peril; that we French and the Spaniards, who were not so cunning, went on further, and that we must be made to see and feel the danger before we would take the alarm; but that even then we could not stick to it. But the Germans and Swiss, more heavy and thick-skulled, had not the sense to look about them, even when the blows were falling about their ears. Peradventure, he only talked so for mirth's sake; and yet it is most certain that in war raw soldiers rush into danger with more precipitancy than after they have been well cudgelled:

"*Haud ignarus . . . quantum nova gloria in armis,
Et prædulce decus, primo certamine possit.*" [12]

[12] " Not ignorant, how hope of glory excites the young soldier in the first essay of arms."—" Æneid," xi. 154.

For this reason it is that, when we judge of a particular action, we are to consider the circumstances, and the whole man by whom it is performed, before we give it a name.

To instance in myself: I have sometimes known my friends call that prudence in me, which was merely fortune; and repute that courage and patience, which was judgment and opinion; and attribute to me one title for another, sometimes to my advantage and sometimes otherwise. As to the rest, I am so far from being arrived at the first and most perfect degree of excellence, where virtue is turned into habit, that even of the second I have made no great proofs. I have not been very solicitous to curb the desires by which I have been importuned. My virtue is a virtue, or rather an innocence, casual and accidental. If I had been born of a more irregular complexion, I am afraid I should have made scurvy work; for I never observed any great stability in my soul to resist passions, if they were never so little vehement: I have not the knack of nourishing quarrels and debates in my own bosom, and, consequently, owe myself no great thanks that I am free from several vices.

"*Si vitiis mediocribus et mea paucis
Mendosa est natura, alioqui recta; velut si
Egregio inspersos reprehendas corpore nævos:*" [13]

I owe it rather to my fortune than my reason. She has caused me to be descended of a race famous for integrity and of a very good father; I know not whether or no he has infused into me part of his humors, or whether domestic examples and the good education of my infancy have insensibly assisted in the work, or, if I was otherwise born so;

"*Seu Libra, seu me Scorpius adspicit
Formidolosus, pars violentior,
Natalis horæ, seutyrannus
Hesperiæ Capricornus undæ:*" [14]

but so it is, that I have naturally a horror for most vices. The answer of Antisthenes to him who asked him, which was the best apprenticeship "to unlearn evil," seems to point at this.

---

[13] "If my nature be chargeable only with slight and few vices, and I am otherwise of rectitude, the venial faults will be no more than moles on a fair body."—Horatius, "Satires," i. 6, 65.

[14] "Whether I was born under the Balance, or under Scorpio, formidable at the natal hour, or under Capricorn, ruler of the occidental seas."—Horace, "Odes," ii. 117.

I have them in horror, I say, with a detestation so natural, and so much my own, that the same instinct and impression I brought of them with me from my nurse, I yet retain, and no temptation whatever has had the power to make me alter it. Not so much as my own discourses, which in some things lashing out of the common road might seem easily to license me to actions that my natural inclination makes me hate. I will say a prodigious thing, but I will say it however: I find myself in many things more under reputation by my manners than by my opinion, and my concupiscence less debauched than my reason. Aristippus instituted opinions so bold in favor of pleasure and riches as set all the philosophers against him: but as to his manners, Dionysius the tyrant, having presented three beautiful women before him, to take his choice, he made answer, that he would choose them all, and that Paris got himself into trouble for having preferred one before the other two: but, having taken them home to his house, he sent them back untouched. His servant finding himself overladen upon the way, with the money he carried after him, he ordered him to pour out and throw away that which troubled him. And Epicurus, whose doctrines were so irreligious and effeminate, was in his life very laborious and devout; he wrote to a friend of his that he lived only upon biscuit and water, entreating him to send him a little cheese, to lie by him against he had a mind to make a feast.[15] Must it be true, that to be a perfect good man, we must be so by an occult, natural, and universal propriety, without law, reason, or example? The debauches wherein I have been engaged, have not been, I thank God, of the worst sort, and I have condemned them in myself, for my judgment was never infected by them; on the contrary, I accuse them more severely in myself than in any other; but that is all, for, as to the rest, I oppose too little resistance and suffer myself to incline too much to the other side of the balance, excepting that I moderate them, and prevent them from mixing with other vices, which, for the most part will cling together, if a man have not a care. I have contracted and curtailed mine, to make them as single and as simple as I can:

"*Nec ultra
Errorem foveo.*"[16]

[15] Diogenes Laertius, x. 11. [16] "Not carry wrong further."—Juvenal, viii. 164.

OF CRUELTY

For as to the opinion of the Stoics, who say, "That the wise man when he works, works by all the virtues together though one be most apparent, according to the nature of the action;" and herein the similitude of a human body might serve them somewhat, for the action of anger cannot work unless all the humors assist it, though choler predominate; if they will thence draw a like consequence, that when the wicked man does wickedly, he does it by all the vices together, I do not believe it to be so, or else I understand them not, for I by effect find the contrary. These are sharp, unsubstantial subtleties, with which philosophy sometimes amuses itself. I follow some vices, but I fly others as much as a saint would do. The Peripatetics also disown this indissoluble connection; and Aristotle is of opinion that a prudent and just man may be intemperate and inconsistent. Socrates confessed to some who had discovered a certain inclination to vice in his physiognomy, that it was, in truth, his natural propension, but that he had by discipline corrected it.[17] And such as were familiar with the philosopher Stilpo said, that being born with addiction to wine and women, he had by study rendered himself very abstinent both from the one and the other.[18]

What I have in me of good, I have, quite contrary, by the chance of my birth; and hold it not either by law, precept, or any other instruction: the innocence that is in me is a simple one; little vigor and no art. Among other vices, I mortally hate cruelty, both by nature and judgment as the very extreme of all vices; nay, with so much tenderness that I cannot see a chicken's neck pulled off, without trouble, and cannot, without impatience, endure the cry of a hare in my dog's teeth, though the chase be a violent pleasure. I conceive that the example of the pleasure of the chase would be more proper; wherein though the pleasure be less, there is the higher excitement of unexpected joy; giving no time for the reason, taken by surprise, to prepare itself for the encounter, when after a long quest the beast starts up on a sudden in a place where, peradventure, we least expected it; the shock and the ardor of the shouts and cries of the hunters so strike us, that it would be hard for those who love this lesser chase, to turn their thoughts, upon the in-

[17] Cicero, "Tusc. Quæs.," iv. 17. [18] Idem, "De Fato," c. 5.

stant, another way; and the poets make Diana triumph over the torch and shafts of Cupid:

> "*Quis non malarum, quas amor curas habet,*
> *Hæc inter obliviscitur?*" [19]

To return to what I was saying before, I am tenderly compassionate of others' afflictions, and should readily cry for company, if, upon any occasion whatever, I could cry at all. Nothing tempts my tears, but tears, and not only those that are real and true, but whatever they are, feigned or painted. I do not much lament the dead, and should envy them rather; but I very much lament the dying. The savages do not so much offend me, in roasting and eating the bodies of the dead, as they do who torment and persecute the living. Nay, I cannot look so much as upon the ordinary executions of justice, how reasonable soever, with a steady eye. Someone having to give testimony of Julius Cæsar's clemency; "he was," says he, "mild in his revenges. Having compelled the pirates to yield by whom he had before been taken prisoner and put to ransom; forasmuch as he had threatened them with the cross, he indeed condemned them to it, but it was after they had been first strangled. He punished his secretary Philemon, who had attempted to poison him, with no greater severity than mere death." Without naming that Latin author,[20] who thus dares to allege as a testimony of mercy the killing only of those by whom we have been offended, it is easy to guess that he was struck with the horrid and inhuman examples of cruelty practised by the Roman tyrants.

For my part, even in justice itself, all that exceeds a simple death appears to me pure cruelty; especially in us who ought, having regard to their souls, to dismiss them in a good and calm condition; which cannot be, when we have agitated them by insufferable torments. Not long since a soldier who was a prisoner, perceiving from a tower where he was shut up that the people began to assemble to the place of execution, and that the carpenters were busy erecting a scaffold, he presently concluded that the preparation was for him; and therefore entered into a resolution to kill himself, but could find no instru-

---

[19] "Who among such delights, would not remove out of his thoughts the anxious cares of love."—Horace, "Epod.," ii. 37.
[20] Suetonius, "Life of Cæsar," c. 74.

OF CRUELTY

ment to assist him in his design except an old rusty cart-nail that fortune presented to him. With this he first gave himself two great wounds about his throat, but finding these would not do, he presently afterwards gave himself a third in the belly, where he left the nail sticking up to the head. The first of his keepers who came in found him in this condition; yet alive, but sunk down and exhausted by his wounds. To make use of time, therefore, before he should die, they made haste to read his sentence; which having done, and he hearing that he was only condemned to be beheaded, he seemed to take new courage, accepted wine which he had before refused, and thanked his judges for the unhoped-for mildness of their sentence; saying, that he had taken a resolution to despatch himself for fear of a more severe and insupportable death, having entertained an opinion, by the preparations he had seen in the place, that they were resolved to torment him with some horrible execution, and seemed to be delivered from death, in having it changed from what he apprehended.

I should advise that those examples of severity, by which 'tis designed to retain the people in their duty, might be exercised upon the dead bodies of criminals; for to see them deprived of sepulture, to see them boiled and divided into quarters, would almost work as much upon the vulgar, as the pain they make the living endure; though that in effect be little or nothing, as God himself says, " Who kill the body, and, after that, have no more that they can do; "[21] and the poets singularly dwell upon the horrors of this picture, as something worse than death:

"*Heu! reliquias semiassi regis, denudatis ossibus,
Per terram sanie delibutas fœde divexarier.*"[22]

I happened to come by one day, accidentally, at Rome, just as they were upon executing Catena, a notorious robber: he was strangled without any emotion of the spectators, but when they came to cut him in quarters the hangman gave not a blow that the people did not follow with a doleful cry and exclamation, as if everyone had lent his sense of feeling to the miserable carcass. Those inhuman excesses ought to be exercised upon the bark,

[21] Luke xii. 4.
[22] " Alas! that the half-burned remains of these kings, and their bared bones, should be shamefully dragged through the dirt."—Cicero, " Tusc. Quæs.," i. 44.

and not upon the quick. Artaxerxes, in almost a like case, moderated the severity of the ancient laws of Persia, ordaining that the nobility who had committed a fault, instead of being whipped, as they were used to be, should be stripped only and their clothes whipped for them; and that whereas they were wont to tear off their hair, they should only take off their high-crowned tiara.[23] The so devout Egyptians thought they sufficiently satisfied the divine justice by sacrificing hogs in effigy and representation; a bold invention to pay God, so essential a substance, in picture only and in show.

I live in a time wherein we abound in incredible examples of this vice, through the license of our civil wars; and we see nothing in ancient histories more extreme than what we have proof of every day, but I cannot, any the more, get used to it. I could hardly persuade myself, before I saw it with my eyes, that there could be found souls so cruel and fell, who, for the sole pleasure of murder, would commit it; would hack and lop off the limbs of others; sharpen their wits to invent unusual torments and new kinds of death, without hatred, without profit, and for no other end but only to enjoy the pleasant spectacle of the gestures and motions, the lamentable groans and cries of a man dying in anguish. For this is the utmost point to which cruelty can arrive: "*Ut homo hominem, non iratus, non timens, tantum spectaturus, occidat.*"[24] For my own part, I cannot without grief see so much as an innocent beast pursued and killed that has no defence; and from which we have received no offence at all; and that which frequently happens, that the stag we hunt, finding himself weak and out of breath, and seeing no other remedy, surrenders himself to us who pursue him, imploring mercy by his tears,

"*Questuque cruentus,
Atque imploranti similis,*"[25]

has ever been to me a very unpleasing sight; and I hardly ever take a beast alive that I do not presently turn out again. Pythagoras bought them of fishermen and fowlers to do the same:

---

[23] Plutarch, "Notable Sayings of the Ancient Kings."
[24] "That a man should kill a man without being angry, or without fear, only for the pleasure of the spectacle."—Seneca, "Epistolæ ad Lucilium," 90.
[25] "Who, bleeding, by his tears seems to crave mercy."—"Æneid," vii. 501.

OF CRUELTY

"Primoque a cæde ferarum,
Incaluisse puto maculatum sanguine ferrum." [26]

Those natures that are sanguinary toward beasts discover a natural propension to cruelty. After they had accustomed themselves at Rome to spectacles of the slaughter of animals, they proceeded to those of the slaughter of men, to the gladiators. Nature has, herself, I fear, imprinted in man a kind of instinct to inhumanity; nobody takes pleasure in seeing beasts play with and caress one another, but everyone is delighted with seeing them dismember and tear one another to pieces. And that I may not be laughed at for the sympathy I have with them, theology itself enjoins us some favor in their behalf; and considering that one and the same master has lodged us together in this palace for his service, and that they, as well as we, are of his family, it has reason to enjoin us some affection and regard to them. Pythagoras borrowed the metempsychosis from the Egyptians; but it has since been received by several nations, and particularly by our Druids:

" Morte carent animæ; semperque, priore relicta
Sede, novis domibus vivunt, habitantque receptæ." [27]

The religion of our ancient Gauls maintained that souls, being eternal, never ceased to remove and shift their places from one body to another; mixing moreover with this fancy some consideration of divine justice; for according to the deportments of the soul, while it had been in Alexander, they said that God assigned it another body to inhabit, more or less painful, and proper for its condition.

"Muta ferarum
Cogit vincla pati; truculentos ingerit ursis,
Prædonesque lupis; fallaces vulpibus addit:
Atque ubi per varios annos, per mille figuras
Egit, Lethæo purgatos flumine, tandem
Rursus ad humanæ revocat primordia formæ:" [28]

[26] "I think 'twas slaughter of wild beasts that first stained the steel of man with blood."—Ovid, "Metamorphoses," xv. 106.
[27] "Souls never die, but, having left one seat, are received into new houses."—Ovid, "Metamorphoses," xv. 158.
[28] "He made them wear the silent chains of brutes, the bloodthirsty souls he enclosed in bears; the thieves in wolves; the sly in foxes; where after having, through successive years and a thousand forms, finished these careers, purging them well in Lethe's flood, at last he replaces them in human bodies."—Claudian, "Contra Ruf.," ii. 482.

if it had been valiant, he lodged it in the body of a lion; if voluptuous, in that of a hog; if timorous, in that of a hart or hare; if malicious, in that of a fox, and so of the rest, till having purified it by this chastisement, it again entered into the body of some other man:

> "*Ipse ego, nam memini, Trojani tempore belli*
> *Panthoïdes Euphorbus eram.*" [29]

As to the relationship between us and beasts, I do not much admit of it; nor of that which several nations, and those among the most ancient and most noble, have practised, who have not only received brutes into their society and companionship, but have given them a rank infinitely above themselves, esteeming them one while familiars and favorites of the gods, and having them in more than human reverence and respect; others acknowledged no other god or divinity than they. "*Belluæ a barbaris propter beneficium consecratæ:*" [30]

> "*Crocodilon adorat*
> *Pars hæc; illa pavet saturam serpentibus ibin:*
> *Effigies sacri hic nitet aurea cercopitheci;*
> *Hic piscem fluminis, illic*
> *Oppida tota canem venerantur.*" [31]

And the very interpretation that Plutarch [32] gives to this error, which is very well conceived, is advantageous to them: for he says that it was not the cat or the ox, for example, that the Egyptians adored: but that they, in those beasts, adored some image of the divine faculties: in this, patience and utility; in that vivacity, or, as with our neighbors the Burgundians and all the Germans, impatience to see themselves shut up; by which they represented liberty, which they loved and adored above all other godlike attributes, and so of the rest. But when, among the more moderate opinions, I meet with arguments that endeavor to demonstrate the near resemblance between us and animals, how large a share they have in our greatest privileges,

---

[29] "For I myself remember that in the days of the Trojan war, I was Euphorbus, son of Pantheus."—Ovid, "Metamorphoses," xv. 160; and see Diogenes Laertius, "Life of Pythagoras."

[30] "The barbarians consecrated beasts, out of opinion of some benefit received by them."—Cicero, "De Natura Deor.," i. 36.

[31] "This place adores the crocodile; another dreads the ibis, feeder on serpents: here you may behold the statue of a monkey shining in gold: here men venerate a river fish; there whole towns worship a dog."—Juvenal, xv. 2.

[32] "On Isis and Osiris," c. 39.

and with how much probability they compare us together, truly I abate a great deal of our presumption, and willingly resign that imaginary sovereignty that is attributed to us over other creatures.

But supposing all this were not true, there is, nevertheless, a certain respect, a general duty of humanity, not only to beasts that have life and sense, but even to trees and plants. We owe justice to men, and graciousness and benignity to other creatures that are capable of it; there is a certain commerce and mutual obligation between them and us. Nor shall I be afraid to confess the tenderness of my nature so childish, that I cannot well refuse to play with my dog, when he the most unseasonably importunes me so to do. The Turks have alms and hospitals for beasts. The Romans had public care to the nourishment of geese, by whose vigilance their capital had been preserved. The Athenians made a decree that the mules and moyles which had served at the building of the temple called Hecatompedon should be free and suffered to pasture at their own choice, without hinderance.[33] The Agrigentines[34] had a common use solemnly to inter the beasts they had a kindness for, as horses of some rare quality, dogs, and useful birds, and even those that had only been kept to divert their children; and the magnificence that was ordinary with them in all other things, also particularly appeared in the sumptuosity and numbers of monuments erected to this end, and which remained in their beauty several ages after. The Egyptians[35] buried wolves, bears, crocodiles, dogs, and cats in sacred places, embalmed their bodies, and put on mourning at their death. Cimon gave an honorable sepulture to the mares with which he had three times gained the prize of the course at the Olympic Games.[36] The ancient Xantippus caused his dog to be interred on an eminence near the sea, which has ever since retained the name,[37] and Plutarch says, that he had a scruple about selling for a small profit to the slaughterer an ox that had been long in his service.[38]

[33] Plutarch, "Life of Cato the Censor," c. 3.
[34] Diogenes Siculus, xiii. 17.
[35] Idem, Ibid.
[36] Herodotus, book ii.
[37] Plutarch, ut supra.
[38] Idem, Ibid.

OF REPENTANCE

OTHERS form man; I only report him: and represent a particular one, ill-fashioned enough, and whom, if I had to model him anew, I should certainly make something else than what he is: but that's past recalling. Now, though the features of my picture alter and change, 'tis not, however, unlike: the world eternally turns round; all things therein are incessantly moving, the earth, the rocks of Caucasus, and the pyramids of Egypt, both by the public motion and their own. Even constancy itself is no other but a slower and more languishing motion. I cannot fix my object; 'tis always tottering and reeling by a natural giddiness: I take it as it is at the instant I consider it; I do not paint its being, I paint its passage; not a passing from one age to another, or, as the people say, from seven to seven years, but from day to day, from minute to minute. I must accommodate my history to the hour: I may presently change, not only by fortune, but also by intention. 'Tis a counterpart of various and changeable accidents, and of irresolute imaginations, and, as it falls out, sometimes contrary: whether it be that I am then another self, or that I take subjects by other circumstances and considerations: so it is, that I may peradventure contradict myself, but, as Demades said, I never contradict the truth. Could my soul once take footing, I would not essay but resolve: but it is always learning and making trial.

I propose a life ordinary and without lustre: 'tis all one; all moral philosophy may as well be applied to a common and private life, as to one of richer composition: every man carries the entire form of human condition. Authors communicate themselves to the people by some especial and extrinsic mark; I, the first of any, by my universal being; as Michel de Montaigne, not as a grammarian, a poet, or a lawyer. If the world find fault that I speak too much of myself, I find fault that they do not so much as think of themselves. But is it reason, that being so particular in my way of living, I should pretend to recommend myself to the public knowledge? And is it also reason that I should produce to the world, where art and handling have so much credit and authority, crude and simple effects of nature, and of a weak nature to boot? Is it not to build a wall without stone or brick, or some such thing, to write books without learning and without art? The fancies of music are carried on by art; mine by chance. I have this, at least, according to discipline, that never any man treated of a subject he better understood and knew, than I what I have undertaken, and that in this I am the most understanding man alive: secondly, that never any man penetrated farther into his matter, nor better and more distinctly sifted the parts and sequences of it, nor ever more exactly and fully arrived at the end he proposed to himself. To perfect it, I need bring nothing but fidelity to the work; and that is there, and the most pure and sincere that is anywhere to be found. I speak truth, not so much as I would, but as much as I dare; and I dare a little the more, as I grow older; for, methinks, custom allows to age more liberty of prating, and more indiscretion of talking of a man's self. That cannot fall out here, which I often see elsewhere, that the work and the artificer contradict one another: " Can a man of such sober conversation have written so foolish a book?" Or " Do so learned writings proceed from a man of so weak conversation?" He who talks at a very ordinary rate, and writes rare matter, 'tis to say that his capacity is borrowed and not his own. A learned man is not learned in all things: but a sufficient man is sufficient throughout, even to ignorance itself; here my book and I go hand in hand together. Elsewhere men may commend or censure the work, without reference to the workman; here they cannot: who touches the one, touches the other. He who shall judge of it without knowing him, will more wrong himself than me; he who does know him, gives me all the satisfaction I desire. I shall be happy beyond my desert, if I can obtain only thus much from the public approbation, as to make men of understanding perceive that I was capable of profiting by knowledge, had I had it; and that I deserved to have been assisted by a better memory.

Be pleased here to excuse what I often repeat, that I very

rarely repent, and that my conscience is satisfied with itself, not as the conscience of an angel, or that of a horse, but as the conscience of a man, always adding this clause, not one of ceremony, but a true and real submission, that I speak inquiring and doubting, purely and simply referring myself to the common and accepted beliefs for the resolution. I do not teach, I only relate.

There is no vice that is absolutely a vice which does not offend, and that a sound judgment does not accuse; for there is in it so manifest a deformity and inconvenience, that, peradventure, they are in the right who say that it is chiefly begotten by stupidity and ignorance: so hard is it to imagine that a man can know without abhorring it. Malice sucks up the greatest part of its own venom, and poisons itself.[1] Vice leaves repentance in the soul, like an ulcer in the flesh, which is always scratching and lacerating itself: for reason effaces all other grief and sorrows, but it begets that of repentance, which is so much the more grievous, by reason it springs within, as the cold and heat of fevers are more sharp than those that only strike upon the outward skin. I hold for vices (but every one according to its proportion), not only those which reason and nature condemn, but those also which the opinion of men, though false and erroneous, have made such, if authorized by law and custom.

There is likewise no virtue which does not rejoice a well-descended nature; there is a kind of, I know not what, congratulation in well-doing that gives us an inward satisfaction, and a generous boldness that accompanies a good conscience: a soul daringly vicious may, peradventure, arm itself with security, but it cannot supply itself with this complacency and satisfaction. 'Tis no little satisfaction to feel a man's self preserved from the contagion of so depraved an age, and to say to himself: "Whoever could penetrate into my soul would not there find me guilty either of the affliction or ruin of anyone, or of revenge or envy, or any offence against the public laws, or of innovation or disturbance, or failure of my word; and though the license of the time permits and teaches everyone so to do, yet have I not plundered any Frenchman's goods, or taken his money, and have lived upon what is my own, in war as well as in peace; neither have I set any man to work without paying him his

[1] Seneca, "Epistolæ ad Lucilium," 81.

hire." These testimonies of a good conscience please, and this natural rejoicing is very beneficial to us, and the only reward that we can never fail of.

To ground the recompense of virtuous actions upon the approbation of others is too uncertain and unsafe a foundation, especially in so corrupt and ignorant an age as this, wherein the good opinion of the vulgar is injurious: upon whom do you rely to show you what is recommendable? God defend me from being an honest man, according to the descriptions of honor I daily see everyone make of himself. "*Quæ fuerant vitia, mores sunt.*"[2] Some of my friends have at times schooled and scolded me with great sincerity and plainness, either of their own voluntary motion, or by me entreated to it as to an office, which to a well-composed soul surpasses not only in utility, but in kindness all other offices of friendship: I have always received them with the most open arms, both of courtesy and acknowledgment; but, to say the truth, I have often found so much false measure, both in their reproaches and praises, that I had not done much amiss, rather to have done ill, than to have done well according to their notions. We, who live private lives, not exposed to any other view than our own, ought chiefly to have settled a pattern within ourselves by which to try our actions; and according to that, sometimes to encourage and sometimes to correct ourselves. I have my laws and my judicature to judge of myself, and apply myself more to these than to any other rules: I do, indeed, restrain my actions according to others; but extend them not by any other rule than my own. You yourself only know if you are cowardly and cruel, loyal and devout: others see you not, and only guess at you by uncertain conjectures, and do not so much see your nature as your art; rely not therefore upon their opinions, but stick to your own: "*Tuo tibi judicio est utendum. . . . Virtutis et vitiorum grave ipsius conscientiæ pondus est: qua sublata, jacent omnia.*"[3]

But the saying that repentance immediately follows the sin seems not to have respect to sin in its high estate, which is lodged in us as in its own proper habitation. One may disown

---

[2] "What before were vices are now right manners."—Seneca, "Epistolæ ad Lucilium," 39.
[3] "Thou must employ thy own judgment upon thyself; great is the weight of thy own conscience in the discovery of thy own virtues and vices that, being taken away, all things are lost."—Cicero, "De Nat. Dei," iii. 35; "Tusc. Quæs.," i. 25.

and retract the vices that surprise us, and to which we are hurried by passions; but those which by a long habit are rooted in a strong and vigorous will are not subject to contradiction. Repentance is no other but a recanting of the will and an opposition to our fancies, which lead us which way they please. It makes this person disown his former virtue and continency:

> "*Quæ mens est hodie, cur eadem non puero fuit?*
> *Vel cur his animis incolumes non redeunt genæ?*"[4]

'Tis an exact life that maintains itself in due order in private. Everyone may juggle his part, and represent an honest man upon the stage: but within, and in his own bosom, where all may do as they list, where all is concealed, to be regular—there's the point. The next degree is to be so in his house, and in his ordinary actions, for which we are accountable to none, and where there is no study nor artifice. And therefore Bias, setting forth the excellent state of a private family, says: "of which [5] the master is the same within, by his own virtue and temper, that he is abroad, for fear of the laws and report of men." And it was a worthy saying of Julius Drusus,[6] to the masons who offered him, for three thousand crowns, to put his house in such a posture that his neighbors should no longer have the same inspection into it as before; "I will give you," said he, "six thousand to make it so that everybody may see into every room." 'Tis honorably recorded of Agesilaus,[7] that he used in his journeys always to take up his lodgings in temples, to the end that the people and the gods themselves might pry into his most private actions. Such a one has been a miracle to the world, in whom neither his wife nor servant has ever seen anything so much as remarkable; few men have been admired by their own domestics; no one was ever a prophet, not merely in his own house, but in his own country, says the experience of histories:[8] 'tis the same in things of naught, and in this low example the image of a greater is to be seen. In my country of Gascony they look upon it as a drollery to see me in print; the further

---

[4] "Why was I not of the same mind when I was a boy that I am now? or why do not the ruddy cheeks of my youth return to help me now?"—Horace, "Odes," iv. 10, 7.
[5] Plutarch, "Banquet of the Seven Sages."
[6] He is called so by Plutarch in his "Instructions to those who Manage State Affairs," but he was, in reality, Marcus Livius Drusus, the famous tribune, as we find in Paterculus.
[7] Plutarch, in vita, c. 5.
[8] No man is a hero to his valet-de-chambre, said Marshal Catinat.

off I am read from my own home, the better I am esteemed. I am fain to purchase printers in Guienne; elsewhere they purchase me. Upon this it is that they lay their foundation who conceal themselves present and living, to obtain a name when they are absent and dead. I had rather have a great deal less in hand, and do not expose myself to the world upon any other account than my present share; when I leave it I quit the rest. See this functionary whom the people escort in state, with wonder and applause, to his very door; he puts off the pageant with his robe, and falls so much the lower by how much he was higher exalted: in himself within, all is tumult and degraded. And though all should be regular there, it will require a vivid and well-chosen judgment to perceive it in these low and private actions; to which may be added, that order is a dull, sombre virtue. To enter a breach, conduct an embassy, govern a people, are actions of renown: to reprehend, laugh, sell, pay, love, hate, and gently and justly converse with a man's own family, and with himself; not to relax, not to give a man's self the lie is more rare and hard, and less remarkable. By which means, retired lives, whatever is said to the contrary, undergo duties of as great or greater difficulty than the others do; and private men, says Aristotle,[9] serve virtue more painfully and highly, than those in authority do: we prepare ourselves for eminent occasions, more out of glory than conscience. The shortest way to arrive at glory would be to do that for conscience which we do for glory: and the virtue of Alexander appears to me of much less vigor in his great theatre, than that of Socrates in his mean and obscure employment. I can easily conceive Socrates in the place of Alexander, but Alexander in that of Socrates, I cannot. Who shall ask the one what he can do, he will answer, " Subdue the world:" and who shall put the same question to the other, he will say, " Carry on human life conformably with its natural condition;"[10] a much more general, weighty, and legitimate science than the other.

The virtue of the soul does not consist in flying high, but in walking orderly; its grandeur does not exercise itself in grandeur, but in mediocrity. As they who judge and try us within make no great account of the lustre of our public actions,

[9] " Moral. ad Nicom.," x. 7.
[10] Montaigne added here, " To do for the world that for which he came into the world," but he afterwards erased these words from the manuscript.—Naigeon.

and see they are only streaks and rays of clear water springing from a slimy and muddy bottom: so, likewise, they who judge of us by this gallant outward appearance, in like manner conclude of our internal constitution; and cannot couple common faculties, and like their own, with the other faculties that astonish them, and are so far out of their sight. Therefore it is that we give such savage forms to demons: and who does not give Tamerlane great eyebrows, wide nostrils, a dreadful visage, and a prodigious stature, according to the imagination he has conceived by the report of his name? Had anyone formerly brought me to Erasmus, I should hardly have believed but that all was adage and apothegm he spoke to his man or his hostess. We much more aptly imagine an artisan having a call of nature, or having a wife, than a great president venerable by his port and sufficiency: we fancy that they, from their high tribunals, will not abase themselves so much as to live. As vicious souls are often incited by some foreign impulse to do well, so are virtuous souls to do ill; they are therefore to be judged by their settled state, when they are at home, whenever that may be; and, at all events, when they are nearer repose, and in their native station.

Natural inclinations are much assisted and fortified by education: but they seldom alter and overcome their institution: a thousand natures of my time have escaped toward virtue or vice, through a quite contrary discipline;

> "*Sic ubi desuetæ silvis in carcere clausæ*
> *Mansuevere feræ, et vultus posuere minaces,*
> *Atque hominem didicere pati, si torrida parvus*
> *Venit in ora cruor, redeunt rabiesque furorque,*
> *Admonitæque tument gustato sanguine fauces;*
> *Fervet, et a trepido vix abstinet ira magistro;*" [11]

these original qualities are not to be rooted out; they may be covered and concealed. The Latin tongue is as it were natural to me; I understand it better than French; but I have not been used to speak it, nor hardly to write it these forty years. Yet, upon extreme and sudden emotions which I have fallen into

---

[11] "So savage beasts, when shut up in cages, and grown unaccustomed to the woods, become tame, and lay aside their fierce looks, and submit to the rule of man; if again they taste blood, their rage and fury return, their jaws are erected by thirst of blood, and they scarcely forbear to assail their trembling masters."—Lucan, iv. 237.

twice or thrice in my life, and once, seeing my father in perfect health fall upon me in a swoon, I have always uttered my first outcries and ejaculations in Latin; nature starting up, and forcibly expressing itself, in spite of so long a discontinuation; and this example is said of many others.

They who in my time have attempted to correct the manners of the world by new opinions, reform seeming vices, but the essential vices they leave as they were, if indeed, they do not augment them; and augmentation is, therein, to be feared; we defer all other well-doing upon the account of these external reformations, of less cost and greater show, and thereby expiate cheaply, for the other natural consubstantial and intestine vices. Look a little into our experience: there is no man, if he listen to himself, who does not in himself discover a particular and governing form of his own, that jostles his education, and wrestles with the tempest of passions that are contrary to it. For my part, I seldom find myself agitated with surprises; I always find myself in my place, as heavy and unwieldy bodies do; if I am not at home, I am always near at hand, my dissipations do not transport me very far, there is nothing strange nor extreme in the case; and yet I have sound and vigorous turns.

The true condemnation, and which touches the common practice of men, is, that their very retirement itself is full of filth and corruption; the idea of their reformation composed; their repentance sick and faulty, very nearly as much as their sin. Some, either from having been linked to vice by a natural propension, or long practice, cannot see its deformity. Others (of which constitution I am) do indeed feel the weight of vice, but they counterbalance it with pleasure, or some other occasion; and suffer, and lend themselves to it, for a certain price, but viciously and basely. Yet there might, haply, be imagined so vast a disproportion of measure, where with justice the pleasure might excuse the sin, as we say of utility; not only if accidental, and out of sin, as in thefts, but the very exercise of sin, where the temptation is violent, and 'tis said, sometimes not to be overcome.

Being the other day at Armaignac, on the estate of a kinsman of mine, I there saw a country fellow who was by everyone nicknamed the thief. He thus related the story of his life; that being born a beggar, and finding that he should not be able, so as to be clear of indigence, to get his living by the sweat of his brow, he resolved to turn thief, and by means of his strength of body, had exercised this trade all the time of his youth in great security; for he ever made his harvest and vintage in other men's grounds, but a great way off, and in so great quantities, that it was not to be imagined one man could have carried away so much in one night upon his shoulders; and, moreover, was careful equally to divide and distribute the mischief he did, that the loss was of less importance to every particular man. He is now grown old, and rich for a man of his condition, thanks to his trade, which he openly confesses to everyone. And to make his peace with God, he says, that he is daily ready by good offices to make satisfaction to the successors of those he has robbed, and if he do not finish (for to do it all at once he is not able) he will then leave it in charge to his heirs to perform the rest, proportionably to the wrong he himself only knows he has done to each. By this description, true or false, this man looks upon theft as a dishonest action, and hates it, but less than poverty, and simply repents; but to the extent he has thus recompensed, he repents not. This is not that habit which incorporates us into vice, and conforms even our understanding itself to it; nor is it that impetuous whirlwind that by gusts troubles and blinds our souls and for the time precipitates us, judgment and all, into the power of vice.

I customarily do what I do thoroughly and make but one step on't; I have rarely any movement that hides itself and steals away from my reason, and that does not proceed in the matter by the consent of all my faculties, without division or intestine sedition; my judgment is to have all the blame or all the praise; and the blame it once has, it has always; for almost from my infancy it has ever been one; the same inclination, the same turn, the same force; and as to universal opinions, I fixed myself from my childhood in the place where I resolved to stick. There are some sins that are impetuous, prompt, and sudden; let us set them aside; but in these other sins so often repeated, deliberated, and contrived, whether sins of complexion or sins of profession and vocation, I cannot conceive that they should have so long been settled in the same resolution, unless the reason and conscience of him who has them, be constant to have them; and the repentance he boasts to be inspired with on a sudden, is very hard for me to imagine or form. I follow not the opinion of the Pythagorean sect, "that men take up a new soul when they repair to the images of the gods to receive their oracles," unless he mean that it must needs be extrinsic, new, and lent for the time; our own showing so little sign of purification and cleanness, fit for such an office.

They act quite contrary to the stoical precepts, who do, indeed, command us to correct the imperfections and vices we know ourselves guilty of, but forbid us therefore to disturb the repose of our souls; these make us believe that they have great grief and remorse within; but of amendment, correction, or interruption, they make nothing appear. It cannot be a cure if the malady be not wholly discharged; if repentance were laid upon the scale of the balance, it would weigh down sin. I find no quality so easy to counterfeit as devotion, if men do not conform their manners and life to the profession; its essence is abstruse and occult; the appearances easy and ostentatious.

For my own part, I may desire in general to be other than I am; I may condemn and dislike my whole form, and beg of Almighty God for an entire reformation, and that He will please to pardon my natural infirmity: but I ought not to call this repentance, methinks, no more, than the being dissatisfied that I am not an angel or Cato. My actions are regular, and conformable with what I am, and to my condition; I can do no better; and repentance does not properly touch things that are not in our power; sorrow does. I imagine an infinite number of natures more elevated and regular than mine; and yet I do not for all that improve my faculties, no more than my arm or will grows more strong and vigorous for conceiving those of another to be so. If to conceive and wish a nobler way of acting than that we have should produce a repentance of our own, we must then repent us of our most innocent actions, forasmuch as we may well suppose that in a more excellent nature they would have been carried on with greater dignity and perfection; and we would that ours were so. When I reflect upon the deportments of my youth, with that of my old age, I find that I have commonly behaved myself with equal order in both, according to what I understand: this is all that my resistance can do. I do not flatter myself; in the same circumstances I should do the same things. It is not a patch, but rather a universal tincture, with which I am stained. I know no repentance, superficial, half-way, and ceremonious; it must sting me all over before I can call it so, and must prick my bowels as deeply and universally as God sees into me.

As to business, many excellent opportunities have escaped me for want of good management; and yet my deliberations were sound enough, according to the occurrences presented to me: 'tis their way to choose always the easiest and safest course. I find that, in my former resolves, I have proceeded with discretion, according to my own rule, and according to the state of the subject proposed, and should do the same a thousand years hence in like occasions; I do not consider what it is now, but what it was then, when I deliberated on it: the force of all counsel consists in the time; occasions and things eternally shift and change. I have in my life committed some important errors, not for want of good understanding, but for want of good luck. There are secret, and not to be foreseen, parts in matters we have in hand, especially in the nature of men; mute conditions, that make no show, unknown sometimes even to the possessors themselves, that spring and start up by incidental occasions; if my prudence could not penetrate into nor foresee them, I blame it not: 'tis commissioned no further than its own limits; if the event be too hard for me, and take the side I have refused, there is no remedy; I do not blame myself, I accuse my fortune, and not my work; this cannot be called repentance.

Phocion, having given the Athenians an advice that was not followed, and the affair nevertheless succeeding contrary to his opinion, someone said to him: "Well, Phocion, art thou content that matters go so well?" "I am very well content," replied he, "that this has happened so well, but I do not repent that I counselled the other." [12] When any of my friends address themselves to me for advice, I give it candidly and clearly, without sticking, as almost all other men do, at the hazard of the thing's falling out contrary to my opin-

[12] Plutarch, "Apothegm."

ion, and that I may be reproached for my counsel; I am very indifferent as to that, for the fault will be theirs for having consulted me, and I could not refuse them that office.

I, for my own part, can rarely blame anyone but myself for my oversights and misfortunes, for indeed I seldom solicit the advice of another, if not by honor of ceremony, or excepting where I stand in need of information, special science, or as to matter of fact. But in things wherein I stand in need of nothing but judgment, other men's reasons may serve to fortify my own, but have little power to dissuade me; I hear them all with civility and patience: but to my recollection, I never made use of any but my own. With me, they are but flies and atoms, that confound and distract my will; I lay no great stress upon my opinions; but I lay as little upon those of others, and fortune rewards me accordingly: if I receive but little advice, I also give but little. I am seldom consulted, and still more seldom believed, and know no concern, either public or private, that has been mended or bettered by my advice. Even they whom fortune had in some sort tied to my direction, have more willingly suffered themselves to be governed by any other counsels than mine. And as a man who am as jealous of my repose as of my authority, I am better pleased that it should be so; in leaving me there, they humor what I profess, which is to settle and wholly contain myself within myself. I take a pleasure in being uninterested in other men's affairs, and disengaged from being their warranty, and responsible for what they do.

In all affairs that are past, be it how it will, I have very little regret; for this imagination puts me out of my pain, that they were so to fall out; they are in the great revolution of the world, and in the chain of stoical causes: your fancy cannot, by wish and imagination, move one tittle, but that the great current of things will not reverse both the past and the future.

As to the rest, I abominate that incidental repentance which old age brings along with it. He, who said of old,[13] that he was obliged to his age for having weaned him from pleasure, was of another opinion than I am; I can never think myself beholden to impotency, for any good it can do to me; "*Nec tam aversa unquam videbitur ab opere suo providentia, ut de-*

[13] Sophocles, "Cicero, De Senectute," c. 14.

bilitas inter optima inventa sit." [14] Our appetites are rare in old age; a profound satiety seizes us after the act; in this I see nothing of conscience; chagrin and weakness imprint in us a drowsy and rheumatic virtue. We must not suffer ourselves to be so wholly carried away by natural alterations, as to suffer our judgments to be imposed upon by them. Youth and pleasure have not formerly so far prevailed with me, that I did not well enough discern the face of vice in pleasure; neither does the distaste that years have brought me, so far prevail with me now, that I cannot discern pleasure in vice. Now that I am no more in my flourishing age, I judge as well of these things as if I were.[15] I, who narrowly and strictly examine it, find my reason the very same it was in my most licentious age, except, perhaps, that 'tis weaker and more decayed by being grown older; and I find that the pleasure it refuses me upon the account of my bodily health, it would no more refuse now, in consideration of the health of my soul, than at any time heretofore. I do not repute it the more valiant for not being able to combat; my temptations are so broken and mortified, that they are not worth its opposition; holding but out my hands, I repel them. Should one present the old concupiscence before it, I fear it would have less power to resist it than heretofore; I do not discern that in itself it judges anything otherwise now, than it formerly did, nor that it has acquired any new light: wherefore, if there be convalescence, 'tis an enchanted one. Miserable kind of remedy, to owe one's health to one's disease! 'Tis not that our misfortune should perform this office, but the good fortune of our judgment. I am not to be made to do anything by persecutions and afflictions, but to curse them: that is for people who cannot be roused but by a whip. My reason is much more free in prosperity, and much more distracted, and put to't to digest pains than pleasures: I see best in a clear sky; health admonishes me more cheerfully, and to better purpose, than sickness. I did all that in me lay to reform and regulate myself from pleasures, at a time when I had health and vigor to enjoy them; I should be ashamed and envious, that the misery and misfor-

---

[14] " Nor can Providence ever be seen so averse to her own work, that debility should be ranked among the best things."—Quintilian, " Instit. Orat.," v. 12.

[15] " Old though I am, for ladies' love unfit, The power of beauty I remember yet." —Chaucer.

tune of my old age should have credit over my good, healthful, sprightly, and vigorous years; and that men should estimate me, not by what I have been, but by what I have ceased to be.

In my opinion, 'tis the happy living, and not (as Antisthenes [16] said) the happy dying, in which human felicity consists. I have not made it my business to make a monstrous addition of a philosopher's tail to the head and body of a libertine; nor would I have this wretched remainder give the lie to the pleasant, sound, and long part of my life: I would present myself uniformly throughout. Were I to live my life over again, I should live it just as I have lived it; I neither complain of the past, nor do I fear the future; and if I am not much deceived, I am the same within that I am without. 'Tis one main obligation I have to my fortune, that the succession of my bodily estate has been carried on according to the natural seasons; I have seen the grass, the blossom, and the fruit; and now see the withering; happily, however, because naturally. I bear the infirmities I have the better, because they came not till I had reason to expect them, and because also they make me with greater pleasure remember that long felicity of my past life. My wisdom may have been just the same in both ages; but it was more active, and of better grace while young and sprightly, than now it is when broken, peevish, and uneasy. I repudiate, then, these casual and painful reformations. God must touch our hearts; our consciences must amend of themselves, by the aid of our reason, and not by the decay of our appetites; pleasure is, in itself, neither pale nor discolored, to be discerned by dim and decayed eyes.

We ought to love temperance for itself, and because God has commanded that and chastity; but that which we are reduced to by catarrhs, and for which I am indebted to the stone, is neither chastity nor temperance; a man cannot boast that he despises and resists pleasure, if he cannot see it, if he knows not what it is, and cannot discern its graces, its force, and most alluring beauties; I know both the one and the other, and may therefore the better say it. But, methinks, ours souls, in old age, are subject to more troublesome maladies and imperfections than in youth; I said the same when young and when I was reproached with the want of a beard; and I say so now

[16] Diogenes Laertius, vi. 5.

OF REPENTANCE

that my gray hairs give me some authority. We call the difficulty of our humors and the disrelish of present things wisdom; but, in truth, we do not so much forsake vices as we change them, and, in my opinion, for worse. Besides a foolish and feeble pride, an impertinent prating, froward and insociable humors, superstition, and a ridiculous desire of riches when we have lost the use of them, I find there more envy, injustice, and malice. Age imprints more wrinkles in the mind than it does on the face; and souls are never, or very rarely seen, that in growing old do not smell sour and musty. Man moves all together, both toward his perfection and decay. In observing the wisdom of Socrates, and many circumstances of his condemnation, I should dare to believe that he in some sort himself purposely, by collusion, contributed to it, seeing that, at the age of seventy years, he might fear to suffer the lofty motions of his mind to be cramped, and his wonted lustre obscured.[17] What strange metamorphoses do I see age every day make in many of my acquaintance! 'Tis a potent malady, and that naturally and imperceptibly steals into us; a vast provision of study and great precaution are required to evade the imperfections it loads us with, or at least, to weaken their progress. I find that, notwithstanding all my entrenchments, it gets foot by foot upon me; I make the best resistance I can, but I do not know to what at last it will reduce me. But fall out what will, I am content the world may know, when I am fallen, from what I fell.

[17] Xenophon, indeed, tells us expressly that this was the purpose of Socrates in making so haughty a defence.

OF THE INCONVENIENCE OF GREATNESS

SINCE we cannot attain unto it, let us revenge ourselves by railing at it; and yet it is not absolutely railing against anything, to proclaim its defects, because they are in all things to be found, how beautiful or how much to be coveted soever. Greatness has in general this manifest advantage, that it can lower itself when it pleases, and has, very near, the choice of both the one and the other condition; for a man does not fall from all heights; there are several from which one may descend without falling down. It does, indeed, appear to me that we value it at too high a rate, and also overvalue the resolution of those whom we have either seen, or heard, have condemned it, or displaced themselves of their own accord: its essence is not so evidently commodious that a man may not, without a miracle, refuse it. I find it a very hard thing to undergo misfortunes, but to be content with a moderate measure of fortune and to avoid greatness I think a very easy matter. 'Tis methinks, a virtue to which I, who am no conjurer, could without any great endeavor arrive. What, then, is to be expected from them that would yet put into consideration the glory attending this refusal, wherein there may lurk worse ambition than even in the desire itself, and fruition of greatness? Forasmuch as ambition never comports itself better, according to itself, than when it proceeds by obscure and unfrequented ways.

I incite my courage to patience, but I rein it as much as I can toward desire. I have as much to wish for as another, and allow my wishes as much liberty and indiscretion; but, yet it never befell me to wish for either empire or royalty, or the eminency of those high and commanding fortunes: I do not aim that way; I love myself too well. When I think to grow greater 'tis but very moderately, and by a compelled and timorous advancement, such as is proper for me in resolution, in prudence, in health, in beauty, and even in riches too; but this supreme reputation, this mighty authority, oppress my imagination; and, quite contrary to that other,[1] I should, peradventure, rather choose to be the second or third in Perigord, than the first at Paris: at least, without lying, rather the third at Paris than the first. I would neither dispute, a miserable unknown, with a nobleman's porter, nor make crowds open in adoration as I pass. I am trained up to a moderate condition, as well by my choice as fortune; and have made it appear, in the whole conduct of my life and enterprises, that I have rather avoided than otherwise the climbing above the degree of fortune wherein God has placed me by my birth: all natural constitution is equally just and easy. My soul is so sneaking that I measure not good fortune by the height, but by the facility.

But if my heart be not great enough, 'tis open enough to make amends, at anyone's request, freely to lay open its weakness. Should anyone put me upon comparing the life of L. Thorius Balbus, a brave man, handsome, learned, healthful, understanding, and abounding in all sorts of conveniences and pleasures, leading a quiet life, and all his own, his mind well prepared against death, superstition, pain, and other incumbrances of human necessity, dying at last, in battle, with his sword in his hand, for the defence of his country, on the one part; and on the other part, the life of M. Regulus, so great and high as is known to everyone, and his end admirable; the one without name and without dignity, the other exemplary, and glorious to wonder. I should doubtless say as Cicero did, could I speak as well as he.[2] But if I was to compare them with my own, I should then also say that the first is as much according to my capacity, and from desire, which I conform to my capacity, as the second is far beyond it; that I could not approach the last but with veneration, the other I could readily attain by use.

But let us return to our temporal greatness, from which we are digressed. I disrelish all dominion, whether active or passive. Otanes,[3] one of the seven who had right to pretend to the kingdom of Persia, did, as I should willingly have done,

---

[1] Julius Cæsar.
[2] Cicero, "De Finibus," ii. 20, gives the preference to Regulus, and proclaims him the happier man.
[3] Herodotus, iii. 83.

OF THE INCONVENIENCE OF GREATNESS

which was, that he gave up to his concurrents his right of being promoted to it, either by election or by lot, provided that he and his might live in the empire out of all authority and subjection, those of the ancient laws excepted, and might enjoy all liberty that was not prejudicial to these, being as impatient of commanding as of being commanded.

The most painful and difficult employment in the world, in my opinion, is worthily to discharge the office of a king. I excuse more of their mistakes than men commonly do, in consideration of the intolerable weight of their function, which astounds me. 'Tis hard to keep measure in so immeasurable a power; yet so it is, that it is, even to those who are not of the best nature, a singular incitement to virtue, to be seated in a place where you cannot do the least good that shall not be put upon record; and where the least benefit redounds to so many men, and where your talent of administration, like that of preachers, principally addresses itself to the people, no very exact judge, easy to deceive, and easily content. There are few things wherein we can give a sincere judgment, by reason that there are few wherein we have not, in some sort, a private interest. Superiority and inferiority, dominion and subjection, are bound to a natural envy and contest, and must of necessity perpetually intrench upon one another. I believe neither the one nor the other touching the rights of the other party; let reason, therefore, which is inflexible and without passion, determine when we can avail ourselves of it. 'Tis not above a month ago that I read over two Scotch authors contending upon this subject, of whom he who stands for the people makes kings to be in a worse condition than a carter; and he who writes for monarchy places them some degrees above God Almighty in power and sovereignty.

Now, the inconveniency of greatness that I have made choice of to consider in this place, upon some occasion that has lately put it into my head, is this: there is not, peradventure, anything more pleasant in the commerce of men than the trials that we make against one another, out of emulation of honor and worth, whether in the exercises of the body or in those of the mind, wherein sovereign greatness can have no true part. And, in earnest, I have often thought that by force of respect itself men use princes disdainfully and injuriously in that particular; for the thing I was infinitely offended at in my childhood, that they who exercised with me forbore to do their best because they found me unworthy of their utmost endeavor, is what we see happen to them daily, everyone finding himself unworthy to contend with them. If we discover that they have the least desire to get the better of us, there is no one who will not make it his business to give it them, and who will not rather betray his own glory than offend theirs; and will, therein, employ so much force only as is necessary to save their honor. What share have they, then, in the engagement, where everyone is on their side? Methinks I see those Paladins of ancient times presenting themselves to jousts and battle with enchanted arms and bodies. Brisson,[4] running against Alexander, purposely missed his blow, and made a fault in his career; Alexander chid him for it, but he ought to have had him whipped. Upon this consideration Carneades said, that "the sons of princes learned nothing right but to ride; by reason that, in all their other exercises, everyone bends and yields to them; but a horse, that is neither a flatterer nor a courtier, throws the son of a king with no more ceremony than he would throw that of a porter."

Homer was fain to consent that Venus, so sweet and delicate a goddess as she was, should be wounded at the battle of Troy, thereby to ascribe courage and boldness to her; qualities that cannot possibly be in those who are exempt from danger. The gods are made to be angry, to fear, to run away, to be jealous, to grieve, to be transported with passions, to honor them with the virtues that, among us, are built upon these imperfections. Who does not participate in the hazard and difficulty can claim no interest in the honor and pleasure that are the consequences of hazardous actions. 'Tis pity a man should be so potent that all things must give way to him; fortune therein sets you too remote from society, and places you in too great a solitude. This easiness and mean facility of making all things bow under you is an enemy to all sorts of pleasure: 'tis to slide, not to go; 'tis to sleep, and not to live. Conceive man accompanied with omnipotence: you overwhelm him; he must beg

---

[4] Plutarch, "On Satisfaction or Tranquillity of the Mind." But in his essay, "How a Man may Distinguish a Flatterer from a Friend," he calls him Christo.

disturbance and opposition as an alms: his being and his good are in indigence.[5]

Their good qualities are dead and lost; for they can only be perceived by comparison, and we put them out of this: they have little knowledge of true praise, having their ears deafened with so continual and uniform an approbation. Have they to do with the stupidest of all their subjects? they have no means to take any advantage of him, if he but say: " 'Tis because he is my king," he thinks he has said enough to express, that he, therefore, suffered himself to be overcome. This quality stifles and consumes the other true and essential qualities: they are sunk in the royalty; and leave them nothing to recommend themselves with but actions that directly concern and serve the function of their place; 'tis so much to be a king, that this alone remains to them. The outer glare that environs him conceals and shrouds him from us; our sight is there repelled and dissipated, being filled and stopped by this prevailing light. The senate awarded the prize of eloquence to Tiberius; he refused it, esteeming that though it had been just, he could derive no advantage from a judgment so partial, and that was so little free to judge.

As we give them all advantages of honor, so do we soothe and authorize all their vices and defects, not only by approbation, but by imitation also. Every one of Alexander's followers carried his head on one side, as he did; and the flatterers of Dionysius ran against one another in his presence, and stumbled at and overturned whatever was under foot, to show they were as purblind as he. Hernia itself has also served to recommend a man to favor; I have seen deafness affected; and because the master hated his wife, Plutarch has seen his courtiers repudiate theirs, whom they loved: and, which is yet more, uncleanliness and all manner of dissolution have so been in fashion; as also disloyalty, blasphemy, cruelty, heresy, superstition, irreligion, effeminacy, and worse, if worse there be: and by an example yet more dangerous than that of Mithridates's flatterers, who, as their master pretended to the honor of a good physician, came to him to have incisions and cauteries

---

[5] In the Bordeaux copy, Montaigne here adds, "Evil to man is, in its turn, good; and good, evil. Neither is pain always to be shunned, nor pleasure always to be pursued."

made in their limbs; for these others suffered the soul, a more delicate and noble part, to be cauterized.

But to end where I began; the Emperor Adrian, disputing with the philosopher Favorinus about the interpretation of some word, Favorinus soon yielded him the victory; for which his friends rebuking him: "You talk simply," said he, "would you not have him wiser than I, who commands thirty legions?"[6] Augustus wrote verses against Asinius Pollio, and "I," said Pollio, "say nothing, for it is not prudence to write in contest with him who has power to prescribe;" and he had reason; for Dionysius, because he could not equal Philoxenus in poesy and Plato in discourse, condemned the one to the quarries, and sent the other to be sold for a slave into the island of Ægina.

[6] Spartian, "Life of Adrian," c. 15.

OF MANAGING THE WILL

FEW things, in comparison of what commonly affect other men, move, or to say better, possess me: for 'tis but reason they should concern a man, provided they do not possess him. I am very solicitous, both by study and argument, to enlarge this privilege of insensibility, which is in me naturally raised to a pretty degree, so that consequently I espouse and am very much moved with very few things. I have a clear sight enough, but I fix it upon very few objects; I have a sense delicate and tender enough; but an apprehension and application hard and negligent. I am very unwilling to engage myself; as much as in me lies, I employ myself wholly on myself, and even in that subject should rather choose to curb and restrain my affection from plunging itself over head and ears into it, it being a subject that I possess at the mercy of others, and over which fortune has more right than I; so that even as to health, which I so much value, 'tis all the more necessary for me not so passionately to covet and heed it, than to find diseases so insupportable. A man ought to moderate himself between the hatred of pain and the love of pleasure; and Plato[1] lets down a middle path of life between the two. But against such affections as wholly carry me away from myself, and fix me elsewhere, against those, I say, I oppose myself with my utmost power. 'Tis my opinion that a man should lend himself to others, and only give himself to himself. Were my will easy to lend itself out, and to be swayed, I should not stick there; I am too tender, both by nature and use:

"*Fugax rerum, securaque in otia natus.*"[2]

Hot and obstinate disputes wherein my adversary would at last have the better, the issue that would render my heat and obsti-

[1] "Laws," vii.
[2] "Born and bred up in negligence and ease."—Ovid, "De Trist.," iii. 2, 9.

nacy disgraceful, would peradventure vex me to the last degree. Should I set myself to it at the rate that others do, my soul would never have the force to bear the emotion and alarms of those who grasp at so much; it would immediately be disordered by this inward agitation. If, sometimes, I have been put upon the management of other men's affairs, I have promised to take them in hand, but not into my lungs and liver; to take them upon me, not to incorporate them: to take pains, yes: to be impassioned about it, by no means; I have a care of them, but I will not sit upon them. I have enough to do to order and govern the domestic throng of those that I have in my own veins and bowels, without introducing a crowd of other men's affairs; and am sufficiently concerned about my own proper and natural business, without meddling with the concerns of others. Such as know how much they owe to themselves, and how many offices they are bound to of their own, find that nature has cut them out work enough of their own to keep them from being idle. "Thou hast business enough at home, look to that."

Men let themselves out to hire; their faculties are not for themselves, but for those to whom they have enslaved themselves; 'tis their tenants occupy them, not themselves. This common humor pleases not me. We must be thrifty of the liberty of our souls, and never let it out but upon just occasions, which are very few, if we judge aright. Do but observe such as have accustomed themselves to be at everyone's call; they do it indifferently upon all, as well little as great occasions; in that which nothing concerns them, as much as in what imports them most. They thrust themselves in indifferently wherever there is work to do and obligation; and are without life when not in tumultuous bustle: *"In negotiis sunt, negotii causa."* [3] It is not so much that they will go, as it is that they cannot stand still; like a rolling stone that cannot stop till it can go no further. Occupation, with a certain sort of men, is a mark of understanding and dignity; their souls seek repose in agitation, as children do by being rocked in a cradle; they may pronounce themselves as serviceable to their friends, as they are troublesome to themselves. No one distributes his money to others, but everyone distributes his time and his life; there is

[3] "They only seek business for business' sake."—Seneca, "Epistolæ ad Lucilium," 22.

nothing of which we are so prodigal as of these two things, of which to be thrifty would be both commendable and useful. I am of a quite contrary humor; I look to myself, and commonly covet with no great ardor what I do desire; and desire little; and I employ and busy myself at the same rate, rarely and temperately. Whatever they take in hand, they do it with their utmost will and vehemence. There are so many dangerous steps, that, for the more safety, we must a little lightly and superficially glide over the world, and not rush through it. Pleasure itself is painful in profundity:

> "*Incedis per ignes,*
> *Suppositos cineri doloso.*" [4]

The parliament of Bordeaux chose me mayor of their city at a time when I was at a distance from France,[5] and still more remote from any such thought. I entreated to be excused, but I was told by my friends that I had committed an error in so doing, and the greater because the King had, moreover, interposed his command in that affair. 'Tis an office that ought to be looked upon so much more honorable, as it has no other salary nor advantage than the bare honor of its execution. It continues two years, but may be extended by a second election, which very rarely happens; it was to me, and had never been so but twice before; some years ago to Monsieur de Lanssac, and lately to Monsieur de Biron, marshal of France, in whose place I succeeded; and I left mine to Monsieur de Matignon, marshal of France also; proud of so noble a fraternity—

> "*Uterque bonus pacis bellique minister.*" [6]

Fortune would have a hand in my promotion, by this particular circumstance which she put in of her own, not altogether vain; for Alexander disdained the ambassadors of Corinth, who came to offer him a burgess-ship of their city; but when they proceeded to lay before him that Bacchus and Hercules were also in the register, he graciously accepted the offer.

At my arrival, I faithfully and conscientiously represented

[4] "You tread on fire, hidden under deceitful ashes."—Horace, "Odes," ii. 1, 7.
[5] At the baths Della Villa, near Lucca, September, 1581; see Montaigne's "Travels," ii. 448.
[16] "Both able ministers in peace, and good in war."—"Æneid," xi. 658.

myself to them for such as I find myself to be—a man without memory, without vigilance, without experience, and without vigor; but withal, without hatred, without ambition, without avarice, and without violence; that they might be informed of my qualities, and know what they were to expect from my service. And the knowledge they had had of my father, and the honor they had for his memory, having been the only motive to confer this favor upon me, I plainly told them that I should be very sorry anything should make so great an impression upon me as their affairs and the concerns of their city had made upon him, while he held the government to which they had preferred me. I remembered, when a boy, to have seen him in his old age cruelly tormented with these public affairs, neglecting the soft repose of his own house, to which the declension of his age had reduced him for several years before, the management of his own affairs, and his health; and certainly despising his own life, which was in great danger of being lost, by being engaged in long and painful journeys on their behalf. Such was he; and this humor of his proceeded from a marvellous good-nature; never was there a more charitable and popular soul. Yet this proceeding which I commend in others, I do not love to follow myself, and am not without excuse.

He had learned that a man must forget himself for his neighbor, and that the particular was of no manner of consideration in comparison with the general. Most of the rules and precepts of the world run this way; to drive us out of ourselves into the street for the benefit of public society: they thought to do a great feat to divert and remove us from ourselves, assuming we were but too much fixed there, and by a too natural inclination; and have said all they could to that purpose: for 'tis no new thing for the sages to preach things as they serve, not as they are. Truth has its obstructions, inconveniences, and incompatibilities with us; we must often deceive, that we may not deceive ourselves; and shut our eyes and our understandings, to redress and amend them: "*Imperiti enim judicant, et qui frequenter in hoc ipsum fallendi sunt, ne errent.*" [7] When they order us to love three, four, or fifty degrees of things above ourselves, they do like archers, who, to hit the white, take their

---

[7] "For the ignorant judge, and therefore are oft to be deceived lest they should err."—Quintilian, "Inst. Orat.," xi. 17.

aim a great deal higher than the butt; to make a crooked stick straight, we bend it the contrary way.

I believe that in the Temple of Pallas, as we see in all other religions, there were apparent mysteries to be exposed to the people; and others, more secret and high, that were only to be shown to such as were professed; 'tis likely that in these the true point of friendship that everyone owes to himself is to be found; not a false friendship, that makes us embrace glory, knowledge, riches, and the like, with a principal and immoderate affection, as members of our being; nor an indiscreet and effeminate friendship, wherein it happens, as with ivy, that it decays and ruins the walls it embraces; but a sound and regular friendship, equally useful and pleasant. He who knows the duties of this friendship and practices them is truly of the cabinet council of the Muses, and has attained to the height of human wisdom and of our happiness; such a one, exactly knowing what he owes to himself, will on his part find that he ought to apply to himself the use of the world and of other men; and to do this, to contribute to public society the duties and offices appertaining to him. He who does not in some sort live for others does not live much for himself: " *Qui sibi amicus est, scito hunc amicum omnibus esse.*" [8] The principal charge we have, is, to everyone his own conduct; and 'tis for this only that we here are. As he who should forget to live a virtuous and holy life, and should think he acquitted himself of his duty in instructing and training others up to it, would be a fool; even so he who abandons his own particular healthful and pleasant living, to serve others therewith, takes, in my opinion, a wrong and unnatural course.

I would not that men should refuse, in the employments they take upon them, their attention, pains, eloquence, sweat, and blood if need be:

"Non ipse pro caris amicis
Aut patria, timidus perire:" [9]

but 'tis only borrowed, and accidentally; his mind being always in repose and in health; not without action, but without vexation, without passion. To be simply acting costs him so little

---

[8] " He who is his own friend is a friend to everybody else." — Seneca, " Epistolæ ad Lucilium," 6.

[9] " Not afraid to die for beloved friends, and for his country."—Horace, " Odes," iv. 9, 51.

that he acts even sleeping; but it must be set on going with discretion; for the body receives the offices imposed upon it, just according to what they are; the mind often extends and makes them heavier at its own expense, giving them what measure it pleases. Men perform like things with several sorts of endeavor, and different contention of will; the one does well enough without the other: for how many people hazard themselves every day in war without any concern which way it goes; and thrust themselves into the dangers of battles, the loss of which will not break their next night's sleep? and such a man may be at home, out of the danger which he dared not have looked upon, who is more passionately concerned for the issue of this war, and whose soul is more anxious about events, than the soldier who therein stakes his blood and his life. I could have engaged myself in public employments without quitting my own matters a nail's breadth, and have given myself to others, without abandoning myself. This sharpness and violence of desires more hinder than they advance the execution of what they undertake; fill us with impatience against slow or contrary events, and with heat and suspicion against those with whom we have to do. We never carry on that thing well by which we are prepossessed and led:

"Male cuncta ministrat Impetus." [10]

He who therein employs only his judgment and address proceeds more cheerfully: he counterfeits, he gives way, he defers quite at his ease, according to the necessities of occasions; he fails in his attempt without trouble and affliction, ready and entire for a new enterprise; he always marches with the bridle in his hand. In him who is drunk with this violent and tyrannic intention, we discover, of necessity, much imprudence and injustice; the impetuosity of his desire carries him away; these are rash motions, and, if fortune do not very much assist, of very little fruit. Philosophy directs that, in the revenge of injuries received, we should strip ourselves of choler; not that the chastisement should be less, but, on the contrary, that the revenge may be the better and more heavily laid on, which, it

[10] "Passionate heat carries on things ill."—Statius, "Thebaid," x. 704.

conceives, will be by this impetuosity hindered. For anger not only disturbs, but, of itself, also wearies the arms of those who chastise; this fire benumbs and wastes their force; as in precipitation, "*festinatio tarda est*"[11]—"haste trips up its own heels," fetters, and stops itself; "*Ipsa se velocitas implicat.*"[12] For example, according to what I commonly see, avarice has no greater impediment than itself; the more bent and vigorous it is, the less it rakes together, and commonly sooner grows rich when disguised in a visor of liberality.

A very honest gentleman, and a particular friend of mine, had liked to have cracked his brains by a too passionate attention and affection to the affairs of a certain prince, his master; which master [13] has thus set himself out to me; "that he foresees the weight of accidents as well as another, but that in those for which there is no remedy he presently resolves upon suffering; in others, having taken all the necessary precautions which by the vivacity of his understanding he can presently do, he quietly awaits what may follow." And, in truth, I have accordingly seen him maintain a great indifferency and liberty of actions and serenity of countenance in very great and difficult affairs: I find him much greater, and of greater capacity in adverse than in prosperous fortune: his defeats are to him more glorious than his victories, and his mourning than his triumph.

Do but consider, that even in vain and frivolous actions, as at chess, tennis, and the like, this eager and ardent engaging with an impetuous desire immediately throws the mind and members into indiscretion and disorder: a man astounds and hinders himself; he who carries himself more moderately both toward gain and loss has always his wits about him: the less peevish and passionate he is at play, he plays much more advantageously and surely.

As to the rest, we hinder the mind's seizure and hold, in giving it so many things to seize upon: some things we should only offer to it; tie it to others, and with others incorporate it. It can feel and discern all things, but ought to feed upon nothing but itself; and should be instructed in what properly concerns itself, and that is properly of its own having and substance. The laws of nature teach us what justly we need. After the

[11] Quintus Curtius, ix. 9, 12.
[12] Seneca, "Epistolæ ad Lucilium," 44.
[13] Probably the King of Navarre, afterward Henry IV.

sages have told us that no one is indigent according to nature, and that everyone is so according to opinion,[14] they very subtly distinguish between the desires that proceed from her, and those that proceed from the disorder of our own fancy: those of which we can see the end are hers; those that fly before us, and of which we can see no end, are our own: the poverty of goods is easily cured; the poverty of the soul is irreparable:

> "*Nam si, quod satis est homini, id satis esse potesset*
> *Hoc sat erat; nunc, quum hoc non est, qui credimus porro*
> *Divitias ullas animum mi explere potesse?*" [15]

Socrates, seeing a great quantity of riches, jewels, and furniture carried in pomp through the city: "How many things are there," said he, "that I do not want." [16] Metrodorus lived on twelve ounces a day; Epicurus upon less: Metrocles slept in winter abroad among sheep; in summer in the cloisters of churches; "*Sufficit ad id natura, quod poscit.*" [17] Cleanthes lived by the labor of his own hands, and boasted that Cleanthes, if he would, could yet maintain another Cleanthes.

If that which nature exactly and originally requires of us for the conservation of our being, be too little (as in truth what it is, and how good cheap life may be maintained, cannot be better expressed than by this consideration that it is so little that by its littleness it escapes the gripe and shock of fortune), let us allow ourselves a little more; let us call every one of our habits and conditions, nature; let us rate and treat ourselves by this measure; let us stretch our appurtenances and accounts so far; for so far, I fancy, we have some excuse. Custom is a second nature, and no less powerful. What is wanting to my custom, I reckon is wanting to me; and I should be almost as well content that they took away my life, as cut me short in the way wherein I have so long lived. I am no longer in condition for any great change, nor to put myself into a new and unwonted course, not even to augmentation. 'Tis past the time for me to become other than what I am; and as I should

---

[14] Seneca, "Epistolæ ad Lucilium," 16.
[15] "For if what is for man enough, could be enough, it were enough; but since it is not so, how can I believe than any wealth can give my mind content?"—Lucilius, apud Nonium Marcellinum, v. sec. 98.
[16] Cicero, "Tusc. Quæs.," v. 32.
[17] "Nature suffices for what it requires."—Seneca, "Epistolæ ad Lucilium," 90.

OF MANAGING THE WILL

complain of any great good hap that should now befall me, that it came not in time to be enjoyed:

"*Quo mihi fortunas, si non conceditur uti?*" [18]

so should I complain of any inward acquisition. It were almost better never, than so late, to become an honest man, and well fit to live, when one has no longer to live. I, who am about to make my exit out of the world, would easily resign to any newcomer, who should desire it, all the prudence I am now acquiring in the world's commerce; after meat, mustard. I have no need of goods, of which I can make no use; of what use is knowledge to him who has lost his head? 'Tis an injury and unkindness in fortune to tender us presents that will only inspire us with a just despite that we had them not in their due season. Guide me no more; I can no longer go. Of so many parts as make up a sufficiency, patience is the most sufficient. Give the capacity of an excellent treble to a chorister who has rotten lungs, and eloquence to a hermit, exiled into the deserts of Arabia. There needs no art to help a fall; the end finds itself of itself at the conclusion of every affair. My world is at an end, my form expired; I am totally of the past, and am bound to authorize it, and to conform my outgoing to it. I will here declare, by way of example, that the pope's late ten days' diminution [19] has taken me so aback that I cannot well reconcile myself to it; I belong to the years wherein we kept another kind of account. So ancient and so long a custom challenges my adherence to it, so that I am constrained to be somewhat heretical on that point: incapable of any, though corrective, innovation. My imagination, in spite of my teeth, always pushes me ten days forward or backward, and is ever murmuring in my ears: "This rule concerns those who are to begin to be." If health itself, sweet as it is, returns to me by fits, 'tis rather to give me cause of regret than possession of it; I have no place left to keep it in. Time leaves me; without which nothing can be possessed. Oh, what little account should I make of those great elective dignities that I see in such esteem in the world, that are never conferred but upon men who are taking leave of it;

---

[18] "What is the good of fortune to me if I can't use it?"—Horace, "Ep.," i. 5, 12.
[19] Gregory XIII, in 1582, reformed the calendar, and, in consequence, in France they all at once passed from the ninth to the twentieth of December.

wherein they do not so much regard how well the man will discharge his trust, as how short his administration will be: from the very entry they look at the exit. In short, I am about finishing this man, and not rebuilding another. By long use, this form is in me turned into substance, and fortune into nature.

I say, therefore, that every one of us feeble creatures is excusable in thinking that to be his own which is comprised under this measure; but withal, beyond these limits, 'tis nothing but confusion; 'tis the largest extent we can grant to our own claims. The more we amplify our need and our possession, so much the more do we expose ourselves to the blows and adversities of fortune.[20] The career of our desires ought to be circumscribed and restrained to a short limit of near and contiguous commodities; and their course ought, moreover, to be performed not in a right line that ends elsewhere, but in a circle, of which the two points, by a short wheel, meet and terminate in ourselves. Actions that are carried on without this reflection—a near and essential reflection, I mean—such as those of ambitious and avaricious men, and so many more as run point-blank, and whose career always carries them before themselves, such actions, I say, are erroneous and sickly.

Most of our business is farce: "*Mundus universus exercet histrionam.*" [21] We must play our part properly, but withal as the part of a borrowed personage; we must not make real essence of a mask and outward appearance; nor of a strange person, our own; we cannot distinguish the skin from the shirt: 'tis enough to meal the face, without mealing the breast. I see some who transform and transubstantiate themselves into as many new shapes and new beings as they undertake new employments; and who strut and fume even to the heart and liver, and carry their state along with them even in their dressing-gowns. I cannot make them distinguish the salutations made to themselves from those made to their commission, their train, or their mule: "*Tantum se fortunæ permittunt, etiam ut naturam dediscant.*" [22] They swell and puff up their souls, and their natural way of speaking, according to the height of their magisterial place. The mayor of Bordeaux and Montaigne have ever

---

[20] "L'homme tient par ses vœux à mille choses: plus il augmentes ses attachements, plus il multiplie ses peines."—Rousseau, "Émile," liv. v.

[21] Petronius Arbiter, iii. 8.

[22] "They so much give themselves up to fortune, as even to forget their nature."—Quintus Curtius, ii. 2.

OF MANAGING THE WILL

been two by very manifest separation. Because one is an advocate or a financier, he must not ignore the knavery there is in such callings; an honest man is not accountable for the vice or absurdity of his employment, and ought not on that account refuse to take the calling upon him: 'tis the usage of his country, and then there is money to be got by it; a man must live by the world, and make his best of it, such as it is. But the judgment of an emperor ought to be above his empire, and see and consider it as a foreign accident; and he ought to know how to enjoy himself apart from it, and to communicate himself as James and Peter, to himself, at all events.

I cannot engage myself so deep and so entire; when my will gives me to anything, 'tis not with so violent an obligation that my judgment is infected with it. In the present broils of this kingdom my own interest has not made me blind to the laudable qualities of our adversaries, nor to those that are reproachable in those of men of our party. Others adore all of their own side; for my part, I do not so much as excuse most things in those of mine: a good work has never the worse grace with me for being made against me. The knot of the controversy excepted, I have always kept myself in equanimity and pure indifference: "*Neque extra necessitates velli, præcipuum odium gero;*"[23] for which I am pleased with myself; and the more, because I see others commonly fail in the contrary direction. Such as extend their anger and hatred beyond the dispute in question, as most men do, show that they spring from some other occasion and private cause; like one, who, being cured of an ulcer, has yet a fever remaining, by which it appears that the ulcer had another more concealed beginning. The reason is that they are not concerned in the common cause; because it is wounding to the state and general interest; but are only nettled by reason of their particular concern. This is why they are so especially animated, and to a degree so far beyond justice and public reason: "*Non tam omnia universi, quam ea quæ ad quemque pertinent, singuli carpebant.*"[24] I would have the advantage on our side, but if it be not, I shall not run mad. I am heartily for the right party; but I do not want to be taken

---

[23] "And have no express hatred beyond the necessity of war."
[24] "Everyone was not so much angry against things in general, as against those that particularly concerned himself."—Livy, xxxiv. 36.

notice of as an especial enemy to others, and beyond the general quarrel. I am a mortal enemy to this vicious form of censure: " He is of the League, because he admires the Duke of Guise; he is astonished at the King of Navarre's energy, and therefore he is a Huguenot; he finds such and such faults in the King's conduct, he is therefore seditious in his heart;" and I would not grant to the magistrate himself that he did well in condemning a book because it had placed a heretic [25] among the best poets of the time. Shall we not dare to say of a thief, that he has a handsome leg? If a woman be a strumpet, must it needs follow that she has a stinking breath? Did they in the wisest ages revoke the proud title of Capitolinus they had before conferred on Marcus Manlius, as conservator of religion and the public liberty, and stifle the memory of his liberality, his feats of arms, and military recompenses granted to his valor, because he afterward aspired to the sovereignty, to the prejudice of the laws of his country? If we take a hatred against an advocate, he will not be allowed, the next day, to be eloquent. I have elsewhere spoken of the zeal that pushed on worthy men to the like faults. For my part, I can say, " Such a one does this thing ill, and another thing virtuously and well." So in the prognostics, or sinister events of affairs, they would have everyone in his party blind or a blockhead, and that our persuasion and judgment should subserve not truth, but to the project of our desires. I should rather incline toward the other extreme; so much I fear being suborned by my desire; to which may be added that I am a little tenderly distrustful of things that I wish.

I have in my time seen wonders in the indiscreet and prodigious facility of people in suffering their hopes and belief to be led and governed, which way has best pleased and served their leaders, despite a hundred mistakes one upon another, despite mere dreams and phantasms. I no more wonder at those who have been blinded and seduced by the fooleries of Appollonius and Mahomet. Their sense and understanding are absolutely taken away by their passion; their discretion has no more any other choice than that which smiles upon them, and encourages their cause. I had principally observed this in the beginning of our intestine distempers; that other, which has sprung up

[25] Theodore de Beza.

since, in imitating, has surpassed it; by which I am satisfied that it is a quality inseparable from popular errors; after the first that rolls, opinions drive on one another like waves with the wind: a man is not a member of the body, if it be in his power to forsake it, and if he do not roll the common way. But, doubtless, they wrong the just side, when they go about to assist it with fraud; I have ever been against that practice: 'tis only fit to work upon weak heads; for the sound, there are surer and more honest ways to keep up their courage and to excuse adverse accidents.

Heaven never saw a greater animosity than that between Cæsar and Pompey, nor ever shall; and yet I observe, methinks, in those brave souls, a great moderation toward one another; it was a jealousy of honor and command which did not transport them to a furious and indiscreet hatred, and was without malignity and detraction; in their hottest exploits upon one another, I discover some remains of respect and good-will; and am therefore of opinion that, had it been possible, each of them would rather have done his business without the ruin of the other than with it. Take notice how much otherwise matters went with Marius and Sylla.

We must not precipitate ourselves so headlong after our affections and interests. As, when I was young, I opposed myself to the progress of love which I perceived to advance too fast upon me, and had a care lest it should at last become so pleasing as to force, captivate, and wholly reduce me to its mercy; so I do the same upon all other occasions where my will is running on with too warm an appetite. I lean opposite to the side it inclines to, as I find it going to plunge and make itself drunk with its own wine; I evade nourishing its pleasure so far, that I cannot recover it without infinite loss. Souls that, through their own stupidity, only discern things by halves, have this happiness that they smart less with hurtful things; 'tis a spiritual leprosy that has some show of health, and such a health as philosophy does not altogether contemn, but yet we have no reason to call it wisdom, as we often do. And after this manner someone anciently mocked Diogenes, who, in the depth of winter and stark naked, went hugging an image of snow for a trial of his endurance; the other seeing him in this position, " Art thou now very cold?" said he. " Not at all," replied Diogenes. "Why then," said the other, "what difficult and exemplary thing dost thou think thou doest in embracing that snow?"[26] To take a true measure of constancy, one must necessarily know what the suffering is.

But souls that are to meet with adverse events and the injuries of fortune, in their depth and sharpness, that are to weigh and taste them according to their natural weight and bitterness, let such show their skill in avoiding the causes and diverting the blow. What did King Cotys do?[27] He paid liberally for the rich and beautiful vessel that had been presented to him, but, seeing it was exceedingly brittle, he immediately broke it, betimes to prevent so easy a matter of displeasure against his servants. In like manner, I have willingly avoided all confusion in my affairs, and never coveted to have my estate contiguous to those of my relations, and such with whom I coveted a strict friendship; for thence matter of unkindness and falling out often proceed. I formerly loved the hazardous games of cards and dice; but have long since left them off, only for this reason, that, with whatever good air I carried my losses, I could not help feeling vexed within. A man of honor, who ought to be touchingly sensible of the lie or of an insult, and who is not to take a scurvy excuse for satisfaction, should avoid occasions of dispute. I shun melancholy, crabbed men, as I would the plague; and in matters I cannot talk of without emotion and concern, I never meddle, if not compelled by my duty: "*Melius non incipient, quam desinent.*"[28] The surest way, therefore, is to prepare one's self beforehand for occasions.

I know very well that some wise men have taken another way, and have not feared to grapple and engage to the utmost upon several subjects; these are confident of their own strength, under which they protect themselves in all ill successes, making their patience wrestle and contend with disaster:

> "*Velut rupes, vastum quæ prodit in æquor,*
> *Obvia ventorum furiis, expostaque ponto,*
> *Vim cunctam atque minas perfert cœlique marisque;*
> *Ipsa immota manens.*"[29]

---

[26] Plutarch, "Notable Sayings of the Lacedæmonians": Diogenes Laertius, vi. 25.

[27] Plutarch, "Notable Sayings of the Ancient Kings": Cotys.

[28] "A man had better never to have begun, than to have to desist."—Seneca, "Epistolæ ad Lucilium," 72.

[29] "As a rock standing among the vast billows, exposed to the furious winds and the raging flood, remains unmoved, and defies all the force of seas and skies."—Vergil, "Æneid," x. 693.

OF MANAGING THE WILL

Let us not attempt these examples; we shall never come up to them. They set themselves resolutely, and without agitation, to behold the ruin of their country, which possessed and commanded all their will; this is too much and too hard a task for our commoner souls. Cato gave up the noblest life that ever was upon this account; we meaner spirits must fly from the storm as far as we can; we must provide for sentiment, and not for patience, and evade the blows we cannot meet. Zeno, seeing Chremonides, a young man whom he loved, draw near to sit down by him, suddenly started up; and Cleanthes demanding of him the reason why he did so, " I hear," said he, " that physicians especially order repose, and forbid emotion in all tumors." [30] Socrates does not say, " Do not surrender to the charms of beauty; stand your ground, and do your utmost to oppose it." " Fly it," says he; " shun the fight and encounter of it, as of a powerful poison that darts and wounds at a distance." [31] And his good disciple,[32] feigning or reciting, but, in my opinion, rather reciting than feigning the rare perfections of the great Cyrus, makes him distrustful of his own strength to resist the charms of the divine beauty of that illustrious Panthea, his captive, and committing the visiting and keeping her to another, who could not have so much liberty as himself. And the Holy Ghost in like manner: " *Ne nos inducas in tentationem.*" [33] We do not pray that our reason may not be combated and overcome by concupiscence, but that it should not be so much as tried by it; that we should not be brought into a state wherein we are so much as to suffer the approaches, solicitations, and temptations of sin; and we beg of Almighty God to keep our consciences quiet, fully and perfectly delivered from all commerce of evil.

Such as say that they have reason for their revenging passion, or any other sort of troublesome agitation of mind, often say true, as things now are, but not as they were: they speak to us when the causes of their error are by themselves nourished and advanced; but look backward—recall these causes to their beginning—and there you will put them to a nonplus. Will they have their faults less, for being of longer continuance; and that of an unjust beginning, the sequel can be just? Who-

[30] Diogenes Laertius, vii. 17.
[31] Xenophon, " Mem. of Socrates," i. 3, 13.
[32] Idem, " Cyropædia," i. 3, 3.
[33] " Lead us not into temptation."— St. Matthew, vi. 13.

ever shall desire the good of his country, as I do, without fretting or pining himself, will be troubled, but will not swoon to see it threatening either its own ruin, or a no less ruinous continuance; poor vessel, that the waves, the winds, and the pilot toss and steer to so contrary designs!

*"In tam diversa, magister,
Ventus, et unda, trahunt."* [34]

He who does not gape after the favor of princes, as after a thing he cannot live without, does not much concern himself at the coldness of their reception and countenance, nor at the inconstancy of their wills. He who does not brood over his children or his honors, with a slavish propension, ceases not to live commodiously enough after their loss. He who does good principally for his own satisfaction, will not be much troubled to see men judge of his actions contrary to his merit. A quarter of an ounce of patience will provide sufficiently against such inconveniences. I find ease in this receipt, redeeming myself in the beginning as cheap as I can; and find that by this means I have escaped much trouble and many difficulties. With very little ado I stop the first sally of my emotions, and leave the subject that begins to be troublesome, before it transports me. He who stops not the start, will never be able to stop the career; he, who cannot keep them out, will never get them out when they are once got in; and he who cannot crush them at the beginning, will never do it after; nor ever keep himself from falling, if he cannot recover himself when he first begins to totter: *" Etenim ipsæ se impellunt; ubi semel a ratione discessum est; ipsaque sibi imbecillitas indulget, in altumque provehitur imprudens, nec reperit locum consistendi."* [35] I am betimes sensible of the little breezes that begin to sing and whistle in the shrouds, the fore-runners of the storm:

*"Ceu flamina prima
Quum deprensa fremunt sylvis, et cæca voluntant
Murmura, venturos nautis prodentia ventos."* [36]

---

[34] Buchanan. The translation is in the previous passage.

[35] "For they throw themselves headlong when once they loose their reason, and frailty so far indulges itself, that it is unawares carried out into the deep, and can find no port wherein to come to an anchor."—Cicero, "Tusc. Quæs.," iv. 18.

[36] "As when the rising winds, checked by woods, send out dull murmurs, portending a storm to the mariner."—"Æneid," x. 97.

How often have I done myself a manifest injustice, to avoid the hazard of having yet a worse done me by the judges, after an age of vexations, dirty and vile practices, more enemies to my nature than fire or the rack? *"Convenit a litibus, quantum licet, et nescio an paulo plus etiam, quam licet, abhorrentem esse: est enim non modo liberale, paululum nonnunquam de suo jure decedere, sed interdum etiam fructuosum."* [37] Were we wise, we ought to rejoice and boast, as I one day heard a young gentleman of a good family very innocently do, that his mother had lost her cause, as if it had been a cough, a fever, or something very troublesome to keep. Even the favors that fortune might have given me through relationship or acquaintance with those who have sovereign authority in those affairs, I have very conscientiously and very carefully avoided employing them to the prejudice of others, and of advancing my pretensions above their true right. In fine, I have so much prevailed by my endeavors (and happily I may say it) that I am to this day a virgin from all suits in law; though I have had very fair offers made me, and with very just title would I have hearkened to them; and a virgin from quarrels, too. I have almost passed over a long life without any offence of moment, either active or passive, or without ever hearing a worse word than my own name: a rare favor of heaven.

Our greatest agitations have ridiculous springs and causes: what ruin did our last Duke of Burgundy run into about a cartload of sheepskins? [38] And was not the graving of a seal the first and principal cause of the greatest commotion that this machine of the world ever underwent? [39] for Pompey and Cæsar were but the offsets and continuation of the two others: and I have in my time seen the wisest heads in this kingdom assembled with great ceremony, and at the public expense, about treaties and agreements, of which the true decision, in the mean time, absolutely depended upon the ladies' cabinet council, and the inclination of some foolish woman.

The poets very well understood this, when they put all Greece and Asia to fire and sword about an apple. Inquire

---

[37] "A man should be an enemy to all lawsuits as much as he may, and I know not whether not something more; for 'tis not only liberal, but sometimes also advantageous, too, a little to recede from one's right."—Cicero, "De Offic.," ii. 18.

[38] "Mem. de Comines," lib. v. c. 1.

[39] The civil war between Marius and Sylla; see Plutarch's "Life of Marius," c. 3.

why that man hazards his life and honor upon the fortune of his rapier and dagger; let him acquaint you with the occasion of the quarrel; he cannot do it without blushing; 'tis so idle and frivolous.

A little thing will engage you in it; but being once embarked, all the cords draw; great provisions are then required, more hard and more important. How much easier is it not to enter in, than it is to get out? Now we should proceed contrary to the reed, which, at its first springing produces a long and straight shoot, but afterward, as if tired and out of breath, it runs into thick and frequent joints and knots, as so many pauses which demonstrate that it has no more its first vigor and firmness; 'twere better to begin gently and coldly, and to keep one's breath and vigorous efforts for the height and stress of the business. We guide affairs in their beginnings, and have them in our own power; but afterward, when they are once at work, 'tis they that guide and govern us, and we are to follow them.

Yet do I not mean to say that this counsel has discharged me of all difficulty, and that I have not often had enough to do to curb and restrain my passions; they are not always to be governed according to the measure of occasions, and often have their entries very sharp and violent. But still good fruit and profit may thence be reaped; except for those who in well-doing are not satisfied with any benefit, if reputation be wanting; for, in truth, such an effect is not valued but by everyone to himself; you are better contented, but not more esteemed, seeing you reformed yourself before you got into the whirl of the dance, or that the provocative matter was in sight. Yet not in this only, but in all other duties of life also, the way of those who aim at honor is very different from that they proceed by, who propose to themselves order and reason. I find some, who rashly and furiously rush into the lists, and cool in the course. As Plutarch says, that those who, through false shame, are soft and facile to grant whatever is desired of them, are afterward as facile to break their word and to recant; so he who enters lightly into a quarrel is apt to go as lightly out of it. The same difficulty that keeps me from entering into it, would, when once hot and engaged in quarrel, incite me to maintain it with great obstinacy and resolution. 'Tis the

OF MANAGING THE WILL 59

tyranny of custom; when a man is once engaged, he must go through with it, or die. " Undertake coldly," said Bias, " but pursue with ardor." [40] For want of prudence, men fall into want of courage, which is still more intolerable.

Most accommodations of the quarrels of these days of ours are shameful and false; we only seek to save appearances, and in the mean time betray and disavow our true intentions; we salve over the fact. We know very well how we said the thing, and in what sense we spoke it, and the company know it, and our friends whom we have wished to make sensible of our advantage, understand it well enough too: 'tis at the expense of our frankness and of the honor of our courage, that we disown our thoughts, and seek refuge in falsities, to make matters up. We give ourselves the lie, to excuse the lie we have given to another. You are not to consider if your word or action may admit of another interpretation; 'tis your own true and sincere interpretation, your real meaning in what you said or did, that you are thenceforward to maintain, whatever it cost you. Men speak to your virtue and conscience, which are not things to be put under a mask; let us leave these pitiful ways and expedients to the jugglers of the law. The excuses and reparations that I see every day made and given to repair indiscretion, seem to me more scandalous than the indiscretion itself. It were better to affront your adversary a second time, than to offend yourself by giving him so unmanly a satisfaction. You have braved him in your heat and anger, and you would flatter and appease him in your cooler and better sense; and by that means lay yourself lower and at his feet, whom before you pretended to overtop. I do not find anything a gentleman can say so vicious in him, as unsaying what he has said is infamous, when to unsay it is authoritatively extracted from him; forasmuch as obstinacy is more excusable in a man of honor than pusillanimity. Passions are as easy for me to evade, as they are hard for me to moderate: "*Exscinduntur facilius animo, quam temperantur.*" [41] He, who cannot attain the noble stoical impassibility, let him secure himself in the bosom of this popular stolidity of mine; what they performed by virtue, I inure myself to do by temperament. The middle region harbors storms

---
[40] Diogenes Laertius, i. 87.
[41] " They are more easily to be eradicated than governed."

and tempests; the two extremes, of philosophers and peasants, concur in tranquillity and happiness:

> *"Felix, qui potuit rerum cognoscere causas,*
> *Atque metus omnes et inexorabile fatum*
> *Subjecit pedibus, strepitumque Acherontis avari!*
> *Fortunatus et ille, Deos qui novit agrestes,*
> *Panaque, Sylvanumque senem, Nymphasque sorores!"* [42]

The births of all things are weak and tender; and therefore we should have our eyes intent on beginnings; for as when, in its infancy, the danger is not perceived, so when it is grown up, the remedy is as little to be found. I had every day encountered a million of crosses, harder to digest in the progress of ambition, than it has been hard for me to curb the natural propension that inclined me to it:

> *" Jure perhorrui*
> *Late conspicuum tollere verticem."* [43]

All public actions are subject to various and uncertain interpretations; for too many heads judge of them. Some say of this civic employment of mine [44] (and I am willing to say a word or two about it, not that it is worth so much, but to give an account of my manners in such things), that I have behaved myself in it as a man not sufficiently easy to be moved, and with a languishing affection; and they have some color for what they say. I endeavored to keep my mind and my thoughts in repose, *" Cum semper natura, tum etiam ætate jam quietus;"* [45] and if they sometimes lash out upon some rude and sensible impression, 'tis in truth without my advice. Yet from this natural heaviness of mine, men ought not to conclude a total inability in me (for want of care and want of sense are two very different things), and much less any unkindness or ingratitude toward that corporation, who employed the utmost means they had in their power to oblige me, both before they knew me and after; and they did much more for me in choosing me anew, than in con-

---

[42] " Happy is he who has discovered the causes of things, and tramples under foot all fear, all concern, as to inexorable fate, or as to the roaring of greedy Acheron: he is blest who knows the country gods, Pan, old Sylvanus, and the sister nymphs."—Vergil, " Georgics," ii. 490.

[43] " I ever justly feared to raise my head too high."—Horace, " Odes," iii. 16, 18.

[44] The Bordeaux mayoralty.

[45] " As being always quiet by nature, so also now by age."—Cicero, " De Petit. Consul.," c. 2.

ferring that honor upon me at first. I wish them all imaginable good; and assuredly had occasion been, there is nothing I would have spared for their service; I did for them, as I would have done for myself. 'Tis a good, warlike, and generous people, but capable of obedience and discipline, and of whom the best use may be made, if well guided. They say also that my administration passed over without leaving any mark or trace. Good! They moreover accuse my cessation in a time when everybody almost was convicted of doing too much. I am impatient to be doing where my will spurs me on; but this itself is an enemy to perseverance. Let him who will make use of me according to my own way, employ me in affairs where vigor and liberty are required, where a direct, short, and, moreover, a hazardous conduct is necessary; I may do something; but if it must be long, subtle, laborious, artificial, and intricate, he had better call in somebody else. All important offices are not necessarily difficult: I came prepared to do somewhat rougher work, had there been great occasion; for it is in my power to do something more than I do, or than I love to do. I did not, to my knowledge, omit anything that my duty really required. I easily forgot those offices that ambition mixes with duty and palliates with its title; these are they that, for the most part, fill the eyes and ears, and give men the most satisfaction; not the thing but the appearance contents them; if they hear no noise, they think men sleep. My humor is no friend to tumult; I could appease a commotion without commotion and chastise a disorder without being myself disorderly; if I stand in need of anger and inflammation, I borrow it, and put it on. My manners are languid, rather faint than sharp. I do not condemn a magistrate who sleeps, provided the people under his charge sleep as well as he: the laws in that case sleep, too. For my part, I commend a gliding, staid, and silent life: "*Neque submissam et abjectam, neque se efferentem;*" [46] my fortune will have it so. I am descended from a family that has lived without lustre or tumult, and, time out of mind, particularly ambitious of a character for probity.

Our people nowadays are so bred up to bustle and ostentation, that good nature, moderation, equability, constancy, and such like quiet and obscure qualities, are no more thought on or re-

[46] "Not subject, nor abject, but not obtrusive."—Cicero, "De Offic.," i. 34.

garded. Rough bodies make themselves felt; the smooth are imperceptibly handled: sickness is felt, health little or not at all; no more than the oils that foment us, in comparison of the pains for which we are fomented. 'Tis acting for one's particular reputation and profit, not for the public good, to refer that to be done in the public squares which one may do in the council chamber; and to noonday what might have been done the night before; and to be jealous to do that himself which his colleague can do as well as he; so were some surgeons of Greece wont to perform their operations upon scaffolds in the sight of the people, to draw more practice and profit. They think that good rules cannot be understood but by the sound of trumpet. Ambition is not a vice of little people nor of such modest means as ours. One said to Alexander: " Your father will leave you a great dominion, easy and pacific;" this youth was emulous of his father's victories, and of the justice of his government; he would not have enjoyed the empire of the world in ease and peace. Alcibiades, in Plato, had rather die young, beautiful, rich, noble, and learned, and all this in full excellence, than to stop short of such condition; this disease is, peradventure, excusable in so strong and so full a soul. When wretched and dwarfish souls gull and deceive themselves, and think to spread their fame for having given right judgment in an affair, or maintained the discipline of the guard of a gate of their city, the more they think to exalt their heads the more they show their tails. This little well-doing has neither body nor life; it vanishes in the first mouth, and goes no farther than from one street to another. Talk of it by all means to your son or your servant, like that old fellow who, having no other auditor of his praises, nor approver of his valor, boasted to his chambermaid, crying, " Oh, Perrette, what a brave, clever man hast thou for thy master!" At the worst, talk of it to yourself, like a councillor of my acquaintance, who, having disgorged a whole cartful of law jargon with great heat and as great folly, coming out of the council chamber to a retiring room, was heard very complacently to mutter between his teeth: *" Non nobis, Domine, non nobis, sed nomini tuo da gloriam:"* [47] He who gets it of nobody else, let him pay himself out of his own purse.

[47] " Not unto us, O Lord, not to us; but unto Thy name be the glory."— Psalm cxiii. 1.

OF MANAGING THE WILL

Fame is not prostituted at so cheap a rate; rare and exemplary actions, to which it is due, would not endure the company of this prodigious crowd of petty daily performances. Marble may exalt your titles, as much as you please, for having repaired a rod of wall or cleansed a public sewer; but not men of sense. Renown does not follow all good deads, if novelty and difficulty be not conjoined; nay, so much as mere esteem, according to the Stoics, is not due to every action that proceeds from virtue; nor will they allow him bare thanks, who, out of temperance, abstains from an old blear-eyed hag. Those who have known the admirable qualities of Scipio Africanus deny him the glory that Panætius attributes to him, of being abstinent from gifts, as a glory not so much his as that of the age he lived in.[48] We have pleasures suitable to our lot; let us not usurp those of grandeur; our own are more natural, and by so much more solid and sure, as they are lower. If not for that of conscience, yet at least for ambition's sake, let us reject ambition; let us disdain that thirst of honor and renown, so low and mendicant, that it makes us beg it of all sorts of people ("*Quæ est ista laus quæ pessit e macello peti?*"[49]) by abject means, and at what cheap rate soever: 'tis dishonor to be so honored. Let us learn to be no more greedy, than we are capable, of glory. To be puffed up with every action that is innocent or of use, is only for those with whom such things are extraordinary and rare; they will value it as it costs them. The more a good effect makes a noise the more do I abate of its goodness as I suspect that it was more performed for the noise, than upon account of the goodness; exposed upon the stall, 'tis half sold. Those actions have much more grace and lustre, that slip from the hand of him that does them, negligently and without noise, and that some honest man thereafter finds out and raises from the shade, to produce it to the light upon its own account. "*Mihi quidem laudabiliora videntur omnia, quæ sine venditatoine, et sine populo teste fiunt,*"[50] says the most ostentatious man that ever lived.

I had but to conserve and to continue, which are silent and

---

[48] Cicero, "De Offic.," ii. 22.
[49] "What praise is that which is to be got in the market-place?"—Cicero, "De Fin.," ii. 15.
[50] "All things truly seem more laudable to me that are performed without ostentation, and without the testimony of the people."—Idem, "Tusc. Quæs.," ii. 26.

insensible effects; innovation is of great lustre; but 'tis interdicted in this age, when we are pressed upon and have nothing to defend ourselves from but novelties. To forbear doing is often as generous as to do; but 'tis less in the light, and the little good that I have in me is of this kind. In fine occasions in this employment of mine have been confederate with my humor, and I heartily thank them for it. Is there any who desires to be sick, that he may see his physician at work? and would not that physician deserve to be whipped, who should wish the plague among us, that he might put his art in practice? I have never been of that wicked humor, and common enough, to desire that troubles and disorders in this city should elevate and honor my government; I have ever heartily contributed all I could to their tranquillity and ease. He who will not thank me for the order, the sweet and silent calm that has accompanied my administration, cannot, however, deprive me of the share that belongs to me, by title of my good fortune. And I am of such a composition that I would as willingly be lucky as wise, and had rather owe my successes purely to the favor of Almighty God than to any operation of my own. I had sufficiently published to the world my unfitness for such public offices; but I have something in me yet worse than incapacity itself; which is, that I am not much displeased at it, and that I do not much go about to cure it, considering the course of life that I have proposed to myself. Neither have I satisfied myself in this employment; but I have very near arrived at what I expected from my own performance, and have much surpassed what I promised them with whom I had to do; for I am apt to promise something less than what I am able to do and than what I hope to make good. I assure myself that I have left no offence or hatred behind me; to leave regret or desire for me among them, I at least know very well that I never much aimed at it:

"*Mene huic confidere monstro!*
Mene salis placidi vultum, fluctusque quietos
Ignorare?" [51]

[51] "Should I place confidence in this monster? Should I be ignorant of the dangers of that seeming placid sea, those now quiet waves?" — Vergil, "Æneid," v. 849.

OF CEREMONIES

ON CROMWELL

BY

VOLTAIRE
(François-Marie Arouet)

FRANÇOIS-MARIE VOLTAIRE
1694—1778

The father of the great French writer universally known as Voltaire was a notary of good family by the name of Arouet. His famous son, who was born at Châtenay in 1694, was baptized François-Marie Arouet. He took the name Voltaire in 1718, shortly after the production of his tragedy " Œdipe." The origin of his assumed name has never been definitely traced. Voltaire's early education was in charge of the Jesuits at the Collège Louis-le-Grand in Paris. He began the writing of verses while at college, and his wit, seconded by the influence of his godfather, the Abbé de Châteauneuf, secured for him an introduction into the most aristocratic circles of Parisian society. The freedom of his satirical utterances soon made enemies for him. Between 1716 and 1726 he was twice expelled from Paris, and twice imprisoned in the Bastile. His second imprisonment was due to a quarrel with an influential but unscrupulous nobleman. These differences eventually caused his expulsion from the country.

During his exile Voltaire spent nearly two years in England. At that time the group of literary men who made the reign of Queen Anne illustrious was at the height of its activity, and London was the foremost literary centre in Europe. Here Voltaire wrote his " Histoire de Charles XII " and a number of tragedies, of which " Zaïre " was the most successful, and published his " Henriade." His " Lettres philosophiques " produced such a storm in France that they were ordered to be destroyed by the public executioner. In 1734 Voltaire went to live at the château of the Marquise du Châtelet at Cirey in Champagne. The Marquise, who was devoted to science and literature, had conceived a great admiration for Voltaire, and sought to surround him with the external conditions most favorable to sustain literary effort. With the exception of some brief excursions Voltaire remained at Cirey until the death of his patroness in 1749. During this period he wrote the dramas " Zulime," " L'enfant prodigue," " Mahomet," " Mérope," and the " Essai sur les mœurs." In 1746, being again in favor with the Court, he was elected a member of the Academy.

From 1750 to 1753 Voltaire resided at the Court of Frederick the Great, where he completed and published one of his most important works, " Le siècle de Louis XIV." After quarrelling with his royal master he returned to France. In 1758 he purchased the château of Ferney, in France, near the Swiss frontier, where he passed the remainder of his life. Of his later works the most notable were his " Histoire de la Russie sous Pierre le Grand," his tragedy " Tancrède," and the novels " Candide," " Zadig," and " L'Ingénu." In 1778 Voltaire was invited to Paris, where he was received like a conquering hero. The fatigue of the journey and the excitement of his enthusiastic reception were too great a strain on his weakened frame, and he died at Paris on May 30, 1778.

Numerous volumes of Voltaire's works fail to reveal the secret of the vast influence he exerted. He attacked institutions that were already tottering in their foundations, and addressed minds already ripe for the principles he preached. His writings are, however, remarkable for their wit and versatility, and for their easy, graceful style, of which his essays " On Cromwell " and " On Ceremonies " are excellent examples.

OF CEREMONIES

THE arm-chair, the easy-chair, the court-stool, the right and the left hand, have for several ages been considered as important objects of policy and illustrious subjects for disputes. I fancy that the ancient ceremonial relating to arm-chairs took its rise from our barbarous ancestors having but one of these chairs at most in a house, and that this was commonly appropriated to the use of any person who was sick. There are still several provinces in France, and countries in England, where the arm-chair is called a groaning-chair.

Long after the times of Attila and Dagobert, when luxury began to creep into courts, and the great ones of the earth had two or three arm-chairs in their mighty dungeons, it was esteemed a singular mark of distinction to sit on one of these thrones; and the master of a castle took care to have preserved among the records of his family that having been to pay his court to such a count, he had been received by him in an arm-chair.

We may read in the "Memoirs" of mademoiselle, sister to Louis XIV, that this august princess passed at least a fourth part of her life in mortal agonies occasioned by disputes about easy-chairs; and a whole court was taken up in caballing whether it was proper to sit on a chair or a stool in such or such a room, or whether to sit at all. At present our manners are more uniform; and ladies make use indifferently of couches or sofas, without the peace of society being disturbed.

When Cardinal Richelieu was negotiating the marriage between Henrietta of France and Charles I of England, with the ambassador of that nation, the affair was on the point of being broken off, on account of two or three steps nearer to a door that was claimed by the ambassador, till the cardinal, to get over the mighty difficulty, received him in bed; and this precious anecdote has been carefully preserved in history. I am of opinion that, if it had been proposed to Scipio to place himself at his length naked between two sheets to receive Hannibal's visit, he would have thought it a droll ceremony.

One coach going before another, and what is called taking the way in a street or a road, has also been a mark of grandeur, and occasioned claims, disputes, and petty combats, for a whole century together; and it was esteemed a singular victory for the equipage of one person to oblige that of another to yield the way. When foreign ambassadors passed through a street it was like disputing the prize in a circus; and if a Spanish minister made a Portuguese coachman back his horses, he immediately despatched a courier post haste to Madrid, to inform the King his master of the advantage he had gained.

In proportion as a nation is more or less barbarous, or the court weak or powerful, these ceremonies are more or less in vogue. True power and real politeness despise ostentation.

It is probable that we shall one time or other see an end to the ridiculous custom which still prevails among the ambassadors of some courts, to beggar themselves for the sake of going in procession through the streets with a number of hired coaches, vamped up and new-gilt, and preceded by a crowd of servants walking on foot. This is called making their entry; and it is pleasant enough to hear of a person making his entry into a city seven or eight months after his arrival.

The important affair of the *punctilio*, which constitutes the grandeur of the modern Romans—the theory of the number of paces to be made in conducting a signor to the door at his departure; of opening a curtain half way, or altogether; of taking the right or left hand of a person in a room—this noble art, I say, which would never have entered the head of a Fabius or a Cato, begins now to give way; and the train-bearers to the Cardinals lament, with tears in their eyes, that everything seems to denounce a general lapse of these essential ceremonials.

A French colonel happening to be at Brussels, about a year ago, and not knowing how to spend his time, proposed going to the public assembly; one of his acquaintances told him it was held at the house of a princess. "Very true," replied the officer; "but what of that?" "Why, princes go there." "Are you a prince?" "Pish, man!" said he, "they are a very good kind of princes; last year, when we took the town, I had a dozen of them waiting in my ante-chamber; they are the civilest creatures breathing."

ON CROMWELL

CROMWELL is commonly represented as one who was an impostor through the whole course of his life. This is what I can hardly believe. My opinion of the matter is that he was, first of all, an enthusiast, but that afterwards he made his very fanaticism subservient to his greatness. A novice possessed of extreme religious fervor at twenty often becomes a consummate knave at forty. In the great game of human life men begin with being dupes, but end knaves. A statesman shall sometimes take for his chaplain a monk covered over with the little pedantry of his convent; fanatic, devout, credulous, awkward, and quite raw in the world; the monk acquires knowledge, politeness, learns to intrigue, till at last he supplants his patron.

Cromwell at first hardly knew what to make of himself, and was puzzled whether to be a churchman or a soldier. He was actually both. He made a campaign with Frederick Henry, Prince of Orange, in 1622, who was not only a man of great capacity himself, but also brother to two illustrious personages. When he returned to England he entered into the service of Bishop Williams, and was my lord's chaplain, whilst my lord was thought to be rather to great with his wife. His religious principles were those of the puritanical sect; so that he could not but mortally hate the bishop, nor could he have any great affection for kings. He was banished from the bishop's family on account of his being a puritan, and this accident was properly the foundation and first beginning of all his grandeur. The English Parliament had declared against royalty and episcopacy when some friends Cromwell had in that Parliament succeeded in having him chosen for a borough. He may be said to have existed only from this time and was turned of forty before he made any noise in the world. In vain had he studied the Bible, learned to wrangle about the institution of priests and deacons, and made some wretched sermons and libels: he was still in obscurity. I have seen a sermon of his pretty much like one of the Quakers' harangues, in which one cannot discover the smallest traces of that persuasive eloquence by which he afterwards swayed the Parliaments. The true reason of this is, he was much better qualified for the State than the Church. But his eloquence consisted wholly in his air and in the tone of his voice; the single motion of that hand, that won so many battles, and killed so many Royalists, was more persuasive than all the studied periods of Cicero. It must also be acknowledged that the reputation he acquired was wholly owing to his incomparable valor, which laid the first steps of that ladder, by which he reached the highest summit of human grandeur.

He began with serving as a volunteer, desirous of making his fortune in the city of Hull, which was then besieged by the King. Here he performed so many gallant and successful exploits that he was rewarded by the Parliament with a gratification of about six thousand livres of our money. Such a present, bestowed by the Parliament on a simple volunteer, was a sure prognostic that their party must one day get the better. The King was not then in a condition to make such a present to his general officers as the Parliament gave on this occasion to their volunteers. With money and fanaticism, they must, in the long run, overcome all that stood in their way: they made Cromwell a colonel: then it was that his great talents for war began to display themselves, insomuch that, when the Parliament made the Earl of Manchester their general, they made Cromwell a lieutenant-general, without passing through the intermediate ranks. Never did man seem more worthy of command; never was there seen a greater share of prudence and activity, or a more daring and undaunted spirit, joined to such an infinity of resources as were in Cromwell.

He was wounded in the battle of York; and whilst the surgeons were beginning to dress his wound he was told that his general, Lord Manchester, was retreating, and the battle entirely lost. He runs to Lord Manchester, whom he finds flying with some of his officers: he immediately takes him by the arm; and, with an air of intrepidity and greatness, told him, "You are mistaken, my lord; this is not the way the enemy have fled." He leads him back near to the spot on which the battle was fought; rallies in the night upwards of twelve thousand men; exhorts them in the name of the Lord; cites the examples of Moses, Gideon, and Joshua; beseeches them by all means not to neglect to engage the victorious Royalists at break of day; and entirely defeats them. Almost all the officers in his army were enthusiasts, who carried their Bibles tied to the pommel of their saddles: There was nothing talked of, either in the army or in Parliament, but the overthrowing of Babylon, establishing the Lord's worship in the new Jerusalem, and breaking the great idol. Cromwell, though amidst a host of fools, grew wise at last, and bethought himself that it was better to guide them than to be governed by them. The habit, however, of preaching like one inspired still remained with him. Imagine to yourself a fakir, with his loins bound about with a girdle of iron out of mere mortification, who afterwards pulls off his girdle and falls to knocking down his brother fakirs. This is Cromwell: he became full as good a politician as he was a soldier: he enters into an association with all the colonels of the army; and thus he forms his soldiers into a kind of republic, who force their general to abdicate. Another generalissimo is named, with whom he is presently dissatisfied; he governs the army, and with them the Parliament, whom he at last compels to create him generalissimo. All this is certainly a great deal; but what is more remarkable is, that he gained every battle he fought, whether in Scotland, England, or Ireland; and gained them not like other generals, by being a mere spectator, solicitous about his own safety, but by continually charging the enemy in person; rallying his troops; by being present everywhere; often wounded, killing several of the Royalists with his own hand; like some furious grenadier, that delights in carnage.

In the midst of this cruel and bloody war, Cromwell was making love, and went with his Bible under his arm to lie with the wife of his major-general, Lambert. This lady was in love with the Earl of Holland, who was then serving in the royal army. Cromwell takes him prisoner in one of his battles, and has the pleasure to cut off his rival's head. His maxim was to cut off every enemy of any consequence, either in the field of battle, or by the hand of the executioner. He increased his power on every occasion by perpetually abusing it; and the depth of his designs wants nothing of his natural ferocity. He enters the Parliament, and taking out his watch, throws it on the ground, and breaks it into pieces, with this expression, "I will break you, just as I have done that watch." Some time after he returns, and dissolves them by his own authority, making them file off, as it were, in review, before him. Each member was obliged, as he passed him, to make him a profound bow. One of them, it seems, thought proper to pass him with his hat on; when Cromwell, taking it off, threw it on the ground. "Learn," says he, "to show me the proper respect."

After having insulted every crowned head, by cutting off that of the King, his lawful sovereign, and when he had even begun his own reign, he sent his picture to Queen Christina of Sweden. Marvel, a famous English poet, who made very good Latin verses, composed six lines on the occasion, which were to accompany that present, in which he introduced Cromwell himself. Cromwell corrected the two last, which are these:

> "*At tibï submittit frontem reverentior umbia*
> *Non sunt bi vultus regibus usque truces.*"

The bold sentiment expressed in those three couplets may be turned in this manner:

> "*Les armes à la main j'ai défendu les loix ;*
> *D'un peuple audacieux j'ai vengé la querelle ;*
> *Regardez sans frémir cette image fidèle ;*
> *Mon front n'est pas toujours l'épouvante des rois.*"
>
> Behold the chief who fought for dying laws,
> And shunned no dangers in his country's cause;
> To kings no longer dreadful, sues to you,
> And smooths the terrors of his awful brow.

This queen was the first who acknowledged him on his being made protector of the three kingdoms. Almost every sovereign in Europe sent ambassadors to their brother Cromwell, to this once menial servant of a bishop, who had put his sovereign, who was of their blood, to death by the hands of the executioner: Nay, they disputed who should have the honor of being in alliance with him. Cardinal Mazarin, to please him, banished the two sons of Charles I, the two grandsons of Henry IV, the two cousins-germain of Louis XIV, of France; conquered Dunkirk for him, and the keys of that place were accordingly sent him. When he died, Louis XIV, with his whole court.

put on mourning, except mademoiselle, who had the courage to come to the circle in colors, thus singly maintaining the honor of her family.

Never was there a king more absolute than Cromwell. He said he liked better to govern under the quality of protector than that of king, because the power of the latter was well known to the people of England, whereas that of a protector was not. This showed a thorough knowledge of mankind, who are slaves to opinion, which opinion often depends on a mere name. He had conceived a thorough contempt for religion, though he was indebted to it for all the power and honors he enjoyed. We have an undeniable anecdote of this preserved in the St. John family, which is a sufficient proof of the sovereign contempt Cromwell entertained for that instrument which had produced such wonderful effects in his hands. He was one day cracking a bottle with Ireton Fleetwood and St. John. They wanted to draw the cork of a bottle, when the corkscrew happened to fall under the table; they were, all of them in search of it, but could not find it. In the mean time word was brought in that a deputation from the Presbyterian churches waited for an audience in the ante-chamber. "Tell them," says Cromwell, "that I am *in private seeking the Lord.*" This was the canting expression of those fanatics for being at prayers. When he had in this manner dismissed the deputation of ministers, he made use of these very words to his companions: "Those knaves think we are seeking the Lord, whereas in truth we are looking for the corkscrew."

Europe has no other example of a man who raised himself to such a height of glory from so humble an original. What could such a man want? Success. This success he enjoyed; but was he happy with all his good fortune? He lived in very narrow and uneasy circumstances till past forty; he then bathed himself in blood, passed the rest of his days in perpetual anxieties, and died at last in his seven and fiftieth year. Let any man but compare the life of this man with that of Newton, who lived four-score and four years, in perfect tranquillity, full of honor, the light and guide of all intelligent beings, his reputation and fortune daily increasing, without care or remorse; and then tell me whose was the happier lot of the two.

O curas hominum, o quantum est in rebus inane!

CHOICE EXAMPLES OF EARLY PRINTING AND ENGRAVING.

Fac-similes from Rare and Curious Books.

EARLY VENETIAN PRINTING.

Page from Appian's Roman History.

This page, which is the work of the printers Bernardo Pictor and Erhardt Ratdolt, shows all the characteristics of printing at Venice in the fifteenth century—beauty and regularity of letters—boldness of leading, and fine initial and border adornments. The branching and looping of the woodcut decorations are notable for ease and flexibility, and are models of what such work ought to be. Appian's "Roman History," from which this page is taken, was printed at Venice in 1477.

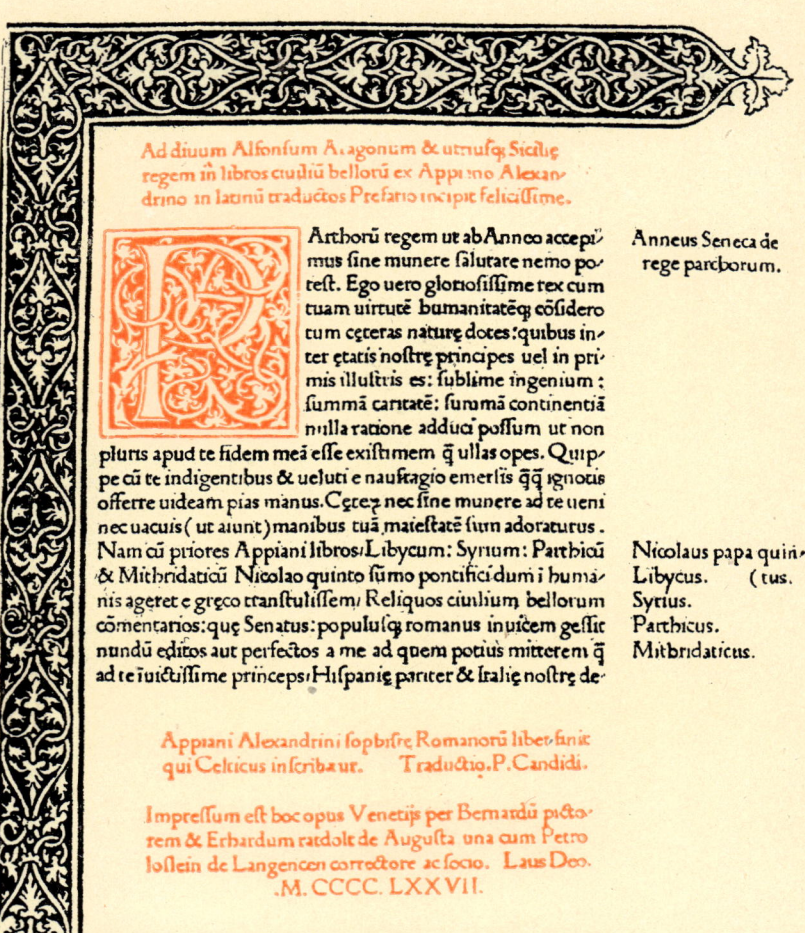

Ad diuum Alfonsum Aragonum & utriusq; Sicilię
regem in libros ciuiliu bellorū ex Appiano Alexan-
drino in latinū traductos Prefatio incipit felicissime.

Arthorū regem ut ab Anneo accepi-
mus sine munere salutare nemo potest. Ego uero gloriosissime rex cum
tuam uirtutē humanitatēq; cōsidero
tum cęteras naturę dotes: quibus inter ętatis nostrę principes uel in pri-
mis illustris es: sublime ingenium:
summā caritatē: summā continentiā
nulla ratione adduci possum ut non
pluris apud te fidem meā esse existimem q̄ ullas opes. Quip-
pe cū te indigentibus & ueluti e naufragio emersis q̄q̄ ignotis
offerre uideam pias manus. Cęterꝫ nec sine munere ad te ueni
nec uacuis (ut aiunt) manibus tuā maiestatē sum adoraturus.
Nam cū priores Appiani libros, Libycum: Syrium: Parthicū
& Mithridaticū Nicolao quinto sūmo pontifici dum i huma-
nis ageret e greco transtulissem: Reliquos ciuilium bellorum
cōmentarios: quę Senatus: populusq; romanus inuicem gessit
nundū ęditos aut perfectos a me ad quem potius mitterem q̄
ad te inuictissime princeps, Hispaniꝫ pariter & Italię nostrę de

Anneus Seneca de
rege parthorum.

Nicolaus papa quin-
Libycus. (tus.
Syrius.
Parthicus.
Mithridaticus.

Appiani Alexandrini sophistę Romanorū liber finit
qui Celticus inscribatur.   Traductio. P. Candidi.

Impressum est hoc opus Venetijs per Bernardū picto-
rem & Erhardum ratdolt de Augusta una cum Petro
loslein de Langencen correctore ac socio. Laus Deo.
.M. CCCC. LXXVII.

THE PEOPLE

—

BY

JEAN JACQUES ROUSSEAU

JEAN JACQUES ROUSSEAU
1712—1778

Jean Jacques Rousseau was born at Geneva in 1712. His early education was sadly neglected, but he acquired a great deal of knowledge by reading, which, though unsystematic, was extensive. His father was a watchmaker, and young Rousseau was, therefore, apprenticed to a watchmaker in his native town. But the boy soon ran away from his master, and figured successively in the capacity of an engraver's apprentice, a lackey, a musician, a student in a seminary, a clerk, a private tutor, and a music copyist. From time to time he lived at the houses of various patrons—Madame de Warens, Madame d'Epinay, the Duke of Luxembourg, Marshall Keith, David Hume, Madame d'Enghien—and quarrelled with all. His last home was with M. de Giradin, near Paris, where he died in 1778.

The first period of Rousseau's life, covering nearly twenty years, has been characterized as one of vagabondage. The next period, ending about 1741, was devoted to ardent study; and during this time he evidenced a steadily growing interest in literature. The nine succeeding years were the period of his lighter writings, operas, and comedies. None of them have proved of permanent interest, but they gave him a considerable reputation among the literary circles of his day. Some articles on music contributed to the "Encyclopédie" secured for him an introduction to Diderot, who probably influenced him in turning his mind toward more serious subjects.

In 1749 Rousseau wrote an essay to compete for a prize offered by the Academy of Dijon, entitled "Discours sur les sciences et les arts," which was crowned and brought him great fame. During the following ten years he wrote in rapid succession the works that have given him lasting fame. His romance "Julie, ou la nouvelle Heloïse" appeared in 1761. The year following he published "Émile, ou de l'éducation," and the "Contrat social." The ideas expressed in "Émile" led to Rousseau's exile from France, but it is credited with having laid the foundation of modern pedagogy.

The "Contrat social" voiced the popular protest against the injustice of a social state already rotten and trembling on the brink of ruin. Rousseau's brilliant social philosophy, though superficial and often false, was hailed by the downtrodden masses as an inspired message, and became the gospel of the Revolution.

The vast influence of Rousseau's work on the social and political history of France overshadows but should not blind us to the far-reaching influence of his style and methods upon literature. His novels popularized the analysis of the emotions, and he was the first writer to make word-painting of nature an indispensable element of fiction. His style, both in his romances and in his more serious writings, is simple, direct, unconventional, yet full of passion and eloquence.

His teachings and his literary manner exerted a strong influence on the orators of the French Revolution. The essay on "The People" is taken from the "Social Contract," and is a characteristic example of his work in his best and most effective vein. After Rousseau's expulsion from France he lived in Switzerland and England until he was allowed to return in 1767, on condition that he would henceforth cease to write for publication. Accordingly, his last works of consequence, "Les confessions" and "Rêveries d'un promeneur solitaire," were not published until four years after his death. He died of apoplexy at Ermenonville, near Paris, on July 2, 1778.

THE PEOPLE

AS an architect, before erecting a large edifice, examines and tests the soil in order to see whether it can support the weight, so a wise lawgiver does not begin by drawing up laws that are good in themselves, but considers first whether the people for whom he designs them are fit to endure them. It is on this account that Plato refused to legislate for the Arcadians and Cyrenians, knowing that these two peoples were rich and could not tolerate equality; and it is on this account that good laws and worthless men were to be found in Crete, for Minos had only disciplined a people steeped in vice.

A thousand nations that have flourished on the earth could never have borne good laws; and even those that might have done so could have succeeded for only a very short period of their whole duration. The majority of nations, as well as of men, are tractable only in their youth; they become incorrigible as they grow old. When once customs are established and prejudices have taken root, it is a perilous and futile enterprise to try and reform them; for the people cannot even endure that their evils should be touched with a view to their removal, like those stupid and cowardly patients that shudder at the sight of a physician.

But just as some diseases unhinge men's minds and deprive them of all remembrance of the past, so we sometimes find, during the existence of States, epochs of violence, in which revolutions produce an influence upon nations such as certain crises produce upon individuals, in which horror of the past supplies the place of forgetfulness, and in which the State, inflamed by civil wars, springs forth so to speak from its ashes, and regains the vigor of youth in issuing from the arms of death. Such was Sparta in the time of Lycurgus, such was

Rome after the Tarquins, and such among us moderns were Holland and Switzerland after the expulsion of their tyrants.

But these events are rare; they are exceptions, the explanation of which is always found in the particular constitution of the excepted State. They could not even happen twice with the same nation; for it may render itself free so long as it is merely barbarous, but can no longer do so when the resources of the State are exhausted. Then commotions may destroy it without revolutions being able to restore it, and as soon as its chains are broken, it falls in pieces and ceases to exist; henceforward it requires a master and not a deliverer. Free nations, remember this maxim: "Liberty may be acquired but never recovered."

Youth is not infancy. There is for nations as for men a period of youth, or, if you will, of maturity, which they must await before they are subjected to laws; but it is not always easy to discern when a people is mature, and if the time is anticipated, the labor is abortive. One nation is governable from its origin, another is not so at the end of ten centuries. The Russians will never be really civilized, because they have been civilized too early. Peter had an imitative genius; he had not the true genius that creates and produces anything from nothing. Some of his measures were beneficial, but the majority were ill-timed. He saw that his people were barbarous, but he did not see that they were unripe for civilization; he wished to civilize them, when it was necessary only to discipline them. He wished to produce at once Germans or Englishmen, when, he should have begun by making Russians; he prevented his subjects from ever becoming what they might have been, by persuading them that they were what they were not. It is in this way that a French tutor trains his pupil to shine for a moment in childhood, and then to be forever a nonentity. The Russian Empire will desire to subjugate Europe, and will itself be subjugated. The Tartars, its subjects or neighbors, will become its masters and ours. This revolution appears to me inevitable. All the kings of Europe are working in concert to accelerate it.

As nature has set limits to the stature of a properly formed man, outside which it produces only giants and dwarfs; so likewise, with regard to the best constitution of a State, there are limits to its possible extent so that it may be neither too great to enable it to be well governed, nor too small to enable it to maintain itself single-handed. There is in every body politic a maximum of force which it cannot exceed, and which is often diminished as the State is aggrandized. The more the social bond is extended, the more it is weakened; and, in general, a small State is proportionally stronger than a large one.

A thousand reasons demonstrate the truth of this maxim. In the first place, administration becomes more difficult at great distances, as a weight becomes heavier at the end of a longer lever. It also becomes more burdensome in proportion as its parts are multiplied; for every town has first its own administration, for which the people pay; every district has its administration, still paid for by the people; next, every province, then the superior governments, the satrapies, the viceroyalties, which must be paid for more dearly as we ascend, and always at the cost of the unfortunate people; lastly comes the supreme administration, which overwhelms everything. So many additional burdens perpetually exhaust the subjects; and far from being better governed by all these different orders, they are much worse governed than if they had but a single superior. Meanwhile, hardly any resources remain for cases of emergency; and when it is necessary to have recourse to them the State trembles on the brink of ruin.

Nor is this all; not only has the government less vigor and activity in enforcing observance of the laws, in putting a stop to vexations, in reforming abuses, and in forestalling seditious enterprises which may be entered upon in distant places; but the people have less affection for their chiefs whom they never see, for their country, which is in their eyes like the world, and for their fellow-citizens, most of whom are strangers to them. The same laws cannot be suitable to so many different provinces, which have different customs and different climates, and cannot tolerate the same form of government. Different laws beget only trouble and confusion among the nations which, living under the same chiefs and in constant communication, mingle or intermarry with one another, and, when subjected to other usages, never know whether their patrimony is really theirs. Talents are hidden, virtues ignored, vices unpunished, in that multitude of men, unknown to one another, whom the seat of the supreme administration gathers together in one place. The chiefs, overwhelmed with business, see nothing themselves; clerks rule the State. In a word, the measures that must be taken to maintain the general authority, which so many officers at a distance wish to evade or impose upon, absorb all the public attention; no regard for the welfare of the people remains, and scarcely any for their defence in time of need; and thus a body too huge for its constitution sinks and perishes, crushed by its own weight.

On the other hand, the State must secure a certain foundation, that it may possess stability and resist the shocks which it will infallibly experience, as well as sustain the efforts which it will be forced to make in order to maintain itself; for all nations have a kind of centrifugal force, by which they continually act one against another, and tend to aggrandize themselves at the expense of their neighbors, like the vortices of Descartes. Thus the weak are in danger of being quickly swallowed up, and none can preserve itself long except by putting itself in a kind of equilibrium with all, which renders the compression almost equal everywhere.

Hence we see that there are reasons for expansion and reasons for contraction; and it is not the least of a statesman's talents to find the proportion between the two which is most advantageous for the preservation of the State. We may say, in general, that the former, being only external and relative, ought to be subordinated to the others, which are internal and absolute. A healthy and strong constitution is the first thing to be sought; and we should rely more on the vigor that springs from a good government than on the resources furnished by an extensive territory.

States have, however, been constituted in such a way that the necessity of making conquests entered into their very constitution, and in order to maintain themselves they were forced to enlarge themselves continually. Perhaps they rejoiced greatly at this happy necessity, which nevertheless revealed to them, with the limit of their greatness, the inevitable moment of their fall.

A body politic may be measured in two ways, viz., by the extent of its territory, and by the number of its people; and there is between these two modes of measurement a suitable relation according to which the State may be assigned its true dimensions. It is the men that constitute the State, and it is the soil that sustains the men; the due relation, then, is that the land should suffice for the maintenance of its inhabitants, and that there should be as many inhabitants as the land can sustain. In this proportion is found the maximum power of a given number of people; for if there is too much land, the care of it is burdensome, the cultivation inadequate, and the produce superfluous, and this is the proximate cause of defensive wars. If there is not enough land, the State is at the mercy of its neighbors for the additional quantity; and this is the proximate cause of offensive wars. Any nation which has, by its position, only the alternative between commerce and war is weak in itself; it is dependent on its neighbors and on events; it has only a short and precarious existence. It conquers and changes its situation, or it is conquered and reduced to nothing. It can preserve its freedom only by virtue of being small or great.

It is impossible to express numerically a fixed ratio between the extent of land and the number of men which are reciprocally sufficient, on account of the differences that are found in the quality of the soil, in its degrees of fertility, in the nature of its products, and in the influence of climate, as well as on account of those which we observe in the constitutions of the inhabitants, of whom some consume little in a fertile country, while others consume much on an unfruitful soil. Further, attention must be paid to the greater or less fecundity of the women, to the conditions of the country, whether more or less favorable to population, and to the numbers which the legislator may hope to draw thither by his institutions; so that an opinion should be based not on what is seen, but on what is foreseen, while the actual state of the people should be less observed than that which it ought naturally to attain. In short, there are a thousand occasions on which the particular accidents of situation require or permit that more territory than appears necessary should be taken up. Thus men will spread out a good deal in a mountainous country, where the natural productions, viz., woods and pastures, require less labor, where experience teaches that women are more fecund than in the plains, and where with an extensive inclined surface there is only a small horizontal base, which alone should count for vegetation. On the other hand, people may inhabit a smaller space on the seashore, even among rocks and sands that are almost barren, because fishing can, in great measure, supply the deficiency in the productions of the earth, because men ought to be more concentrated in order to repel pirates, and because, further, it is easier to relieve the country, by means of colonies, of the inhabitants with which it is overburdened.

In order to establish a nation, it is necessary to add to these conditions one which cannot supply the place of any other, but without which they are all useless—it is that the people should enjoy abundance and peace; for the time of a State's formation is, like that of forming soldiers in a square, the time when the body is least capable of resistance and most easy to destroy. Resistance would be greater in a state of absolute disorder than at a moment of fermentation, when each is occupied with his own position and not with the common danger. Should a war, a famine, or a sedition supervene at this critical period, the State is inevitably overthrown.

Many governments, indeed, may be established during such storms, but then it is these very governments that destroy the State. Usurpers always bring about or select troublous times for passing, under cover of the public agitation, destructive laws which the people would never adopt when soberminded. The choice of the moment for the establishment of a government is one of the surest marks for distinguishing the work of the legislator from that of the tyrant.

What nation, then, is adapted for legislation? That which is already united by some bond of interest, origin, or convention, but has not yet borne the real yoke of the laws; that which has neither customs nor superstitions firmly rooted; that which has no fear of being overwhelmed by a sudden invasion, but which, without entering into disputes of its neighbors, can single-handed resist either of them, or aid one in repelling the other; that in which every member can be known by all, and in which there is no necessity to lay on a man a greater burden than a man can bear; that which can subsist without other nations, and without which every other nation can subsist;[1] that which is neither rich nor poor and is self-sufficing; lastly, that which combines the stability of an old nation with the docility of a new one. The work of legislation is rendered arduous not so much by what must be established as by what must be destroyed; and that which makes success so rare is the impossibility of finding the simplicity of nature conjoined with the necessities of society. All these conditions, it is true, are with difficulty combined; hence few well-constituted States are seen.

There is still one country in Europe capable of legislation; it is the island of Corsica. The courage and firmness which that brave nation has exhibited in recovering and defending its freedom would well deserve that some wise man should teach it how to preserve it. I have some presentiment that this small island will one day astonish Europe.

[1] If of two neighboring nations one could not subsist without the other, it would be a very hard situation for the first, and a very dangerous one for the second. Every wise nation in such a case will endeavor very quickly to free the other from this dependence. The republic of Tlascala, enclosed in the empire of Mexico, preferred to do without salt rather than buy it of the Mexicans or even accept it gratuitously. The wise Tlascalans saw a trap hidden beneath this generosity. They kept themselves free; and this small State, enclosed in that great empire, was at last the instrument of its downfall.

ARISTOTLE AND TRAGEDY

BY

GOTTHOLD EPHRAIM LESSING

GOTTHOLD EPHRAIM LESSING

1729—1781

Gotthold Ephraim Lessing was born in the little Saxon town of Kamenz, in 1729, and received his education at the universities of Leipsic and Wittenberg. His father intended him for the ministry, but his ability lay in other directions. At the universities he displayed marked literary ability. In 1748 he went to Berlin, where he succeeded in gaining a precarious livelihood by his pen. As the years went on recognition came, and by 1755, when he published "Miss Sara Sampson," a tragedy, Lessing had already become a celebrated man, a dreaded critic, and an admired dramatist and poet of some distinction. In 1759 he commenced the publication of the "Literary Letters," a series of literary criticisms of remarkable acumen and force, which he continued during nearly seven years. Meantime he had left Berlin to become the private secretary of the Governor of Silesia. While at Breslau, "Minna von Barnhelm," one of the masterpieces of the German drama, was published. After his return to Berlin, in 1766, "Laocoön," his masterly treatise on æsthetic criticism, was given to the world. In 1767 Lessing was called to Hamburg to assist in establishing a stage for the national drama. The result of his activity there caused him to write his famous "Dramatic Notes," a series of essays that exerted a profound influence on the German drama. They were written in Lessing's best vein and in the fulness of his powers. "Aristotle and Tragedy" is a good example of these remarkable essays as well as of Lessing's style. In 1770 he was appointed by the Duke of Brunswick librarian at Wolfenbüttel, a position he held until his death in 1781. Here he wrote the two excellent plays, "Emilia Galotti" and "Nathan the Wise," besides numerous treatises, chiefly on theological questions and polemic in character.

The key-note of Lessing's character and writings is truth. Hence his impatience with cant and hypocrisy, the unsparing severity displayed in his theological controversies, and the lucidity of his dramatic and literary criticisms. As a critic Lessing may justly be regarded as the greatest Germany has produced. Although not exclusively destructive in his criticisms, it was as a critic of this school that he produced his most lasting works. His dramatic criticisms did much toward the development of the modern German Drama and his literary criticisms prepared the way for Goethe and Schiller. His theological and philosophical writings are less important, but they in turn served in preparing the way for Kant and Fichte.

Lessing's literary style is distinguished by clearness and precision, in marked contrast to that in vogue with German prose writers of his time. He avoided long and intricate sentences and constructions. "Write as you speak," was his motto, and in all his writings he displays a most astonishing power of clear and concise statement and a wealth of logical argument that make his works models of expository and argumentative style.

ARISTOTLE AND TRAGEDY

CRÉBILLON is known among the French as "the Terrible." I greatly fear that he has received this name more on account of the terror which should not exist in tragedy, than on account of that legitimate terror which the philosopher includes amongst the essentials of tragedy.

And this ought not to have been named terror at all. The word used by Aristotle means fear: fear and pity, he says, should be provoked by tragedy, not terror and pity. Terror is, it is true, a species of fear; it is a sudden, overwhelming fear. But this very suddenness, this surprise, which is included in the conception of the term, clearly shows that those who here substituted the word terror for fear did not understand to what kind of fear Aristotle was referring.

"Pity," says Aristotle, "demands a person who suffers undeservedly, and fear requires him to be one of ourselves. The villain is neither the one nor the other, and his misfortunes consequently do not excite either pity or fear."[1]

Fear, as I have said, has been called terror by modern commentators and translators; and this substitution has enabled them to bring the most extraordinary charges against the philosopher.

"It has not been found possible," says one of this crowd,[2] "to agree as to the explanation of terror; and indeed it contains in every respect one superfluous link which hampers its universality and limits it too much. If Aristotle, in adding the words 'one of ourselves,' was merely thinking of the similarity of mankind, in the sense that the spectator and the acting personage are both human beings, however widely they may differ from each other in character, dignity, and rank: then such an addition was unnecessary, for the fact was self-

[1] "Poetics," cap. xiii.
[2] Schmidt, in his Introduction to "The Comic Theatre."

evident. If, on the contrary, he was of opinion that terror could only be excited by virtuous persons or by such as are afflicted with venial faults: then he was mistaken, for commonsense and experience are opposed to him. Terror undoubtedly springs from a feeling of humanity; for every human being is subject to it, and every human being is touched by this feeling at the adverse fortunes of a fellow-creature. There may possibly be persons who deny this with regard to themselves; but such a denial would only be a disavowal of their natural sensibility, a mere boast founded upon defective principles, and therefore no argument. Now if a vicious person, upon whom our attention is centred, meets with an unexpected misfortune, we lose sight of the reprobate and behold only the human being. The sight of human suffering in general makes us sad, and this sudden feeling of sadness which comes over us is terror."

All this is perfectly true, but it is out of place. For what does it prove against Aristotle? Nothing at all. Aristotle is not thinking of this kind of terror when he speaks of that fear which can only be evoked by one of our fellow-creatures. Such fear, with which we are seized when we are suddenly brought face to face with a misfortune that threatens another person, is a sympathetic fear, and should therefore be included in the term pity. Aristotle would not say " Pity and Fear," if by the latter he understood no more than merely a modified form of pity.

" Pity," says the author of " Letters on the Emotions,"[3] " is a compound emotion consisting of love for an object and displeasure at its misfortunes. The movements by which pity manifests itself differ from the simple symptoms of love as well as from those of displeasure; for pity is a mere manifestation. But how varied this manifestation may be! Let the one limitation of time be but changed in a commiserated misfortune, and pity will manifest itself by totally different signs. The sight of Electra, weeping over her brother's urn, fills us with compassionate grief; for she thinks that the misfortune has taken place and is lamenting the loss which she has sustained. The sufferings of Philoctetes likewise call forth our pity, but in this case it is pity of a somewhat different nature; for the

[3] Moses Mendelssohn.

afflictions which overtake this virtuous man are actually present and seize him before our very eyes. But what do we feel when Œdipus is seized with terror, as the fatal secret is suddenly revealed; when Monime is alarmed at seeing the jealous Mithridates turn pale; when the virtuous Desdemona becomes frightened as she hears the threatening words of her Othello, erstwhile so tender? We still feel pity. But pitiful terror, pitiful alarm, pitiful fear. The movements are various; but the essence of the emotion is in all cases identical. For since love is ever connected with a willingness to put ourselves in the place of the person whom we love, we must share every kind of misfortune with that person; and this is very expressively termed compassion or pity. Why then should not also fear, terror, wrath, jealousy, revenge—in fact, all kinds of unpleasant emotions, even envy not excepted, spring from pity? We may hereby see how unskilfully the majority of critics divide the tragic passions into terror and pity. Terror and pity! Is theatrical terror no pity, then? For whom does the spectator tremble when Merope draws the dagger upon her own son? Certainly not for himself, but for Ægisthus, whose preservation he so earnestly desires, and for the deluded queen who regards him as the murderer of her son. But if we apply the name of pity to the mere displeasure which the present misfortunes of a fellow-creature excite in us: then we must draw a distinction between pity properly so called, on the one hand, and not only terror, but all other feelings communicated to us by a fellow-creature, on the other."

These ideas are so correct, so clear, so perspicuous, that everyone, it seems to us, could and ought to hold them. Nevertheless I will not ascribe the acute observations of the new philosopher to the ancient one; I am too well acquainted with the former's contributions to the doctrine of mixed sensations, for the true theory of which we are indebted to him alone. But what he has explained so thoroughly, Aristotle may also, on the whole, have experienced; at all events it cannot be denied that Aristotle must either have believed that tragedy could and should excite nothing but genuine pity, nothing but the displeasure experienced at the present misfortunes of a fellow-creature, which seems highly improbable; or else he included under the term pity all passions in general that can be communicated to us by another.

For it certainly was not Aristotle who made the division, so justly censured, of the tragic passions into pity and terror. He has been misread and mistranslated. He speaks of pity and fear, not of pity and terror; and the fear to which he refers is not that which an impending misfortune to another person excites in us on his behalf, but that which, from our resemblance to the victim, we feel on our own behalf; it is the fear that the disasters which we see threatening him may overtake us also; it is the fear that we may ourselves become the objects of commiseration. In a word: this fear is pity referred back to ourselves.

Aristotle always requires to be interpreted through himself. If any person were thinking of giving us a new commentary upon his "Poetics," which should excel that of Dacier, I would strongly advise him, before so doing, to read the philosopher's works from beginning to end. He will come across explanations bearing upon the art of poetry where he least expects to find them; and he must above all things study the treatises on rhetoric and ethics. It might indeed be supposed that the schoolmen, who had the writings of Aristotle at their finger ends, would long ago have discovered these explanatory passages. Yet the "Poetics" was the very work to which they paid the least attention. They moreover lacked other knowledge without which the explanations referred to could not have borne fruit; they were not acquainted with the theatre and its masterpieces.

The true explanation of this fear, which Aristotle mentions in conjunction with tragic pity, is to be found in the fifth and eighth chapters of the second book of his "Rhetoric." It would have been an easy matter to remember these chapters; yet not one of his commentators seems to have called them to mind; at any rate not one has made that use of them which they afford. For even those who perceived, without their aid, that this fear was not the same as compassionate terror, might still have learnt an important fact from them—viz., the reason why the Stagyrite here combines pity with fear, why he combines it with fear alone, and not with any other passion or passions. Of the reason of this they know nothing, and I for my part should like to hear what answer their own intelligence would suggest to them, if they were asked, for example, the following question: Why cannot and may not tragedy excite pity and admiration equally as well as pity and fear?

All, however, depends upon the conception which Aristotle framed of pity. Now he was of opinion that a misfortune which is intended as the object of our pity, must of necessity be of such a nature that we are capable of dreading its happening to ourselves also, or to one of our friends. And where there was not this fear, he argued, there could be no pity; for neither he whom misfortune had so overwhelmed that he saw nothing further to fear, nor he who considered his happiness so complete that he could not imagine any misfortune overtaking him; neither the desperate man nor the over-confident one is in the habit of feeling pity for others. He therefore explains the fearful and the pitiable by means of each other. We find those things fearful, he says, which would awaken our pity if they had befallen, or were about to befall, another person; and we find those things pitiable which we should fear if they were about to happen to ourselves. It is not enough, therefore, that the sufferer, for whom we are to feel pity, may not deserve his misfortune, though he may have brought it upon himself by his own weakness: his injured innocence, or rather his error, for which he is made to pay too severe a penalty, would lose its effect upon us, would fail to excite our pity, unless we saw that there was a possibility of his calamity overtaking us also. Now this possibility arises, and it becomes the more probable, if the poet does not represent him worse than mankind in general; if he lets him think and act exactly as we should have thought and acted in his place, or as we imagine we should have done; if, in short, he makes him of the same flesh and blood as ourselves. It is this resemblance that gives rise to the fear that our fate may as easily become like his as we feel ourselves to be like him; and it is this fear that serves as it were to mature our pity.

Such were Aristotle's thoughts concerning pity, and by their aid alone can we arrive at the true reason why, in his definition of tragedy, fear was the only emotion which he named in conjunction with pity. It is not that this fear is a separate passion independent of pity, which might be excited now with pity, and now without it, in the same way as pity can be excited now with and now without fear. This was Corneille's error. Aristotle's reason was that, in his definition of pity, fear was of necessity included, because nothing could awaken our pity which did not at the same time excite our fear.

Corneille had already written all his plays before he set himself to commentate upon the "Poetics" of Aristotle.[4] For half a century he had been working for the theatre, and after such experience he might undoubtedly have furnished us with much valuable information concerning the ancient dramatic code, if, during the time of his labors, he had but studied it a little more diligently. But this he appears only to have done in so far as the mechanical rules of his art were concerned. In the more essential points he disregarded it; and when he found in the end that he had violated its laws, a thing which he was by no means disposed to admit, he sought to clear himself by the help of comments, and caused his pretended master to say things of which he had never thought.

Corneille had brought martyrs upon the stage and portrayed them as the most perfect and immaculate of human beings; he had produced the most repulsive monsters in Prusias, Phocas, and Cleopatra; and of both these species Aristotle declares that they are unsuitable for tragedy, since neither of them can awaken pity or fear. What does Corneille say in answer to this? How does he contrive to prevent both his own authority and that of Aristotle from being disparaged by this contradiction? "We can easily come to terms with Aristotle," he says;[5] "we need only assume that he did not mean to maintain that both fear and pity were required at the same time to effect the purification of our passions, which according to him should be the chief aim of tragedy, but that one of these means would suffice. We can find this explanation confirmed in his own writings," he continues, "if we carefully weigh the reasons given by him for the exclusion of those events which he censures in tragedies. He never says: this or that event is out of place in tragedy because it merely awakens pity, and not fear; or again, such a thing is intolerable because it simply produces fear, without calling forth pity. No; he excludes

---

[4] He says: "Je hasarderai quelque chose sur cinquante ans de travail pour la scène," in his dissertation on the Drama. His first play, "Mélite," dates from 1625, and his last, "Suréna," from 1675. This makes exactly fifty years, so that in his commentaries upon Aristotle he was certainly able to have an eye to all his plays.
[5] "Il est aisé de nous accommoder avec Aristote," etc.

such events because, as he says, they fail to excite either pity or fear; and he thereby gives us to understand that he finds them unsuitable because the one is wanting as well as the other, and that he would not condemn them if they did but produce one of these effects."

Now this it utterly wrong. And I cannot understand why Dacier, who, as a rule, did not fail to observe the false interpretations which Corneille tried to place upon the text of Aristotle to suit his own purpose, should have overlooked this, the worst example of all. Yet, after all, how could he help overlooking it, since it never occurred to him to study the philosopher's definition of pity? Corneille's ideas on this point are, as I have said, utterly wrong. Aristotle cannot have meant anything of the kind, or else we must believe that he could have so far forgotten his own definitions as to contradict himself in the most flagrant manner. If, according to his doctrine, no misfortune that befalls another can excite our pity, unless we are afraid that it may also overtake ourselves: then no action in tragedy, which could only excite pity, and not fear, would have appeared suitable to him; for he deemed the thing itself an impossibility. Such actions did not exist for him; on the contrary, as soon as they reached a pitch at which they were capable of awakening our pity, they must, he opined, also awaken fear for ourselves; or rather, it was only by means of this fear that they called forth our pity. Still less could he conceive of an action in a tragedy which could awaken fear for ourselves without at the same time calling forth our pity; for he was convinced that anything which awakens in us fear for ourselves, must also call forth our pity, as soon as we see others threatened or overtaken by it; and this is precisely what happens in tragedy, where we see all the evils which we fear, happening not to ourselves, but to others.

In speaking of those actions which are unsuitable for tragedy, Aristotle, it is true, avails himself more than once of the expression that they excite *neither* pity *nor* fear. Yet if Corneille has allowed himself to be misled by this *neither . . . nor*, so much the worse for him. These disjunctive particles do not always express what he intends them to express. For if we use them to deny two or more properties of an object, the existence of the object, notwithstanding that one or other of these properties is wanting to it, depends on whether the latter can be as easily separated in nature as we separate them in the abstract by means of symbolic expressions. If, for example, we say, in speaking of a woman, that she has neither beauty nor wit, we certainly wish to convey that we should be satisfied if she possessed either of these qualities; for wit and beauty cannot only be separated in thought, but they are also separate in reality. But if we say: "This man believes in neither heaven nor hell," do we also wish to imply that we should be satisfied if he did but believe in one of the two; if he believed in heaven, but not in hell; or in hell, but not in heaven? Surely not; for he who believes in the one must of necessity believe in the other also. Heaven and hell, punishment and reward, are correlative terms; if the one exists so must the other. Or, to borrow an example from a sister art, if we say: "This painting is worthless; it has neither outline nor color," do we wish it to be inferred that there could be such a thing as a good painting possessing only one of these properties? All this is very clear.

But what if Aristotle's definition of pity were false? What if we found that we could also feel pity for evils and calamities which we have in nowise to fear for ourselves?

Fear for ourselves is not necessary, it is true, to produce in us a feeling of displeasure at the physical suffering of a person whom we love. Such displeasure arises simply from our perception of the imperfection, just as our love arises from that of the perfections of the individual; and when these feelings of pleasure and displeasure are united, they give rise to that mixed feeling which we term pity.

Yet even then, I do not think that Aristotle's position is at all weakened.

For although we can feel pity for others without experiencing any fear for ourselves, it is indisputable that our pity, when accompanied by such a fear, becomes much stronger and more vivid than it could otherwise be. And what is there to prevent us from assuming that the mixed sensation which we feel on beholding the physical suffering of a beloved object, can only by the addition of fear for ourselves attain a sufficient degree of intensity to deserve the name of an effective force *(Affekt)*.

This is precisely what Aristotle assumed. He did not regard pity according to its primary emotions; he regarded it merely as an effective force *(Affekt)*. Without mistaking the former, he only denied to the spark the name of flame. Compassionate emotions, unaccompanied by fear for ourselves, he terms philanthropy; and he reserves the name of pity for those stronger emotions of the same kind, which are combined with fear for ourselves. According to him, therefore, the misfortunes of a villain will excite neither our pity nor our fear; yet he does not on this account deny him all power of moving us. Even the villain is still a human being possessing, in spite of all his moral imperfections, enough perfections to make us rather hope against his ruin or destruction, and to awaken in us, if we behold it, something akin to pity, the rudiments, as it were, of pity. But this rudimentary feeling, as I have already pointed out, he does not call pity but philanthropy. " A villain," he tells us, " must never be allowed to pass from a state of adversity to one of prosperity; for nothing could be more untragical; he would then lack all that he should have, and would call forth neither philanthropy, nor pity, nor fear. Neither must it be an utter villain who is plunged from a state of prosperity into one of adversity; for such an event might, it is true, excite philanthropy, but not pity, nor yet fear." I know of nothing more feeble and absurd than the common rendering of this word " philanthropy." Its adjective is usually translated into Latin by *hominibus gratum;* into French by *ce qui peut faire quelque plaisir;* and into German by *was Vergnügen machen kann* ("what may give pleasure"). Goulston alone, as far as I can see, appears to have caught the philosopher's meaning; he translates φιλάνθρωπον by *quod humanitatis sensu tangat.* For this word philanthropy is used to signify that feeling which the misfortunes even of a villain can awaken; it is not the satisfaction which we feel at his well-merited punishment, but the common feeling of human sympathy which comes over us when we see him suffer, even though we are given to understand that his suffering is amply deserved. Herr Curtius would indeed confine this feeling of pity for an unfortunate villain to one section only of the evils to which he is liable. " Those accidents to the vicious," he says, " which excite in us neither terror nor pity, must be the results of their vices; for, were they to happen to them by chance, or undeservedly, the sufferers would still retain in the hearts of the spectators the privileges of humanity, which does not withhold its pity from a villain who suffers innocently." But he does not appear to have considered this sufficiently. For even in cases where the misfortune that overtakes the villain is the direct outcome of his crime, we cannot forbear suffering with him at the sight of his punishment. "Behold the mob," says the author of "Letters on the Emotions," as they crowd closely around the condemned criminal! They have heard of all the outrages which the villain has committed; they have been horrified at his conduct, and have perhaps even hated him. Now he is dragged, pale and fainting, to the terrible scaffold. The crowd press forward, some stand on tiptoe, others climb on to the roofs, to see how his features change at the approach of death. His sentence is pronounced; the executioner steps forward; another moment and all will be over. How earnestly all the spectators now wish that he might be pardoned! What? That same person, the object of their hatred, whom but a moment before they would themselves have condemned to death? What has happened to send this sudden ray of human love through their hearts? Is it not his approaching doom, the aspect of the direst physical calamity, that, as it were, reconciles us to the worst offender and secures him our affection? Without love it would be impossible to feel pity for his fate."

And it is this very love for our fellow-creatures, I say, which is never entirely absent from our hearts, which, hidden beneath other and stronger emotions, lies smouldering unceasingly, and needs but a favorable gust, so to speak, of misfortune, pain, or crime, to fan it into a flame of pity; this very love it is that Aristotle understands under the name of philanthropy. We are right in looking upon it as a kind of pity. But neither was Aristotle wrong in giving it a separate name, to distinguish it, as I have said, from the highest grade of compassionate emotions, in which the addition of a probable fear for ourselves converts those emotions into effective forces *(Affekt)*.

I must here meet another objection. If Aristotle conceived of the effectiveness *(Affekt)* of pity as being necessarily combined with fear for ourselves, what necessity was there for him to make special mention of fear? The word pity already included it, and it would have been sufficient for him to say: tragedy ought to effect the purification of our passions by exciting our pity. For the addition of the word fear does not alter the sense, and only makes that which he says ambiguous and uncertain.

I answer: if Aristotle had merely wished to teach us what passions can and ought to be awakened by tragedy, he might indeed have omitted all mention of fear, and would no doubt have done so, for no philosopher was ever more sparing of his words than he. But he wanted to tell us at the same time what passions ought to be purified by means of those which tragedy awakens in us; and for this purpose he was obliged to include fear. For although, according to him, the effective power *(Affekt)* of pity cannot but be connected with fear for ourselves both within and without the theatre; although fear is a necessary ingredient of pity; yet the converse does not hold good, and pity for others is no ingredient of fear for ourselves. As soon as the tragedy is over, our pity ceases; and of all the emotions which we have experienced, none remains save the possible fear which the misfortunes we have pitied have led us to entertain for ourselves. This fear we retain; and whereas before, as an ingredient of pity, it helped to purify our pity, it now helps, as an emotion continuing independently and by itself, to purify itself. Consequently, in order to show that it can and does act thus, Aristotle found it necessary to mention it separately.

It is undeniable that Aristotle never intended to give a strict logical definition of a tragedy. For instead of confining himself merely to those properties which are essential to it, he has included several others which are purely accidental to it, and which had been rendered necessary by the customs of his time. But, leaving these aside and reducing the remaining characteristics to their simplest form, we shall arrive at a concise and exact definition, viz., that a tragedy is, in a word, a poem which excites pity. According to its genus, it is the imitation of an action, like the epic and the comedy; but according to its species, it is the imitation of an action deserving of pity. From these two conceptions all its rules may be clearly deduced, and even its dramatic form may be determined by them.

This latter statement may be doubted. At all events I know

of no critic who ever thought of attempting this. They all look upon the dramatic form of a tragedy as something traditional, which is what it is simply because it happens to be so, and which is left so because it is found to be good. Aristotle alone has discerned the reason of it; but in his definition he assumes it as understood instead of pointing it out clearly. " A tragedy," he tells us, " is the imitation of an action which, not by means of narration, but by means of pity and fear, serves to effect the purification of these and similar passions." These are his actual words. Who could help noticing here the curious antithesis, "not by means of narration, but by means of pity and fear"? Pity and fear are the means employed by tragedy to attain its end, and the narration can only refer to the manner in which these means are employed or avoided. Would not Aristotle, therefore, appear to have omitted something here? Is not the proper antithesis of the narration, namely, the dramatic form, manifestly wanting? Now, how do the translators repair this omission? Some manage carefully to circumvent it; others fill it in, but only with words. They all look upon it as nothing but a carelessly worded sentence, to which they do not consider themselves bound to adhere, provided they convey the philosopher's meaning. Dacier's translation runs as follows: *" d'une action —qui, sans le secours de la narration, par le moyen de la compassion et de la terreur,"* etc. Curtius says, " of an action, which not by the poet's narration, but (by the representation of the action itself) by means of terror and pity serves to purify us of the faults in the passions represented." Quite so! They both say what Aristotle wishes to convey; only they do not say it as he says it. Yet this " as " is of importance; for the sentence is not really so carelessly worded as one might imagine. Briefly stated, the matter stands as follows: Aristotle found that pity of necessity demands some present misfortune; that misfortunes which have happened long ago or may happen in the distant future either fail to awaken our compassion altogether or else awaken it to a far lesser degree than would a present misfortune; that it is consequently necessary to represent the action which is to excite our pity, not as having already occurred, that is to say, in a narrative form, but as actually occurring, that is to say, in a dramatic form. And this fact, that our pity is hardly, if at all, awakened by the narration, but is almost entirely aroused by the actual sight; this fact alone justified him in substituting the thing itself in his definition in place of the form of the thing, because the thing itself is only capable of this one form. Had he considered it possible that our pity could also be awakened by the narration, he would indeed have been guilty of an important omission in saying, "not by means of narration, but by means of pity and fear." Being convinced, however, that in representation, pity and fear can only be excited by means of the dramatic form, he was justified in making that omission for the sake of brevity. I refer my readers to the ninth chapter of the second book of his "Rhetoric."

And lastly, as regards the moral purpose which Aristotle assigns to tragedy and which he thought it necessary to include in his definition of the same, the controversies to which it has given rise, especially in modern times, are well known. Now I am confident of being able to prove that all who have declared themselves against it have failed to grasp Aristotle's meaning. They have invested him with their own particular views, without knowing for certain what his views were. They combat strange notions which originate from themselves, and in refuting the emanations of their own brains they imagine that they incontrovertibly confute the philosopher. I cannot discuss this matter in detail here. But in order not to appear to speak without proof, I will add two observations.

1. They make Aristotle say: "Tragedy should, by means of terror and pity, purify us from the faults of the passions represented." The passions represented? If, therefore, the hero meets with misfortune owing to his curiosity, his ambition, his love, or his wrath: then our curiosity, ambition, love or wrath, is the passion which the tragedy is to purify? Aristotle thought nothing of the kind. And so these gentlemen go on disputing; their imagination transforms windmills into giants; confident in their victory, they tilt at them, nor do they pay the slightest heed to Sancho, who has only common-sense to commend him, and who, seated upon his more cautious quadruped, calls after them urging them not to be over-hasty, but to first look carefully around them. *Τῶν τοιούτων παθημάτων*, says Aristotle; and that does not mean "the passions

represented "; they should have translated it by "these and similar ones," or "the passions awakened." The τοιούτων refers solely to the preceding "pity and fear"; tragedy is to excite our pity and our fear, in order to purify merely these and similar passions, but not all passions without distinction. He, however, uses the word τοιούτων, and not τούτων; he says "these and similar," and not simply "these," in order to show that by the term pity he understands not merely pity properly so called, but all philanthropic feelings in general, and likewise, by the term fear, not merely the displeasure with which we anticipate an impending misfortune, but also every kind of displeasure which is allied to it, the displeasure at present and past misfortunes, sorrows, and griefs. Thus the pity and the fear excited by tragedy are to purify our pity and our fear in a widened sense; they are, however, to purify these alone, and no other passions.

Useful lessons and examples, serving to purify other passions also, may, it is true, be found in tragedy; but these do not form part of its aim; it shares them in common with the epic and the comedy, inasmuch as it is a poem, an imitation of an action in general, but not in so far as it is a tragedy, an imitation of an action deserving of pity in particular. All species of poetry aim at making us better than we are; it is a lamentable thing to have to prove this first, and still more so to find even poets who doubt it. But every species of poetry cannot better everything, or at any rate it cannot better all things equally; but that direction in which each is best capable of effecting improvement, and in which no other species can do so to the same degree, that, and that alone, forms its peculiar aim.

2. Seeing that Aristotle's opponents were not careful to observe what passions he considered that tragedy should purify in us by means of pity and fear: it was but natural that they should misinterpret the purification itself. At the end of his "Politics," where he speaks of the purification of the passions by means of music, Aristotle promises to give a fuller account of this purification in his "Poetics." "Since, however," says Corneille, "there is no mention of it in this work, the majority of his commentators have arrived at the conclusion that it must have reached us in an incomplete form." No mention of it? For my part, I think that even in what remains to us of

his "Poetics," be it much or little, there can be found all that he deemed it necessary to say on this subject to anyone not altogether unacquainted with his other philosophical writings. Corneille himself noticed one passage which he thought sufficiently clear to enable us to discover the manner in which a purification of the passions is effected by tragedy, viz., the passage in which Aristotle says: " Pity demands an innocent sufferer, and fear one of our fellow-creatures." Now this passage is a very important one; only Corneille made a wrong use of it, and he could hardly help doing so, seeing that his thoughts were running on the purification of the passions in general. " Our pity for a misfortune," he says, " with which we see a fellow-creature afflicted, awakens a fear in us lest a similar misfortune overtake ourselves; this fear awakens a desire to evade it, and this desire an endeavor to purify, to moderate, to ameliorate, and even to eradicate entirely that passion owing to which the object of our pity meets with the misfortune before our very eyes. For our common-sense tells us that the cause must be removed if the effect is to be avoided." But this reasoning, whereby fear is made the mere instrument with which pity effects a purification of the passions, is false and cannot possibly be what Aristotle wished to convey. For in that case tragedy would be capable of purifying all the passions except the very two which Aristotle expressly tells us it ought to purify. It would be capable of purifying our wrath, our curiosity, our envy, our ambition, our hatred and our love, accordingly as it is the one or the other of these passions that has brought misfortune upon the object of our pity. Only our pity and our fear would it be unable to purify. For pity and fear are the passions which we, and not the acting personages, feel in tragedy; they are the passions by means of which the acting personages move us; they are not the passions which lead to their own misfortune. I am, of course, quite aware that there might be a play in which they perform both functions. But I have never yet come across one in which the suffering person was plunged into misfortune by means of misconceived pity or misconceived fear. And yet such a play would be the only one embodying, according to Corneille's interpretation, the ideas which Aristotle applied to all tragedies; and even there those ideas would not be carried into practice in the way demanded by the latter. Such a play would form, as it were, the point at which two inclined straight lines intersect never to meet again in all eternity. Dacier could not go so far wrong in interpreting Aristotle's meaning. He was bound to pay more attention to the words of his author, and these distinctly state that our pity and our fear are to be purified by the pity and the fear awakened by tragedy. But thinking, no doubt, that the purpose of tragedy would be very insignificant if it were merely confined to these limitations, he allowed himself to be persuaded, by Corneille's explanation, to assign to it a similar purification of all the other passions. And when Corneille, for his part, denied this and proved by examples that he held it to be a beautiful thought rather than a thing generally attainable, Dacier had to accept these same examples, and thus found himself in such straits that he was forced to make the most violent twists and turns to extricate himself and his Aristotle. I say *his* Aristotle; for the real one stands in no need of such twists and turns. To repeat it once again, the latter thought of no other passions which should be purified in tragedy by means of pity and fear, save only pity and fear themselves; and it was a matter of indifference to him whether a tragedy contributed much or little to the purification of the rest of the passions. Dacier should have confined himself to that purification of which Aristotle speaks; but in that case he would certainly have had to combine it with a broader conception. " It is not difficult to explain," he tells us, " how tragedy excites pity and fear in order to purify pity and fear. It excites these passions by displaying to us the misfortunes into which our fellow-creatures have been plunged through unpremeditated faults; and it purifies them by acquainting us with these misfortunes and by teaching us neither to fear them too much, nor to be too much affected by them, if they should happen to ourselves. It enables persons to bear the most untoward accidents bravely, and causes the most wretched to deem themselves fortunate when they compare their woes with the still greater ones represented in tragedy. For in what condition could a man be found who, on beholding an Œdipus, a Philoctetes, or an Orestes, would not confess that all the evils which he has to suffer are as nothing when compared to those which afflict these men?" This is quite true; and the explanation cannot have cost Dacier much reflection. He found it almost word for word in one of the Stoics who always had an eye to apathy. Without urging that the feeling of our own woe does not leave much room for pity, and that consequently in the case of a sufferer whose pity cannot be awakened, the purification or diminution of his sorrow cannot be brought about by pity: I will allow all his remarks to hold good. I would only ask: to what do all his statements amount? Has he said anything further than that pity purifies our fear? Certainly not; and yet this is but a quarter of what Aristotle intends to convey. For when the latter asserts that tragedy excites pity and fear in order to purify pity and fear, surely anyone can see that this means far more than Dacier has thought it advisable to state. According to the different combinations of these various conceptions, if it is attempted to give the entire meaning of Aristotle, it must be shown successively (1) how tragic pity can, and in reality does, purify our pity; (2) how tragic fear purifies our fear; (3) how tragic pity purifies our fear; and (4) how tragic fear purifies our pity. Now Dacier confined himself merely to the third combination, and even this one he did not treat carefully, but left it only half explained. For if an attempt is made to arrive at a correct and complete conception of the Aristotelian doctrine of the purification of the passions, it will be found that each of the four combinations above mentioned includes in it a two-fold contingency, which may be briefly stated as follows. Since the purification rests upon nothing else but the transformation of passions into virtuous habits, and since, according to our philosopher, every virtue is situated midway between two extremes; it follows that tragedy, if it is to transform our pity into a virtue, must be able to purify us from the two extremes of pity; the same applies in the case of fear. Tragic pity must not only purify the soul of him who feels too much pity, but also of him who feels too little. Tragic fear must not only purify the soul of him who fears no manner of misfortune, but also of him who is afraid of every misfortune, however distant and improbable it may be. In the same way, tragic pity, in regard to fear, must steer between this too much and this too little; and conversely, tragic fear in regard to pity. Dacier, as I have said, has only shown how tragic pity may moderate excessive fear, but not how its entire absence may be remedied, nor how it may be wholesomely increased in him who has too little of it; not to mention that he has omitted to say anything of the rest. Those who came after him have not in the least repaired his omissions; but in order to settle the dispute concerning the utility of tragedy in their own minds, they have drawn matters into it which apply to poetry in general, but in nowise to tragedy as such in particular; they have maintained, for instance, that tragedy is intended to feed and strengthen the feelings of humanity, to inculcate a love of virtue, a hatred of vice, and so on;[6] but, my good sir, what poem should not do the same? Then if this is the intention of every poem, it cannot form the distinctive feature of tragedy; and this cannot therefore be what we were seeking.

To what end the hard work of dramatic form? Why build a theatre, disguise men and women, burden their memories, and assemble the whole town in one place, if I intend my work and its representation to produce nothing more than some of those emotions which could be as well produced by any good story that everyone could read at home for himself?

The dramatic form is the only one in which pity and fear may be aroused; at all events in no other form can these passions be awakened to such a degree. And yet people prefer to awaken in it all other emotions rather than these, and to use it for every other purpose than the one for which it is preeminently adapted.

The public is satisfied; this is well and yet not well. One has no special longing for the food with which one is bound to put up.

It is well known how intent the Greeks and the Romans were upon their plays, especially the former upon their tragedies. What coldness and indifference our public, on the other hand, show towards the theatre! To what must we attribute this difference, if it be not to the fact that the Greeks felt themselves animated by their stage with such intense and extraordinary emotions that they could hardly await the moment to experience them again and again; whereas we, on the other hand, derive such feeble impressions from our stage that we rarely

---

[6] Curtius, in his "Dissertation upon the Aims of Tragedy," appended to Aristotle's "Poetics."

consider it worth the time and the money to procure them? Most of us go to the theatre almost invariably for the sake of satisfying our curiosity or of killing time, for the sake of fashion or of company, from a desire to see and be seen; very few of us, and those but seldom, go from any other motive.

When I say we, our public, our stage, I do not mean the Germans only. We Germans candidly admit that we as yet possess no theatre. What many of our critics, who join us in this confession and who are great admirers of the French theatre, think when they admit it, I am unable to say. But I know what my own views on the matter are. I am of opinion that not only we Germans, but also those who boast of having possessed a theatre for a century already, nay more, who brag of having the best theatre in all Europe—that even the French themselves have as yet no theatre.

At all events, they have no tragic one. The impressions produced by French tragedy are absolutely cold and feeble. Hear what a Frenchman himself has to say of them.

"The surpassing beauties of our theatre," says M. de Voltaire, "were combined with a hidden fault which had escaped notice because the public could not of its own accord have any higher ideas than those imparted to it by the models of the great masters. Saint-Evremond has alone discovered this fault; he says that our plays do not make a sufficient impression, that that which should excite pity only awakens tenderness, that gentle emotion takes the place of agitation, and surprise that of terror; that our feelings, in short, do not attain a sufficient degree of intensity. It cannot be denied that Saint-Evremond has laid his finger upon the secret sore of the French theatre. It may be urged that Saint-Evremond was the author of a wretched comedy, 'Sir Politic Wouldbe,' and of another equally wretched one called 'The Operas'; that his small society verses are the weakest and most trivial of their kind; and that he was nothing but a poetaster. One may not have a spark of genius, and yet possess much wit and taste. Now he had unquestionably a very refined taste; this is borne out by the fact that he divined the true reason why most of our plays are so tame and cold. We have always lacked a certain degree of warmth; everything else we possessed."

In other words: we possessed everything excepting only

that which we most needed; our tragedies were excellent, but for the fact that they were not tragedies at all. And why were they not tragedies?

"This coldness," Voltaire continues, "this monotonous tameness, arose in part from the petty spirit of gallantry which was at that time so prevalent amongst our courtiers, and which transformed a tragedy into a series of amorous dialogues after the taste of Cyrus and Clelie. The only plays that formed an exception to this rule consisted of lengthy political tirades, such as spoilt Sertorius, made Otho cold, Surena and Attila wretched. There was yet another cause that prevented the display of high pathos upon our stage and hindered the action from becoming truly tragic, and that was the narrow, poorly-constructed theatre with its paltry decorations. What room was there for action upon a stage composed of a few dozen boards, which was moreover filled with spectators? How could the eyes of the latter be captivated, dazzled and illuded, by any display of pomp and accessories? How could great tragic actions be performed there? How could the poet's imagination be allowed free play? The pieces had to consist of lengthy descriptions, so that they resembled dialogues rather than plays. Every actor was bent upon shining in a long monologue, and such plays as did not contain any were rejected. In this form all theatrical action disappeared, as did also all intense display of the passions, all powerful pictures of human misery, all harrowing traits which could pierce to the very soul; the spectator's heart, instead of being rent asunder, was scarcely touched."

The first reason is a perfectly correct one. Gallantry and politics always leave a cold impression; and no poet has ever yet succeeded in arousing pity and fear by means of them. The former make us imagine that we hear only the *fat* or the schoolmaster; the latter would have us hear nothing but the human being.

But how about the second reason? Can it be possible that the absence of a spacious theatre and of good scenery should have exercised such an influence upon the genius of the poet? Is it true that every tragic plot requires pomp and accessories? Or should not the poet rather construct his play in such a manner that it could produce its full effect even without these additions?

He certainly should do so, according to Aristotle. "Fear and pity," says the philosopher, "may be awakened by appealing to the organs of sight; but they can also proceed from the connection of the events themselves; the latter is the more excellent method and that adopted by the best poets. For the story must be so constructed that it awakens pity and fear in him who merely listens to the relation of its events; such is the story of Œdipus, which only requires to be heard to arouse the above-mentioned passions. To produce this effect by means of the organs of sight, less art is required; and this should be left to the person who undertakes the representation of the play."

Shakespeare's plays are said to afford a curious proof of the dispensableness of scenic decorations. What plays, it is asked, stand more in need of the whole art of the decorator than these, with their constant interruptions and changes of scene? Yet there was a time when the stages on which they were performed consisted of nothing but a curtain of some coarse material, which, when drawn up, disclosed the walls, which were quite bare or covered, at most, with matting or tapestry. Here there was nothing save the imagination to assist the actors in interpreting the piece and the spectators in comprehending it; yet, in spite of this, it is maintained that Shakespeare's plays were in those days more intelligible without scenery than they afterwards were with it.[7]

If, then, the poet need not trouble himself about scenery; and if the same, even in cases where it would seem necessary, can be omitted without essentially detracting from his play: why should the fact of the French poets not having given us more touching plays be ascribed to the narrow and unfavorable construction of the theatre? The fault did not lie with the theatre; it lay with themselves.

And this is confirmed by experience. For to-day the French

---

[7] Cibber's "Lives of the Poets of Great Britain and Ireland," vol. ii. pp. 78, 79:—"Some have insinuated that fine scenes proved the ruin of acting. In the reign of Charles I there was nothing more than a curtain of very coarse stuff, upon the drawing up of which the stage appeared, either with bare walls on the sides, coarsely matted, or covered with tapestry; so that for the place originally represented, and all the successive changes in which the poets of those times freely indulged themselves, there was nothing to help the spectator's understanding, or to assist the actor's performance, but bare imagination. The spirit and judgment of the actors supplied all deficiencies and made, as some would insinuate, plays more intelligible without scenes than they afterwards were with them."

have a finer and more spacious stage; the spectators are no longer allowed upon it; the wings are kept clear; the decorator has free hands and can paint and construct whatever the poet requires of him. Yet where are those more passionate plays that one might have expected to find? Does M. de Voltaire flatter himself that his "Semiramis" is one of them? There we have pomp and accessories in plenty, and a ghost into the bargain; and notwithstanding all this, I know of no colder play than his "Semiramis."

Now shall I be taken to mean by all this that no Frenchman is capable of writing a really passionate tragedy; that the volatile spirit of that nation is unequal to the task? I should be ashamed of entertaining such an opinion. Germany has not so far made herself ridiculous by any Bouhours; and I, for my part, have not the least inclination for the part. I am convinced that no nation in the world has been specially endowed with any mental gift superior to that of other nations. We often hear of the shrewd Englishman, the witty Frenchman. But who made this distinction? Certainly not Nature, for she distributes all things equally amongst all. There are as many witty Englishmen as witty Frenchmen, and as many shrewd Frenchmen as shrewd Englishmen, whilst the bulk of the people is neither one nor the other.

What, then, do I mean to convey? I merely want to say that the French have not yet got that which they might very well have—viz., true tragedy. And why have they not got it yet? In order to hit upon the correct reason, it would have been necessary for Voltaire to know himself a great deal better.

I mean that they have not got it because they believe that they have had it for a long time. And they are certainly strengthened in this belief by a quality which they possess beyond all other nations, but which is not a gift of nature—namely, their vanity.

As with single individuals, so it is with nations. Gottsched (it will readily be guessed why I mention him here) was in his young days held to be a poet, because at that time people did not know the difference between a mere versifier and a poet. Philosophy and criticism in due course made the distinction clear; and if Gottsched had but tried to keep abreast with the times, if he had but developed and rectified his ideas and his taste according to the ideas and the taste of the age, the versifier might perhaps have grown into a poet. But having so often heard himself styled the greatest poet, and being persuaded by his vanity that such was really the case, he neglected to do this. He could not possibly acquire what he already believed himself to possess; and the older he grew, the more obstinately and unblushingly he asserted his imagined superiority.

The same thing, it appears to me, has happened to the French. No sooner had Corneille raised their theatre a little out of the barbarous conditions in which he found it than they already deemed it close to perfection. Racine appeared to them to add the finishing touch; and from that time forth they never asked themselves for one moment (nor, in fact, had they ever done so) whether it was possible for any tragic poet to be more pathetic, more passionate, than Corneille and Racine. They took it for granted that such a thing was impossible, and all their succeeding poets had to confine their zeal to imitating the one or the other as closely as possible. For a hundred years they have thus deceived themselves and partly also their neighbors. And now let some one tell them so, and see what they will say!

Of the two, Corneille has done the greater harm and exercised the more baneful influence upon their tragic poets. For Racine deceived them by his example only, but Corneille by his example and doctrines together.

The latter especially, which were accepted as oracles by the whole nation (with the exception of one or two pedants, a Hedelin, a Dacier, who, however, often did not themselves know what they wanted) and followed by all subsequent poets, have failed to produce anything but the most shallow, vapid, and untragical stuff. This I would undertake to prove piece by piece.

The rules of Aristotle are well calculated to produce the highest tragic effect. What does Corneille do with them? He brings them forward falsely and inaccurately; and finding them still too severe, he endeavors to discover in one or the other *quelque modération, quelque favorable interprétation,* and weakens and mutilates, misinterprets and frustrates every rule. And why? *Pour n'être pas obligés de condamner beaucoup de poëmes que nous avons vu réussir sur nos théâtres;* " so as not to be obliged to condemn many plays which have met with success upon our stage." A fine reason!

I will rapidly touch upon the chief points. Some of them I have already noticed; but for the sake of consistency I must reiterate them.

1. Aristotle says: tragedy should excite pity and fear. Corneille says: yes, but not necessarily both at the same time; we are quite satisfied with either one or the other, now with pity without fear, now with fear without pity. For else, where should I, the great Corneille, be with my Rodogune and my Chimène? These good children arouse pity, very great pity, but hardly fear. Then again, where should I be, with my Cleopatra, my Prusias, my Phocas? Who can feel any pity for these wretches? And yet they awaken fear. So thought Corneille, and the French thought it after him.

2. Aristotle says: tragedy should excite pity and fear; that is to say, both by means of one and the same person. Corneille says: if this can be so arranged, very good. But it is not absolutely necessary, and one would be perfectly justified in employing several persons to produce these two feelings, as I have done in my "Rodogune." Thus did Corneille, and the French follow his example.

3. Aristotle says: through the pity and the fear which are awakened by tragedy, our pity and our fear, and all our allied feelings, ought to be purified. Corneille knows nothing at all of this, and imagines that Aristotle meant to say that tragedy awakens our pity in order to awaken our fear, and that the latter will serve to purify in us those passions through which the object of our pity has been plunged into misfortune. I will not discuss the value of this aim; suffice it to say that it does not belong to Aristotle, and that, as Corneille assigned to his tragedies an entirely different aim, they could not but become entirely different works from those whence Aristotle had abstracted his theory; they had needs to become **tragedies** which were no true tragedies. And this applies not only to his plays, but to all the French tragedies, for their authors did not set themselves to follow the lines laid down by Aristotle, but those laid down by Corneille. I have already said that Dacier held that both aims could be combined; but by this very combination the former is weakened, and the tragedy falls short of its full

effect. Dacier's conception of the former was, moreover, as I have shown, a very imperfect one, and it was therefore no wonder that he imagined that the French tragedies of his time fulfilled the former aim rather than the latter. "Our tragedy," he says, " is fairly successful in the former aim of exciting and purifying pity and fear. But it rarely succeeds in the latter one, though that is the more important, and it purifies the other passions but little, or, since it ordinarily contains nothing but love-intrigues, if it purified any one of them, it would be the passion of love alone, whence it may be inferred that it is of very small value." [8] Now the truth is exactly the contrary. There are more French tragedies that do justice to the second aim than to the first. I know of several French plays which clearly expose the hurtful consequences resulting from one passion or another, and from which many good lessons may be gathered in regard to such a passion; but I know of none that excite my pity to the extent to which tragedy ought to excite it, and to which several Greek and English plays have conclusively shown me that tragedy can excite it. Some of the French tragedies are very fine and instructive works, and, in my opinion, very praiseworthy; only they are not tragedies. Their authors cannot have been other than very clever men; some of them deserve no mean rank among the poets: only they are not tragic poets; their Corneille and Racine, their Crébillon and Voltaire, have little or nothing of that which makes Sophocles a Sophocles, Euripides a Euripides, and Shakespeare a Shakespeare. These latter are seldom at variance with the essential demands of Aristotle; the former, on the contrary, are often so. For to proceed——

4. Aristotle says: in tragedy a good man must not be plunged into misfortune without any fault on his part; for this would be too terrible. "Precisely," says Corneille, "such an event awakens more displeasure and hatred for him who causes the misfortune, than pity for him who is afflicted by it. The former feeling, which should not be the proper effect of tragedy, would consequently, unless treated with very great skill, stifle the latter feeling, which is the one that tragedy ought to produce. The spectator would go away dissatisfied, because too much wrath would be mingled with his pity, which latter would have

[8] " Poet. d'Arist.," chap. vi., Rem. 8.

satisfied him, if he could but have remained free from any other feelings. But," Corneille hastens to add; for he always has a "but" to follow—"but if this cause is removed; if the poet constructs his play in such a way that the virtuous man who suffers can excite more pity for himself than hatred for him who causes his suffering; what then? Why, then," he goes on to say, " I am of the opinion that no one should hesitate to represent even the most virtuous of men suffering upon the stage." I am at a loss to understand how anyone can deal with the philosopher in such a slipshod manner, and profess to understand him, whilst imputing opinions to him which he has never held. " A totally unmerited misfortune, which overtakes a good man," says Aristotle, " is not suitable for tragedy, because it is terrible." This " because," which leads to the cause, is changed by Corneille into " in so far as," merely a certain condition under which it ceases to be tragic. Aristotle says: it is altogether terrible, and for that very reason untragical. But Corneille says: it is untragical in so far as it is terrible. This terribleness is ascribed by Aristotle to the nature of the misfortune itself; but Corneille sets it down to the displeasure which it awakens towards him who is the cause of it. He does not, or will not, see that this terribleness is something quite different from this displeasure, and that even if the latter were entirely absent, the former might nevertheless be experienced to its fullest extent: it is enough for him that in the first place several of his plays seem to be justified by this *quid pro quo;* plays, which he deems so little at variance with the rules of Aristotle, that he actually has the boldness to imagine that, if Aristotle had but been acquainted with such plays, he would have modified his doctrines accordingly and gathered from them various methods by which the misfortune of a virtuous man may yet be rendered a fitting subject for tragedy. " *En voici,*" he says, " *deux ou trois manières, que peut-être Aristote n'a su prévoir, parcequ'on n'en voyait pas d'exemples sur les théâtres de son temps.*" And whose are these examples? Whose else but his own? And what are those two or three methods? We will see at once. " The first," he says, " consists in representing a very virtuous person as being persecuted by a very vicious one, and yet escaping from his peril, in such a way that the vicious person is himself ensnared by it. This is the case in 'Rodogune' and in 'Heraclius'; and it would have been quite intolerable had Antiochus and Rodogune perished in the first-mentioned play, and Heraclius, Pulcheria and Martian in the second, and Cleopatra and Phocas been left to triumph. The sufferings of the former persons awaken a feeling of pity which our hatred for their persecutors is incapable of stifling, for we keep on hoping that some happy circumstance may intervene to save them from ruin." It is absurd of Corneille to try and make out that Aristotle was unacquainted with this method. On the contrary, he was so well acquainted with it that, if he did not condemn it altogether, he at any rate explicitly declared it to be more suitable for comedy than for tragedy. How could Corneille have forgotten this? But so it is with all who start by assuming their cause to be the cause of truth. Moreover, strictly speaking, this method does not apply to the case in point at all. For it would not have the effect of rendering the virtuous man unfortunate, but would merely lead him along the road to misfortune, and this of itself might perhaps arouse sympathetic anxiety on his behalf, but it would not be terrible.

Now for the second method. "It may also happen," says Corneille, "that a very virtuous man is persecuted and ruined at the instigation of another who is not so vicious as to wholly deserve our displeasure, and whose persecution of the virtuous man reveals more weakness than wickedness. When Felix causes the downfall of his son-in-law Polyeucte, he is prompted not so much by indignant rage against the Christians, which would render him detestable in our eyes, as by servile fear, which hinders him from saving him in the presence of Severus, by whose hatred and vengeance he is awed. Some displeasure will doubtless be awakened against Felix; his conduct will be blamed; yet this displeasure will not outweigh the pity which we entertain for Polyeucte, nor will it prevent his wonderful conversion at the end of the play from reinstating him in the good graces of the spectators." I suppose there have been bunglers in tragedy at all times and even in Athens. Why then should not Aristotle have been acquainted with a play of similar construction, from which he could draw the same conclusions as Corneille? What nonsense! In plays of this kind, timid, vacillating and undecided characters, like Felix, are but an additional fault, for they lend them a certain coldness and repulsiveness on the one hand, without in the least detracting from their terribleness on the other. For, as already mentioned, the terrible does not consist in the displeasure or aversion which they excite, but in the misfortune itself which afflicts the innocent sufferers. The misfortune is in any case equally undeserved, be the persecutors wicked or weak, be their conduct premeditated or unpremeditated. The thought that there may be persons who, from no fault of their own, meet with misfortunes, is in itself a terrible one. And whereas the pagans tried to banish this terrible thought as much as possible, we endeavor to retain it? We try to derive pleasure from plays that confirm it? We, whom religion and common-sense should have convinced that it is as erroneous as it is blasphemous?

The same would no doubt apply to the third method, had not Corneille himself forgotten to state which this is.

5. Aristotle's remarks upon the unfitness of an entirely vicious person to form a tragic hero, inasmuch as his misfortunes would awaken neither pity nor fear, are likewise modified by Corneille. Pity, he tells us, a person of that sort could not excite, but he might very well arouse fear. For although none of the spectators deemed themselves capable of acquiring his vices, and consequently liable to suffer his misfortune in its entirety; yet each one of them might be the victim of some fault more or less akin to one or other of these vices, and would in that case derive a salutary corrective from a fear of its consequences, which, though proportionately less serious, would still be unfortunate. But this argument is based upon the false conception which Corneille formed of fear and of the purification of those passions which are awakened by tragedy. It contradicts itself; for, as I have already pointed out, the excitation of pity is inseparable from the excitation of fear, and if it were possible for a villain to excite our fear, he must of necessity excite our pity also. But since, as Corneille himself admits, he cannot do the latter, he can neither do the former; and he therefore does not serve in the least to fulfil the aim of tragedy. Aristotle even considers him less fitted to do so than the entirely virtuous man; for he clearly maintains that, failing a hero who combines good and bad qualities equally, it is better to choose a good one than a bad one. The reason is very simple;

a man may be very good, and yet possess more faults than one or commit more errors than one, whereby he is plunged into an immeasurable misfortune which fills us with pity and sorrow, without being in the least terrible, because it is the natural consequence of his errors. What Dubos [9] says about the employment of vicious persons in tragedy is not what Corneille means. Dubos would only allow them as subsidiary characters, as merely instrumental in rendering the chief characters less culpable by serving as foils to them. Corneille, on the other hand, would make them the main objects of interest, as he has shown us in " Rodogune "; and it is the latter which is at variance with the aim of tragedy, not the former. Dubos adds the very true remark that the misfortunes of these subsidiary villains make no impression upon us. " In ' Britannicus,' " he says, " we scarcely notice the death of Narcissus." And for this very reason the poet should avoid these characters as far as possible. For if their misfortunes do not directly further the aim of tragedy; if they are merely employed by the poet as instruments to enable him the better to achieve that aim in other characters: it cannot be denied that a play would be all the better, if it produced the same effect without their aid. The simpler a machine, the fewer its springs and wheels and weights, the more perfect it will be.

6. And lastly, as regards the misconception of the first and most essential quality demanded by Aristotle in the moral character of tragic personages. Their morals must be good. " Good? " says Corneille. " Why, if good here means the same as virtuous, what becomes of the majority of ancient and modern tragedies which abound in characters, which if not absolutely bad and vicious, are yet endowed with a weakness that is hardly compatible with virtue? " He is especially alarmed for the safety of Cleopatra in his " Rodogune." So he refuses to regard the goodness demanded by Aristotle as moral goodness; it must be some other kind of goodness, compatible with moral badness as well as with moral goodness. But what Aristotle means is purely moral goodness; only virtuous persons and persons who, under certain circumstances, display moral virtue, are not one and the same thing to him. Corneille, in short, connects the word " moral " with an entirely false idea,

[9] " Réflexions Critiques sur la Poèsie et la Peinture," t. i., sec. xv.

and he has altogether failed to grasp the proæresis, through which alone, according to our philosopher, free actions become moral or immoral. I cannot here furnish an exhaustive proof of any assertion; in order to clearly understand it, one must be familiar with the connection and syllogistic sequence of all the ideas propounded by the Greek critic. I will therefore defer it until another occasion; all that I have to show at present is that Corneille, having missed the proper path, has chosen a very disastrous one instead. The latter leads him to the following conclusion: that by moral goodness Aristotle understood the brilliant and lofty character of some inclination, whether praiseworthy or reprehensible, which might either be the peculiar attribute of the person introduced, or else be skilfully imparted to that person; *le caractère brillant et élevé d'une habitude vertueuse ou criminelle, selon qu'elle est propre et convenable à la personne qu'on introduit.* " Cleopatra in ' Rodogune,' " he says, " is a thoroughly bad person; there is no murder that she fears to commit, if it but serve to maintain her upon the throne, which is dearer to her than anything else in the world; so keen is her love of dominion. But all her crimes are connected with a certain greatness of soul, which is of itself so impressive that, whilst we condemn her actions, we cannot but admire the source from which they originate. I would say the same thing of the Liar. Lying is unquestionably a vicious habit; but Dorante gives vent to his lies with such presence of mind, with such vivacity, that this defect almost appeals in his favor, and the spectators are bound to admit that the ability to tell such lies is a vice whereof no fool could be capable." Corneille could, indeed, hardly have arrived at a more wretched conclusion! Carry it into execution and you will find that all the truth, the illusion and the moral benefit of tragedy vanish entirely. For virtue, which is ever modest and simple, is, by assuming that brilliant character, rendered vain and romantic, whilst vice is thereby shrouded with a certain glamour which always dazzles us, from whichever point of view we regard it. It is absurd to try to employ the mere evil consequences of a vice as a deterrent, if its inner hideousness is kept out of sight. The consequences are accidental, and experience shows us that they are as often favorable as unfavorable. This refers to the purification of the passions, as understood by Corneille. As I imagine it, as Aristotle explained it, it has nothing whatever to do with that deceptive brilliance. The false foil which is by this means given to vice causes us to recognize perfections where none exist, and to feel pity where we should feel none. Dacier, it is true, has already contradicted this explanation, but for less cogent reasons; and the one which he, together with Père Le Bossu, adopts in its place, is not far from being quite as disadvantageous to the poetical perfection of a play. For, according to him, the statement, that the morals should be good, means no more than that they should be clearly defined, *qu'elles soient bien marquées*. This is a rule which, if correctly taken, is, in its proper place, worthy of careful attention on the part of the dramatist. From the French models it would unfortunately appear that *clearly defined* has been taken to mean the same as *strongly defined*. The expression has been overcharged, pressure added to pressure, until the persons characterized have been transformed into personified characters, and vicious or virtuous human beings into haggard skeletons of vice or virtue.

PHILOSOPHY CONSIDERED AS THE ART OF LIFE AND HEALING ART OF THE SOUL

—

BY

CHRISTOPHER MARTIN WIELAND

CHRISTOPHER MARTIN WIELAND

1733—1813

Like Lessing, Christopher Martin Wieland was the son of a clergyman. Born in the village of Oberholzheim, in Würtemberg, in the year 1733, he displayed at an early age a remarkable aptitude for poetry. Some of his youthful productions, written soon after he left the University of Tübingen, awakened Bodmer's interest in him. The Swiss poet and critic invited his young protégé to Zurich, where he remained eight years. During the next decade of the poet's life there were many changes of occupation and residence. But better things were in store for him. In 1769 he was appointed to the chair of philosophy and literature at the University of Erfurt. Three years later he became tutor to the sons of the Duchess Amalia of Saxe-Weimar. It was not long, however, before he was enabled to devote himself entirely to literary pursuits, and thus the great wish of his life had become a reality. Henceforth he lived at Weimar, an intimate companion of the great German poets of his time. He died there in 1813, at the age of eighty.

Wieland was a very prolific writer. In addition to his translations from Shakespeare, Horace, Lucian, and Cicero, we possess more than fifty volumes of writings from his own pen. It cannot be said of him that all his literary productions are of genuine or equal merit. Some have become classical, others are little read now, and almost forgotten. We find in his works a great diversity in form as well as in spirit. He possessed a marked aptitude for versification, as his poetic writings abundantly prove. The spiritual changes he underwent, the progressive views of life he acquired with age and different surroundings are equally manifest in his works. At Zurich the young Wieland was religiously inclined, puritanical, and ascetic. Later in life, and under more liberal influences, associated with men in touch and sympathy with the Encyclopædists, he went to the other extreme, and his spiritual emancipation was complete.

We have already indicated the character of his earlier works. His "Agathon," however, published in 1767, his "Musarion," and a number of other poetical works of less importance, but of great popularity among his contemporaries, placed Wieland at the head of the national literature of his day. Immediately upon his arrival at Weimar he established a monthly literary periodical, "The German Mercury," which he continued to edit for thirty-seven years, and this enterprise greatly increased his literary influence. It was in the pages of this publication that many of his prose writings, chiefly literary and philosophical essays, first appeared, including his essay on "Philosophy Considered as the Art of Life," and that "On the Relation of the Agreeable and the Beautiful to the Useful." Of Wieland's later works the most important is his romantic epic "Oberon," now regarded as the best of his productions.

Both in prose and verse Wieland was a master of literary composition, and most of the younger writers of his day learned much from the clearness, ease, and grace of his style. If Lessing gave precision to modern German prose, Wieland gave it elegance and fluency. His work, at once graceful and fanciful, is pervaded by a quaint humor and delicate irony that give it a lasting charm. Wieland holds an important and even illustrious place in German literature. His share in the development of the epic form of poetry in Germany is undisputed, while, with his universal popularity with all classes, he wielded an influence which it would be difficult to overestimate, and which was attained by few of his contemporaries.

PHILOSOPHY CONSIDERED AS THE ART OF LIFE AND HEALING ART OF THE SOUL

MEN had lived, and perhaps lived many thousand years, before one of them hit upon the thought that life could be an art; and, in all probability, every other art, from the arts of Tubal Cain to the art of catching flies—which Shah Baham, a *peritus in arte,* assures us, is not so easy a matter as some people imagine—had long been invented, when, at last, the sagacious Greeks, along with other fine arts and sciences, invented also this famous art of life, called philosophy: or, if they did not altogether invent it, first reduced it to the form of art, and carried it to a high degree of refinement.

By far the greater part of the children of men never dreamed that there was such an art. People lived without knowing how they did it, very much as Mons. Jourdain in Molière's "Citizen Gentleman," had talked prose all his life, or as we all draw breath, digest, perform various motions, grow and thrive, without one in a thousand knowing or desiring to know by what mechanical laws or by what combination of causes all these things are done. And in this thick fog of ignorance innumerable nations in Asia, Africa, America, and the islands of the South Sea, white and olive, yellow-black and pitch-black, bearded and unbearded, circumcised and uncircumcised, tattooed and untattooed, with and without rings through the nose, from the giants in Patagonia to the dwarfs on Hudson's Bay, etc., etc., live to this hour. And not only so, but even of the greatest portion of the inhabitants of our enlightened Europe, it may be maintained with truth, that they know as little about said art of life and that they care as little about it as the careless people of Otaheite or the half-frozen inhabitants of Terra del Fuego, who are scarcely more than sea-calves.

The strangest part of this business is, that all these people, who, according to a very moderate calculation, constitute nearly the whole human race—like their ancestors as far back as Adam and Eve, who also knew nothing of the aforesaid fine art—notwithstanding their ignorance, live away as courageously as if they were finished masters of it. Nay more, the greater part of these bunglers get on so well, as it respects all the most essential and important functions of human life, that scarcely one of the hired masters and professors of the art can hold a candle to them.

Cicero says somewhere, "Nature is the best guide of life," which probably means, that Nature shows us best how we may help ourselves through this earthly state. Further, he says, "No one can fail who suffers himself to be guided by her." On this guidance, therefore, it would seem that men must always have relied. This same Nature, they thought, which teaches us to breathe, eat, drink, to move hands and feet, etc., teaches us also how to use our senses, our memory, our understanding, and all our other powers; teaches us what is fitting and what is not fitting. It requires only so much attention as every object enforces of itself, to see and feel whether it is friendly or hostile. Our nose and our tongue teach us, without any other instruction, what fruits, herbs, and roots, etc., are good to eat. At a pinch, hunger teaches the same, without much circumstance. Nature has provided for all pressing necessities. Either the thing which we require exists already; and then we have whatever is needed to seize and enjoy it; or, at least, the materials of it exist; and then we have just so much understanding, power, and natural dexterity in our members as is necessary to form those materials to our use and purpose. What does not succeed the first time will succeed the tenth or the twentieth. If two arms are not sufficient, four, six, eight will accomplish it. Every new trial adds something to our knowledge of the thing, and to our faculty. We learn by errors and failures, and become masters by practice, without perceiving how it has come about. And this same Nature which carries us so far, always conceals from us what lies too far to be reached from the place assigned us; makes us happy by ignorance, and has given us this beneficent sluggishness, of which the world-reformers make so much complaint, for no other purpose but that the everlasting desire to improve our condition may not cause us to fall from the frying-pan into the fire, and that we may not fare like that man who, in order to feel better, physicked himself to death, and had for his epitaph: *Per star meglio sto qui.*

So Nature teaches all men how to live, who have not run away from the instruction and discipline of the good Mother. And, in all this, as you perceive, there is no art. It is Nature herself, bodily. The celebrated *Quam multis non ego!* of the ancient philosopher is the native philosophy of all Samoyedes, Laplanders, Esquimaux, etc.—a philosophy in which the New Hollanders or the New Walesmen, as the honest people must suffer themselves to be called, according to the arbitrary pleasure of the gentlemen with the firelocks, who have the command, appear to have made the greatest progress. Let no man come and say that such a life is an oyster-life. Call it, if you please, a continual childhood; but honor Nature who conducts these her children, by the shortest route, to the *beate vivere* at which we enlightened people seldom or never arrive, merely on account of the great multitude of roads which lead to it.

The wise Theophrastus (not Paracelsus, but the scholar and successor of the divine Aristotle) lived ninety years, and when he came to die, he complained against Nature because " she has given man so little time to live, and because an honest fellow must die at the very moment when he has begun to comprehend a little the art of life." When did ever a New Hollander make so unreasonable a complaint? When *he* has come to be a hundred years old (which is nothing rare with them) he has lived just one hundred years, and rises satisfied from the banquet of Nature; and truly, a banquet that, in which Nature furnishes such poor entertainment, that the strictest candidate for canonization need not scruple to share it.

But—let me remark in passing—I am very far from believing that Theophrastus made the foolish speech which is imputed to him. The people around his bed did not exactly understand what he said, and then some schoolmaster came along, a good while after, and tried to make sense of it, and made nonsense. I would bet that Theophrastus meant neither more nor less than this: that he regretted he had not been wise enough, sixty or seventy years before, to see that he might have saved himself the trouble of studying, as art and science, what Nature would have taught him far better and more surely, without study, if he had had the simplicity of mind to heed her instruction. It was not innocent Nature but his own folly that he blamed, as most men are wont to do in his case; although they might as well let it alone; for what is the use of repentance when one has no time left for amendment?

Notwithstanding all that has been said, it is by no means my intention to dispute the value, whatever it may be, of the above-mentioned art of life.

It has somewhere been said, that art is, at bottom, nothing else than Nature herself, who, by means of man, as her most perfect instrument, unfolds and brings to perfection under a different name, what before she had merely sketched, as it were, or hastily begun. If art is that, and so far as it is that, it is worthy of all honor.

Yes, even then, when it merely comes in aid of enfeebled or corrupted Nature, it is, like the art of medicine, sometimes beneficial, although often just as uncertain and just as ineffectual as that. When Nature no longer suffices for the support of life, then, to be sure, art must patch and prop, and plaster and doctor as well as it can. Or, to speak more correctly, even in this case, the good, universal Mother has provided for her darling child. She has remedies in her store-chamber for every wound or disease of the outward or the inward man, so that art has nothing to do but to observe and to exhibit. The simpler then the remedies are, the less they have been tampered with, the better for the sufferer. And still, the successful issue must be expected from Nature alone. If she has strength enough left to raise herself up by the hand of art, well and good; if not, then, for art too, nothing remains, but to let the sick man die and to embalm the dead. Art cannot supply the power of life where it is wanting.

It was long ago that philosophy, on account of this resemblance to the healing art, received the name of "medicine for the soul." And truly, this qualification seems better adapted to secure its acceptance, than when it claims to teach us to live according to the rules of art. For who that has the free use of his natural powers does not feel that he can live without it? On the other hand, when it presents itself only as physician, then the well know that they have nothing to do with it.

The Indians in the islands of the South Sea, it seems, are unacquainted with medicines. With them slight wounds or illnesses heal themselves; and of great ones they die—as we do. And as they are so fortunate as to have no idea of a soul in and of itself, as a man in their apprehension is always a man, made out of one piece, so they know nothing of particular diseases of the soul; or if ever they experience an attack of this kind, the hunger-cure, for which they have but too frequent opportunity, is generally the most effectual remedy.

On the other hand, when the progress of refinement in a nation has gone so far, that body and soul, instead of being as they should be one person, are treated as two powers with different interests, each having its separate establishment, like naughty husbands and wives; what is more natural than that bad consequences should result from such an ill-starred union? Man is then no longer that noble being in whom all is sense and power and soul, in whom, so to speak, everything corporeal is spiritual, and everything spiritual, corporeal. He is an unnatural, centaur-like compound of animal and spirit, in which the one lives at the other's expense, in which the animal creates for itself necessities, the spirit passions, projects, and aims of which the natural man knows nothing. Each oppresses, drags, worries, and exhausts the other as much as it can, and a vast number of bodily and mental diseases are the ultimate fruit of this putting asunder what God had joined together. In such cases, when the evil has reached its height, that "medical art for the soul" may offer its aid with some degree of success; and either relieve the patient by purging, bleeding, and clysters; or, at least, by means of agreeable opiates, procure for him a delusive rest.

But this art has never yet been found able to effect a radical cure; and we may boldly maintain, that when a nation has once fallen into the hands of the two goddesses of healing, it is irrecoverably lost; not because one must needs burst with their medicines, but because whenever they are resorted to, the evil has already proceeded too far to admit of entire restoration.

I said philosophy might the rather maintain its place, as healing art for the soul, because then, the well would know that they had nothing to do with it. But as all arts love to make themselves more important than they are, so this art, too, has found means to impose itself upon all the world as indispensable. Like its sister art, which ministers to the body, it will not allow anyone to be entirely well. According to its doctrine and its ideal of health, the whole earth is one great lazar-house of bodily and mental diseases, and there is no man well enough to dispense with its prescriptions. Happily, this assumption is not conceded to either of these arts. Nature knows nothing of ideals. As long as a man feels himself sound, he has a right to think himself sound; and, without troubling himself whether others object to that view or not, he lives straight forward as a healthy man; and (like Voltaire's Zadig) reads not a letter of all the learned dissertations, in which gentlemen undertake to prove it impossible that he should be well. There are cases, it is true, in which a sick man is only the more dangerously sick, because unconscious of his malady. But these cases are rare, and cannot deprive the great mass of those who feel well, of their traditional right to that feeling.

ON THE NATURE OF MAN

—

OF THE TRUTH OF PHYSIOGNOMY

—

BY

JOHANN KASPAR LAVATER

JOHANN KASPAR LAVATER
1741—1801

Switzerland claims no small share in the literary honors of Germany; one of the most notable of the Swiss contributors to German literature being Johann Kaspar Lavater, who was born at Zurich in 1741. He received his education in the grammar school and university of his native town, and in 1762 was ordained a minister. Nearly his whole life was spent in preaching to various churches in Zurich and in devoting himself to charitable work, for which he displayed an unbounded zeal. In 1798 Lavater's public and outspoken protest against the ravages of the French troops, who were at that time occupying Switzerland, gained the applause of Europe. The following year, while standing in front of his own house, he was shot by a French soldier. He never recovered from the wound, and died from its effects two years later, after much suffering.

Lavater is best known by his works on physiognomy, the first of which was published in 1772. Three years later appeared the first volume of his celebrated " Physiognomical Fragments for the Promotion of Knowledge and Love of Mankind," his most important work. Goethe contributed to it a chapter on the skulls of animals. Besides numerous other treatises on physiognomy he wrote on theology as well. His works were at one time extravagantly praised by his contemporaries, but as original contributions to the fund of human knowledge they have failed to stand the test of time. Lavater is important, however, in the history of German thought and civilization as one of the most interesting literary figures of his generation. His personality was sufficient to impress Goethe, and the observations of the latter would seem to indicate that the man was greater than his works.

Lavater's style is vivid and declamatory, and betrays a genuine depth of conviction that inspired respect and gave him a great personal influence. He is sometimes very abstruse; but he is always entertaining. There is no writer in all literature whose personal character was purer or nobler, or whose life was more unselfish. The essays " On the Nature of Man " and " Of the Truth of Physiognomy " are excellent and representative examples of his style.

ON THE NATURE OF MAN

Which is the Foundation of the Science of Physiognomy

OF all earthly creatures man is the most perfect, the most imbued with the principles of life.

Each particle of matter is an immensity; each leaf a world; each insect an inexplicable compendium. Who then shall enumerate the gradations between insect and man? In him all the powers of nature are united. He is the essence of creation. The son of earth, he is the earth's lord; the summary and central point of all existence, of all powers, and of all life, on that earth which he inhabits.

Of all organized beings with which we are acquainted, man alone excepted, there are none in which are so wonderfully united the three different kinds of life, the animal, the intellectual, and the moral. Each of these lives is the compendium of various faculties, most wonderfully compounded and harmonized.

To know, to desire, to act, or accurately to observe and meditate; to perceive and to wish; to possess the powers of motion and of resistance; these combined, constitute man an animal, intellectual, and moral being.

Man, endowed with these faculties, with this triple life, is in himself the most worthy subject of observation, as he likewise is himself the most worthy observer. Under whatever point of view he may be considered, what is more worthy of contemplation than himself? In him each species of life is conspicuous; yet never can his properties be wholly known, except by the aid of his external form, his body, his superficies. How spiritual, how incorporeal soever, his internal essence may be, still is he only visible and conceivable from the harmony of his constituent parts. From these he is inseparable.

He exists and moves in the body he inhabits, as in his element. This material man must become the subject of observation. All the knowledge we can obtain of man must be gained through the medium of our senses.

This threefold life, which man cannot be denied to possess, necessarily first becomes the subject of disquisition and research, as it presents itself in the form of body, and in such of his faculties as are apparent to sense.

There is no object in nature, the properties and powers of which can be manifest to us in any other manner than by such external appearances as affect the senses. By these all beings are characterized. They are the foundations of all human knowledge. Man must wander in the darkest ignorance, equally with respect to himself and the objects that surround him, did he not become acquainted with their properties and powers by the aid of their externals; and had not each object a character peculiar to its nature and essence, which acquaints us with what it is, and enables us to distinguish it from what it is not.

All bodies which we survey appear to sight under a certain form and superficies. We behold those outlines traced which are the result of their organization. I hope I shall be pardoned the repetition of such commonplace truths, since on these are built the science of physiognomy, or the proper study of man. However true these axioms, with respect to visible objects, and particularly to organized bodies, they are still more extensively true when applied to man, and his nature. The organization of man peculiarly distinguishes him from all other earthly beings; and his physiognomy, that is to say, the superficies and outlines of this organization, show him to be infinitely superior to all those visible beings by which he is surrounded.

We are unacquainted with any form equally noble, equally majestic, with that of man, and in which so many kinds of life, so many powers, so many virtues of action and motion, unite, as in a central point. With firm step he advances over the earth's surface, and with erect body raises his head toward heaven. He looks forward to infinitude; he acts with facility and swiftness inconceivable, and his motions are the most immediate and the most varied. By whom may their varieties be enumerated? He can at once both suffer and perform infinitely more than any other creature. He unites flexibility and fortitude, strength and dexterity, activity and rest. Of all creatures he can the soonest yield, and the longest resist. None resemble him in the variety and harmony of his powers. His faculties, like his form, are peculiar to himself.

How much nobler, more astonishing, and more attractive will this form become, when we discover that it is itself the interpreter of all the high powers it possesses, active and passive! Only in those parts in which animal strength and properties reside does it resemble animals. But how much is it exalted above the brute in those parts in which are the powers of superior origin, the powers of mind, of motion!

The form and proportion of man, his superior height, capable of so many changes, and such variety of motion, prove to the unprejudiced observer his supereminent strength, and astonishing facility of action. The high excellence and physiological unity of human nature are visible at the first glance. The head, especially the face, and the formation of the firm parts, compared to the firm parts of other animals, convince the accurate observer, who is capable of investigating truth, of the greatness and superiority of his intellectual qualities. The eye, the look, the cheeks, the mouth, the forehead, whether considered in a state of entire rest or during their innumerable varieties of motion, in fine, all that is understood by physiognomy, is the most expressive, the most convincing picture of interior sensation, desires, passions, will, and of all those properties which so much exalt moral above animal life.

Although the physiological, intellectual, and moral life of man, with all their subordinate powers and their constituent parts, so eminently unite in one being; although these three kinds of life do not, like three distinct families, reside in separate parts, or stories of the body; but co-exist in one point, and by their combination form one whole; yet is it plain that each of these powers of life has its peculiar station, where it more especially unfolds itself, and acts.

It is beyond contradiction evident that, though physiological or animal life displays itself through all the body, and especially through all the animal parts, yet does it act most conspicuously in the arm, from the shoulder to the ends of the fingers.

It is equally clear that intellectual life, or the powers of the understanding and the mind, make themselves most apparent in the circumference and form of the solid parts of the head, especially the forehead; though they will discover themselves to an attentive and accurate eye in every part and point of the human body, by the congeniality and harmony of the various parts, as will be frequently noticed in the course of this work. Is there any occasion to prove that the power of thinking resides neither in the foot, in the hand, nor in the back; but in the head, and its internal parts?

The moral life of man, particularly, reveals itself in the lines, marks, and transitions of the countenance. His moral powers and desires, his irritability, sympathy, and antipathy; his facility of attracting or repelling the objects that surround him; these are all summed up in, and painted upon, his countenance when at rest. When any passion is called into action, such passion is depicted by the motion of the muscles, and these motions are accompanied by a strong palpitation of the heart. If the countenance be tranquil, it always denotes tranquillity in the region of the heart and breast.

This threefold life of man, so intimately interwoven through his frame, is still capable of being studied in its different appropriate parts; and did we live in a less depraved world we should find sufficient data for the science of physiognomy.

The animal life, the lowest and most earthly, would discover itself from the rim of the belly to the organs of generation, which would become its central or focal point. The middle or moral life would be seated in the breast, and the heart would be its central point. The intellectual life, which of the three is supreme, would reside in the head, and have the eye for its centre. If we take the countenance as the representative and epitome of the three divisions, then will the forehead, to the eyebrows, be the mirror, or image, of the understanding; the nose and cheeks the image of the moral and sensitive life; and the mouth and chin the image of the animal life; while the eye will be to the whole as its summary and centre. I may also add that the closed mouth at the moment of most perfect tranquillity is the central point of the radii of the countenance. It cannot however too often be repeated that these three lives, by their intimate connection with each other, are all, and each, expressed in every part of the body.

What we have hitherto said is so clear, so well known, so universal, that we should blush to insist upon such commonplace truths, were they not, first, the foundation on which we must build all we have to propose; and, again, had not these truths (can it be believed by futurity?) in this our age been so many thousand times mistaken and contested, with the most inconceivable affectation.

The science of physiognomy, whether understood in the most enlarged or most confined sense, indubitably depends on these general and incontrovertible principles; yet, incontrovertible as they are, they have not been without their opponents. Men pretend to doubt of the most striking, the most convincing, the most self-evident truths; although, were these destroyed, neither truth nor knowledge would remain. They do not profess to doubt concerning the physiognomy of other natural objects, yet do they doubt the physiognomy of human nature; the first object, the most worthy of contemplation, and the most animated which the realms of nature contain.

OF THE TRUTH OF PHYSIOGNOMY

ALL countenances, all forms, all created beings, are not only different from each other in their classes, races, and kinds, but are also individually distinct.

Each being differs from every other being of its species. However generally known, it is a truth the most important to our purpose, and necessary to repeat, that, " There is no rose perfectly similar to another rose, no egg to an egg, no eel to an eel, no lion to a lion, no eagle to an eagle, no man to a man."

Confining this proposition to man only, it is the first, the most profound, most secure, and unshaken foundation-stone of physiognomy that, however intimate the analogy and similarity of the innumerable forms of men, no two men can be found who, brought together, and accurately compared, will not appear to be very remarkably different.

Nor is it less incontrovertible that it is equally impossible to find two minds, as two countenances, which perfectly resemble each other.

This consideration alone will be sufficient to make it received as a truth, not requiring farther demonstration, that there must be a certain native analogy between the external varieties of the countenance and form, and the internal varieties of the mind. Shall it be denied that this acknowledged internal variety among all men is the cause of the external variety of their forms and countenances? Shall it be affirmed that the mind does not influence the body, or that the body does not influence the mind?

Anger renders the muscles protuberant; and shall not therefore an angry mind and protuberant muscles be considered as cause and effect?

After repeated observation that an active and vivid eye and an active and acute wit are frequently found in the same person, shall it be supposed that there is no relation between the active eye and the active mind? Is this the effect of accident? Of accident! Ought it not rather to be considered as sympathy, an interchangeable and instantaneous effect, when we perceive that, at the very moment the understanding is most acute and penetrating and the wit the most lively, the motion and fire of the eye undergo, at that moment, the most visible change?

Shall the open, friendly, and unsuspecting eye and the open, friendly, and unsuspecting heart be united in a thousand instances, and shall we say the one is not the cause, the other the effect?

Shall nature discover wisdom and order in all things; shall corresponding causes and effects be everywhere united; shall this be the most clear, the most indubitable of truths; and in the first, the most noble of the works of nature, shall she act arbitrarily, without design, without law? The human countenance, that mirror of the Divinity, that noblest of the works of the Creator—shall not motive and action, shall not the correspondence between the interior and the exterior, the visible and the invisible, the cause and the effect, be there apparent?

Yet this is all denied by those who oppose the truth of the science of physiognomy.

Truth, according to them, is ever at variance with itself. Eternal order is degraded to a juggler, whose purpose it is to deceive.

Calm reason revolts at the supposition that Newton or Leibnitz ever could have the countenance and appearance of an idiot, incapable of a firm step, a meditating eye; of comprehending the least difficult of abstract propositions, or of expressing himself so as to be understood; that one of these in the brain of a Laplander conceived his "Theodica"; and that the other in the head of an Esquimaux, who wants the power to number farther than six, and affirms all beyond to be innumerable, had dissected the rays of light, and weighed worlds.

Calm reason revolts when it is asserted that the strong man may appear perfectly like the weak, the man in full health like another in the last stage of a consumption, or that the rash and irascible may resemble the cold and phlegmatic. It revolts to hear it affirmed that joy and grief, pleasure and pain, love and hatred, all exhibit themselves under the same traits; that is to say, under no traits whatever, on the exterior of man. Yet such are the assertions of those who maintain physiognomy to be a chimerical science. They overturn all that order and combination by which eternal wisdom so highly astonishes and delights the understanding. It cannot be too emphatically repeated that blind chance and arbitrary disorder constitute the philosophy of fools; and that they are the bane of natural knowledge, philosophy and religion. Entirely to banish such a system is the duty of the true inquirer, the sage, and the divine.

All men (this is indisputable), absolutely all men, estimate all things whatever by their physiognomy, their exterior, temporary superficies. By viewing these on every occasion, they draw their conclusions concerning their internal properties.

What merchant, if he be unacquainted with the person of whom he purchases, does not estimate his wares by the physiognomy or appearance of those wares? If he purchase of a distant correspondent, what other means does he use in judging whether they are or are not equal to his expectation? Is not his judgment determined by the color, the fineness, the superficies, the exterior, the physiognomy? Does he not judge money by its physiognomy? Why does he take one guinea and reject another? Why weigh a third in his hand? Does he not determine according to its color, or impression; its outside, its physiognomy? If a stranger enter his shop, as a buyer or seller, will he not observe him? Will he not draw conclusions from his countenance? Will he not, almost before he is out of hearing, pronounce some opinion upon him, and say: "This man has an honest look," "That man has a pleasing, or forbidding, countenance?" What is it to the purpose whether his judgment be right or wrong? He judges. Though not wholly, he depends in part upon the exterior form, and thence draws inferences concerning the mind.

How does the farmer, walking through his grounds, regulate his future expectations by the color, the size, the growth, the exterior; that is to say, by the physiognomy of the bloom, the stalk, or the ear, of his corn; the stem, and shoots of his vine-tree? "This ear of corn is blighted," "That wood is full of sap; this will grow, that not," affirms he, at the first or second glance. "Though these vine-shoots look well, they will bear but few grapes." And wherefore? He remarks, in their appearance, as the physiognomist in the countenances of shallow men, the want of native energy. Does not he judge by the exterior?

Does not the physician pay more attention to the physiognomy of the sick than to all the accounts that are brought him concerning his patient? Zimmermann, among the living, may be brought as a proof of the great perfection at which this kind of judgment has arrived; and among the dead, Kempf, whose son has written a treatise on temperament.

The painter —— Yet of him I will say nothing; his art too evidently reproves the childish and arrogant prejudices of those who pretend to disbelieve physiognomy.

The traveller, the philanthropist, the misanthrope, the lover (and who not?), all act according to their feelings and decisions, true or false, confused or clear, concerning physiognomy. These feelings, these decisions, excite compassion, disgust, joy, love, hatred, suspicion, confidence, reserve, or benevolence.

Do we not daily judge of the sky by its physiognomy? No food, not a glass of wine or beer, not a cup of coffee or tea, comes to table, which is not judged by its physiognomy, its exterior, and of which we do not thence deduce some conclusion respecting its interior, good or bad properties.

Is not all nature physiognomy, superficies and contents; body, and spirit; exterior effect and internal power; invisible beginning and visible ending?

What knowledge is there, of which man is capable, that is not founded on the exterior; the relation that exists between visible and invisible, the perceptible and the imperceptible?

Physiognomy, whether understood in its most extensive or confined signification, is the origin of all human decisions, efforts, actions, expectations, fears, and hopes; of all pleasing and unpleasing sensations, which are occasioned by external objects.

From the cradle to the grave, in all conditions and ages, throughout all nations, from Adam to the last existing man, from the worm we tread on to the most sublime of philosophers (and why not to the angel, why not to the Mediator Christ?), physiognomy is the origin of all we do and suffer.

Each insect is acquainted with its friend and its foe; each child loves and fears, although it knows not why. Physiognomy is the cause; nor is there a man to be found on earth who is not daily influenced by physiognomy; not a man who cannot figure to himself a countenance which shall to him appear exceedingly lovely, or exceedingly hateful; not a man who does not more or less, the first time he is in company with a stranger, observe, estimate, compare, and judge him, according to appearances, although he might never have heard of the word or thing called physiognomy; not a man who does not judge of all things that pass through his hands, by their physiognomy; that is, of their internal worth by their external appearance.

The art of dissimulation itself, which is adduced as so insuperable an objection to the truth of physiognomy, is founded on physiognomy. Why does the hypocrite assume the appearance of an honest man, but because that he is convinced, though not perhaps from any systematic reflection, that all eyes are acquainted with the characteristic marks of honesty.

What judge, wise or unwise, whether he confess or deny the fact, does not sometimes in this sense decide from appearances? Who can, is, or ought to be, absolutely indifferent to the exterior of persons brought before him to be judged? What king would choose a minister without examining his exterior, secretly at least, and to a certain extent? An officer will not enlist a soldier without thus examining his appearance, his height out of the question. What master or mistress of a family will choose a servant without considering the exterior; no matter whether their judgment be or be not just, or whether it be exercised unconsciously?

I am wearied of citing instances so numerous, and so continually before our eyes, to prove that men, tacitly and unanimously, confess the influence which physiognomy has over their sensations and actions. I feel disgust at being obliged to write thus, in order to convince the learned of truths with which every child is or may be acquainted.

He that hath eyes to see, let him see; but should the light, by being brought too close to his eyes, produce frenzy, he may burn himself by endeavoring to extinguish the torch of truth. I use such expressions unwillingly, but I dare do my duty, and my duty is boldly to declare that I believe myself certain of what I now and hereafter shall affirm; and that I think myself capable of convincing all real lovers of truth, by principles which are in themselves incontrovertible. It is also necessary to confute the pretensions of certain literary despots, and to compel them to be more cautious in their decisions. It is therefore proved, not because I say it, but because it is an eternal and manifest truth, and would have been equally truth, had it never been said, that, whether they are or are not sensible of it, all men are daily influenced by physiognomy; that, as Sultzer has affirmed, every man, consciously or inconsciously, understands something of physiognomy; nay, that there is not a living being that does not, at least after its manner, draw some inferences from the external to the internal; that does not judge concerning that which is not, by that which is, apparent to the senses.

This universal, though tacit confession, that the exterior, the visible, the superficies of objects, indicates their nature, their properties, and that every outward sign is the symbol of some inherent quality, I hold to be equally certain and important to the science of physiognomy.

I must once more repeat, when each apple, each apricot, has a physiognomy peculiar to itself, shall man, the lord of earth, have none? The most simple and inanimate object has its characteristic exterior, by which it is not only distinguished as a species, but individually; and shall the first, noblest, best harmonized, and most beauteous of things be denied all characteristic.

But whatever may be objected against the truth and certainty of the science of physiognomy, by the most illiterate, or the most learned; how much soever he who openly professes faith in this science, may be subject to ridicule, to philosophic pity and contempt; it still cannot be contested that there is no object, thus considered, more important, more worthy of observation, more interesting than man, nor any occupation superior to that of disclosing the beauties and perfections of human nature.

Such were my opinions six or eight years ago. Will it in

the next century be believed that it is still, at this time, necessary to repeat these things; or that numerous obscure witlings continue to treat with ridicule and contempt the general feelings of mankind, and observations which not only may be, but are demonstrated; and that they act thus without having refuted any one of the principles at which they laugh; yet that they are, notwithstanding, continually repeating the words, philosophy and enlightened age?

TITHON AND AURORA

BY

JOHANN GOTTFRIED VON HERDER

JOHANN GOTTFRIED VON HERDER
1744—1803

Few men have risen to greatness in spite of such formidable obstacles as confronted Johann Gottfried von Herder in his early career. He was the son of a poor schoolmaster, born in 1744 at Mohrungen, in East Prussia, in the dominions of Frederick the Great, and was educated at the University of Königsberg, where he subsisted literally on charity. Here he came in contact with Kant and Hamann, both of whom influenced his mental development to a marked degree. The strain of his work at the university brought on an affection of the eyes from which he never fully recovered. It was while undergoing a course of treatment for this trouble, at Strasburg in 1769, that he met Goethe, and a friendship sprang up between the two young men that was bound to exert a great influence on the minds and lives of both. Having achieved considerable success in the ministry, his chosen calling, Herder was invited, in 1775, to Weimar as Court preacher. He accepted, and the remainder of his life was spent in that famous centre of literary activity where Wieland and Goethe had already taken up their abode. In 1801 Herder was appointed President of the Consistory, the highest clerical office in the duchy. He also received a patent of nobility from the Elector of Bavaria. He enjoyed these honors only a short time, for two years later he died, in 1803, at the age of fifty-nine.

In 1778 Herder published his "Poetry of the Races" (Dichtung der Völker), a careful selection of popular songs and ballads, taken from nearly every language of Europe, and rendered into his own tongue with poetic sympathy and remarkable accuracy. In 1782 appeared "The Spirit of Hebrew Poetry," and from 1784 to 1791 his greatest work, "Ideas on the Philosophy of the Human Race." He wrote a metrical romance of great power, entitled "The Cid." Herder is also the author of numerous essays and works on theology, philosophy, and criticism, of which "Tithon and Aurora" has been selected as an example.

Herder's success as a translator has already been referred to. In poems of his own composition his style does not show to equal advantage, and in his prose works his style is decidedly inferior in point of clearness to that of his two great contemporaries, Wieland and Goethe. But while his writing lacks occasionally careful attention to detail and form, it often carries with it a peculiar eloquence and profound suggestiveness of thought that give it deservedly a high place in German literature. The genius of Herder was the source of great inspiration to his contemporaries, for the views on art, on history, and life in general that he disseminated were broader than the current views of the eighteenth century. On Goethe and Richter especially his influence was far reaching and happy in its results. The monument erected to Herder by his fellow-philosophers and poets at Weimar bears these three words, "Light, Love, Life," an inscription that expresses most admirably the characteristic aspirations of his soul.

TITHON AND AURORA

ALTHOUGH, in general, no epitaph or panegyric uses to notice how long a man has outlived himself, yet is this one of the most remarkable and not infrequent phenomena in the history of human lives. The earlier the play of the faculties and passions begins, the more impetuously it is continued, and assailed in various ways by external accident, the oftener shall one discover cases of that early exhaustion of the soul—of the warrior laid prostrate without death or wound —of a manly, and, often even, of a youthful extreme age. A man may go about for a long while, with a living body, like the image of his own funeral monument; his spirit gone from him —a shadow and a memory of his former name. Many causes may contribute to this early death: qualities of mind and heart, too great activity and too sluggish patience, relaxation as well as over-tension, too rapid prosperity and too protracted adversity. For it is a general truth, that health, cheerfulness, pleasure, and virtue are ever the medium between two extremes. Either on the precipitous or the shallow shore of the stream the vessel may be wrecked. In the middle, it is easy and pleasant sailing. Many a one has grown old because he wanted the true interior source of activity. He was a brook that contracts its waters into itself and soon dries up and shows its melancholy bed. This one endeavored to make seeming supply the place of being. The darkness passed away, and the glowworms in the hair glittered as sparkling diamonds no longer. That one would accomplish by toil and memory, what intelligence and genius alone can perform. The overloaded memory gave way, excessive labor tired, and the want of the essential was at last painfully apparent. Another, while a youth, overstrained his nobler powers; he piled up mountains of imagination to the skies, and soon, without the lightning of Jupiter, found under them his grave. Still another, whose learning and effort had no object but his own ease, abandoned learning and effort as soon as he had obtained that ease, and buried himself in a blessed decay. Here, one, without desert, has had his brain turned by an unexpected prosperity, a too rapidly acquired fame, an unlooked for success in action. He has no longer any thought beyond this success. His seductive goddess, Fortune, has crowned him at once with laurel, with poplar, and with poppy. He falls asleep or babbles nonsense in her enervating lap. There, one of great merit has suffered too long with undeserved misfortune, until his shoulders are bowed, his breast contracted, his arm paralyzed, and he can no longer stand erect and recruit himself. A thunderbolt from heaven has stricken the oak even to its root and deprived it of the power of life. To this one—a man of manifold capacity—there was wanting a capacious breast to despise envy and to wait for better times. He suffered himself to be drawn into conflict with it, and the flying eagle was unworthily vanquished by the viper that held him in her folds. That one—a man of honest industry—was wanting in intelligence. His more cunning enemies soon made him powerless and wretched. And thus it befell ten other characters, in other situations. Hard by the theatre of civil life there is generally a hospital, and in that the greater part of the actors gradually lose themselves.

Two things especially contribute to this result, and they, too, are extremes. In the first place, the arbitrariness of the ruling great; and, secondly, a too refined delicacy and carefulness. As to the former, it is a well-known and favorite saying, that nothing is so troublesome as gratitude, nothing so insupportable as continued respect and the daily spectacle of acknowledged merit. Accordingly, new favor purchases for itself new gratitude; and creatures whom the great purposely attract to themselves—in whom they even pretend to find gifts and merits which the gods never gave them—have, for them, a peculiar charm, as their own creation. The sap is withdrawn from the old trees that the young world may bloom and thrive. Whoso, in such cases, is not greater than he on whom he depends, dies inwardly with self-consuming vexation. The majestic voice of Philip II, " *Yo el Rey*," has slain many a one of this description. Opposed to this murder of human merits and powers, there is another, which may be termed the most refined species of self-murder. It is the more to be lamented because it occurs only in the case of the most elect of men; suddenly or gradually breaking in pieces their costly mechanism. Men of extreme delicacy of feeling have a "Highest" after which they strive —an idea to which they attach themselves with unspeakable longing—an ideal perfection which they pursue with irresistible impulse. When deprived of this idea, when this fair image is destroyed before their eyes, the heart of their flower is broken, and feeble, withered leaves alone remain. Perhaps more of the dead of this description go about in society, than one might at first suppose, because they, of all men, most carefully conceal their grief, and hide even from their friend the slow poison of their death—that sad secret of the heart. Shakespeare, who depicted all conditions of the soul, has delineated, also, this epoch of the sinking or confusion of the faculties, in various situations and characters, with great truth and exactness. One —perhaps the crown of lamentations over such a state—may serve as an example of all.

> "O! what a noble mind is here o'erthrown!
> The courtier's, soldier's, scholar's eye, tongue, sword,
> The expectancy and rose of the fair State,
> The glass of fashion and the mould of form,
> The observed of all observers! quite, quite down!
> ——Now see that noble and most sovereign reason,
> Like sweet bells jangled out of tune and harsh;
> That unmatched form and stature of blown youth,
> Blasted with ecstasy."

Not only individual persons outlive themselves, but much oftener and longer, those politico-moral persons, so called— institutions, forms of polity, classes, corporations. Often their body remains for centuries, as a show, when the soul of that body has long since fled; or they creep about as shadows among living forms. To be convinced of this, let anyone enter a Jewish synagogue, or read Anquetil's "Zend-Avesta," and the sacred books of the Brahmins. There is no doubt that all these religious institutions were once very useful, and that, in every one of these hulls, lay the germs of a great development. Time has developed each of them more or less—one happily, so that we are disposed perhaps to look for more in it than was there; another imperfectly and feeble; as in the great course of Nature it will fall out. Nevertheless, everything has its goal, and the Rabbi, the Destur, the Mobed—perhaps also the Brahmin—has, in the great whole, outlived himself. In some regions of Mahommedanism something similar is already reported of the Koran, although that is the youngest of bibles. And in Christendom, true as its pure fountain streams, with the water of eternal life, how many a vessel is already broken that was thought to have exhausted this fountain! How many a form which still stands there, had long ago outlived itself! Look at the Romish mass! Listen to many of their litanies and prayers! Into what times do they take us back! What a strange savor of long-perished ages! As, in religion, the priestly order, so in other institutions the orders connected with them follow each its living or its dead. Consider so many institutions and orders of the Middle Ages! Where they could not follow the Genius of opinion and renew their youth with him, they either remained stationary on the shore or else the stream bore them lifeless on, until they found somewhere their place of rest. Even in Cervantes' days the Duke of Bejar would not allow that "Don Quixote" should be dedicated to him, so long as he supposed it to be a serious book of knight-errantry; because the taste for such things had already begun to be ridiculous. He accepted the dedication gladly when, as the book was read to him, he discovered its true character. Time has enacted novels of this kind with several institutions. The princes and heroes of Corneille are for the most part insupportable to us, and we wonder how other times could ever put together, believe, and admire such nonsense. Shakespeare's court-scenes seem to us like capital and state acts. The knights of our day are no longer of the ancient order; and that kingly word of Louis XIV: "*L'Etat? c'est moi!*" will ever remain the appropriate epitaph of that great world-monarch.

"Whatsoever had a birth must die," says the Brahmin; and that, which seeks to defer its downfall by artificial methods, in resorting to such methods, has already outlived itself. In the early spring, the foliage and grass of the former year are often still visible; much of it has retained its place; but, in a short time, the whole is vanished, and a new raiment covers the trees and the bosom of the earth.

If there is anything in the circle of humanity which ought

not to outlive itself, it is science and art. The nature of these is eternal, and they are capable of the purest truth and of infinite extension. And indeed the real essence of art and science never dies, never changes. But their forms are all the more perishable, as they appear, above all things, to depend on their masters and discoverers—to originate, to flourish, and to perish with them. So long as the discoverer lives, so long as the master teaches and directs, men draw living thoughts from his living fountain. In the second and third generation one already wanders through schools that echo and ape him. The image of the master stands there dead. His science and his art has outlived itself, not in his own, but in his successors' works.

Travels give us a long catalogue of things which have thus outlived themselves—travels in the history, as well as in the actual inspection or regions, countries, institutions, persons, classes. Who that enters an ancient castle, and old-fashioned knightly hall, an archive of old diplomas and treaties, of old arms and decorations, old court-houses, churches, convents, palaces, and imperial cities, does not feel himself translated into a perished century? In a tour through Germany, one often finds, within a circle of a few miles, the ancient, the middle, the modern, and *most* modern ages together. Here, we breathe still the air of the twelfth century; there, we hear the melodies of the sixteenth, the tenth, the fourth. All at once, you enter cabinets which have been instituted under the luxurious ducal government—galleries collected under Louis XIV, and end with institutions which seem to have been devised for the twentieth century. Instructive as this chaos may be for the traveller, it would be very confusing and oppressive for the resident, did not human nature accustom itself to all things. "Lord, by this time he stinketh, for he hath been dead four days," said the sorrowing sister; one might say, with regard to many institutions, four centuries, and still they are not offensive to their brothers and sisters. These are accustomed to the odor, and find it nourishing.

Italy seems to me the most instructive theatre of these life-epochs and world-ages. There, you can be with Egyptians, Greeks, Romans, Etruscans, nay, if you please, with Chinese, with Hindoos, and with the people of Madagascar! In Rome, alone, you may follow paganism from Romulus to Diocletian, and Christianity from Constantine to Pius. There, and in the Italian provinces, you may live at pleasure in the fifteenth, the sixteenth, or the eighteenth century. And if you investigate the monuments of nature, you will come upon self-survivals which will take you beyond the bounds of history. It requires a capacious mind to embrace, to distinguish, to classify all these scenes. But, to such a mind, they exhibit a compend of all history, which floods us, at last, with, I know not, what pleasing but dissolving melancholy.

> " The cloud-capped towers, etc., etc.
> ————We are such stuff
> As dreams are made of, and our little life
> Is rounded with a sleep."

Enough of sleep and of dying out! Let us now speak of waking and rejuvenescence! How is this brought about? By revolution?

I confess that, among the misused words of our modern, fashionable vocabulary, few are so displeasing to me as this; because it has entirely departed from its original, pure signification, and carries with it the most mischievous confusion of thought. In astronomy, we call revolution a movement of the great world-bodies which returns into itself—determined by measure, number, and forces; a movement, which is not only the most peaceful order in itself, but, in connection with other harmonious powers, establishes the kingdom of eternal order. Thus the earth revolves around itself and makes day and night, and by means of these, arranges and regulates the sleep and the waking of its creatures, their time for rest and the circle of their occupations. Thus the earth moves around the sun and makes the year, and by means of that, the seasons, and by means of them, the changes of labor and of mortal enjoyment. The revolution of the moon around our earth gives to the sea its ebb and flood, determines the periods of diseases, and perhaps, of the growth of plants. In this sense it is useful to notice revolutions; for, in them, we observe a course of affairs which returns into itself, and, in that course of things, the laws of a perpetual order. In such a course there is nothing abrupt, arbitrary, without reason. There is nothing of destruction in it, but a gently vibrating thread of conservation. Revolutions of this kind are the dance of the Hours around the throne of Jupiter. They are the chaplet of victory on the immortal head of the god, after the conquest of chaos.

Also, if we draw down this idea of revolution from heaven to earth, it can be no other than the idea of a silent progress of things, of a reappearance of certain phenomena, according to their peculiar nature, consequently, of the design of an ever-working Wisdom, Order, and Goodness. In this sense, we speak of the revolutions of arts and sciences, that is, a periodical return of them, the causes of which we endeavor to investigate in history, and, as it were, to calculate astronomically. Thus the Pythagoreans spoke of the revolutions of the human soul, that is, of its periodical return into other forms. Thus have men investigated the laws of the revolution of human thoughts; when they return from oblivion into remembrance; when visions and desires, when activities and passions which had gone to sleep, reappear once more. In all these things, it has been attempted to discover the laws of a hidden, silent order of nature.

But the meaning of this word has undergone a detestable change, because, in the barbarous centuries, men knew of no other revolutions than conquests, overturns, oppressions, confusions without motive, aim, or order. Then it was called revolution, when the nethermost was made uppermost—when, by the so-called right of war, a nation lost more or less of its property, its laws, its goods; or when, by the right of monarchy, all those so-called rights were enforced, which St. Thomas, Machiavel, and Naudé afterwards collected from actual events and brought together in one chapter. Then, finally, it was called a revolution, when the ministers did what the rulers themselves would not do; or when, here and there, the people undertook that which they could rarely execute so well as kings or ministers. Hence the numerous "Histoires des Révolutions"—a kind of book whose title is all the more popular, that its contents are, for the most part, unintelligible or abominable. The notion of an aim or object was almost lost sight of. History became an exhibition of entanglements without a *dénouement*. For, after the conclusion of each revolution, socalled, the confusion, in the kingdoms where they occurred, was greater than before. Revolutions of this sort, whencesoever they may derive their origin, are signs of barbarism, of an insolent force, of a mad wilfulness. The more reason and moderation increase among men, the rarer they will become, until, at last, they entirely disappear. Then the word revolution will revert to its pure and true meaning. Then it will mean, in history also as elsewhere, a course of things arranged according to laws—a course of events which peacefully returns into itself. In this view alone is history worth the study; for, as to the revolutions of wild elephants, when they tear up trees and devastate villages—from these there is not much to be learned.

Not to mislead, therefore, with this abused word, and not to make destructive violence a medicine for mortal ills, we will keep the path of healing Nature. Not revolutions, but evolutions are the silent process of the great mother, wherewith she awakens slumbering powers, brings germs to maturity, gives renewed youth to premature age, and new life to seeming death. Let us see what this remedy comprehends, and how it heals.

If we suppose Nature to have an aim on the earth, that aim can be no other than the development of her powers in all forms, kinds, and ways. These evolutions proceed slowly, often imperceptibly; and, for the most part, they appear periodically. After a night of sleep follows a morning of awakening. Under the shade of the former Nature had re-collected her powers, in order to meet the latter with spirit. In the ages of man, childhood continues long; body and mind advance with a slow growth, until, with collected energies, the flower of youth breaks forth, and the fruit of later years comes gradually to maturity. Very improperly have these periods of development been called revolutions. There is nothing here that revolves, but faculties are evolved, developed. Ever, the more recondite and deeper-lying come forth to view, which, without many a preceding one, could not have been brought into action. Therefore Nature made periods. She gave the creature time to recover itself from one exertion gone through with, in order to begin, with joy, and to accomplish another and more difficult. For when the plant puts forth a flower, or when the fruit is forming in it, unquestionably more inward and finer forces are put in action than when the sap was entering the stem, and the lowest leaves were brought forth. In the ordinary course of things Nature does not leave her work until all its physical powers have been brought into action; the innermost, as it were, turned outward, and the development, which, at every step, is assisted by a kindly *epigenesis,* has become as perfect as it could become, under the given conditions.

Men are accustomed to regard each individual object, and especially each living individual as an isolated whole; but a nearer view shows it to be connected with soil, climate, weather, with the periodical breath of all Nature; and that, according to these, it lasts for a longer or shorter time, grows early old or easily renews its youth. Man, a rational, moral, and political creation, lives, by means of these capacities and powers, in a peculiar and infinitely extended element. His reason is connected with the reason of others, his moral culture with the conduct of others, his capacity to constitute himself a free being—both in himself and in connection with others—is so intimately connected with the way of thinking, the reasonableness, the active enterprise of many, that out of this element, he must needs be like a fish on dry land, or a bird in a space destitute of air. His best powers die out, his capacity remains a dead capability; and all effort, out of time and place, and without the coöperation of the elements, is like a flower in the midst of winter. It is Nature that makes seasons; it is she that furthers capacities. She furthers them also in humankind. Individual men, classes, corporations, whole societies, and nations, can only advance with this stream, they have done all if they steer wisely upon it. Let no one think that, if all the regents of the earth from the proudest negro king to the mightiest khan of the Tartars should combine to make to-day yesterday and to hinder forever the progressive development of the human race, whether it lead to youth or to old age they could ever accomplish their aim. This can never be an aim with wise rulers, simply, because there is no sense in such fruitless endeavor.

A wise ruler then will always regard himself as the householder, not as the antagonist of Nature. He will improve every circumstance which she offers, to the best issues. Here leaves are falling, there a whole autumn of leaves lie already in their shrouds. He will not attempt to restore them again to their former places on limb and twig. Can he give them back their former freshness and sap which made them a living whole with the tree on which they hung? And if he cannot do this, how then? Will he crown himself with a withered wreath of dried leaves, because they were other once than they are now? What Nature could not keep, will the gardener keep it? and that too, not in conformity with the ends of Nature, but in direct opposition to them? Infinitely more beautiful the task to follow Nature, to mark her times, to awaken powers wherever they slumber, to promote thought, activity, invention, joy, and love, in whatsoever field of useful employment. Necessity comes at last and compels with iron sceptre. He who obeys reason and measure will prevent necessity. Often, he will need only to beckon with the lily-staff of Oberon, and here new flowers will spring instead of the withered ones, and there, if the blossom-time is past, nourishing fruits will come to maturity. He will come to the aid of the young shoot and take it under his protection against oppressive weeds. The old wild tree he will not cut down but graft more genial fruits upon it, and the rejuvenized tree will wonder, itself, at its nobler existence. A slight anticipation of this kind, by which one nation had got the start of another, has often secured to it, for centuries, unattainable advantages. England acquired the position which she now occupies, by a somewhat earlier adoption and application of certain points of constitutional finance and commerce, which had long before germinated in other countries, but which folly and passion had suppressed. After many violent revolutions which passed over her, like bloody thunder-showers, it was given to the most peaceful and silent revolution, to awaken a new activity, and thereby to establish, for centuries, the prosperity of a living constitution. If in the time of William III, she had attempted to renew the feudal, military, and forest laws of William the Conqueror, where would she be now?

All orders and arrangements of society are the children of Time. This ancient mother produced, nourished, educated them; she adorned and fitted them out; and after a longer or shorter term of life, she buries them as she buries and renews herself. Whoever therefore confounds his own being with the duration of an order or institution, gives himself unnecessary torment. That which was before thee, will be behind thee too, if it is to be. For thine own part, act understandingly and wisely; time will proceed in its great course and accomplish its own. Be in thine own person more than thine order; and then, however that may grow old, thou wilt be, for thyself and for others, always young. Yea, the darker the night, the brighter shalt thou beam a star! He who does not raise himself above the breastwork of his order, is no hero within it. An order, as such, makes only puppets. Personality makes worth and merit. The more that idle, dead hull which conceals the best as well as the poorest kernel falls away, the more the fair and ripe fruit appears. Assuredly, therefore, it is no retrocession, but an evolution of the times, when the order ceases to be all, and men demand to see, in each order, persons, men, active beings. And since, without a new incursion of barbarism, and with the daily increasing necessities of Europe, this feeling must necessarily increase, there remains only one counsel which can secure each one against the senescence of his order. Be something in your order, and then you will be the first to perceive, to avoid, and to amend its defects. Its old age will appear rejuvenized in you, precisely because there is something in you which would grace every form and live in all.

The excellent Paolo Sarpi wrote a treatise, the title of which attracted me exceedingly: "How opinions are born and die in us." I was very curious to become acquainted with its contents. And although I saw from Foscarini's extract in Grisellini that it was not likely to contain what I had supposed, this capital problem nevertheless was often in my thoughts. Many are the ways in which, from earliest childhood, we arrive at opinions with which we clothe ourselves, body and soul. Many of them cleave to us with great tenacity, and the silliest we generally keep concealed behind our innermost, ninth skin, where, let no one presume to touch them! Unfortunately, however, Time will touch them, and often with very rude hands. And he who, in order to save his life, that is, his reason, peace, and the self-consciousness of internal worth, cannot yield the skin and hair of his opinions to the meddling Satan, is in bad hands. For that which is mere opinion, or even false opinion, will assuredly perish in the fierce fire of purification. But is it not something better that shall arise in its place? Instead of opinions received on authority or even, as Franklin relates, from politeness, knowledge from conviction, reason approved by our own investigation, and a self-acquired felicity shall be our portion. The old man in us must die that a new youth may spring up.

"But how may this be! Can a man return into his mother's womb and be born again?" To this doubt of old Nicodemus, the only answer that can be given is: "*Palingenesia!*"—not revolution, but a happy evolution of the faculties which slumber in us, and by means of which we renew our youth. What we call outliving ourselves—that is, a kind of death—is, with souls of the better sort but sleep, which precedes a new waking, a relaxation of the bow which prepares it for new use. So rests the fallow-field, in order to produce the more plentifully hereafter. So dies the tree in winter, that it may put forth and blossom anew in the spring. Destiny never forsakes the good, as long as he does not forsake himself, and ignobly despair of himself. The Genius which seemed to have departed from him returns to him again, at the right moment, bringing new activity, fortune, and joy. Sometimes the Genius comes in the shape of a friend, sometimes in that of an unexpected change of times. Sacrifice to this Genius even though you see him not! Hope in back-looking, returning Fortune, even when you deem her far off! If the left side is sore, lay yourself on the right; if the storm has bent your sapling one way, bend it the other way, until it attains, once more, the perpendicular medium. You have wearied your memory? Then exercise your understanding. You have striven too diligently after seeming, and it has deceived you? Now seek being. That will not deceive. Unmerited fame has spoiled you? Thank Heaven that you are rid of it, and seek, in your own worth, a fame which cannot be taken away. Nothing is nobler and more venerable than a man, who, in spite of fate, perseveres in his duty, and who, if he is not happy outwardly, at least deserves to be so. He will certainly become so, at the right season. The serpent of time often casts her slough, and brings to the man in his cave, if not the fabled jewel on her head and the rose in her mouth, at least medicinal herbs which procure him oblivion of the past, and restoration to new life.

Philosophy abounds in remedies designed to console us for misfortunes endured, but unquestionably its best remedy is when it strengthens us to bear new misfortunes, and imparts to us a firm reliance on ourselves. The illusion which weakens the faculties of the soul, comes, for the most part, from without. But the objects which environ us are not ourselves. It is sad indeed, when the situation in which a man is placed is so embittered and made so wretched, that he has no desire to touch one of its grapes or flowers, because they crumble to ashes in his hands, like those fruits of Sodom. Nevertheless, the situation is not himself; let him, like the tortoise, draw in his limbs and be what he can and ought. The more he disregards the consequences of his actions, the more repose he has in action. Thereby the soul grows stronger and revivifies itself, like an ever-springing fountain. The fountain does not stop to calculate through what regions of the earth its stream shall flow, what foreign matter it shall take in, and where it shall finally lose itself. It flows from its own fulness, with an irrepressible motion. That which others show us of ourselves is only appearance. It has always some foundation, and is never to be wholly despised; but it is only the reflection of our being in them, mirrored back to us from their own; often a broken and dim form, and not our being itself. Let the little insects creep over and around you, and be at the uttermost pains to make you appear dead; they work in their nature. Work you in yours, and live! In fact, our breast, our character, keeps us always more and longer upright, than all the acumen of the head, than all the cunning of the mind. In the heart we live, and not in the thoughts. The opinions of others may be a favorable or unfavorable wind in our sails. As the ocean its vessels, so circumstances at one time may hold us fast, at another may powerfully further us; but ship and sail, compass, helm, and oar, are still our own. Never, then, like old Tithonus, grow gray in the conceit that your youth has passed away. Rather, with newly awakened activity, let a new Aurora daily spring from your arms.

I ought now to speak to the greater problem, so peculiarly adapted to our times: Whether nations, countries, states, must also decline with old age, or whether they, too, are capable of a new youth? And by what means that youth may be renewed? On this question there is great division of opinion, and, as each opinion knows how to fortify itself with examples from history, this very difference in the answers is itself a proof of the indefiniteness of the question. What is it that can grow old in a nation, a country, a state? What, in them, can or ought to be made young again? Is it the soul, the air, the sky? And how are these changed for the better or worse? Is it the farms, meadows, forests, salt-springs, mines, trees? Or is it the manner of working them, the profit and the application of their products? Is it these alone, or is it man himself, his race, his manners, his education and mode of living, his principles and opinions, his relations and conditions? And how shall these be changed? By speeches and writings, or by institutions and well-directed, consistent, continued action? And what object shall this change accomplish? Superfluity for the few, comfort and idleness for the many, or the happiness of all? And wherein consists the happiness of all? In arts and sciences? In seeming or in being? In loquacious enlightenment or in genuine culture? All these, and perhaps other questions, should be considered with careful reference to place, time and circumstances, and a comparison with more ancient examples and their consequences. And then, it would probably be found:

1. That land and people never grow old, or only at a very late period; but that States, as human institutions, as children of the times, or even, in many cases, as the mere growth of accident, have their age and their youth, and, consequently, an ever-progressive, imperceptible movement toward growth, toward blossoming, or toward dissolution.

2. That man, often individual men, may retard or promote these periods, nay, that they are mostly promoted by opposite measures.

3. That when forces are at work, either for bloom or for dissolution, their progress is rapid, and everything appears to assimilate itself with them, until trivial circumstances—often again, individual men—give the stream a different direction; which new direction, again, is the result of a living presence, although it sometimes appears to be the effect of chance.

4. That, finally, in order to forestall those fearful explosions which are called political revolutions, and which ought to be entirely foreign from the book of human affairs, the State has no other remedy, but to preserve or to restore the natural relation, the healthy action of all its parts, the brisk circulation of its juices, and must not contend against the nature of things. Sooner or later the strongest machine must succumb in that

contest; but Nature never grows old. She only renews her youth periodically, in all her living forces.

The timid nature of man, always compassed about with hope and fear, often prophesies distant evils as near, and calls that death, which is only a wholesome slumber, a necessary, health-bringing relaxation. And so it generally deceives itself in its predictions concerning lands and kingdoms. Powers lie dormant which we do not perceive. Faculties and circumstances are developing themselves, on which we could not calculate. But even when our judgment is true, it usually leans too much to one side. "If this is to live," we say, "that must die." We do not consider whether it may not be possible that both shall live and act favorably on each other?

The good Bishop Berkeley, who was no poet, was inspired, by his beneficent zeal for America, to write the following:

> "Westward the star of empire takes its way;
> The four first acts already past,
> The fifth shall close the drama with the day,
> Time's noblest offspring is the last." [1]

So prophesied the good-natured bishop, and if his spirit could now glance at yonder upstriving America, he would perhaps discover, with that same glance, that, in the arms of the old Tithon, Europe, also, a new Aurora was slumbering. Not four, scarcely three acts in the great drama of this, still youthful, quarter of the globe, are past; and who shall say how many times yet the old Tithon of the human race may and will renew his youth upon our earth!

[1] The original gives the entire poem of which the above is the concluding stanza, together with a German version of it.

THE VICAR OF WAKEFIELD

—

BY

JOHANN WOLFGANG VON GOETHE

JOHANN WOLFGANG VON GOETHE
1749—1832

"Of great men, among so many millions of noted men," says Carlyle, "it is computed that in our time there have been two; one in the practical, another in the speculative, province: Napoleon Bonaparte and Johann Wolfgang von Goethe—Goethe intrinsically of much more unquestionable merit." The man of whom this high estimate was written was born at Frankfort-on-the-Main on August 28, 1749. His father was a man of wealth, culture, and high social position, and his mother, to whom he owed much, was a woman of fine intellect, rare tact and wisdom in all that pertained to the early education of her remarkable son. After two or three years spent in studying law at the University of Leipsic, where he led a life rather unfettered by conventionalities, young Goethe was sent to Strasburg, where he met Herder. In 1773 his first important work was published, the tragedy of "Goetz von Berlichingen." Its popularity was immediate and universal. Soon afterwards he met the young prince, Karl August of Weimar, and a friendship was formed that continued without interruption for fifty-five years. Many of his finest lyrics belong to this period. In 1774 he published his famous novel, "The Sorrows of Werther." The following year his friend, Prince Karl, became Grand Duke of Weimar, and at once summoned Goethe to his Court, where he became the intimate companion of the Duke, was elevated to the dignity of Privy Councillor in 1779, and knighted in 1782. He was made Minister of Finance of the little duchy in the latter year, and in 1815 he became its Prime Minister. The name of Weimar is indelibly linked with Goethe's life and work. After the death of his patron, in 1828, Goethe, then nearly eighty years of age, lived in retirement, but still engaged and interested in literary pursuits so far as his faculties would permit. He died in Weimar in March, 1832, at the ripe age of eighty-three.

In 1786 Goethe set out on a journey to Italy, the country he had long desired to visit. Of his two years' stay, his impressions and experiences, as well as of the journey, we have an account from his own pen. On his return, he wrote in rapid succession the dramas "Egmont," "Iphigenia," "Tasso," and numerous fine poems, chiefly lyrical. He devoted also much attention to science and art. In 1794 a friendship sprang up between Goethe and Schiller that profoundly influenced the work of both, and lasted uninterruptedly till Schiller's death in 1805. In 1796 Goethe completed "Wilhelm Meister," a work he had begun in 1777, and the following year he published "Hermann and Dorothea." At this time also appeared many of his finest ballads. The first part of "Faust," his greatest work and one of the grandest compositions in literature, appeared in 1808. His literary activity continued to the very close of his long life. The second part of "Faust," in the completion of which he labored assiduously during the declining years of his life, appeared only after his death.

Goethe's style is characteristic of the man, marvellously clear and simple, free from all mannerism and eccentricities, yet profoundly impressive, suggestive, and individual. A characteristic example of his prose is given in his essay on "The Vicar of Wakefield." It is as a poet, however, that he achieved his greatest triumphs and his enduring fame. "In Goethe," says Bayard Taylor, "we find a long, rich, and wholly fortunate life, almost unparalleled in its results. In him there is no unfilled promise, no fragmentary destiny: he stands as complete and symmetrical and satisfactory as the Parthenon."

THE VICAR OF WAKEFIELD

HERDER paid us a visit, and together with his great learning, he brought with him many other aids, and the later publications besides. Among these he announced to us the "Vicar of Wakefield" as an excellent work, with the German translation of which he wished to make us acquainted by reading it aloud to us himself.

His method of reading was quite peculiar; one who has heard him preach will easily form an idea of it for himself. He delivered everything, and this romance as well as the rest, in a serious and simple style, perfectly removed from all imitative-dramatic representation, and avoiding even that variety which is not only permitted, but even required, in an epical delivery; I mean that slight change of voice which sets in relief what is spoken by the different characters, and by means of which the interlocutors are distinguished from the narrator. Without being montonous, Herder let everything follow along in the same tone, just as if nothing of it was present before him, but all was only historical; as if the shadows of this poetic creation did not affect him in a life-like manner, but only glided gently by. Yet this manner of delivery had an infinite charm in his mouth: for, as he felt it all most deeply, and knew how to estimate the variety of such a work so its whole merit appeared in perfect purity, and the more clearly, as you were not disturbed by passages sharply spoken out, nor interrupted in the feeling which the whole was meant to produce.

A Protestant country clergyman is, perhaps, the most beautiful subject for a modern idyl; he appears, like Melchizedek, as priest and king in one person. In the most innocent situation which can be imagined in the world, that of a husbandman, he is, for the most part, united to his people by similar occupations, as well as by similar family relationships; he is a father, a master of a family, an agriculturist, and thus a perfect member of the community. On this pure, beautiful, earthly foundation, reposes his higher calling; to him is it given to guide men through life, to take care for their spiritual education, to bless them at all the leading epochs of their existence, to instruct, to strengthen, to console them, and, if present consolation is not sufficient, he calls up before them the hope and firm assurance of a happier future. Imagine to yourself such a man, with feelings of pure humanity, strong enough not to deviate from them under any circumstances, and by this already elevated above the many, of whom one can expect neither purity nor firmness; give him the learning necessary for his office, as well as a cheerful, equable activity which is even passionate, for he neglects no moment for doing good —and you will have him well endowed. But at the same time add the necessary limitedness, so that he must not only labor on in a small circle, but may also, perchance, pass over to a smaller; grant him good-nature, placability, resolution, and everything else praiseworthy that springs from so decided a character, and over all this a serene condescension and a smiling forbearance towards his own failings and those of others: so will you have put together pretty well the image of our excellent Wakefield.

The delineation of this character on his course of life through joys and sorrows, and the ever increasing interest of the plot, by the combination of what is quite natural with the strange and the wonderful, make this romance one of the best which has ever been written; besides this, it has the great superiority of being quite moral, nay, in a pure sense, Christian, for it represents the reward of good intentions and perseverance in the right, it strengthens an unconditional confidence in God, and asserts the final triumph of good over evil, and all this without a trace of cant or pedantry. The author was preserved from both of these by an elevation of mind that shows itself throughout in the form of irony, by reason of which this little work must appear to us as wise as it is amiable. The author, Dr. Goldsmith, has without question great insight into the moral world, into its strength and its infirmities; but at the same time he may thankfully acknowledge that he is an

Englishman,[1] and reckon highly the advantages which his country and his nation afforded him. The family, with whose delineation he has here busied himself, stands upon one of the lowest steps of citizen-comfort, and yet comes in contact with the highest; its narrow circle, which becomes still more contracted, extends its influence into the great world through the natural and common course of things; this little skiff floats full on the agitated waves of English life, and in weal or woe it has to expect injury or help from the vast fleet which sails around it.

I may suppose that my readers know this work and remember it; whoever hears it named for the first time here, as well as he who is induced to read it again, will thank me. For the former I would merely remark, *en passant*, that the vicar's wife is of that busy, good sort, who allows herself and family to want for nothing, but who is also somewhat vain of herself and family. There are two daughters; Olivia, handsome and more devoted to the exterior; and Sophia, charming and more given to her inner self; nor will I omit mentioning an industrious son, Moses, who is somewhat astringent and emulous of his father.

If Herder could be accused of any fault in his reading aloud, it was impatience; he did not wait until the hearer had heard and comprehended a certain part of the details, so as to be able to feel and think correctly about them; he would hurry on immediately to see their effect, and yet he was displeased with this too when it manifested itself in us. He blamed the excess of feeling which overflowed from me at every step in the story. I felt like a man, like a young man; everything was living, true, and present before me. He, considering only the artistic keeping and form, saw clearly, indeed, that I was overpowered by the subject-matter, and this he was unwilling to allow. Peglow's reflections, besides, which were not of the most refined character, were still worse received; but he was especially angry at our want of keenness in not seeing beforehand the contrasts which the author often makes use of, and in suffering ourselves to be moved and carried away by them without remarking the oft-returning art. Nor would he par-

---

[1] Goldsmith was an Irishman by birth, but Goethe presumably meant to refer to him as a British author.

don us for not having seen at once, or at least suspected from the first, where Burchell is on the point of discovering himself by passing over in his narration from the third to the first person, that he himself was the lord whom he was talking about; and when, finally we rejoiced like children at the *dénouement,* and the transformation of the poor, needy wanderer into a rich, powerful lord, he immediately recalled the passage, which, according to the author's plan, we had overlooked, and then he read us a powerful lecture on our stupidity. It will be seen from this that he regarded the work merely as a production of art, and required the same of us who were yet wandering in that state where it is very allowable to let works of art affect us just as if they were productions of nature.

I did not suffer myself to be at all confused by Herder's invectives; for young people have the happiness or unhappiness, that, when anything has produced an effect on them, this effect must be wrought out within themselves; from which much good, as well as much mischief arises. The above work had produced a great impression upon me, for which I could not account. Properly speaking, I felt myself in unison with that ironical tone of mind which elevates itself above every object, above fortune and misfortune, good and evil, death and life, and thus attains to the possession of a truly poetical world. In fact, though I could not become conscious of this until later, it was enough that it gave me much to do at the moment; but I could by no means have expected to see myself so soon transposed from this fictitious world into an actual one so similar.

My fellow-boarder, Weyland, who enlivened his quiet, laborious life by visiting his friends and relations in the country (for he was a native of Alsace), did me many services on my little excursions, by introducing me to different localities and individuals, sometimes in person, sometimes by his recommendations. He had often spoken to me about a country clergyman who lived near Drusenheim, six leagues from Strasburg, in possession of a good benefice, with an intelligent wife and a pair of lovely daughters. The hospitality and agreeableness of this family were always highly extolled. It scarcely needed all this to draw thither a young rider who had already accustomed himself to spend all his leisure days and hours on horseback and in the open air. We decided upon this trip, too, on which my friend had to promise that, on introducing me, he would say neither good nor ill of me, but would treat me with general indifference, and would also allow me to make my appearance clad, if not meanly, yet somewhat poorly and slovenly. He consented to this, and promised himself some sport from it.

It is a pardonable whim in men of consequence to place their exterior advantages in concealment now and then, so as to give the fairer play to the intrinsic worth of their inner man. For this reason the incognito of princes, and the adventures resulting therefrom, are always highly pleasing; they appear like masked divinities, who can nobly reckon at double their value all the good offices shown to them as individuals, and are able either to make light of the disagreeable or to avoid it. That Jupiter should be well pleased in his incognito with Philemon and Baucis, and Henry IV with his peasants after a hunting party, is quite conformable to nature, and we like it well; but that a young man, of no importance or name, should take it into his head to derive any pleasure from an incognito might be construed by many as an unpardonable arrogance. Yet since the question here is not whether such opinions and deeds are praiseworthy or blameable, but how they may have shown themselves and been put into execution, we will pardon the youngster his self-conceit, for this time, for the sake of our own amusement; and the more so as I must here affirm, in my excuse, that from youth up, a love for masquerade had been excited in me even by my stern father himself.

This time too, partly with my own cast-off clothes, partly with some borrowed garments and by the manner of combing my hair, I had, if not disfigured myself, yet at least botched up my accoutrements so outlandishly that my friend could not help laughing along the way, especially since I knew how to take off to the life the bearing and gesture of the Latin riders (as such-looking figures are called) when they sit on horseback. The fine road, the most splendid weather, and the neighborhood of the Rhine, put us in the best humor. We stopped a moment in Drusenheim, he to make himself spruce, and I to rehearse the part I was to play, for I was afraid of speaking now and then out of character. The country here has the characteristics of all the open, level parts of Alsace. We rode by a pleasant foot-path over the meadows, soon reached Sesenheim, left our horses at the tavern, and walked leisurely towards the parsonage. "Do not be put out," said Weyland, showing me the house from a distance, "that it looks like an old and miserable farm-house; it is so much the younger inside." We stepped into the court-yard; the whole pleased me well: for it was just what is called picturesque, and what had so magically interested me in the Dutch school of art. The effect which time produces on all the works of man was strongly perceptible. House, barn, and stable were just at that point of dilapidation where, in doubtful hesitation betwixt repairing and rebuilding, men often neglect the one without being able to accomplish the other.

As in the village, so in the court-yard of the parsonage, everything was quiet and deserted. We found the father quite alone, a little man, wrapped up within himself, but friendly notwithstanding; the family were then in the field. He bade us welcome, and offered us some refreshment, which we declined. My friend hurried away to look after the ladies, and I remained alone with our host. "Perhaps," said he, "you are surprised to find me so miserably quartered in a wealthy village, and with a lucrative benefice; but," continued he, "it proceeds from irresolution. Long since it has been promised me by the parish, and even by those in higher places, that the house should be rebuilt; many plans have been already drawn, examined, and altered, none of them altogether rejected, and none carried into execution. This has lasted so many years, that I scarcely know how to command my impatience." I answered him whatever I thought likely to cherish his hopes, and encourage him to take up the affair more vigorously. Thereupon he proceeded to describe familiarly the personages on whom such matters depend, and although he was no great hand at the delineation of character, yet I could easily comprehend how the whole business must have been delayed. The confidentialness of the man was something peculiar; he talked to me as if he had known me for ten years, though there was nothing in his look from which I could have suspected that he was directing any particular scrutiny to my character. At last my friend came in with the mother. She seemed to look at me with altogether different eyes. Her countenance was regular, and its expression intelligent; she must have been handsome in her youth. Her figure was tall and spare, but not more so than became her years, and when seen from behind she had yet quite a youthful and pleasing appearance. The elder daughter then came bouncing in briskly; she inquired after Frederica, just as both the others had also done. The father assured them that he had not seen her since all three had gone out together. The daughter again went out to the door to look for her sister; the mother brought us some refreshment, and Weyland continued the conversation with the old couple, which referred to nothing but known persons and circumstances; for it is usually the case, when acquaintances meet after some length of time, that they make inquiries about the members of a large circle, and mutually give each other information. I listened, and now learned how much I had to promise myself from this circle.

The elder daughter came hastily back into the room, anxious at not having found her sister. They felt uneasy about her, and scolded at this or that bad habit; only the father said, very composedly: "Always let her alone; she is back again already!" At this instant, in fact, she entered the door; and then truly a most charming star arose in this terrestrial heaven. Both daughters still wore nothing but German, as they used to call it, and this almost obsolete national costume became Frederica particularly well. A short, white, full skirt, with a furbelow, not so long but it left the neatest little foot visible up to the ankle; a tight white bodice and a black taffeta apron—there she stood, on the boundary between country beauty and city belle. Slender and airy, she tripped along as if she had nothing to carry, and her neck seemed almost too delicate for the luxuriant braids of flaxen hair on her elegant little head. A free, open glance beamed from her calm blue eyes, and her pretty little turned-up nose peered inquiringly into the air with as much unconcern as if there could be nothing like care in the world; her straw hat dangled on her arm, and thus, at the first glance, I had the delight of seeing her perfect grace, and acknowledging her perfect loveliness.

I now began to act my character subduedly, half ashamed

to have played a joke on such good people, whom I had leisure enough to observe: for the girls continued the previous conversation, and that with feeling and humor. All the neighbors and connections were again brought upon the tapis, and to my imagination there seemed such a swarm of uncles and aunts, relations, cousins, comers and goers, gossips and guests, that I thought myself lodged in the liveliest world possible. All the members of the family had spoken some words with me, the mother looked at me every time she came in or went out, but Frederica first entered into conversation with me, and as I took up and glanced through the music that was lying around, she asked me if I played also? When I told her "Yes," she requested me to perform something; but the father would not allow this, for he maintained that it was becoming in her to serve her guest first, with some piece of music or other, or a song.

She played several things with some execution, in the style which one usually hears in the country, and on a harpsichord, too, that the schoolmaster should have tuned long since, if he had only had time. She was now to sing a song also, something of the tender-melancholy; but she could not succeed with it. She rose up and said, smiling, or rather with that touch of serene joy which ever reposed on her countenance: "If I sing poorly, I cannot lay the blame on the harpsichord or the schoolmaster; but let us go out of doors, then you shall hear my Alsatian and Swiss songs, they sound much better."

During tea, an idea which had already struck me before, occupied me to such a degree, that I became meditative and silent, although the liveliness of the elder sister, and the gracefulness of the younger, shook me often enough out of my contemplations. My astonishment at finding myself so actually in the Wakefield family was beyond all expression. The father, indeed, could not be compared with that excellent man; but where will you find his like? On the other hand, all the worth which is peculiar to the husband there, here appeared in the wife. You could not see her without at once reverencing and fearing her. In her we saw the fruits of a good education; her demeanor was quiet, easy, cheerful, and inviting.

If the elder daughter had not the celebrated beauty of Olivia, yet she possessed a fine figure, was lively, and rather impetuous; she everywhere showed herself active, and lent a helping hand to her mother in all things. It was not hard to put Frederica in the place of Primrose's Sophia: for of her there is little said, we take it for granted that she is lovely; and this girl was lovely indeed. Now as the same occupation and the same general situation, wherever they can occur, produce similar, if not the same effects, so here too many things were talked about and happened which had already taken place in the Wakefield family. But when a younger son, long spoken of and impatiently expected by the father, at last sprang into the room, and boldly sat himself down by us, taking but little notice of the guests, I could scarcely help exclaiming: "Moses, are you here, too?"

The conversation at table extended my insight into this country and family circle, as they chatted about various pleasant incidents which had happened here and there. Frederica, who sat next to me, took occasion from that circumstance to describe to me different localities which it might be worth my while to visit. As one little story always calls out another, I was able to mingle in the conversation the better, and relate similar incidents, and as, besides this, a good country wine was by on means spared, I stood in danger of slipping out of my character, for which reason my provident friend took advantage of the beautiful moonlight, and proposed a walk, which was immediately resolved on. He gave his arm to the elder, I to the younger, and thus we went through the wide plains, paying more attention to the heavens above than to the earth beneath, which lost itself in extension around us. There was nothing of moonshine about Frederica's conversation, however; by the clearness with which she spoke she turned night into day, and there was nothing in it which hinted at or would have excited feeling, only her expressions addressed themselves more than ever to me, while, as I walked by her side, she represented to me her own situation, as well as the neighborhood and her acquaintances, just as I wished to be made acquainted with them; then she added that she hoped I would make no exception, and would visit them again, as all strangers had willingly done who had once lodged at the parsonage.

It was very pleasant to me to listen silently to the descriptions which she gave of the little world in which she moved, and of the persons whom she particularly valued. She thereby imparted to me a clear, and, at the same time, such an amiable idea of her situation, that it had a very strange effect on me: for I felt at once a deep regret that I had not lived with her sooner, and at the same time a right painful jealous feeling towards all who had hitherto had the good fortune to surround her. I also watched closely, as if I had had a right to do so, all her descriptions of men, whether they appeared under the names of neighbors, cousins, or familiar friends, and my conjectures inclined now to one, now to another; but how should I have discovered anything in my complete ignorance of all the circumstances? She at last became more and more talkative, and I constantly more and more silent. It was so good to listen to her, and as I heard only her voice, while the outlines of her countenance, like the rest of the world around, floated dimly in the twilight, it seemed to me as if I could see into her heart, and that I could not but find it very pure, since it unbosomed itself to me in such unembarrassed prattle.

When my companion and I retired to the guest-chamber which was prepared for us, he, with self-complacency, immediately broke out into pleasant jesting, and took great credit to himself for having surprised me so much with the likeness of the Primrose family. I chimed in with him, by showing myself thankful. "Truly," cried he, "the story is all here together. This family may well be compared to that, and the gentleman in disguise here, may assume the honor of passing for Mr. Burchell; moreover, since scoundrels are not so necessary in every-day life as in romances, I will for this time undertake the *rôle* of the nephew, and will behave myself better than he did." However, I immediately changed this conversation, pleasant as it was to me, and first of all asked him, on his conscience, if he had not betrayed me? He answered me "No!" and I ventured to believe him. They had rather inquired, said he, after the jovial table-companion who boarded at the same house with him in Strasburg, and of whom they had heard all sorts of preposterous stuff. I now went to other questions: Had she ever been in love? Was she now in love? Was she engaged? He said "No" to them all. "In truth," replied I, "that such a serenity should come by nature is inconceivable to me. If she had loved and lost, and again recovered herself, or if she was betrothed, in both these cases I could account for it."

Thus we chatted together till deep in the night, and I was awake again at the dawn. My longing to see her once more seemed unconquerable; but while I was dressing I was horrified at the confounded wardrobe I had so capriciously selected. The further I advanced in putting on my clothes, the meaner I seemed in my own eyes: for everything was calculated for just that effect. I might perchance have set my hair to rights; but when at last I forced my arms into the borrowed, worn-out gray coat, the short sleeves of which gave me the most absurd appearance, I fell decidedly into despair, and the more so since I could see myself only piece-meal, in a little looking-glass, and then each part always looked more ridiculous than the rest.

During this toilette my friend awoke, and with the satisfaction of a good conscience, and in the feeling of pleasurable hopes for the day, he looked out at me from under the quilted silk coverlet. I had envied his fine clothes for a long time already, as they hung over the chair, and had he been of my size, I would have carried them off before his very eyes, dressed myself in them, and hurrying into the garden, left my cursed husks for him; he would have had good humor enough to deck himself out in my clothes, and our tale would have found a merry ending early in the morning. But that was not now to be thought of, as little as any other feasible accommodation. To appear again before Frederica in such a figure that my friend could give me out as a laborious and accomplished but poor student of theology—before Frederica, who yesterday evening had spoken so friendly to my disguised self—that was altogether impossible. There I stood, vexed and thoughtful, and summoned up all my power of invention; alas! it deserted me! But now when he, comfortably stretched out in bed, after fixing his eyes upon me for a while, all at once burst out into a loud laugh, and exclaimed: "Yes! it is true, you do look most confoundedly!" I replied impetuously: "And I know what I will do. Good-by, and make my excuses!" "Are you crazy!" cried he, springing out of bed and trying to detain me. But I was already out of the door, down the stairs, out of the house and yard, to the tavern; in an instant my horse was saddled, and I hurried away in mad vexation, galloping towards Drusenheim, dashed through the place, and still onwards!

As I thought myself by this time in safety, I began to ride more leisurely, and now first felt how infinitely against my will I was going away. But I resigned myself to my fate, recalled to mind the promenade of yesterday evening with the greatest calmness, and cherished the secret hope of seeing her soon again. Yet this quiet feeling again changed itself into impatience, and I now determined to ride rapidly into the city, change my dress, take a good fresh horse, and then, as my passion made me believe, I could at all events return before dinner, or, as was more probable, to the dessert or towards evening, and beg my forgiveness.

I was just about to put spurs to my horse to execute this resolve, when another, and, as seemed to me, a happier thought came into my head. In the tavern at Drusenheim, the day before, I had noticed a son of the landlord very nicely dressed, who, up early to-day and busied about his rural arrangements, had saluted me from his court-yard as I rode by. He was of my size, and had slightly reminded me of myself. Thought, done! My horse was hardly turned around, when I found myself in Drusenheim; I brought him into the stable, and made the fellow my proposal in brief: that he should lend me his clothes, as I had something merry on foot at Sesenheim. I had no need to talk long; he agreed to the proposition with joy, and praised me for wishing to make some sport for the Mamselles; they were so gallant and good, especially Mamselle Rica, and the parents, too, liked to see everything go on merry and pleasant. He considered me attentively, and as from my appearance he might have taken me for a poor starveling, he said: "If you wish to insinuate yourself into their good graces, this is the right way." Meanwhile we had already made rapid advances in our toilette; he could not indeed trust me with his holiday clothes on the strength of mine; but he was honest-hearted, and had my horse in his stable. I soon stood there right trig, threw back my shoulders, and my friend seemed to contemplate his likeness with complacency. "Well, Mr. Brother!" said he, giving me his hand, which I grasped heartily, "don't come too near my gal, she might mistake you!"

My hair, which now had its full growth again, I could part at top pretty much like his, and as I looked at him repeatedly, I found it comical to imitate closely his thicker eyebrows, with a burnt cork, and bring mine nearer together in the middle, so as with my enigmatical intentions, to make myself an external riddle likewise. "Now have you not," said I, as he handed me his beribboned hat, "something or other to be done at the parsonage, so that I may announce myself there in a natural manner?" "Good!" replied he, "but then you must wait two hours yet. There is a confinement at our house; I will offer to take the cake to the parson's wife,[2] and you might carry it over there. Pride must be paid for, and so must a joke." I concluded to wait, but these two hours were infinitely long, and I was dying of impatience when the third hour passed by before the cake came out of the oven. I got it at last, quite hot, and hastened away with my credentials in the most beautiful sunshine, accompanied for a space by my ditto, who promised to come after me in the evening and bring me my clothes, which however, I briskly declined, and reserved to myself the privilege of returning him his own when I was done with them.

I had not skipped far with my present, which I carried neatly tied up in a napkin, when, in the distance, I saw my friend approaching with the two ladies. My heart was uneasy, although in fact it was unnecessary under this jacket. I stood still, took breath, and tried to think how I should begin; and now I first remarked that the nature of the ground was very much in my favor; for they were walking on the other side of the brook, which, together with the strips of meadow through which it ran, kept the two foot-paths pretty far apart. When they were just opposite to me, Frederica, who had already perceived me long before, cried: "George, what have you got there?" I was clever enough to cover my face with my hat, which I took off, at the same time holding up the loaded napkin high in the air. "A christening-cake!" cried she at that; "how does your sister do!" "Gooed," said I, for I tried to talk strange, if not exactly in the Alsatian dialect. "Carry it to the house!" said the elder, "and if you do not

[2] [This was the general custom of the **country villages in Protestant Germany** on such occasions.]

find mother, give it to the maid; but wait for us, we will be back soon, do you hear?" I hastened along my path in the joyous feeling of the best hope that, as the beginning was so lucky, all would go off well, and I soon reached the parsonage. I found nobody either in the house or the kitchen; I did not wish to disturb the old gentleman, whom I might have supposed busy in the study; I therefore sat me down on the bench before the door, placed the cake beside me, and pressed my hat upon my face.

I cannot easily recall more delightful sensations. To sit here again on this threshold, over which, a short time before, I had blundered out in despair; to have seen her already, to have heard her dear voice again so soon after my chagrin had pictured to me a long separation, to be expecting every moment herself, and a discovery at which my heart throbbed fast, and yet, in this ambiguous case, it would be an exposure without shame; for from its very beginning it was a merrier prank than any of those they had laughed at so much yesterday. Love and necessity are yet the best masters; they both worked together here, and their pupil was not unworthy of them.

But the maid came stepping out of the barn. "Now! did the cake turn out well!" cried she to me; "how does your sister do?" "All gooed," said I, and pointed to the cake without looking up. She took up the napkin and muttered: "Now what's the matter with you to-day again? Has little Barbara been looking at somebody else once more? Don't let us suffer for that! A happy couple you will make, if you carry on so!" As she spoke pretty loud, the parson came to the window and asked: "What's the matter?" She showed him; I stood up and turned myself towards him, but yet kept the hat over my face. As he spoke rather kindly to me and had asked me to remain, I went towards the garden, and was just going in when the parson's wife, who was entering the court-yard gate, called to me. As the sun shone right in my face, I once more took advantage of my hat, and saluted her with a ploughman's scrape; but she went into the house after she had bidden me not go away without eating something. I now walked up and down in the garden; everything had hitherto had the best success, yet I drew a deep breath when I reflected that the young people would soon return. But the mother unexpectedly stepped up to me, and was just going to ask me a question, when she looked me in the face so that I could not conceal myself any longer, and the question stuck in her mouth. "I was looking for George," said she, after a pause, "and whom do I find? Is it you, young sir? How many forms have you, then?" "In earnest only one," replied I; "in sport as many as you like." "Which sport I will not spoil," smiled she; "go out behind the garden and into the meadow until it strikes twelve, then come back, and I will already have contrived the joke." I did so; but when I was outside of the hedge that bounds the village gardens, and was going into the meadow, I saw some country people coming along the footpath towards me, who embarrassed me. I therefore turned aside into a little grove which crowned an elevation near by, in order to conceal myself there till the appointed time. Yet how strangely was I surprised when I entered it! for it appeared to be a neatly trimmed place, with benches, from every one of which could be enjoyed a fine view of the country. Here were the village and the church tower, here Drusenheim, and behind it the woody islands of the Rhine, in the opposite direction was the Vosgian mountain-range, and at last the minster of Strasburg. These different heaven-bright pictures were surrounded by frames of foliage, so that one could imagine nothing more joyous and more pleasing. I sat me down upon one of the benches and noticed on the largest tree an oblong little board with the inscription: "Frederica's Repose." It never entered into my head that I could have come to disturb this repose: for a budding passion has this beauty about it, that, as it is unconscious of its origin, neither does it spend any thought upon its end, and as it feels itself glad and cheerful, it can have no presentiment that it may make mischief too.

Scarcely had I had time to look about me and lose myself in sweet reveries, when I heard somebody coming; it was Frederica herself. "George, what are you doing here?" she cried from a distance. "Not George!" cried I, running towards her, "but one who craves forgiveness of you a thousand times." She looked at me with astonishment, but soon collected herself and said, after drawing a deeper breath: "You abominable fellow, how you frighten me!" "The first disguise has led me into the second," exclaimed I; "the former would have been unpardonable if I had only known in any manner whom I was going to see, but this one you will certainly forgive, for it is the form of a man whom you meet in so friendly a manner." Her pale cheeks had colored up with the loveliest rosy red. "You shall not be treated worse than George, at all events! But let us sit down! I confess that the fright has thrilled through all my limbs." I sat down beside her, exceedingly agitated. "We know everything already from your friend, up to this morning," said she, "now do you tell me the rest." I did not suffer her to ask twice, but described to her my horror at my yesterday's figure, and my rushing out of the house, so comically that she laughed heartily and delightedly; then I went on with what followed, with all modesty, indeed, yet passionately enough to have well passed for a declaration of love in historical form. At last I solemnized my pleasure at finding her again, by a kiss upon her hand, which she suffered to remain in mine. If she had taken upon herself the expense of the conversation during yesterday evening's moonlight walk, I now, on my part, richly repaid the debt. The pleasure of seeing her again, and being able to say to her everything that I had kept back yesterday, was so great, that, in my eloquence, I did not remark how meditative and silent she was becoming. Once more she drew a deep breath, and over and over again I begged her forgiveness for the fright which I had caused her. How long we may have sat here I know not; but all at once we heard someone call, "Rica! Rica!" It was the voice of her sister. "That will be a pretty story to tell," said the dear girl, restored to her perfect serenity again; "she is coming hither from the side next to me," added she, bending over so as half to conceal me: "turn yourself away, so that she will not recognize you at once." The sister came up to the spot, but not alone; Weyland was with her, and both, as soon as they saw us, stood still as if petrified.

If we should all at once see a powerful flame burst out from a quiet roof, or should meet a monster whose deformity was at the same time revolting and fearful, we should not be struck with such massive astonishment as seizes us, when, unexpectedly, we see with our own eyes something we had believed morally impossible. " What is this? " cried the elder, with the rapidity of one who is frightened to death. " What is this? you with George! Hand-in-hand! How am I to understand this? " " Dear sister," replied Frederica, very doubtfully, " the poor fellow is begging something of me; he has something to beg of you, too, you must forgive him beforehand." " I don't understand—I don't comprehend——" said her sister, shaking her head and looking at Weyland, who, in his quiet way, stood by in perfect tranquillity, and contemplated the scene without any kind of expression. Frederica arose and drew me after her. " No hesitating! " cried she. " Pardon begged and granted! " " Now do! " said I, stepping pretty near the elder, " I have need of pardon! " She drew back, gave a loud shriek, and blushed over and over, then threw herself down on the grass, burst into a roar of laughter, and could not get enough of it. Weyland smiled as if pleased, and cried: " You are a rare youth! " Then he shook my hand in his. He was not usually liberal with his caresses, but his shake of the hand had something hearty and enlivening about it; yet he was sparing of this also.

After taking some time to recover and collect ourselves, we set out on our return to the village. On the way I learned how this singular rencounter had been occasioned. Frederica had at last parted from the promenaders to rest herself in her little nook for a moment before dinner, and when the other two came back to the house, the mother had sent them to call Frederica in the greatest haste, as dinner was ready.

The elder sister manifested the most extravagant delight, and when she learned that the mother had already discovered the secret, she exclaimed: " All that is left now is that father, brother, servant-man, and maid should be cheated likewise." When we were at the garden-hedge, Frederica insisted upon going beforehand into the house with my friend. The maid was busy in the kitchen-garden, and Olivia (for so I may be allowed to name the elder sister here) called out to her: " Here, I have something to tell you! " She left me standing by the hedge, and went towards the maid. I saw that she was speaking to her very earnestly. Olivia represented to her that George had quarrelled with Barbara, and seemed desirous of marrying her. The lass was not displeased at this; I was now called, and was to confirm what had been said. The handsome, stout girl cast down her eyes, and remained so till I stood quite near before her. But when, all at once, she looked into the strange face, she too gave a loud scream and ran away. Olivia bade me run after her and hold her fast, so that she should not get into the house and give the alarm; while she herself wished to go and see how it was with her father. On the way Olivia met the servant-boy, who was in love with the maid; I had in the mean time hurried after the maid, and held her fast. "Only think! what good luck!" cried Olivia: "it's all over with Barbara, and George marries Liese." "I have thought he would for a long while," said the good fellow, and stood there disconsolate.

I had given the maid to understand, that all we had yet to do was to cheat the father. We went up to the lad, who turned away and would have walked off; but Liese took him aside, and he, too, when he was undeceived, made the most extraordinary gestures. We went together to the house. The table was covered, and the father already in the room. Olivia, who kept me behind her, stepped to the threshold and said: "Father, you have no objections to George's dining with us to-day? but you must let him keep his hat on." "With all my heart!" said the old man, "but why such an unusual thing? Has he hurt himself?" She led me forward as I stood, with my hat on. "No!" said she, handing me into the room, "but he has a bird-cage under it, and the birds might fly out and make a deuce of a fuss; for there are nothing but loose wild birds there." The father was pleased with the joke, without precisely knowing what it meant. At this instant she took off my hat, made a ploughman's scrape, and required me to do the same. The old man looked at me, recognized me, but was not put out of his priestly self-possession. "Ay, ay, Mr. Candidate!" exclaimed he, raising a threatening finger at me: "You have changed saddles very quickly, and over-night I have lost an assistant, who yesterday promised me so faithfully that he would often mount my pulpit on week-days." Thereupon he laughed heartily, bade me welcome, and we sat down to table. Moses came in much later; for, as the youngest and spoiled child, he had accustomed himself not to hear the dinner-bell. Besides, he took very little notice of the company, scarce even when he contradicted them. In order to make surer of him, they had placed me, not between the sisters, but at the end of the table, where George often used to sit. As he came in at the door, which was behind me, he slapped me smartly on the shoulder, and said: " Good dinner to you, George! " " Many thanks, youngster! " replied I. The strange voice and the strange face startled him. " What say you? " cried Olivia: " does he not look very like his brother? " " Yes, from behind," replied Moses, who managed to recover his composure immediately, like other folk. He did not look at me again, and busied himself merely with zealously devouring the dishes, in order to make up for lost time. Then, too, he thought proper occasionally to find something for himself to do in the yard and the garden. At the dessert the genuine George came in, and made the scene still more lively. They rallied him for his jealousy, and would not praise him for having gotten himself a rival in me; but he was modest and clever enough, and, in a half-confused manner, he mixed up himself, his sweetheart, his ditto, and the Mamselles with each other to such a degree that at last nobody could tell whom he was talking about, so that they were glad to give him a glass of wine and a piece of his own cake to eat, to keep him quiet.

At table there was some talk about going to walk; which however did not suit me very well in my peasant's clothes. But the ladies, early on that day already, when they learned who had run away in such a desperate hurry, had remembered that a hunting-coat of a cousin of theirs, in which he used to go sporting when he was here, was hanging in a clothes-press. Yet I declined, apparently with all sorts of jokes, but with a feeling of secret vanity, not wishing, as cousin, to disturb the good impression I had made in the character of peasant. The father had gone to take his afternoon nap; the mother, as always, was busy about her housewifery. But my friend proposed that I should tell them some story, to which I immediately agreed. We repaired to a spacious arbor, and I gave them a tale which I have since written out under the title of " The New Melusina." It bears about the same relation to " The New Paris " as the youth bears to the boy, and I would insert it here, were I not afraid of injuring, by its outlandish play of fancy, the rural reality and simplicity which agreeably surround us. Enough: I succeeded in that which rewards the inventors and narrators of such productions, I succeeded in awakening curiosity, in fixing the attention, in inciting them to give over-hasty solutions of impenetrable riddles, in deceiving their expectations, in confusing them by making that wonderful which was merely strange, in arousing sympathy and fear, in making them anxious, in moving them; and at last, by the inversion of what was apparently sober earnest into an ingenious and cheerful jest, this little tale satisfied the mind, leaving behind it materials for new images to the imagination, and to the understanding for further reflection.

Should anyone hereafter read this tale in print, and doubt whether it could have and produce such an effect, let him remember that, properly speaking, man is only intended to have influence while present. Writing is an abuse of language, reading silently to one's self is a pitiful succedaneum of speech. The strongest influence in a man's power is made by his personal presence, youth is the most powerful upon youth, and hence too arise the purest influences. These are they which enliven the world, and can perish neither morally nor physically. I had inherited from my father a certain loquacious fondness for teaching; from my mother the faculty of representing, clearly and powerfully, everything that the imagination can produce or grasp, of giving a freshness to known stories, of inventing and relating others, and even making them up as I went along. By my paternal endowment I was for the most part rather a bore to the company: for who likes to listen to the opinions and sentiments of another, especially a youth, whose judgment, on account of his fragmentary experience, seems constantly insufficient? My mother, on the contrary, had thoroughly qualified me for social conversations. For to the imagination even the emptiest tale has an elevated charm, and even the smallest quantity of solid matter is thankfully received by the understanding.

By such recitals, which cost me nothing, I made myself beloved by children, I excited and delighted youth, and drew upon me the attention of older persons. But in society, such as it commonly is, I was soon obliged to stop these practices, and I have thereby lost but too much of the enjoyment of the world and of intellectual improvement; yet both these parental gifts accompanied me throughout my whole life, united with a third, namely the necessity of expressing myself figuratively and by comparisons. In consideration of these peculiarities, Doctor Gall, a man of as much profundity as acuteness, discovering them by his theory, assured me that I was properly speaking born for a popular orator. At this disclosure I was not a little confounded: for as I discovered, in my nation, no opportunity to harangue about anything, it would follow, if his assertion were well grounded, that everything else I could undertake would have been, alas, but a mistaken vocation!

UPON NAÏVE AND SENTIMENTAL POETRY

—

BY

FRIEDRICH VON SCHILLER

JOHANN CHRISTOPH FRIEDRICH VON SCHILLER

1759—1805

The most popular of German poets, Johann Christoph Friedrich von Schiller, was born at Marbach, in the duchy of Würtemberg, in 1759. His own tastes and the wishes of his father inclined him to the ministry, but poverty forced him to accept the offer of the Duke of Würtemberg to educate him at the Karlschule in Stuttgart. The narrow repressive discipline of this institution fostered in the fiery youth a spirit of rebellion, which found vent in his first drama, "The Robbers," written when he was nineteen, and published three years later. This stormy, impetuous tragedy startled not only Germany, but all Europe. Translations soon appeared in several languages, and its author, like Byron after the publication of "English Bards and Scotch Reviewers," awoke one morning to find himself famous. The revolutionary spirit pervading the play, however, brought on him the displeasure of the Duke, and, to escape persecution and possible imprisonment, Schiller fled to Mannheim, and soon afterward to Leipsic. During the period following he wrote many of his lyrics, but an incessant struggle with poverty prevented him from devoting his best energies to literature. One of the great events of his life was his first visit to Weimar, in 1787, where he made the acquaintance of Wieland and Herder. In the following year he met Goethe. There seemed to be at that time a wide difference in the tendencies, mode of thought, and literary aims of the two poets, and their first meeting resulted in little more than the exchange of formal courtesies and the beginning of a formal correspondence. It was not until 1794, after a conversation on scientific subjects, that the eyes of the older poet were opened to the worth of the younger. After this their friendship grew strong and fast, ripening into one of the most beautiful examples to be found in the history of literature. To this friendship Goethe ascribes what he calls his second youth. The publication of his "History of the Revolt of the Netherlands," in 1788, called attention to Schiller as an original investigator; and in recognition of this he was appointed to the chair of history at Jena. Here he wrote his "History of the Thirty Years' War." Influenced by Kant, he abandoned history for philosophical investigation, chiefly along the line of æsthetics and criticism. In his essay "On Naive and Sentimental Poetry," Goethe thought Schiller had laid the foundation of modern criticism. His intimacy with Goethe after 1794 was the cause of an increased lyrical activity, and scarcely a year passed without remarkable poetical works coming from his pen. For seven years he worked at his trilogy of "Wallenstein," and in 1798-99 the work was produced at Weimar. In 1799 he removed to Weimar to be in close touch with Goethe. Here he wrote "Marie Stuart," "The Maid of Orleans," "The Bride of Messina," and, in 1804, "Wilhelm Tell," his last drama. The following year he died, at the early age of forty-six. In 1802 he received a patent of nobility.

As a dramatist, among the modern writers, Schiller has been surpassed only by Goethe and Shakespeare. As a poet, not even Goethe ranks so high in the estimation of the German people. Schiller's poems appeal decidedly more to popular sympathy, although Goethe undoubtedly touched chords that were more profound. In his style, both in poetry and prose, Schiller is clear and methodical, a master of words, and always effective.

UPON NAÏVE AND SENTIMENTAL POETRY

THERE are moments in our life when we feel a kind of love and tender respect for nature in plants, minerals, animals, landscapes, and for human nature in children, in the manners of rustics and of the primitive times: not on account of its sensuous interest, nor because it satisfies our intellect or taste, for the opposite may often occur with both, but solely because it is nature. Every cultivated man, not entirely deficient in feeling, is sensible of this, when he walks in the open air, or is living in the country, or lingers near the monuments of past time: in short, when he is overtaken, in the midst of artificial relations and situations, by the simplicity of nature. It is this interest, often amounting to a want, which underlies many of our passions for flowers and creatures, for simple gardens, for walks, for the country and its inhabitants, for many products of distant antiquity, and the like. But this presupposes that neither affection nor an otherwise accidental interest comes into play. Then this kind of interest in nature occurs only under two conditions. In the first place it is absolutely necessary that the object which excites it should be nature, or taken for such by us: secondly, that, in the widest signification of the term, it should be naïve, that is, that nature should stand in contrast with art, and rebuke it. Nature becomes naïve as soon as these two conditions are combined.

From this point of view nature becomes for us nothing more nor less than independent being, the persistence of things by themselves, existence according to peculiar and immutable laws.

This conception is absolutely prerequisite, if we would take interest in like phenomena. Could one, with the completest deception, give a natural look to an artificial flower, or carry the imitation of naïve manners to the highest point of illusion, the discovery that it was all imitation would entirely destroy the feeling of which we speak.[1] Whence it is clear that this kind of pleasure in nature is moral and not æsthetic: for it is mediated by an idea, and is not created by direct contemplation. Besides which, it is by no means directed towards beauty of form. For instance: what attraction would a colorless flower, a fountain, a mossy stone, the twitter of birds, the humming of bees, have for us in themselves? What could give them a claim to our love? We do not love the objects themselves, but the ideas they represent. We love in each of them the still, creative life, the tranquil production out of itself, existence according to its own laws, eternal unity with itself.

They are what we were; they are what we again should be. Like them, we were nature; and our culture ought to lead us back to nature, by the path of reason and freedom. Then they are at the same time the representation of our lost childhood, which forever remains the dearest to us: hence, they fill us with a certain sadness; and at the same time the representation of our loftiest completion in the ideal: hence, they give us a sublime emotion.

But their completeness is not their merit, since it is not the work of their own choice. They secure for us, then, this entirely peculiar pleasure, that without making us ashamed, they are our model. They surround us, as a continual divine manifestation, but more refreshing than dazzling. What makes their character complete is exactly that in which our own is deficient: what distinguishes us from them is exactly that of divinity in which they fail. We are free, and they are necessary: we alter, they remain one. But the divine or the ideal obtains, only when the differences are blended, when the will follows freely the law of necessity, and the reason maintains its sway through every change of fancy. Then we forever perceive in them that which we lack, but for which we are invited to strive, and to which, even though we never attain it, we may yet hope to approximate in an infinite progression. We

---

[1] Kant, the first to my knowledge who directed reflection expressly towards this phenomenon, remarks, that if we heard a man imitate with complete success the note of a nightingale, and yielded to the impression with profound emotion, all our pleasure would vanish with the dissipation of this illusion. See the chapter in the " Critique of Æsthetic Judgment," upon intellectual interest in the beautiful. Whoever has learned to admire the author only as a great thinker, will here be delighted to meet with a trace of his heart; and to be convinced, by the discovery, of his fitness for this lofty vocation, which unquestionably demands the union of both those qualities.

perceive in ourselves a superiority, which they lack, but which they can either never share, like the senseless creation, or only as they proceed in our path, like the state of childhood. Hence, as idea, they create for us the sweetest enjoyment of our manhood, although they must of necessity humiliate us with respect to each determinate condition of our manhood.

As this interest for nature is based upon an idea, it can be shown only in dispositions susceptible of ideas, that is, in moral ones. By far the majority of men only affect it; and the universality of this sentimental taste in our times, which displays itself, especially since the appearance of certain writings, in affected travels, gardens of like sort, walks and other fondnesses of the kind, is no proof at all for the universality of the true sentiment. Yet nature will always exert something of this influence upon the most insensible, since for that the common bias of all men to the moral is adequate; and all of us without distinction, however great a disproportion there may be between our acts and the simplicity and truth of nature, are compelled to that in idea. This sentiment for nature and incitement from objects standing in a close relation with us—as for example, children and childlike people—and bringing nearer to us both self-retrospection and our own *unnature*, is especially strong and universal. It is erroneous to suppose that it is only the appearance of helplessness which makes us, at certain times, linger with so much emotion near children. Perhaps that may be the case with some, who are wont to feel, in the presence of weakness, nothing but their own superiority. But the feeling of which I speak occurring only in entirely moral dispositions, and not to be confounded with that excited by the playful activity of children, is rather humiliating than gratifying to self-love; and indeed if any superiority is noticeable at all, it is by no means on our side. We experience emotion, not while we look down upon the child from the height of our power and perfection, but while we look up, out of the limitation of our condition which is inseparable from the definite mode to which we have attained, at the child's boundless determinableness and its perfect innocence. And, at such a moment, our feeling is too plainly mingled with a certain sadness, to allow us to mistake its source. The child represents the bias and determination, we represent the fulfilment, which forever remains infinitely far behind the former. Hence the child is an actualization of the ideal, not indeed of one fulfilled, but of one proposed; and so it is by no means the appearance of its neediness and limits which moves us, but, on the contrary, the appearance of its free and pure power, its integrity, its infinity. For this reason, a child will be a holy object to the man of morality and feeling, that is, an object which, by the magnitude of an idea, abolishes every actual magnitude, and which wins again in rich measure from the estimation of the reason all that it may lose in the estimation of the understanding.

Out of this very contradiction between the judgment of the reason and of the understanding, proceeds the entirely peculiar phenomenon of mixed feeling, which a naïve disposition excites in us. It unites childlike with childish simplicity. By the latter, it gives the understanding an idea of weakness, and produces that laughter by which we make known our (theoretic) superiority. But as soon as we have reason to believe that childish simplicity is at the same time childlike, and that consequently its source is not folly, or imbecility, but a loftier (practical) strength, a heart full of innocence and truth, which makes ashamed, by its internal greatness, the mediation of art—then that triumph of the understanding is over, and a jest at simpleness passes over into admiration of simplicity. We feel ourselves compelled to respect the object at which we previously laughed, and, while casting a look into ourselves, to lament that we are not like it. Thus arises the entirely peculiar appearance of a feeling, in which are blended gay derision, reverence, and sadness.[2] The naïve demands that nature

[2] Kant, in a note to the "Analysis of the Sublime" ("Critique of Æsthetic Judgment," p. 225, 1st Ed.), in like manner distinguishes this threefold composition in the perception of the naïve, but he gives another explanation of it. "Something of both (the animal feeling of pleasure, and the spiritual feeling of respect) united, is found in naiveté, which is the outbreak of the originally natural uprightness of humanity against the art of dissimulation become a second nature. We laugh at the simplicity which does not yet understand how to dissimulate, and still we enjoy that natural simplicity which disappoints such arts. If we expected the every-day style of an affected expression that is prudently established upon æsthetic show, behold, it is unsophisticated, blameless nature, which we were not at all prepared to meet, and which, it would seem, was not meant to be exposed. And because the æsthetic, but false, show, which commonly counts for much in our judgment, here suddenly vanishes, and because, so to speak, our waggery is exposed, this brings out in two opposite directions, a mental agitation, which at the same time gives the body a salutary shaking. But because something, which is infinitely better than all assumed style, that is, mental sincerity (at least the tendency thereto), is not yet entirely extinguished in human nature—this it is which mingles seriousness and regard in this play of the judgment. But since the phenomenon lasts only for a little while, and the veil of dissimulation is soon again

should bear away the victory over art,[3] whether it happen without the knowledge and will of the person, or with his full consciousness. In the first case it is the naïve of surprise, and delights: in the other case it is the naïve of disposition, and moves.

In the naïve of surprise, the person must be morally able to deny nature; in the naïve of disposition he need not be so, and yet, if it would affect us as naïveté, we need not imagine him as physically unable to do so. Hence the talk and actions of children give us the pure impression of naïveté, only so long as we do not remember their incapacity for art, but merely regard the contrast of their naturalness with the art in us. A childishness, where it is no longer expected, is naïve, and therefore that cannot be ascribed, in strictness of meaning, to actual childhood.

But in the cases, both of naïveté of surprise and that of disposition, nature must be right, but art be wrong.

The conception of the naïve is only completed by this final definition. Feeling is also nature, and the rule of propriety is something artificial; but yet the victory of feeling over propriety is nothing less than naïve. If, on the other hand, the same feeling overcomes artifice, false propriety, dissimulation, we do not hesitate to call that naïve.[4] It is necessary, then,

drawn before it, a regret, which is an emotion of tenderness, mingles also with our feeling; and it does not refuse to unite as play with a hearty laugh, at the same time relieving the embarrassment of the person who is the object of it, because he has not yet learned the way of the world." I must confess the explanation does not entirely satisfy me, and particularly for this reason, that it asserts something of the naïve in general, which is chiefly true of one species, the naïve of surprise, of which I shall afterwards speak. It certainly excites laughter, when anybody exposes himself by naïveté; and in many cases this laughter may result from a previous expectation which is resolved into nothing. But also naïveté of the noblest kind, the naïve of disposition, always excites a smile, which can hardly have for its cause an expectation resolved into nothing; but it is generally to be explained only by the contrast of a certain demeanor with the once assumed and expected forms. I also doubt, whether the pity, which is blended in our feeling at the naïve of the latter kind, relates to the naïve person, and not rather to ourselves, or rather to mankind in general, of whose deterioration we are reminded by such a circumstance. It is too plainly a moral sadness, which must have a nobler object than the physical weakness with which sincerity is threatened in the customary routine of life; and this object cannot well be other than the decay of truth and simplicity in humanity.

[3] Perhaps I should briefly say, " truth over dissimulation." But the idea of the naïve appears to me to include still something more, while the simplicity which prevails over artifice, and the natural freedom which conquers stiffness and constraint, excite in us a similar perception.

[4] A child is ill bred if it resists the precepts of a good education from desire, caprice, or passion: but it is naïve, if it releases itself by virtue of a free and healthy nature, from the mannerism of an unwise education, from the stiff postures of the dancing-master, and the like. The same also occurs with that loosely defined naïveté which results from the transmission of humanity to the irrational. If the weeds got the upper hand in a badly kept garden, no one would find the appearance naïve; but there is something positively naïve

that nature should triumph over art not as a dynamic magnitude, by its blind force, but as a moral magnitude, by its form. The impropriety, and not the insufficing of art, must have afforded the victory to nature; for nothing which results from deficiency can command respect. It is true, that in the naïve of surprise it is always the overplus of feeling and a deficiency of restraint which causes nature to be recognized: but this deficiency and that overplus by no means create the naïve, for they only afford an opportunity for nature to follow unimpeded its moral capacity, that is, the law of harmony.

The naïve of surprise can only appertain to man, and to man alone, in so far as at that moment he is no longer pure and innocent nature. It presupposes a will which does not harmonize with that which nature does spontaneously. Such a person, if rendered conscious of it, will be frightened at himself: on the contrary, he who is naïve by disposition, will be surprised at men and at their astonishment. Then, as the truth does not here recognize the personal and moral character, but only the natural character released by feeling, so we attribute no merit to the man for his uprightness, and our laughter, which is restrained by no personal veneration for him, is merited sport. But as here also it is the uprightness of nature which breaks through the veil of falseness, a satisfaction of a higher kind unites with the mischievous pleasure at having surprised a man. For nature, in opposition to artifice, and truth, in opposition to deception, must always excite respect. We feel, then, in the naïve of surprise also, an actual moral pleasure, though not from a moral character.[5]

It is true, we always respect nature in the naïve of surprise, since we must respect the truth. On the contrary, we respect the person in the naïve of disposition, and then we enjoy not only a moral pleasure, but also at a moral object. In the one

when the free growth of outspreading branches destroys the laborious work of the shears in a French garden. And so it is not at all naïve when a trained horse repeats his lesson badly out of natural fatness, but there is something naïve when he forgets it out of natural freedom.

[5] As the naïve depends only upon the form in which something is said or done, this property disappears, as soon as the thing itself, either through its causes or through its effects, makes a preponderating or indeed contradictory impression. By naïveté of this kind even a crime can be detected, but then we have neither the quiet nor the leisure to direct our attention to the form of the detection: and aversion for the personal character absorbs all our satisfaction at the nature. And as a revolted feeling steals the moral pleasure at the uprightness of nature, as soon as naïveté gives knowledge of a crime, just so does an excited compassion destroy our mischievous pleasure, as soon as we see anybody placed in peril by his naïveté.

as in the other case nature is right, so that she speaks the truth: but in the latter case nature is not only right, but the person is also worthy of respect. In the first case the uprightness of nature always redounds to the shame of the person, because it is involuntary; in the second it always redounds to his merit, even supposing that he incurs odium by what it expresses.

We ascribe a naïve disposition to a man, if in his judgments of things, he overlooks their artificial and forced relations, and adheres only to simple nature. We demand from him all the judgments that can be made within the limits of healthy nature; and we completely discharge him only from that which presupposes a separation from, at least a knowledge of, nature, whether in feeling or in thought.

If a father tells his child that this or that man is pining in poverty, and the child hastens to carry to the man his father's purse of gold, the action is naïve, for healthy nature acts out of the child: and it would be perfectly right so to proceed in a world where healthy nature rules. He only regards the need and the nearest method of satisfying it: such an extension of the right of property whereby a part of humanity are left to perish, is not founded in simple nature. The action of the child, then, is a rebuke of the actual world, and our heart also confesses it by the satisfaction which the action causes it to feel.

If a man without knowledge of the world, but otherwise of good capacity, confesses his secrets to another, who betrays him—but who knows how to artfully dissimulate—and by this very candor lends him the means of doing him an injury, we find it naïve. We laugh at him, but yet we cannot resist for that reason highly prizing him. For his confidence in the other results from the honesty of his own intentions: at least he is naïve only so far as that is the case.

Hence the naïve of reflection can never be a property of corrupted men, but can only belong to children and men with childlike dispositions. The latter often act and think naïvely in the most artificial relations of the great world. Out of their own fine humanity they forget that they have to do with a corrupted world, and they demean themselves at the courts of kings with an ingenuous innocence only to be found among a race of shepherds.

Now it is not so easy always correctly to distinguish childish from childlike innocence, since there are actions which waver between the extreme limits of both, and which actually leave us in doubt, whether we ought to laugh at simpleness or reverence a noble simplicity. A very remarkable instance of this kind is found in the political history of Pope Adrian VI, which Schröckh has described for us with the thoroughness and pragmatic truth peculiar to himself. This pope, a Netherlander by birth, administered the pontificate at a critical moment for the hierarchy, when an embittered party exposed without mercy the weak points in the Roman Church, and the adverse party was deeply interested to conceal them. What the truly naïve character, if such a one ever strayed into the holy chair of Peter, would have to do in this case, is not the question: but rather, how far such a naïveté of disposition might be compatible with the function of a pope. This, by the way, was something which by no means embarrassed the predecessors and followers of Adrian. With perfect uniformity they adhered to the Romish system once for all accepted, nowhere to concede anything. But Adrian really had the simple character of his nation and the innocence of his former rank. He was elevated from the narrow sphere of the student to his exalted post, and had never been false to the simplicity of that character on the eminence of his new dignity. The abuses in the Church disturbed him, and he was much too honest openly to dissimulate his private convictions. In conformity to such a mood he suffered himself, in the instruction with which he furnished his legate to Germany, to fall into confessions, before unheard of from any pope, and to flatly impugn the principles of this court. Among other things it says: " We know well that for many years past much that is odious has been perpetrated in this holy chair: no wonder if the sickness has been transmitted from the head to the members, from the pope to the prelates. We have all fallen away, and for a long time past there has not been one of us who has done a good thing, no, not one." Again, elsewhere, he enjoins the legate to declare in his name, " that he, Adrian, cannot be blamed on account of that which happened through former popes, and that such excesses had always displeased him, even when he filled an inferior station," etc. We can easily imagine what reception the Roman clergy gave to such naïveté on the part of the pope. The least which they imputed to him was that he had betrayed the church to the heretics. Now this highly impolitic measure of the pope would compel our whole respect and admiration, if we could only be convinced that he was actually naïve, that is, that he had been forced to it only through the natural truth of his character, without any regard to the possible consequences, and that he would have done it none the less if he had anticipated the whole extent of its unseemliness. But we have some grounds for believing that he did not deem this step so very impolitic, and in his innocence went so far as to hope that he might gain a very important advantage for the church by his condescension toward the opposition. He not only presumed that as an honest man he ought to take this step, but to be able also as pope to justify it: and while he forgot that the most artificial of all structures could actually be sustained by a systematic denial of the truth, he committed the unpardonable error of using precepts in a position completely the reverse of those natural relations in which they might have been valid. This certainly modifies our judgment seriously: and although we cannot withhold our respect from the honesty of heart, out of which that action flowed, it is not a little weakened by the reflection that nature had in art, and the heart in the head, a feeble rival.

That is not a true genius which is not naïve. Nothing but its naïveté makes it genius; and what it is in taste and intellect it cannot contradict in its morality. Unacquainted with rules, the crutches of weakness and the taskmasters of perversity, guided only by nature or by instinct, its guardian angel, it passes tranquilly and safely through all the snares of a vicious taste, in which the pseudo-genius is inevitably caught, unless it is acute enough to anticipate them from afar. It is only granted to genius to be always at home beyond the limits of the familiar, and to extend, without transgressing, nature. It is true the greatest genius now and then commits the latter fault, but only because it also has its moments of fantasy, when protecting nature leaves it: only because the force of example wins it, or the corrupt taste of its age seduces it.

Genius must solve the most complicated problems with unpretending simplicity and skill. The egg of Columbus is a sample of every method of true spirit. It legitimates itself as genius only by triumphing through simplicity over the most factitious art. It proceeds not according to familiar principles, but by impulses and feelings. But its impulses are suggestions of a god—all which healthy nature does, is divine—and its feelings are laws for all ages and for every race of men.

The childlike character which genius stamps upon its works, it also manifests in its manners and its private life. It is chaste, because nature is always so: but it is not decent, because decency is only native to depravity. It is intelligent, for nature can never be the opposite; but it is not cunning, for only art can be so. It is true to its character and its inclinations, but not so much because it has principles, as because nature always returns through every vacillation to its first position, always restores the old necessity. It is modest, even bashful, because genius itself is always a mystery, but it is not anxious, because it does not know the perils of the road on which it travels. We know little of the private life of the greatest geniuses, but even that little which has been preserved, for example, concerning Sophocles, Archimedes, Hippocrates, among the ancients, and Ariosto, Dante and Tasso, Raphael, Albert Dürer, Cervantes, Shakespeare, Fielding, Sterne, and others of modern times, confirms this assertion.

And even, a fact which seems to present for greater difficulty, the great statesman and general will exhibit a naïve character, as soon as their genius makes them great. Among the ancients, I will only here allude to Epaminondas and Julius Cæsar, and to Henry IV of France, Gustavus Adolphus of Sweden, and Peter the Great, among the moderns. The Duke of Marlborough, Turenne, Vendome, all display this character. And in the other sex, nature has indicated her highest perfection of naïveté. Feminine coquetry strives for nothing so much as for the appearance of naïveté: proof enough, if we had no other, that the chief power of the sex rests upon this quality. But since the prevalent principles of female education are in lasting opposition to this character, it is as hard for the woman morally, as for the man intellectually, to maintain that noble gift of nature with the advantages bestowed by generous culture. The woman who unites this naïveté of manners with a demeanor appropriate to the world merits our reverence as much as the scholar who combines a genial freedom of thought with all the severity of the schools.

A naïve expression necessarily flows out of naïve reflection, both in words and gestures: and it is the most important element of grace. Genius expresses thus naïvely its sublimest and deepest thoughts: they are oracles from the mouth of a child. While common-sense, always afraid of error, nails its words and conceptions upon the cross of logic and grammar, while it is hard and stiff in order to be definite, multiplies words lest it say too much, and prefers to extract all the force and keenness from its thought, from dread of being inconsiderate, genius, with a single happy dash of the pencil, gives to its thought a firm, forever definite, and yet flowing outline. If, on the one hand, the symbol and the thing symbolized remain forever foreign and heterogeneous, on the other, the speech issues from the thought as by an inward necessity, and is so entirely one with it, that the spirit seems exposed even under its material veil. In composition, it is expression of this kind, where the symbol entirely vanishes in the thing symbolized, and where the language still leaves the thought which it expressed naked, while another never can present without at the same time concealing it, that we style by eminence spirited and genial.

Innocence of heart expresses itself freely and naturally in daily life, like genius in its works of thought. It is notorious that in social life a man eschews simplicity and severe integrity of expression in the same proportion as he lacks purity of intention: and where offence is so readily incurred, and the imagination so easily corrupted, a constrained demeanor is a necessity. Without being false, we often say what we do not think: we invent circumlocutions in order to say things which can offend only a sickly vanity, or injure only a corrupt imagination. An ignorance of these conventional laws, united with natural uprightness, which despises every labyrinth and show of falsehood (and not rudeness, which only rejects those laws because they incommode it), creates a naïveté of expression in intercourse, which consists in calling things, which we either may not designate at all or only artfully, by their right names and in the curtest way. The customary expressions of children are of this kind. They create laughter from their contrast with our customs; and yet in our hearts we confess that the child is right.

It is true that, strictly speaking, a naïve disposition can be attributed to man only as a being not positively subject to nature, though still only so far as pure nature really acts in him. And yet, by an effect of the poetizing imagination, it is often transferred from the rational to the irrational. Thus we often attribute a naïve character to an animal, a landscape, a building, and to nature generally, in opposition to the caprice and fantasy of man. But this always demands that we should subjectively lend a will to that which has none, and have regard to its strict direction according to necessary laws. Dissatisfaction at our own ill-exercised moral freedom, and at the lack of moral harmony in our actions, easily induces that kind of mood in which we address an irrational thing as a person, and imagine its eternal uniformity a merit, and envy its tranquil tenor, as if it really had to struggle with a temptation to be otherwise. At such a moment it jumps with our humor to consider our prerogative of reason an evil and a curse, and to deny justice to our capacity and destiny, from a vivid sense of the meagreness of our actual execution.

Then we see in irrational nature only a more fortunate sister, who remained in the maternal house, from which we stormed forth into the distance, in the exuberance of our freedom. With sorrowful longing we yearn to be back again, as soon as we begin to feel the oppressiveness of culture, and to hear in the foreign remoteness of art the winning voice of the mother. While we were only nature's children we were happy and perfect; we became free and ceased to be both. Hence results a twofold and very dissimilar longing for nature, longing for her happiness, longing for her perfection. The loss of the former is lamented only by the sensuous man; but the moral man alone can mourn over the loss of the latter.

Ask yourself strictly then, sympathizing friend of nature, does your indolence pine for her repose? does your offended moral sense desire her harmony? Ask yourself candidly, does art disgust you, and do you take refuge in the solitude of inanimate nature from the abuses of society? do you abhor its privations, its burdens, its difficulties, or its moral anarchy, its disorders, its caprice? You must meet the former with joy and courage, and your compensation must be the very freedom out of which they flow. You may well propose the tranquil joy of nature for your distant goal, but only such as is the prize of your own worthiness. Then complain no longer of the hardship of life, of the inequality of conditions, of the stress of circumstances, of the insecurity of property, of ingratitude, oppression, persecution. You must submit to all the evils of culture with free resignation, you must respect them as the natural conditions of the only Good: you must lament only over its wickedness, but not with unmanly tears. Much rather care to act purely amid those contaminations, freely under that slavery, firmly through that fickle mutability, loyally through that anarchy. Do not fear external, but internal confusion: strive for unity, but seek it not in uniformity: strive for repose, but through the equipose, not through the cessation, of your activity. That nature, which you begrudge to the irrational, deserves neither longing nor respect. It lies behind you: it must forever lie behind you. When you no longer feel the ladder which upheld you, there remains for you no choice but to grasp the law with free consciousness and volition, or else to fall beyond deliverance into a fathomless abyss.

But if you become consoled for the loss of nature's happiness, then let her perfection be your heart's ideal. If you step forth unto her from your sphere of art, and see her before you in her great tranquillity, in her naïve beauty, in her childlike innocence and simplicity, linger before the picture, cherish that feeling: it is worthy of your noblest manhood. Do not longer indulge the wish or fancy to exchange with her, but receive her into yourself, and strive to wed her infinite superiority to your own infinite prerogative, and create from that union the divine. Let her encompass you like a tender Idyll, in which you may always find yourself again out of the distractions of art, from which you may gather new courage and confidence for the race, and kindle afresh in your heart the flame of the Ideal, which flickers and sinks so soon in the storms of life.

If we call to mind the beautiful nature which surrounded the ancient Greeks, if we recollect how confidingly that people could live under their fortunate heaven with free nature, how much nearer their conception, their sentiment, their manners lay to simple nature, and what a true reflection of her their works of fancy are, it must seem strange to observe that we find so few traces among them of that sentimental interest with which we moderns can cling to natural scenes and characters. It is true, the Greek is in the highest degree strict, true, circumstantial, in his description of nature, but yet not a whit more and with no heartier sympathy, than he is also in the description of an array, a shield, a suit of armor, a domestic utensil, or of any product of mechanics. He seems to make no distinction in his love for the object, between that which is in itself and that which is through art and human will. Nature seems to interest his intellect and curiosity more than his moral sense: he does not cling to her as we do, with heartiness, with sensibility, with a sweet sadness. And even when he personifies and deifies her single manifestations, and represents their effects as actions of a free being, he abolishes in her that tranquil necessity, by which precisely she is so attractive to us. His impatient fancy bears him away over her to the drama of human life. Nothing satisfies him but the free and living, nothing but characters, actions, fates, and manners. And while we, in certain moral moods of mind, could wish to give up the superiority of our free volition, which causes us so much strife with ourselves, so much unrest and confusion, for the choiceless but tranquil necessity of the irrational, the Greek fancy, precisely the reverse, is busy making human nature inchoate even within the inanimate world, and giving influence to will in the province of blind necessity.

Whence indeed this diversity of spirit? How comes it that we who are so far surpassed by the ancients in everything that is nature, can precisely here honor nature in a higher sense, cling to her with heartfulness, and embrace even the inanimate world with warmest sensibility? It is because with us nature has vanished out of humanity, and we meet her again in her truth only beyond the latter, in the world of matter. It is not our greater conformity with nature, but, quite the contrary, the incongruity of our relations, conditions, and manners, which impels us to procure in the physical world that which is hopeless in the moral world, namely, satisfaction for the growing impulse for truth and simplicity, which lies incorruptible and ineffaceable in all human hearts, like the moral disposition whence it flows. It is for this reason that the feeling with which we cling to nature is so nearly akin to the feeling which laments the vanished age of childhood and of childlike innocence. Our childhood is the only unmutilated nature which we still find in cultivated manhood: then it is no wonder if every vestige of external nature conducts us back to our childhood.

It was very different with the ancient Greeks.[6] Their culture had not so far degenerated that nature was abandoned. The whole structure of their social life was based upon feelings, and not upon a composition of art: their mythology itself was the suggestion of a naïve sentiment, the creation of a joyous fancy, and not of a refining reason, like the religion of later nations. Then as the Greek had not lost the nature in humanity, he could not be surprised by her beyond the limits of the latter: and so he could have no pressing necessity for objects in which he might recover her. In unison with himself, and happy in the feeling of his humanity, he fain held silently to that as his maximum, and approached all else with difficulty: while we, not in unison with ourselves, and unhappy in our experiences of humanity, have no pressing interest except to escape from it, and to thrust from our vision a form so unsuccessful.

The feeling to which we here allude, is not then, that which the ancients had: it is rather identical with that which we have for the ancients. They perceived naturally: we perceive the natural. Without doubt, the feeling which filled Homer's soul when he let his celestial swineherd entertain Ulysses was quite different from that which moved the soul of the young Werther, when he read the passage after a tedious company. Our sentiment for nature is like the feeling of the invalid for health.

In the same degree that nature vanished out of human life as experience and as the (active and perceptive) subject, we see her appearing in the poetic world as idea and as object.

---

[6] But with the Greeks only: for just such a lively animation and such a rich fulness of human life as surrounded the Greek, were requisite, in order to transfer life into the lifeless also, and to pursue with that zeal the image of humanity. Ossian's human world, for example, was needy and monotonous: the inanimate around him was great, colossal, mighty. Thus it was imperative, and maintained its rights over man himself: and hence inanimate nature (in opposition to man) appears in the songs of this poet much more as an object of sentiment. But Ossian too laments a falling away of humanity; and however small was the circle of his people's culture and their corruptions, its experience was still lively and impressive enough, to repel the singer, with his tenderness and purity, back towards the inanimate, and to pour over his songs that elegiac tone which we find so moving and attractive.

That nation which has proceeded furthest both in unnature and in reflection upon it must have been the first to be most strongly moved by the phenomenon of naïveté, and to give to it a name. This nation, so far as I know, was the French. But perception of, and interest in, the naïve, is naturally much earlier, and dates from the very commencement of moral and æsthetic depravation. This change in the perceptive mode is extremely striking even so early as Euripides; for example, when we compare him with his predecessors and with Æschylus especially, and yet that poet was the favorite of his age. The same revolution is apparent also among the old historians. Horace, the poet of a cultivated and corrupted age, extols tranquil happiness in his Tibur; and we may designate him as the true founder of this sentimental school of poetry, while as a model he has not yet been surpassed. We also find traces of this perception in Propertius, Vergil, and others, but few in Ovid, who lacked heartfulness, and who mourns, in his exile at Tomi, the loss of that happiness which Horace so readily dispenses with in his Tibur.

Poets are universally, by their very conception, the guardians of nature. Where they can no longer be so, and already feel in themselves the destructive influence of capricious and artificial forms, or at least have had to struggle with it, they will then appear as the witnesses and as the avengers of nature. They will either be, or they will seek, a lost nature. Thus two very different schools of poetry arise, which cover and exhaust the whole province of that art. All who are really poets will belong either to the naïve or to the sentimental school, according to the constitution of the age in which they flourish, or as contingent circumstances affect their general culture and predominating neutral tone.

The early poet of a naïve and spiritual world, and he, in an age of artificial culture, who is nearest to him, is austere and coy, like the virgin Diana in her forests. With no familiar manners, he eludes the heart that seeks him, and the longing that would embrace him. The homely truthfulness with which he handles an object often seems like insensibility. The object possesses him entirely: his heart does not lie, like a base metal, just beneath the surface, but will be sought after in the depths, like gold. He stands behind his work like the

Infinite behind the structure of the world. He is the work and the work is him. We must first be unworthy of the work, or unequal to it, or weary, only to ask for him.

So appears, for example, Homer among the ancients and Shakespeare among the moderns; two very different natures, separated by the immeasurable lapse of ages, but in this particular characteristic completely one. When I first became acquainted with the latter poet, at a very early age, I was troubled at the coldness, the insensibility, which permitted him to jest in the deepest pathos, to disturb with a clown the heart-rending scenes in " Hamlet," " King Lear," " Macbeth," and others, which now held him fast where my feelings hurried on, and now coldly hastened forward where the heart would so willingly have rested. Led by acquaintance with the later writers, to seek for the poet in the work, to meet his heart, to reflect familiarly with him concerning his object, in short, to contemplate the object in the subject, it was intolerable to me that the poet would nowhere suffer contact, and never deign to talk with me. And for many years he had all my reverence and my study too, before I learned to win his personality. I was yet incapable of understanding nature at first hand. I could only tolerate her image reflected through the intellect and adjusted by the rules; and the sentimental poets both of the French and Germans, from 1750 to 1780, were just the proper subjects for that end. But I am not ashamed of this puerile judgment, since the mature critic passed a similar one, and was naïve enough to publish it to the world.

The same thing happened to me with respect to Homer, also, whom I knew at a still later period. I remember now the remarkable place in the sixth book of the " Iliad," where Glaucus and Diomed attack each other, and after one recognizes the other as his guest, exchange presents. This affecting picture of the piety with which the laws of hospitality were observed in war itself, can be matched with a description of knightly magnanimity in Ariosto, where two knights and rivals, Ferran and Rinaldo, the one a Saracen, the other a Christian, make peace after being covered with wounds in a violent conflict, and mount the same horse in order to seek and bring back the flying Angelica. Different as both examples are, they still coincide in the effect upon our hearts, since both depict the beautiful triumph of manners over passion, and affect us with their naïveté of disposition. But how differently do the poets undertake the description of this same action. Ariosto, the citizen of a later age, whose manners had deteriorated in simplicity, cannot conceal his own admiration and emotion at the relation of this event. The feeling of the remoteness of these manners from those which characterize his age overpowers him. He abandons at once the delineation of the object and appears in his own person. The beautiful stanzas are well known, and have always excited special admiration:

> " O noble minds, by knights of old possess'd!
> Two faiths they knew, one love their hearts profess'd:
> And still their limbs the smarting anguish feel
> Of strokes inflicted by the hostile steel.
> Through winding paths and lonely woods they go,
> Yet no suspicion their brave bosoms know.
> At length the horse, with double spurring, drew
> To where diverging ways appeared in view."

And now old Homer! Hardly does Diomed learn from the relation of Glaucus, his rival, that the latter is a guest of his family from the father's times downward, when he buries his spear in the ground, talks cordially with him, and they agree in future to avoid each other during battle. But hear Homer himself:

> " Henceforth let our spears
> Avoid each other in tumultuous war;
> For many Trojans and renown'd allies
> Have I to slay, whom to this arm some god
> May bring, or else my speed may overtake;
> And many Greeks there are for thee to slay,
> Whome'er thou canst; but let us arms exchange,
> That all who see our conference may know
> We boast to be hereditary guests.
> This said, both heroes leaping from their cars,
> With mutual kindness joined their hands and pledged
> The faith of friendship!"

A modern poet (at least one who is so in the moral sense of that word) would have hardly waited until now, in order to testify his pleasure at the action. And we should the easier pardon him for it, since our heart also makes a pause in the reading, and withdraws from the object, in order to contemplate itself. But no trace of all this in Homer: he proceeds in his barren truthfulness, as if he had announced an every-day affair, nay, as if he bore no heart in his bosom:

> "Then Saturnian love
> Exalted Glaucus' liberal mind, who gave
> His golden for Tydides' brazen arms,
> Although a hundred oxen his were worth,
> And those of Diomed no more than nine."

Poets of this naïve kind are properly no longer in their place in an artificial age. In fact they are hardly possible there, at least only if they run wild, and are saved from the crippling influence of their times by a fortunate destiny. They can never proceed out of society itself; but they sometimes appear beyond its limits, yet rather as strangers who astonish us, and as untamed children of nature who scandalize us. Beneficial as such phenomena are for the artist who studies them, and for the genuine connoisseur who knows how to estimate them, they prosper little on the whole with their period. The seal of ruler rests upon their brow; but we prefer to be rocked and carried by the muses. The critics, who are the special hedge-trimmers of taste, hate them as bound-breakers, and would fain suppress them. For Homer himself need thank only the power of more than a millennium of evidence, for the toleration of these æsthetic judges: it would harass them not a little to maintain their rules against his example, and his reputation against their rules.

I said that the poet either is nature, or he will seek her. If the former, he is naïve; if the latter, he is sentimental.

The poetic spirit is immortal and inalienable in humanity: it cannot fail except simultaneously with that and with the poetic inclination. For when the man removes himself, by the freedom of his fancy and his understanding, from the simplicity, truth, and necessity of nature, not only the road to her remains forever open to him, but a mightier and more indestructible instinct, the moral, also impels him constantly back to her; and the poetic capacity stands in the closest relationship with this very instinct. That, then, is not also lost together with natural simplicity, but only operates in another channel.

Nature is still the only flame which nourishes the poetic

spirit; it creates its whole energy out of her alone, and speaks to her even in the artificial man comprised within his culture. Every other mode of operation is foreign to the poetic spirit; hence, by the way, all so-called works of humor are improperly styled poetic, although, guided by the reputation of French literature, we have for a long time confounded the two qualities. It is still nature, I say, that even in the artificial conditions of culture, gives energy to the poetic spirit; only she stands in a relation to it entirely new.

It is evident that, while man continues to be pure and not rude nature, he acts as an undivided sensuous unity and as a harmonizing whole. Sense and reason, the receptive and the creative faculty, are not yet separate in their operations, much less do they stand in opposition. The perceptions of the one are not the formless sport of chance, the ideas of the other are not the barren play of fancy; the former result from the law of necessity, the latter from reality. When man has passed into the state of culture, and art has lain her hand upon him, that sensuous harmony within him is removed, and he can only express himself as a moral unity, that is, as striving after unity. The agreement between his perception and reflection, which took place in the first condition actually, now exists only ideally. It is no longer in him, but out of him; as a thought which has yet to be realized, and no longer as a fact of his life. If now we apply the conception of poetry, which is none other than to give humanity its completest possible expression, to both the above conditions, the result is, that in the condition of natural simplicity, where the man still acts with all his powers at once as a harmonious unity, and where therefore the totality of his nature fully expresses itself in reality, the completest possible imitation of the actual must make the poet; that on the contrary, in the condition of culture, where that harmonious coöperation of his whole nature is only an idea, the elevation of reality to the ideal or what amounts to the same thing, the representation of the ideal, must make the poet. And these are also the two only possible modes in which the poetic genius can find expression. They are, as we see, entirely distinct; but there is a higher conception which comprehends them both, and we need not be surprised to find this conception coinciding with the idea of humanity.

This is not the place to pursue further this thought, which only a special discussion can place in its full light. But whoever knows how to institute a comparison between the ancient and modern poets,[7] not only according to accidental forms, but according to the spirit, can easily be satisfied of its truth. The former affect us through their nature, through sensuous truth, through living presence: the latter affect us through ideas.

Moreover, this path which the modern poets travel is the same which man must commonly pursue, as well in the part as in the whole. Nature makes him one with himself, art separates and divides him, the ideal restores his unity. But since the ideal is an infinity which man never reaches, the cultivated man can never become perfect in his mode, as the natural man is able to become in his. Then he must be infinitely inferior to the latter in perfection, if regard is had only to the relation in which both stand to their mode and their maximum. On the contrary, if we compare together the modes themselves, it is evident that the goal for which the man strives through culture is infinitely superior to that which he attains through nature. The one then acquires his value through positive attainment of a finite, the other desires it through approximation to an infinite, magnitude. But since the latter has only degree and progress, the relative worth of the cultivated man, taken as a whole, is never determinable, although when partially regarded he is found in necessary inferiority to him in whom nature acts in her whole perfection. But in so far as the final goal of humanity can only be reached through that progress, and the natural man can only proceed according as he cultivates himself, and consequently passes over into the other condition—there is no question to which of the two the preference is to be awarded, with respect to that final goal.

What has here been said of the two distinct forms of humanity may also be applied to both those poetic forms corresponding to them.

---

[7] Perhaps it is not superfluous to mention, that if the modern poets are here set opposite to the ancient, we are to understand not so much the difference in time as the difference in manner. We have also in modern and even in the latest times, naïve poems in all classes, though no longer of a style entirely pure; and there is no want of the sentimental among the old Latin, and even Grecian poets. We frequently find both kinds united, not only in the same poet, but even in the same work, as for example in the "Sorrows of Werther." Productions of this kind will always have a superior effect.

For this reason we ought not to compare together ancient and modern—naïve and sentimental—poets, or, if we do, only beneath a higher conception common to both: for such a one there really is. For certainly, if we have once partially abstracted the generic conception of poetry from the old poets, nothing is easier, but nothing also is more trivial, than to undervalue the moderns in comparison. If we only call that poetry which has uniformly affected simple nature in all times, the only result will be to render dubious the name of poet as applied to moderns exactly in their highest and most peculiar beauty, because it is precisely here that they speak only to the disciple of art, and have nothing to say to simple nature.[8] The richest contents will be empty show, and the highest flight of poetry will be exaggeration to him whose mind is not already prepared to pass out of reality into the province of ideas. The wish can never occur to a reasonable man to set a modern side by side with that in which Homer is great; and it sounds laughable enough to hear a Milton or a Klopstock styled the modern Homer. And just as little would any ancient poet, least of all Homer, be able to maintain a comparison with the modern poet in *his* characteristics. The former, if I may so express it, is powerful through the art of limitation; the latter through the art of illimitation.

And from the fact that the strength of the ancient artist (for what has here been said of the poet, can also be applied in general to the liberal artist, under the restrictions which naturally occur) consisted in limitation, we may explain the high superiority which the plastic art of antiquity asserts over that of modern times; and, in general, the unequal relation of value in which modern poetry and modern plastic art stand to both species of art in antiquity. A work for the eye finds its perfection only in limitation: a work for the imagination can also attain it through the unlimited. Hence a modern's preponderance in ideas helps him little in plastic works; he is com-

---

[8] It became Molière at any rate, as a naïve poet, to leave to the decision of his maid-servant what should stand in his comedies and what should be subtracted. It were to be wished that the masters of the French cothurn had also tried that test upon their tragedies. But I do not mean to propose that a similar test should be applied to the odes of Klopstock, to the finest passages in the "Messiah," in "Paradise Lost," in "Nathan the Wise," and many other pieces. But what do I say? This test is actually applied, and Molière's maid reasons at full sweep, in our critical libraries, philosophical and literary annals and travels, upon poetry, art, and the like; only as is reasonable, a little more insipidly on German than on French soil, and in keeping with the style in the savants' hall of German literature.

pelled here to define in space most rigidly the image of his fancy, and consequently to measure himself with the ancient artist precisely in that quality, in which the latter holds the indisputable palm. It is otherwise in poetic works; and though the ancient poets conquer here also in the simplicity of their means, and in that which is sensuously presentable and corporeal—the moderns in their turn leave them behind in profusion of material, in that which is irrepresentable and ineffable, and in short, in that which we call spirit in a work of art.

As the naïve poet follows only simple nature and perception, and confines himself only to imitation of reality, he can only hold a single relation to his subject, and in this respect, he has no choice in his mode of handling. The different impression of naïve poems depends (presupposing that we abstract all therein which pertains to the contents, and regard that impression only as the pure effect of the poetic handling) only, I remark, upon the different degree of one and the same perceptive method. Even the difference in the external forms can make no alteration in the quality of that æsthetic impression. Let the form be lyric or epic, dramatic or descriptive, we may indeed experience emotions more or less powerful, but never of different kinds, supposing the contents abstracted. Our emotion is altogether the same, composed entirely of one element, so that we can distinguish in it nothing else. Even the difference of tongues and times makes no alteration in this respect; for this pure unity of their origin and their effect is precisely one characteristic of naïve poetry.

The case is entirely different with the sentimental poet. He reflects upon the impression which the objects make upon him, and the emotion into which he throws us and is thrown himself, is only based upon that reflection. Here the object is related to an idea, and its poetic power only rests upon that relation. Hence the sentimental poet is always involved with two conflicting representations and perceptions, with reality as a limit and with his idea as the unlimited: and the mingled feeling which he excites will always betray this twofold source.[9] Since, then, a plurality of principles here occurs, it

---

[9] Whoever notices the impression which naïve poems make upon himself, and is able to disconnect therefrom the sympathy created by the contents, will

depends upon which of the two predominates in the poet's perception and in his representation, and a difference in the handling is consequently possible. For now the question arises whether he will be more occupied with the real, or more with the ideal, whether he will treat the former as an object of aversion, or the latter as an object of inclination. Then his representation will either be satirical, or it will be elegiac (in a wider signification of this word, hereafter to be explained). Every sentimental poet will conform to one of these two methods of perception.

find this impression, even in very pathetic subjects, always cheerful, always pure, always tranquil: while that of sentimental poems is always somewhat grave and intensive. The reason is, that while in the case of naïve representations, be the action what it will, we always rejoice at the truth, at the living presence of the object in our imagination, and seek nothing more than this—in the sentimental, on the contrary, we have to unite the presentation of the imagination with an idea of the reason, which always leaves us irresolute between two different conditions.

ON CONSOLATION

—

BY

JEAN PAUL FRIEDRICH RICHTER

JEAN PAUL FRIEDRICH RICHTER

1763—1825

The remarkable writer whose name, among his contemporaries and admirers, has been shortened to "Jean Paul," but who was christened Johann Paul Friedrich Richter, was born in the village of Wunsiedel, in the heart of the Franconian mountains, in 1763. He was the son of a poor clergyman blessed with a large family, and his early years were passed amid grinding poverty. Part of his education was obtained in the gymnasium of Hof; later he studied at Leipsic. During the two years spent there he was seriously hampered in his studies by the struggle to obtain the bare necessities of life. His first book was written in 1783—a collection of witty, satirical sketches entitled "The Greenland Lawsuits." It was only after long search that he found a publisher for the book. Owing to its extravagantly eccentric style, the book was little read and less appreciated. His next book was the "Selections from the Devil's Papers," which no publisher would consider. Still his determination to devote himself to literature remained unshaken. His mother was now living at Hof, as poor as himself, and he joined in the effort to keep the family from starvation. As buying books was out of the question, he borrowed them, making copious extracts from others, and combining the sheets thus gathered into a most extraordinary sort of "cyclopædia." Everything was there, Bayard Taylor tells us—theology and tinware, art and artichokes, science, cookery, ideas of heaven, making of horse-shoes, æsthetics, edible mushrooms, mythology, millinery. This *magnum opus* Richter kept always at his side when working, and from it he, no doubt, drew many of his seemingly far-fetched and incongruous allusions and illustrations.

In 1793 Richter wrote "The Invisible Lodge." His next book, "Hesperus," brought him to the knowledge of every author and critic in Germany. In 1796 he visited Weimar and met its literary celebrities. In 1800 he married, and before long settled permanently in Bayreuth, where he remained till his death, in 1825. He was comparatively prosperous during the latter part of his life. He was the guest of princes and the idol of the somewhat limited circle of his admirers. Besides "Hesperus," his most important romances were "Titan," "Flegeljahre" (Wild Oats), and "Siebenkäs." He also wrote a number of essays, of which "On Consolation" is a good example, and he achieved a considerable degree of success in his numerous shorter tales.

Richter's style is the despair of readers and translators. As Carlyle has said, there is "probably not in any modern language so intricate a writer; abounding, without measure, in obscure allusions, in the most twisted phraseology; perplexed into endless entanglements and dislocations, parenthesis within parenthesis; not forgetting elisions, sudden whirls, quips, conceits, and all manner of inexplicable crotchets; the whole moving on in the gayest manner." His fine humor, his deep and tender humanity, his rich poetical imagination, the exquisite delicacy and sprightliness of his fancy are, however, qualities that have rescued Richter's work from oblivion in spite of his style. And, after all, the style is a part of the man. It is the amazing combination of strength and weakness, delicacy and coarseness, knowledge and ignorance, sentiment and grotesque humor that make "Jean Paul" what his admirers love to call him—"the Unique" ("Der Einzige").

ON CONSOLATION

A TIME will come, that is, must come, when we shall be commanded by morality not only to cease tormenting others, but also ourselves. A time must come when man, even on earth, shall wipe away most of his tears, were it only from pride.

Nature, indeed, draws tears out of the eyes, and sighs out of the breast, so quickly, that the wise man can never wholly lay aside the garb of mourning from his body; but let his soul wear none. For if it is over a merit to bear a small suffering with cheerfulness, so must the calm and patient endurance of the worst be a merit, and will only differ in being a greater one; as the same reason which is valid for the forgiveness of small injuries is equally valid for the forgiveness of the greatest.

The first thing that we have to contend against and despise, in sorrow as in anger, is its poisonous enervating sweetness, which we are so loath to exchange for the labor of consoling ourselves, and to drive away by the effort of reason.

We must not exact of philosophy, that with one stroke of the pen it shall reverse the transformation of Rubens, who, with one stroke of his brush, changed a laughing child into a weeping one. It is enough if it change the full-mourning of the soul into half-mourning; it is enough if I can say to myself, I will be content to endure the sorrow that philosophy has left me; without it, it would be greater, and the gnat's bite would be a wasp's sting.

Even physical pain shoots its sparks upon us out of the electrical condenser of the imagination. We could endure the most acute pangs calmly if they only lasted the sixtieth part of a second; but, in fact, we never have to endure an hour of pain, but only a succession of the sixtieth parts of a second, the sixty beams of which are collected into the burning focus of a second, and directed upon our nerves by the imagination alone. The most painful part of our bodily pain is that which is bodiless, or immaterial, namely, our impatience, and the delusion that it will last forever.

There is many a loss over which we all know for certain that we shall no longer grieve in twenty—ten—two years. Why do we not say to ourselves: I will at once then, to-day, throw away an opinion which I shall abandon in twenty years? Why should I be able to abandon errors of twenty years' standing, and not of twenty hours?

When I awake from a dream which an Otaheite has painted for me on the dark ground of the night, and find the flowery land melted away, I scarcely sigh, thinking to myself, "It was only a dream." Why is it that if I had really possessed this island while awake, and it had been swallowed up by an earthquake, why is it that I do not then exclaim, "The island was only a dream"? Wherefore am I more inconsolable at the loss of a longer dream than at the loss of a shorter?—for that is the difference; and why does man find a great loss less probable and less a matter of necessity, when it occurs, than a small one?

The reason is, that every sentiment and every emotion is mad, and exacts and builds its own world. A man can vex himself that it is already, or only, twelve o'clock. What folly! The mood not only exacts its own world, its own individual [1] consciousness, but its own time. I beg everyone to let his passions, for once, speak out plainly within himself, and to probe and question them to the bottom, as to what they really desire. He will be terror-struck at the enormity of these hitherto only half-muttered wishes. Anger wishes that all mankind had only one neck; love, that it had only one heart; grief, two tear-glands; and pride, two bent knees.

When I read in Widman's "Court Chronicle" of the terrible bloody times of the Thirty Years' War, and as it were lived them over again; when I heard once more the cries of the tortured for help, as they struggled in the Danube-whirlpools of their age, and again beheld the clasping of hands, and the delirious wandering to and fro on the several pillars of the crumbling bridges, against which struck foaming billows and fiercely-driven fields of ice—and thus reflected, "All the waves have subsided, the ice has melted, the storm is mute, and the human

[1] "Sein eignes ich."

beings also with their sighs," I was filled with a peculiar melancholy feeling of consolation for all times; and I asked, " Was and is, then, this fleeting misery beneath the churchyard-gate of life, which three steps into the nearest cavern could put an end to, worth all this cowardly lamentation?" Verily, if there be, as I believe there is, true constancy under an eternal sorrow, then is patience under a fleeting one scarcely worthy of the name.

A great and unmerited national calamity should not humble us, as the theologians demand, but rather make us proud. When the long heavy sword of war falls upon humanity, and when a thousand pale hearts are riven and bleeding; or when, on a blue serene evening, the hot smoky cloud of a city, cast on the funereal pyre, hangs darkly on the sky—as though it were the cloud of ashes of a thousand consumed hearts and joys— then be thy spirit lifted up in pride, and let it contemn the tear and that for which it falls, saying, " Thou art much too insignificant, thou every-day life, for the inconsolableness of an immortal—thou tattered, misshapen, wholesale existence! Upon this sphere, which is rounded with the ashes of thousands of years, amid the storms of earth, made up of vapors, it is a disgrace that the sigh should only be dissipated together with the bosom that gives it birth, and not sooner; and that the tear should not perish except with the eye whence it flows."

But then, moderate thy sublime indignation, and put this question to thyself: If the hidden Infinite One, who is encompassed by gleaming abysses without bounds, and who himself creates the bounds, were now to lay immensity open to thy view, and to reveal himself to thee in his distribution of the suns, the lofty spirits, the little human hearts, and our days and some tears therein—wouldst thou rise up out of thy dust against him, and say, " Almighty! be other than Thou art!"

But be one sorrow alone forgiven thee, or made good to thee —the sorrow for thy dead ones; for this sweet sorrow for the lost is itself but another form of consolation. When the heart is full of longing for them, it is but another mode of continuing to love them; and we shed tears as well when we think of their departure, as when we picture to ourselves our joyful reunion and the tears, methinks, differ not.

CHOICE EXAMPLES OF EARLY PRINTING AND ENGRAVING.

Fac-similes from Rare and Curious Books.

DE BOEC DES GULDEN THROENS.

The clearness and regularity of early Dutch printing are finely exemplified in this work, which issued from the press of Otto van Passau at Haarlem in 1484. Haarlem, the native place of the great printing pioneer, Koster, kept her special pre-eminence as the cradle of the art up to the end of the fifteenth century, as is testified by the very handsome typography of this book. This fragment of typography exhibits the style of Dutch printing in its second epoch. The miniature is a wood engraving, and represents a kneeling woman making a petition to a King. The initial capital is red, and inserted by hand, while a touch of the same color rubricates the capitals throughout the text.

Gemael veel goets
heeft v minnēde sie
le mijn ghesellē dē
sesten oudē geleert
voer mi hoe ghi vā
buten leuen selt vo
re den mēschen tot
enen goeden exempel te geuen Ech
ter ick seuende oude wil v minnende
siel leren die const die v inwendich en̄
vtwēdich nut en̄ nootruftich is daer
ghi mede ghestoert moecht werden.
dat v leuen den gulden throen mach
vdienen des ewighen leuens ¶Want
nu te mael veel goets en̄ veel quaets
ontspringhet ende gegeuen wert vā
quaden ghedachten en̄ woerden. en̄
dat daer toe horet dat seer veel is soe
xviij

is minnende siel seer nootruftich dz
ghi gheestelike dingē daer in wel be
siet daer om dat ghi toecomende sca
de des te bet ontlopen ende ontuliē
moghet ¶Dat seyt iheronimus totter
ioncfrouwen demetriades Also wat
ghi v scamet te seggē dat seldi v oeck
scamen te dencken en̄ een seker en̄ eē
volcomen ghewoentheit houdē dat
uwe moet vlitich si en̄ wakende en̄ be
hoedich hoe ghi wel bekennen moghet alsulcke ghedachten .welc men
behouden sel .of welck men verwer
pen sel ¶Of echter dat ghi quade ghe
dachten verdriuet en̄ goede gedachten vaste behout want dencken is eē
versprōc ende beghinsel alre daden
ende oec boser sonden . En̄ wat goed
of quader wercken ymmermeer ghe
daen werden dat wert voer ontfan-
ghen indē becoringhen der ghedachten. ¶Daer om raet ons cesarius wa-
ringhe en̄ spreect Wi sellen aenuaen
goede gedachten te hebben en̄ te mi
nen soe werden wi verledicht vandē
bosen ghedachten die ons aen woer
den ende aen wercken aen siel en̄ aen
lijf ghescaden moghen want nu dye
ghedachten sijn een oersproncк ende
een saeck van vele goets en̄ quaets.
en̄ hoer ynemāt in deser tijt can noch
en mach ledich staen Hoe leer ic leue
de oude v minnēde siel hoe ghi in al-
len ghedachten houdē selt en̄ welc v
goet sijn of scadelic sijn wāt tē is ghe
ne dinc soe goet ghi en moecht daer
quaet wt dencken en̄ sondelike ghedachten daer wt trecke en̄ maken en
de die wise comen vā des mēschen ō-
c ij

ON AUTHORSHIP AND STYLE

—

BY

ARTHUR SCHOPENHAUER

ARTHUR SCHOPENHAUER
1788—1860

Arthur Schopenhauer was born at Dantzic in 1788. His father, a member of the mercantile aristocracy of the city, was successful in business and a man of unusual intelligence, but was afflicted with hereditary mental disorder, which culminated in suicide. His mother, who was twenty years younger than her husband, was a woman of considerable intellectual power, a novelist of some reputation among her contemporaries, and a friend of Goethe. During his boyhood Schopenhauer travelled extensively with his parents. In 1805 he entered his father's business, but this proved so extremely distasteful to him that his mother gave him permission to attend the lectures at the University of Göttingen, where he devoted himself chiefly to the study of Kant and Plato. He had, when still young, determined that his life should be one given to philosophical speculation, saying to Wieland, who once suggested doubts as to the wisdom of his choice: " Life is a ticklish business; I have resolved to spend it in reflecting upon it."

After two years spent at Göttingen, Schopenhauer went to Berlin, where Fichte and Schleiermacher were his teachers, and in 1813 submitted as a thesis for the degree of doctor of philosophy a treatise " On the Fourfold Root of the Principle of Sufficient Reason." In 1819 he published his *magnum opus,* " The World as Will and Idea."

After this he led an eccentric and solitary existence in various German cities, interrupted only by a journey to Italy, finally settling in Frankfort, in 1831, where he lived till his death, in 1860.

In 1836 Schopenhauer published a book entitled " Will in Nature," and in 1841 " The Two Main Problems of Ethics "—both works of minor importance and of interest chiefly to students of his philosophy. In 1844 a second edition of " The World as Will and Idea " was published, a new volume being added, consisting of commentaries on the first. Although Schopenhauer's work now holds a high place in German philosophical literature and has profoundly influenced certain channels of modern thought, it was many years before its merits were recognized. This undeserved neglect intensified Schopenhauer's psychological peculiarities and made him still more retired and morose. The old philosopher, waiting for a sign that his great message to mankind had at last found appreciative hearers, living meanwhile alone with his dog and his daily paper as the only visible means of his intercourse with the world without, is one of the most striking figures in the annals of literature. During his last years the importance of his system began to be recognized, and he suddenly became famous, his death being a sort of apotheosis. As a thinker Schopenhauer ranks among the first of the post-Kantian philosophers. His literary style is perhaps superior to that of any of the other German writers on philosophy, being notably clear and brilliant. His illustrations are especially apt and forcible. The essay on " Authorship and Style " is a characteristic example of his literary method.

ON AUTHORSHIP AND STYLE

THERE are, first of all, two kinds of authors: those who write for the subject's sake, and those who write for writing's sake. The first kind have had thoughts or experiences which seem to them worth communicating, while the second kind need money and consequently write for money. They think in order to write, and they may be recognized by their spinning out their thoughts to the greatest possible length, and also by the way they work out their thoughts, which are half-true, perverse, forced, and vacillating; then also by their love of evasion, so that they may seem what they are not; and this is why their writing is lacking in definiteness and clearness.

Consequently, it is soon recognized that they write for the sake of filling up the paper, and this is the case sometimes with the best authors; for example, in parts of Lessing's "Dramaturgie," and even in many of Jean Paul's romances. As soon as this is perceived the book should be thrown away, for time is precious. As a matter of fact, the author is cheating the reader as soon as he writes for the sake of filling up paper; because his pretext for writing is that he has something to impart. Writing for money and preservation of copyright are, at bottom, the ruin of literature. It is only the man who writes absolutely for the sake of the subject that writes anything worth writing. What an inestimable advantage it would be, if, in every branch of literature, there existed only a few but excellent books! This can never come to pass so long as money is to be made by writing. It seems as if money lay under a curse, for every author deteriorates directly he writes in any way for the sake of money. The best works of great men all come from the time when they had to write either for nothing or for very little pay. This is confirmed by the Spanish proverb: "*Honra y provecho no caben en un saco*" (Honor and money are not to be found in the same purse). The deplorable condition of the literature of to-day, both in Germany and other countries, is due to the fact that books are written for the sake of earning money. Everyone who is in want of money sits down and writes a book, and the public is stupid enough to buy it. The secondary effect of this is the ruin of language.

A great number of bad authors eke out their existence entirely by the foolishness of the public, which only will read what has just been printed. I refer to journalists, who have been appropriately so called. In other words it would be " day laborer."

Again, it may be said that there are three kinds of authors. In the first place, there are those who write without thinking. They write from memory, from reminiscences, or even direct from other people's books. This class is the most numerous. In the second, those who think whilst they are writing. They think in order to write; and they are numerous. In the third place, there are those who have thought before they begin to write. They write solely because they have thought; and they are rare.

Authors of the second class, who postpone their thinking until they begin to write, are like a sportsman who goes out at random—he is not likely to bring home very much. While the writing of an author of the third, the rare class, is like a chase where the game has been captured beforehand and cooped up in some enclosure from which it is afterwards set free, so many at a time, into another enclosure, where it is not possible for it to escape, and the sportsman has now nothing to do but to aim and fire—that is to say, put his thoughts on paper. This is the kind of sport which yields something.

But although the number of those authors who really and seriously think before they write is small, only extremely few of them think about the subject itself; the rest think only about the books written on this subject, and what has been said by others upon it, I mean. In order to think, they must have the more direct and powerful incentive of other people's thoughts. These become their next theme, and therefore they always remain under their influence and are never, strictly speaking, original. On the contrary, the former are roused to thought through the subject itself, hence their thinking is directed immediately to it. It is only among them that we find the authors whose names become immortal. Let it be understood that I am speaking here of writers of the higher branches of literature, and not of writers on the method of distilling brandy.

It is only the writer who takes the material on which he writes direct out of his own head that is worth reading. Book manufacturers, compilers, and the ordinary history writers, and others like them, take their material straight out of books; it passes into their fingers without its having paid transit duty or undergone inspection when it was in their heads, to say nothing of elaboration. (How learned many a man would be if he knew everything that was in his own books!) Hence their talk is often of such a vague nature that one racks one's brains in vain to understand of what they are really thinking. They are not thinking at all. The book from which they copy is sometimes composed in the same way: so that writing of this kind is like a plaster cast of a cast of a cast, and so on, until finally all that is left is a scarcely recognizable outline of the face of Antinous. Therefore, compilations should be read as seldom as possible: it is difficult to avoid them entirely, since compendia, which contain in a small space knowledge that has been collected in the course of several centuries, are included in compilations.

No greater mistake can be made than to imagine that what has been written latest is always the more correct; that what is written later on is an improvement on what was written previously; and that every change means progress. Men who think and have correct judgment, and people who treat their subject earnestly, are all exceptions only. Vermin is the rule everywhere in the world: it is always at hand and busily engaged in trying to improve in its own way upon the mature deliberations of the thinkers. So that if a man wishes to improve himself in any subject he must guard against immediately seizing the newest books written upon it, in the assumption that science is always advancing and that the older books have been made use of in the compiling of the new. They have, it is true, been used; but how? The writer often does not thoroughly understand the old books; he will, at the same time, not use their exact words, so that the result is he spoils and bungles what has been said in a much better and clearer way by the old writers; since they wrote from their own lively knowledge of the subject. He often leaves out the best things they have written, their most striking elucidations of the matter, their happiest remarks, because he does not recognize their value or feel how pregnant they are. It is only what is stupid and shallow that appeals to him. An old and excellent book is frequently shelved for new and bad ones; which, written for the sake of money, wear a pretentious air and are much eulogized by the authors' friends. In science, a man who wishes to distinguish himself brings something new to market; this frequently consists in his denouncing some principle that has been previously held as correct, so that he may establish a wrong one of his own. Sometimes his attempt is successful for a short time, when a return is made to the old and correct doctrine. These innovators are serious about nothing else in the world than their own priceless person, and it is this that they wish to make its mark. They bring this quickly about by beginning a paradox; the sterility of their own heads suggests their taking the path of negation; and truths that have long been recognized are now denied—for instance, the vital power, the sympathetic nervous system, *generatio equivoca,* Bichat's distinction between the working of the passions and the working of intelligence, or they return to crass atomism, etc., etc. Hence the course of science is often retrogressive.

To this class of writers belong also those translators who, besides translating their author, at the same time correct and alter him, a thing that always seems to me impertinent. Write books yourself which are worth translating and leave the books of other people as they are. One should read, if it is possible, the real authors, the founders and discoverers of things, or at any rate the recognized great masters in every branch of learning, and buy second-hand books rather than read their contents in new ones.

It is true that *inventis aliquid addere facile est,* therefore a man, after having studied the principles of his subject, will have to make himself acquainted with the more recent information written upon it. In general, the following rule holds good here as elsewhere, namely: what is new is seldom good; because a good thing is only new for a short time.

What the address is to a letter the title should be to a book—

that is, its immediate aim should be to bring the book to that part of the public that will be interested in its contents. Therefore, the title should be effective, and since it is essentially short, it should be concise, laconic, pregnant, and if possible express the contents in a word. Therefore a title that is prolix, or means nothing at all, or that is indirect or ambiguous, is bad; so is one that is false and misleading: this last may prepare for the book the same fate as that which awaits a wrongly addressed letter. The worst titles are those that are stolen, such titles that is to say that other books already bear; for in the first place they are a plagiarism, and in the second a most convincing proof of an absolute want of originality. A man who has not enough originality to think out a new title for his book will be much less capable of giving it new contents. Akin to these are those titles which have been imitated, in other words, half stolen; for instance, a long time after I had written " On Will in Nature," Oersted wrote " On Mind in Nature."

A book can never be anything more than the impression of its author's thoughts. The value of these thoughts lies either in the matter about which he has thought, or in the form in which he develops his matter—that is to say, what he has thought about it.

The matter of books is very various, as also are the merits conferred on books on account of their matter. All matter that is the outcome of experience, in other words everything that is founded on fact, whether it be historical or physical, taken by itself and in its widest sense, is included in the term matter. It is the *motif* that gives its peculiar character to the book, so that a book can be important whoever the author may have been; while with form the peculiar character of a book rests with the author of it. The subjects may be of such a nature as to be accessible and well known to everybody; but the form in which they are expounded, what has been thought about them, gives the book its value, and this depends upon the author. Therefore if a book, from this point of view, is excellent and without a rival, so also is its author. From this it follows that the merit of a writer worth reading is all the greater the less he is dependent on matter—and the better known and worn out this matter, the greater will be his merit. The three great Grecian tragedians, for instance, all worked at the same subject.

So that when a book becomes famous one should carefully distinguish whether it is so on account of its matter or its form.

Quite ordinary and shallow men are able to produce books of very great importance because of their matter, which was accessible to them alone. Take, for instance, books which give descriptions of foreign countries, rare natural phenomena, experiments that have been made, historical events of which they were witnesses, or have spent both time and trouble in inquiring into and specially studying the authorities for them.

On the other hand, it is on form that we are dependent where the matter is accessible to everyone or very well known; and it is what has been thought about the matter that will give any value to the achievement; it will only be an eminent man who will be able to write anything that is worth reading. For the others will only think what is possible for every other man to think. They give the impress of their own mind; but everyone already possesses the original of this impression.

However, the public is very much more interested in matter than in form, and it is for this very reason that it is behindhand in any high degree of culture. It is most laughable the way the public reveals its liking for matter in poetic works; it carefully investigates the real events or personal circumstances of the poet's life which served to give the *motif* of his works; nay, finally, it finds these more interesting than the works themselves; it reads more about Goethe than what has been written by Goethe, and industriously studies the legend of Faust in preference to Goethe's " Faust " itself. And when Bürger said that " people would make learned expositions as to who Leonora really was," we see this literally fulfilled in Goethe's case, for we now have many learned expositions on Faust and the Faust legend. They are and will remain of a purely material character. This preference for matter to form is the same as a man ignoring the shape and painting of a fine Etruscan vase in order to make a chemical examination of the clay and colors of which it is made. The attempt to be effective by means of the matter used, thereby ministering to this evil propensity of the public, is absolutely to be censured in branches of writing where the merit must lie expressly in the form; as, for instance, in poetical writing. However, there are numerous bad dramatic authors striving to fill the theatre by means of the matter they are treating. For instance, they place on the stage any kind of celebrated man, however stripped of dramatic incidents his life may have been, nay, sometimes without waiting until the persons who appear with him are dead.

The distinction between matter and form, of which I am here speaking, is true also in regard to conversation. It is chiefly intelligence, judgment, wit, and vivacity that enable a man to converse; they give form to the conversation. However, the matter of the conversation must soon come into notice—in other words, that about which one can talk to the man, namely, his knowledge. If this is very small, it will only be his possessing the above-named formal qualities in a quite exceptionally high degree that will make his conversation of any value, for his matter will be restricted to things concerning humanity and nature which are known generally. It is just the reverse if a man is wanting in these formal qualities, but has, on the other hand, knowledge of such a kind that it lends value to his conversation; this value, however, will then entirely rest on the matter of his conversation, for, according to the Spanish proverb, "*Mas sabe el necio en su casa, que el sabio en la agena.*"

A thought only really lives until it has reached the boundary line of words; it then becomes petrified and dies immediately; yet it is as everlasting as the fossilized animals and plants of former ages. Its existence, which is really momentary, may be compared to a crystal the instant it becomes crystallized.

As soon as a thought has found words it no longer exists in us or is serious in its deepest sense.

When it begins to exist for others it ceases to live in us; just as a child frees itself from its mother when it comes into existence. The poet has also said:

"*Ihr müsst mich nicht durch Widerspruch verwirren!*
Sobald man spricht, beginnt man schon zu irren."

The pen is to thought what the stick is to walking, but one walks most easily without a stick, and thinks most perfectly when no pen is at hand. It is only when a man begins to get old that he likes to make use of a stick and his pen.

A hypothesis that has once gained a position in the mind,

or been born in it, leads a life resembling that of an organism, in so far as it receives from the outer world matter only that is advantageous and homogeneous to it; on the other hand, matter that is harmful and heterogeneous to it is either rejected, or if it must be received, cast off again entirely.

Abstract and indefinite terms should be employed in satire only as they are in algebra, in place of concrete and specified quantities. Moreover, it should be used as sparingly as the dissecting knife on the body of a living man. At the risk of forfeiting his life it is an unsafe experiment.

For a work to become immortal it must possess so many excellences that it will not be easy to find a man who understands and values them all; so that there will be in all ages men who recognize and appreciate some of these excellences; by this means the credit of the work will be retained throughout the long course of centuries and ever-changing interests, for, as it is appreciated first in this sense, then in that, the interest is never exhausted.

An author like this, in other words, an author who has a claim to live on in posterity, can only be a man who seeks in vain his like among his contemporaries over the wide world, his marked distinction making him a striking contrast to everyone else. Even if he existed through several generations, like the Wandering Jew, he would still occupy the same position; in short, he would be, as Ariosto has put it, "*lo fece natura, e poi ruppe lo stampo.*" If this were not so, one would not be able to understand why his thoughts should not perish like those of other men.

In almost every age, whether it be in literature or art, we find that if a thoroughly wrong idea, or a fashion, or a manner is in vogue, it is admired. Those of ordinary intelligence trouble themselves inordinately to acquire it and put it in practice. An intelligent man sees through it and despises it, consequently he remains out of the fashion. Some years later the public sees through it and takes the sham for what it is worth; it now laughs at it, and the much-admired color of all these works of fashion falls off like the plaster from a badly-built wall: and they are in the same dilapidated condition. We should be glad and not sorry when a fundamentally wrong notion of which we have been secretly conscious for a long time finally gains a footing and is proclaimed both loudly and openly. The falseness of it will soon be felt and eventually proclaimed equally loudly and openly. It is as if an abscess had burst.

The man who publishes and edits an article written by an anonymous critic should be held as immediately responsible for it as if he had written it himself; just as one holds a manager responsible for bad work done by his workmen. In this way the fellow would be treated as he deserves to be—namely, without any ceremony.

An anonymous writer is a literary fraud against whom one should immediately cry out, "Wretch, if you do not wish to admit what it is you say against other people, hold your slanderous tongue."

An anonymous criticism carries no more weight than an anonymous letter, and should therefore be looked upon with equal mistrust. Or do we wish to accept the assumed name of a man, who in reality represents a *société anonyme,* as a guarantee for the veracity of his friends?

The little honesty that exists among authors is discernible in the unconscionable way they misquote from the writings of others. I find whole passages in my works wrongly quoted, and it is only in my appendix, which is absolutely lucid, that an exception is made. The misquotation is frequently due to carelessness, the pen of such people has been used to write down such trivial and banal phrases that it goes on writing them out of force of habit. Sometimes the misquotation is due to impertinence on the part of someone who wants to improve upon my work; but a bad motive only too often prompts the misquotation—it is then horrid baseness and roguery, and, like a man who commits forgery, he loses the character for being an honest man forever.

Style is the physiognomy of the mind. It is a more reliable key to character than the physiognomy of the body. To imitate another person's style is like wearing a mask. However fine the mask, it soon becomes insipid and intolerable because it is without life; so that even the ugliest living face is better. Therefore authors who write in Latin and imitate the style of the old writers essentially wear a mask; one certainly hears what they say, but one cannot watch their physiognomy—that is to say their style. One observes, however, the style in the

Latin writings of men who think for themselves, those who have not deigned to imitate, as, for instance, Scotus Erigena, Petrarch, Bacon, Descartes, Spinoza, etc.

Affectation in style is like making grimaces. The language in which a man writes is the physiognomy of his nation; it establishes a great many differences, beginning from the language of the Greeks down to that of the Caribbean islanders.

We should seek for the faults in the style of another author's works, so that we may avoid committing the same in our own.

In order to get a provisional estimate of the value of an author's productions it is not exactly necessary to know the matter on which he has thought or what it is he has thought about it—this would compel one to read the whole of his works—but it will be sufficient to know how he has thought. His style is an exact expression of how he has thought, of the essential state and general quality of his thoughts. It shows the formal nature—which must always remain the same—of all the thoughts of a man, whatever the subject on which he has thought or what it is he has said about it. It is the dough out of which all his ideas are kneaded, however various they may be. When Eulenspiegel was asked by a man how long he would have to walk before reaching the next place, and gave the apparently absurd answer, "Walk," his intention was to judge from the man's walking how far he would go in a given time. And so it is when I have read a few pages of an author, I know about how far he can help me.

In the secret consciousness that this is the condition of things, every mediocre writer tries to mask his own natural style. This instantly necessitates his giving up all idea of being naïve, a privilege which belongs to superior minds sensible of their superiority, and therefore sure of themselves. For instance, it is absolutely impossible for men of ordinary intelligence to make up their minds to write as they think; they resent the idea of their work looking too simple. It would always be of some value, however. If they would only go honestly to work and in a simple way express the few and ordinary ideas they have really thought, they would be readable and even instructive in their own sphere. But instead of that they try to appear to have thought much more deeply than is the case. The result is, they put what they have to say into forced and involved language, create new words and prolix periods which go round the thought and cover it up. They hesitate between the two attempts of communicating the thought and of concealing it. They want to make it look grand so that it has the appearance of being learned and profound, thereby giving one the idea that there is much more in it than one perceives at the moment. Accordingly, they sometimes put down their thoughts in bits, in short, equivocal, and paradoxical sentences which appear to mean much more than they say (a splendid example of this kind of writing is furnished by Schelling's treatises on natural philosophy); sometimes they express their thoughts in a crowd of words and the most intolerable diffuseness, as if it were necessary to make a sensation in order to make the profound meaning of their phrases intelligible—while it is quite a simple idea if not a trivial one (examples without number are supplied in Fichte's popular works and in the philosophical pamphlets of a hundred other miserable blockheads that are not worth mentioning), or else they endeavor to use a certain style in writing which it has pleased them to adopt—for example, a style that is so thoroughly κατ' ἐξοχήν profound and scientific, where one is tortured to death by the narcotic effect of long-spun periods that are void of all thought (examples of this are specially supplied by those most impertinent of all mortals, the Hegelians in their Hegel newspaper commonly known as " Jahrbücher der wissenschaftlichen Literatur "); or again, they aim at an intellectual style where it seems then as if they wish to go crazy, and so on. All such efforts whereby they try to postpone the *nascetur ridiculus mus* make it frequently difficult to understand what they really mean. Moreover, they write down words, nay, whole periods, which mean nothing in themselves, in the hope, however, that someone else will understand something from them. Nothing else is at the bottom of all such endeavors but the inexhaustible attempt which is always venturing on new paths, to sell words for thoughts, and by means of new expressions, or expressions used in a new sense, turns of phrases and combinations of all kinds, to produce the appearance of intellect in order to compensate for the want of it which is so painfully felt. It is amusing to see how, with this aim in view, first this mannerism and then that is tried; these they intend to represent the mask of intellect: this mask may possibly deceive the inexperienced for a while, until it is recognized as being nothing but a dead mask, when it is laughed at and exchanged for another.

We find a writer of this kind sometimes writing in a dithyrambic style, as if he were intoxicated; at other times, nay, on the very next page, he will be high-sounding, severe, and deeply learned, prolix to the last degree of dulness, and cutting everything very small, like the late Christian Wolf, only in a modern garment. The mask of unintelligibility holds out the longest; this is only in Germany, however, where it was introduced by Fichte, perfected by Schelling, and attained its highest climax finally in Hegel, always with the happiest results. And yet nothing is easier than to write so that no one can understand; on the other hand, nothing is more difficult than to express learned ideas so that everyone must understand them. All the arts I have cited above are superfluous if the writer really possesses any intellect, for it allows a man to show himself as he is and verifies for all time what Horace said: *"Scribendi recte sapere est et principium et fons."*

But this class of authors is like certain workers in metal, who try a hundred different compositions to take the place of gold, which is the only metal that can never have a substitute. On the contrary, there is nothing an author should guard against more than the apparent endeavor to show more intellect than he has; because this rouses the suspicion in the reader that he has very little, since a man always affects something, be its nature what it may, that he does not really possess. And this is why it is praise to an author to call him naïve, for it signifies that he may show himself as he is. In general, naïveté attracts, while anything that is unnatural everywhere repels. We also find that every true thinker endeavors to express his thoughts as purely, clearly, definitely, and concisely as ever possible. This is why simplicity has always been looked upon as a token, not only of truth, but also of genius. Style receives its beauty from the thought expressed, while with those writers who only pretend to think it is their thoughts that are said to be fine because of their style. Style is merely the silhouette of thought; and to write in a vague or bad style means a stupid or confused mind.

Hence, the first rule—nay, this in itself is almost sufficient for a good style—is this, that the author should have something to say. Ah! this implies a great deal. The neglect of this rule is a fundamental characteristic of the philosophical, and generally speaking of all the reflective authors in Germany, especially since the time of Fichte. It is obvious that all these writers wish to appear to have something to say, while they have nothing to say. This mannerism was introduced by the pseudo-philosophers of the universities and may be discerned everywhere, even among the first literary notabilities of the age. It is the mother of that forced and vague style which seems to have two, nay, many meanings, as well as of that prolix and ponderous style, *le stile empesé;* and of that no less useless bombastic style, and finally of that mode of concealing the most awful poverty of thought under a babble of inexhaustible chatter that resembles a clacking mill and is just as stupefying: one may read for hours together without getting hold of a single clearly defined and definite idea. The "Halleschen," afterwards called the "Deutschen Jahrbücher," furnishes almost throughout excellent examples of this style of writing. The Germans, by the way, from force of habit read page after page of all kinds of such verbiage without getting any definite idea of what the author really means: they think it all very proper and do not discover that he is writing merely for the sake of writing. On the other hand, a good author who is rich in ideas soon gains the reader's credit of having really and truly something to say; and this gives the intelligent reader patience to follow him attentively. An author of this kind will always express himself in the simplest and most direct manner, for the very reason that he really has something to say; because he wishes to awaken in the reader the same idea he has in his own mind and no other. Accordingly he will be able to say with Boileau—

" *Ma pensée au grand jour partout s'offre et s'expose,*
Et mon vers, bien ou mal, dit toujours quelque chose ; "

while of those previously described writers it may be said, in the words of the same poet, " *et qui parlant beaucoup ne disent jamais rien.*" It is also a characteristic of such writers to avoid, if it is possible, expressing themselves definitely, so that they may be always able in case of need to get out of a difficulty; this is why they always choose the more abstract expressions:

while people of intellect choose the more concrete; because the latter bring the matter closer to view, which is the source of all evidence. This preference for abstract expressions may be confirmed by numerous examples: a specially ridiculous example is the following. Throughout German literature of the last ten years we find " to condition " almost everywhere used in place of " to cause " or " to effect." Since it is more abstract and indefinite it says less than it implies, and consequently leaves a little back door open to please those whose secret consciousness of their own incapacity inspires them with a continual fear of all definite expressions. While with other people it is merely the effect of that national tendency to immediately imitate everything that is stupid in literature and wicked in life; this is shown in either case by the quick way in which it spreads. The Englishman depends on his own judgment both in what he writes and what he does, but this applies less to the German than to any other nation. In consequence of the state of things referred to, the words " to cause " and " to effect " have almost entirely disappeared from the literature of the last ten years, and people everywhere talk of " to condition." The fact is worth mentioning because it is characteristically ridiculous. Every-day authors are only half conscious when they write, a fact which accounts for their want of intellect and the tediousness of their writings; they do not really themselves understand the meaning of their own words, because they take ready-made words and learn them. Hence they combine whole phrases more than words—*phrases banales*. This accounts for that obviously characteristic want of clearly defined thought; in fact, they lack the die that stamps their thoughts, they have no clear thought of their own; in place of it we find an indefinite, obscure interweaving of words, current phrases, worn-out terms of speech, and fashionable expressions. The result is that their foggy kind or writing is like print that has been done with old type. On the other hand, intelligent people really speak to us in their writings, and this is why they are able to both move and entertain us. It is only intelligent writers who place individual words together with a full consciousness of their use and select them with deliberation. Hence their style of writing bears the same relation to that of those authors described above, as a picture that is really painted does to one that has been executed with stencil. In the first instance every word, just as every stroke of the brush, has some special significance, while in the other everything is done mechanically. The same distinction may be observed in music. For it is the omnipresence of intellect that always and everywhere characterizes the works of the genius; and analogous to this is Lichtenberg's observation, namely, that Garrick's soul was omnipresent in all the muscles of his body. With regard to the tediousness of the writings referred to above, it is to be observed in general that there are two kinds of tediousness—an objective and a subjective. The objective form of tediousness springs from the deficiency of which we have been speaking—that is to say, where the author has no perfectly clear thought or knowledge to communicate. For if a writer possesses any clear thought or knowledge it will be his aim to communicate it, and he will work with this end in view; consequently the ideas he furnishes are everywhere clearly defined, so that he is neither diffuse, unmeaning, nor confused, and consequently not tedious. Even if his fundamental idea is wrong, yet in such a case it will be clearly thought out and well pondered; in other words, it is at least formally correct, and the writing is always of some value. While, for the same reason, a work that is objectively tedious is at all times without value. Again, subjective tediousness is merely relative: this is because the reader is not interested in the subject of the work, and that what he takes an interest in is of a very limited nature. The most excellent work may therefore be tedious subjectively to this or that person, just as, *vice versa,* the worst work may be subjectively diverting to this or that person: because he is interested in either the subject or the writer of the book.

It would be of general service to German authors if they discerned that while a man should, if possible, think like a great mind, he should speak the same language as every other person. Men should use common words to say uncommon things, but they do the reverse. We find them trying to envelop trivial ideas in grand words and to dress their very ordinary thoughts in the most extraordinary expressions and the most outlandish, artificial, and rarest phrases. Their sentences perpetually stalk about on stilts. With regard to their delight in bombast, and to their writing generally in a grand, puffed-up, unreal, hyperbolical, and acrobatic style, their prototype is Pistol, who was once impatiently requested by Falstaff, his friend, to " say what you have to say, like a man of this world!" [1]

There is no expression in the German language exactly corresponding to *stile empesé;* but the thing itself is all the more prevalent. When combined with unnaturalness it is in works what affected gravity, grandness, and unnaturalness are in social intercourse; and it is just as intolerable. Poverty of intellect is fond of wearing this dress; just as stupid people in every-day life are fond of assuming gravity and formality.

A man who writes in this *preziös* style is like a person who dresses himself up to avoid being mistaken for or confounded with the mob; a danger which a gentleman, even in his worst clothes, does not run. Hence just as a plebeian is recognized by a certain display in his dress and his *tiré à quatre épingles,* so is an ordinary writer recognized by his style.

If a man has something to say that is worth saying, he need not envelop it in affected expressions, involved phrases, and enigmatical innuendoes; but he may rest assured that by expressing himself in a simple, clear, and naïve manner he will not fail to produce the right effect. A man who makes use of such artifices as have been alluded to betrays his poverty of ideas, mind, and knowledge.

Nevertheless, it is a mistake to attempt to write exactly as one speaks. Every style of writing should bear a certain trace of relationship with the monumental style, which is, indeed, the ancestor of all styles; so that to write as one speaks is just as faulty as to do the reverse, that is to say, to try and speak as one writes. This makes the author pedantic, and at the same time difficult to understand.

Obscurity and vagueness of expression are at all times and everywhere a very bad sign. In ninety-nine cases out of a hundred they arise from vagueness of thought, which, in its turn, is almost always fundamentally discordant, inconsistent, and therefore wrong. When a right thought springs up in the mind it strives after clearness of expression, and it soon attains it, for clear thought easily finds its appropriate expression. A man who is capable of thinking can express himself at all times in clear, comprehensible, and unambiguous words. Those

[1] [Schopenhauer here gives an example of this bombastic style which would be of little interest to English readers.]

writers who construct difficult, obscure, involved, and ambiguous phrases most certainly do not rightly know what it is they wish to say: they have only a dull consciousness of it, which is still struggling to put itself into thought; they also often wish to conceal from themselves and other people that in reality they have nothing to say. Like Fichte, Schelling, and Hegel, they wish to appear to know what they do not know, to think what they do not think, and to say what they do not say.

Will a man, then, who has something real to impart endeavor to say it in a clear or an indistinct way? Quintilian has already said, "*plerumque accidit ut faciliora sint ad intelligendum et lucidiora multo, quæ a doctissimo quoque dicuntur. . . . Erit ergo etiam obscurior, quo quisque deterior.*"

A man's way of expressing himself should not be enigmatical, but he should know whether he has something to say or whether he has not. It is an uncertainty of expression which makes German writers so dull. The only exceptional cases are those where a man wishes to express something that is in some respect of an illicit nature. As anything that is far-fetched generally produces the reverse of what the writer has aimed at, so do words serve to make thought comprehensible; but only up to a certain point. If words are piled up beyond this point they make the thought that is being communicated more and more obscure. To hit that point is the problem of style and a matter of discernment; for every superfluous word prevents its purpose being carried out. Voltaire means this when he says: "*L'adjectif est l'ennemi du substantif.*" (But, truly, many authors try to hide their poverty of thought under a superfluity of words.)

Accordingly, all prolixity and all binding together of unmeaning observations that are not worth reading should be avoided. A writer must be sparing with the reader's time, concentration, and patience; in this way he makes him believe that what he has before him is worth his careful reading, and will repay the trouble he has spent upon it. It is always better to leave out something that is good than to write down something that is not worth saying. Hesiod's πλέον ἥμισυ παντός [2] finds its right application. In fact, not to say everything! *Le secret pour être ennuyeux, c'est de tout dire.* Therefore, if

[2] "Opera et dies," v. 40.

possible, the quintessence only! the chief matter only! nothing that the reader would think for himself. The use of many words in order to express little thought is everywhere the infallible sign of mediocrity; while to clothe much thought in a few words is the infallible sign of distinguished minds.

Truth that is naked is the most beautiful, and the simpler its expression the deeper is the impression it makes; this is partly because it gets unobstructed hold of the hearer's mind without his being distracted by secondary thoughts, and partly because he feels that here he is not being corrupted or deceived by the arts of rhetoric, but that the whole effect is got from the thing itself. For instance, what declamation on the emptiness of human existence could be more impressive than Job's: "*Homo, natus de muliere, brevi vivit tempore, repletus multis miseriis, qui, tanquam flos, egreditur et conteritur, et fugit velut umbra.*" It is for this very reason that the naïve poetry of Goethe is so incomparably greater than the rhetorical of Schiller. This is also why many folk-songs have so great an effect upon us. An author should guard against using all unnecessary rhetorical adornment, all useless amplification, and in general, just as in architecture he should guard against an excess of decoration, all superfluity of expression—in other words, he must aim at chastity of style. Everything that is redundant has a harmful effect. The law of simplicity and naïveté applies to all fine art, for it is compatible with what is most sublime.

True brevity of expression consists in a man only saying what is worth saying, while avoiding all diffuse explanations of things which everyone can think out for himself; that is, it consists in his correctly distinguishing between what is necessary and what is superfluous. On the other hand, one should never sacrifice clearness, to say nothing of grammar, for the sake of being brief. To impoverish the expression of a thought, or to obscure or spoil the meaning of a period for the sake of using fewer words shows a lamentable want of judgment. And this is precisely what that false brevity nowadays in vogue is trying to do, for writers not only leave out words that are to the purpose, but even grammatical and logical essentials.

Subjectivity, which is an error of style in German literature, is, through the deteriorated condition of literature and neglect of old languages, becoming more common. By subjectivity I mean when a writer thinks it sufficient for himself to know what he means and wants to say, and it is left to the reader to discover what is meant. Without troubling himself about his reader, he writes as if he were holding a monologue; whereas it should be a dialogue, and, moreover, a dialogue in which he must express himself all the more clearly as the questions of the reader cannot be heard. And it is for this very reason that style should not be subjective, but objective, and for it to be objective the words must be written in such a way as to directly compel the reader to think precisely the same as the author thought. This will only be the case when the author has borne in mind that thoughts, inasmuch as they follow the law of gravity, pass more easily from head to paper than from paper to head. Therefore the journey from paper to head must be helped by every means at his command. When he does this his words have a purely objective effect, like that of a completed oil painting; while the subjective style is not much more certain in its effect than spots on the wall, and it is only the man whose fantasy is accidentally aroused by them that sees figures; other people only see blurs. The difference referred to applies to every style of writing as a whole, and it is also often met with in particular instances; for example, I read in a book that has just been published: "I have not written to increase the number of existing books." This means exactly the opposite of what the writer had in view, and is nonsense into the bargain.

A man who writes carelessly at once proves that he himself puts no great value on his own thoughts. For it is only by being convinced of the truth and importance of our thoughts that there arises in us the inspiration necessary for the inexhaustible patience to discover the clearest, finest, and most powerful expression for them; just as one puts holy relics or priceless works of art in silvern or golden receptacles. It was for this reason that the old writers—whose thoughts, expressed in their own words, have lasted for thousands of years and hence bear the honored title of classics—wrote with universal care. Plato, indeed, is said to have written the introduction to his "Republic" seven times with different modifications. On the other hand, the Germans are conspicuous above all other nations for neglect of style in writing, as they are for neglect of dress, both kinds of slovenliness which have their source in the German national character. Just as neglect of dress betrays contempt for the society in which a man moves, so does a hasty, careless, and bad style show shocking disrespect for the reader, who then rightly punishes it by not reading the book.

THE ACADEMY OF SYLLOGRAPHS

—

BY

GIACOMO LEOPARDI

GIACOMO LEOPARDI

1798—1837

Giacomo Leopardi was born in 1798 in the ancestral mansion of his family at Recanati, a small town not far from Ancona, in Italy. Both his parents were of ancient and patrician lineage, but of impaired worldly fortunes. They appear never to have understood their gifted son, and much of his lifelong misery was due to their narrowness and severity. During his boyhood Leopardi was taught by the two priests of his village, but at fourteen he had mastered all they could teach him and had begun to absorb a vast store of erudition by omnivorous reading in his father's library. The amazing industry with which he read was only equalled by his tenacity of memory. While in his teens he had mastered Latin, Greek, English, French, and Spanish, and had acquired a considerable knowledge of Hebrew. All this was the more remarkable, as he was largely self-taught. In 1814 he wrote a revision of Porphyry's "Life of Plotinus," with a commentary which was found serviceable by the ablest scholars of the day. In 1815 he wrote a treatise on "The Popular Errors of the Ancients," in which he displayed a profound erudition. During the next few years he wrote many volumes of philological research and criticism, but his constitution, never strong, broke down under the excessive strain this work involved. From the age of seventeen he was a hopeless invalid; at times even his eyesight failed him, while his mental tortures were terribly acute. His parents, meanwhile, were deaf to his appeals to be permitted to leave Recanati, until, goaded to madness, he actually ran away. He was soon brought back, and fell for a time into a stupor of despair. At length, in 1822, his father permitted him to visit Rome, where he was cordially received by men of letters. The next ten years he devoted to poetry and philosophy, residing for varying periods at Bologna, Pisa, Florence, Milan, and Recanati. In 1830 he was elected an academician of the Accademia della Crusca. Soon afterwards he settled in Naples, where some of his best works were written. For a time his health improved; but he suffered a relapse in 1836, and died the following year. His grave is not far from the reputed resting-place of Vergil, in a suburb of Naples.

As a poet, Leopardi is universally recoginzed as one of the greatest of modern Italy. Some of his odes rank among the most finished in all literature, and all his poetical writings are distinguished for a felicity of expression and a perfection in style that raise them to the rank of masterpieces. His most celebrated prose works are his "Dialogues" and "Thoughts." "The Academy of Syllographs" is a representative example of his work as an essayist and gives an excellent idea of his prose style, which is noted for its simplicity and chasteness, and is on a par with the excellence of his poetry.

THE ACADEMY OF SYLLOGRAPHS

THE Academy of Syllographs, ever mindful of the primary aim of its constitution, and having always at heart the promotion of the public good, has come to the conclusion that it could not more effectually conduce to this end than by aiding in the development of the distinguishing tendencies of what an illustrious poet has characterized as the happy age in which we live.

For this reason it has diligently diagnosed the genius of the present time, and after prolonged and searching investigation it has arrived at the conviction that the present age ought to be characterized as preëminently the age of machines. And this not only because the men of to-day live and move more mechanically than did those of any former period, but also by reason of the infinite number of mechanical contrivances continually being invented, and daily being applied to so many various purposes, that nowadays it may almost be said that human affairs and all the operations of life are governed and regulated, not by men at all, but by machines.

This feature of the age is hailed by the Academy with peculiar satisfaction, not only in view of the manifest general convenience which flows from it, but also for two special reasons of a most important character, though not generally recognized by society. In the first place, the Academy feels confident that in course of time the agency of mechanism may be so extended as to embrace not only the material but the moral world; and that, just as mechanical inventions now protect us from lightning and other atmospherical disturbances, so, in time, some sort of apparatus may be invented calculated to shield us from envy, calumny, perfidy, and fraud; some species of moral lightning-conductors, so to speak, which may protect us from the effects of egotism, from the dominion of mediocrity, from the arrogance of bloated imbecility, from the ribaldry of the base, from the cynical pessimism of pedants, from the indifferentism engendered by over-culture, and from numerous other such-like inconveniences, which of late have become as difficult to ward off as formerly were the lightnings and storms of the physical world.

The next consideration just referred to is this; and it is one of paramount importance. It is well known that philosophers have come to despair of remedying the manifold defects of humanity, and are convinced that it would be more difficult to amend these than it would be to recast things on an entirely fresh basis, and to substitute an entirely fresh agency as the motive power of life. The Academy of Syllographs, concurring in this opinion, hold that it would be in the highest degree expedient that men should retire as far as possible from the conduct of the business of the world, and should gradually give place to mechanical agency for the direction of human affairs. Accordingly, resolved to contribute as far as lies in its power to this consummation, it has determined to offer three prizes to be awarded to the persons who shall invent the best examples of the three machines now to be described.

The scope and object of the first of these automata shall be to represent the person and discharge the functions of a friend who shall not calumniate or jeer at his absent associate; who shall not fail to take his part when he hears him censured or ridiculed; who shall not prefer a reputation for wit, and the applause of men, to his duty to friendship; who shall never, from love of gossip or mere ostentation of superior knowledge, divulge a secret committed to his keeping; who shall not abuse the intimacy or confidence of his fellow in order to supplant or surpass him; who shall harbor no envy against his friend; who shall guard his interests and help to repair his losses, and shall be prompt to answer his call, and minister to his needs more substantially than by empty professions.

In the construction of this piece of mechanism it will be well to study, among other things, the treatise on friendship by Cicero, as well as that of Madame de Lambert. The Academy is of opinion that the manufacture of such a machine ought not to prove impracticable or even particularly difficult, for, besides the automata of Regiomontanus and Vaucanson, there was at one time exhibited in London a mechanical figure which drew portraits, and wrote to dictation; while there have been more than one example of such machines capable of playing at chess. Now, in the opinion of many philosophers human life is but a game; nay, some hold that it is more shallow and more frivolous than many other games, and that the principles of chess, for example, are more in accordance with reason, and that its various moves are more governed by wisdom, than are the actions of mankind; while we have it on the authority of Pindar that human action is no more substantial than the shadow of a dream; and this being so, the intelligence of an automaton ought to prove quite equal to the discharge of the functions which have just been described.

As to power of speech, it seems unreasonable to doubt that men should have the power of communicating it to machines constructed by themselves, seeing that this may be said to have been established by sundry precedents, such, for example, as in the case of the statue of Memnon, and of the human head manufactured by Albertus Magnus, which actually became so loquacious that Saint Thomas Aquinas, losing all patience with it, smashed it to pieces. Then, too, there was the instance of the parrot of Nevers, though *it* was a living creature; but if it could be taught to converse reasonably, how much more may it be supposed that a machine devised by the mind of man, and constructed by his hands, should do as much; while it would have the advantage that it might be made less garrulous than the parrot of Nevers or the head of Albertus, and therefore it need not irritate its acquaintances and provoke them to smash it.

The inventor of the best example of such a machine shall be decorated with a gold medallion of four hundred zecchins in weight, bearing on its face the images of Pylades and Orestes, and on the reverse the name of the successful competitor, surrounded by the legend, *First Realizer of the Fables of Antiquity.*

The second machine called for by the Academy is to be an artificial steam man, so constructed and regulated as to perform virtuous and magnanimous actions. The Academy is of opinion that in the absence of all other adequate motive power to that end, the properties of steam might prove effective to inspire an automaton, and direct it to the attainment of virtue and true glory. The inventor who shall undertake the construction of such a machine should study the poets and the writers of romance, who will best guide him as to the qualities and functions most essential to such a piece of mechanism. The prize shall be a gold medal weighing four hundred and fifty zecchins, bearing on its obverse a figure symbolical of the golden age, and on its reverse the name of the inventor, with the following inscription borrowed from the fourth eclogue of Vergil:

*"Quo Ferrea Primum
Desinet Ac Toto Surget Gens Aurea Mundo."*

The third automaton should be so constituted as to perform the duties of woman such as she was conceived by the Count Baldassar Castiglione, and described by him in his treatise entitled "The Courtier," as well as by other writers in other works on the subject, which will be readily found, and which, as well as that of the count, will have to be carefully consulted and followed. The construction of a machine of this nature, too, ought not to appear impossible to the inventors of our time, when they reflect on the fact that in the most ancient times, and times destitute of science, Pygmalion was able to fabricate for himself, with his own hands, a wife of such rare gifts that she has never since been equalled down to the present day. The successful inventor of this machine shall be rewarded with a gold medal weighing five hundred zecchins, bearing on one face the figure of the Arabian Phœnix of Metastasio, couched on a tree of a European species, while its other side will bear the name of the inventor, with the title, *Inventor of Faithful Women and of Conjugal Happiness.*

Finally, the Academy has resolved that the funds necessary to defray the expenses incidental to this competition shall be supplemented by all that was found in the purse of Diogenes, its first secretary, together with one of the three golden asses which were the property of three of its former members—namely, Apuleius, Firenzuola, and Machiavelli, but which came into the possession of the Academy by the last wills and testaments of the aforementioned, as duly recorded in its minutes.

ABOUT CATHERINE DE MEDICI

BY

HONORÉ DE BALZAC

HONORÉ DE BALZAC

1799—1850

Born at Tours in 1799, Honoré de Balzac was at first destined for his father's profession, the law. He attended the College of Vendôme, but while there he devoted far more time to reading fiction and mystic books than to the law. He then attended the law school at the Sorbonne, and studied also in one or two law offices, where he learned much about the chicanery of disreputable practice. At the age of twenty he gave up the study of law altogether and devoted himself to literature, for which he incurred for a time the disfavor of his father. Ten years of poverty followed, during which he found "three sous for bread, two for milk, and three for fuel" sufficed for his daily subsistence. In spite of his untiring activity, however, Balzac produced nothing during these years that received or deserved recognition.

It was not until 1829 that his genius found its true expression. In that year he wrote his first successful book, "Le dernier Chouan," and in the following year he began the amazing series of volumes that followed one after another in rapid succession down to the year of his death. This series he has been pleased to call the "Comédie Humaine." His manner of working was extraordinary. It is said of him that he usually retired at six in the evening, rising to begin work at midnight, and, stimulated by copious draughts of black coffee, worked without intermission till noon. Sometimes he would shut himself up for months with his manuscripts, seeing no one except his printer. Then again for months he would disappear, studying at first hand the life he sought to portray in his pages, in all its varied forms and surroundings. He had a mania for speculative enterprises, prompted by the desire, no doubt, to be relieved of the anxiety of providing immediate necessities. For the greater part of his life, however, he was burdened with a mountain of debt. At last, on March 14, 1850, he married a wealthy Russian lady, and now a rest seemed possible. His debts were paid, and he now looked forward to some years of ease and contentment. His iron constitution, sapped by overwork, however, succumbed suddenly, and he died six months after his marriage on August 18, 1850.

It is impossible to give in brief space an adequate estimate of the literary genius of Balzac. In his writings he scales every height and sounds every depth of human character. His own ambition was "by infinite patience and courage, to compose for the France of the nineteenth century that history of morals which the old civilizations of Rome, Athens, Memphis, and India have left untold." He aimed to give a complete picture of human life of his day in all its phases. "The administration of government, the church, the army, the judiciary, the aristocracy, the bourgeoisie, the proletariat, the peasantry; artists, journalists, men of letters, actors, shopkeepers of every station, criminals," all play their part in his vast "Human Comedy." This work he left in a sense incomplete, for, when death ended his career, he had plans in his fertile brain for more than thirty additional novels. But as it stands it is a lasting monument to his genius. Of his novels the most powerful are "Le Père Goriot," "Eugénie Grandet," "La Cousine Bette," "La peau de chagrin," "La recherche de l'absolu," "Seraphita," and "Le médecin de campagne." His short stories, some of which are of the highest literary merit, deserve mention here. Balzac's style is at times clumsy and inelastic. He has succeeded nevertheless in giving life to the two thousand characters that move in his works. And his great genius, in leaving us what is without question the greatest and most comprehensive portrayal of human life and passion ever attempted, cannot be disputed.

ABOUT CATHERINE DE MEDICI

WHEN men of learning are struck by a historical blunder, and try to correct it, "Paradox!" is generally the cry; but to those who thoroughly examine the history of modern times it is evident that historians are privileged liars, who lend their pen to popular beliefs, exactly as most of the newspapers of the day express nothing but the opinions of their readers.[1]

Historical independence of thought has been far less conspicuous among lay writers than among the priesthood. The purest light thrown on history has come from the Benedictines, one of the glories of France—so long, that is to say, as the interests of the monastic orders are not in question. Since the middle of the eighteenth century some great and learned controversialists have arisen who, struck by the need for rectifying certain popular errors to which historians have lent credit, have published some remarkable works. Thus Monsieur Launoy, nicknamed the Evicter of Saints, made ruthless war on certain saints who have sneaked into the Church Calendar. Thus the rivals of the Benedictines, the too little known members of the *Académie des Inscriptions et Belles-lettres,* began their *mémoires,* their studious notes, full of patience, erudition, and logic, on certain obscure passages of history. Thus Voltaire, with an unfortunate bias, and sadly perverted passions, often brought the light of his intellect to bear on historical prejudices. Diderot, with this end in view, began a book—much too long—on a period of the history of Imperial Rome. But for the French Revolution, criticism, as applied to history, might perhaps have laid up the materials for a good and true history of France, for which evidence had long been amassed by the great French Benedictines. Louis XVI, a man of clear mind, himself translated the English work which so much agitated

---

[1] This essay was written as an introduction to Balzac's three historical studies which were written in the form of historical novelettes and published under the general title of "Catherine de Medicis Expliquée."

the last century, in which Walpole tried to explain the career of Richard III.

How is it that persons so famous as kings and queens, so important as generals of great armies, become objects of aversion or derision? Half the world hesitates between the song on Marlborough and the history of England, as they do between popular tradition and history as concerning Charles IX.

At all periods when great battles are fought between the masses and the authorities the populace creates an *ogresque* figure—to coin a word for the sake of its exactitude. Thus in our own time, but for the "Memorials of Saint Helena," and the controversies of Royalists and Bonapartists, there was scarcely a chance but that Napoleon would have been misunderstood. Another Abbé de Pradt or two, a few more newspaper articles, and Napoleon from an emperor would have become an ogre.

How is error propagated and accredited? The mystery is accomplished under our eyes without our discerning the process. No one suspects how greatly printing has helped to give body both to the envy which attends persons in high places, and to the popular irony which sums up the converse view of every great historical fact. For instance, every bad horse in France that needs flogging is called after the Prince de Polignac; and so who knows what opinion the future may hold as to the Prince de Polignac's *coup d'état?* In consequence of a caprice of Shakespeare's—a stroke of revenge perhaps, like that of Beaumarchais on Bergasse (Begearss)—Falstaff, in England, is a type of the grotesque; his name raises a laugh, he is the King of Buffoons. Now, instead of being enormously fat, ridiculously amorous, vain, old, drunken, and a corrupter of youth, Falstaff was one of the most important figures of his time, a Knight of the Garter, holding high command. At the date of Henry V's accession Falstaff was at most four-and-thirty. This general, who distinguished himself at the battle of Agincourt, where he took the Duc d'Alençon prisoner, in 1420 took the town of Montereau, which was stoutly defended. Finally, under Henry VI, he beat ten thousand Frenchmen with fifteen hundred men who were dropping with fatigue and hunger. So much for valor!

If we turn to literature, Rabelais, among the French, a sober man who drank nothing but water, is thought of as a lover of good cheer and a persistent sot. Hundreds of absurd stories have been coined concerning the author of one of the finest books in French literature, "Pantagruel."

Aretino, Titian's friend, and the Voltaire of his day, is now credited with a reputation, in complete antagonism with his works and character, which he acquired by his over-free wit, characteristic of the writings of an age when gross jests were held in honor, and queens and cardinals indited tales which are now considered licentious. Instances might be infinitely multiplied.

In France, and at the most important period of our history, Catherine De Medici has suffered more from popular error than any other woman, unless it be Brunehaut or Frédégonde; while Marie De Medici, whose every action was prejudicial to France, has escaped the disgrace that should cover her name. Marie dissipated the treasure amassed by Henri IV; she never purged herself of the suspicion that she was cognizant of his murder; Epernon, who had long known Ravaillac, and who did not parry his blow, was in favor with the queen; she compelled her son to banish her from France, where she was fostering the rebellion of her other son, Gaston; and Richelieu's triumph over her on the *Journée des Dupes* was due solely to the Cardinal's revealing to Louis XIII certain documents secreted after the death of Henry IV.

Catherine De Medici, on the contrary, saved the throne of France, she maintained the royal authority under circumstances to which more than one great prince would have succumbed. Face to face with such leaders of the factions and ambitions of the Houses of Guise and of Bourbon as the two Cardinals de Lorraine and the two "Balafrés," the two Princes de Condé, Queen Jeanne d'Albret, Henri IV, the Connétable de Montmorency, Calvin, the Colignys, and Théodore de Bèze, she was forced to put forth the rarest fine qualities, the most essential gifts of statesmanship, under the fire of the Calvinist press. These, at any rate, are indisputable facts. And to the student who digs deep into the history of the sixteenth century in France, the figure of Catherine De Medici stands out as that of a great king.

When once calumnies are undermined by facts laboriously

brought to light from under the contradictions of pamphlets and false anecdotes, everything is explained to the glory of this wonderful woman, who had none of the weakness of her sex, who lived chaste in the midst of the gallantries of the most licentious Court in Europe, and who, notwithstanding her lack of money, erected noble buildings, as if to make good the losses caused by the destructive Calvinists, who injured art as deeply as they did the body politic.

Hemmed in between a race of princes who proclaimed themselves the heirs of Charlemagne, and a factious younger branch that was eager to bury the Connétable de Bourbon's treason under the throne; obliged, too, to fight down a heresy on the verge of devouring the monarchy, without friends, and aware of treachery in the chiefs of the Catholic party and of republicanism in the Calvinists, Catherine used the most dangerous but the surest of political weapons—craft. She determined to deceive by turns the party that was anxious to secure the downfall of the House of Valois, the Bourbons who aimed at the Crown, and the Reformers—the Radicals of that day, who dreamed of an impossible republic, like those of our own day, who, however, have nothing to reform. Indeed, so long as she lived, the Valois sat on the throne. The great De Thou understood the worth of this woman when he exclaimed, on hearing of her death:

"It is not a woman, it is royalty that dies in her!"

Catherine had, in fact, the sense of royalty in the highest degree, and she defended it with admirable courage and persistency. The reproaches flung at her by Calvinist writers are indeed her glory; she earned them solely by her triumphs. And how was she to triumph but by cunning? Here lies the whole question.

As to violence—that method bears on one of the most hotly disputed points of policy, which, in recent days, has been answered here, on the spot where a big stone from Egypt has been placed to wipe out the memory of regicide, and to stand as an emblem of the materialistic policy which now rules us; it was answered at Les Carmes and at the Abbaye; it was answered on the steps of Saint Roch; it was answered in front of the Louvre in 1830, and again by the people against the King, as it has since been answered once more by La Fayette's "best of all republics" against the republican rebellion, at Saint-Merri and the Rue Transnonnain.

Every power, whether legitimate or illegitimate, must defend itself when it is attacked; but, strange to say, while the people is heroic when it triumphs over the nobility, the authorities are murderers when they oppose the people! And, finally, if after their appeal to force they succumb, they are regarded as effete idiots. The present Government (1840) will try to save itself, by two laws, from the same evil as attacked Charles X, and which he tried to scotch by two decrees. Is not this a bitter mockery? May those in power meet cunning with cunning? Ought they to kill those who try to kill them?

The massacres of the Revolution are the reply to the massacre of Saint-Bartholomew. The People, being King, did by the nobility and the King as the King and the nobility did by the rebels in the sixteenth century. And popular writers, who know full well that, under similar conditions, the people would do the same again, are inexcusable when they blame Catherine De Medici and Charles IX.

"All power is a permanent conspiracy," said Casimir Périer, when teaching what power ought to be. We admire the antisocial maxims published by audacious writers; why, then, are social truths received in France with such disfavor when they are boldly stated? This question alone sufficiently accounts for historical mistakes. Apply the solution of this problem to the devastating doctrines which flatter popular passion, and to the conservative doctrines which would repress the ferocious or foolish attempts of the populace, and you will see the reason why certain personages are popular or unpopular. Laubardemont and Laffemas, like some people now living, were devoted to the maintenance of the power they believed in. Soldiers and judges, they obeyed a royal authority. D'Orthez, in our day, would be discharged from office for misinterpreting orders from the ministry, but Charles X left him to govern his province. The power of the masses is accountable to no one; the power of one is obliged to account to its subjects, great and small alike.

Catherine, like Philip II and the Duke of Alva, like the Guises and Cardinal Granvelle, foresaw the future to which the Reformation was dooming Europe. They saw monarchies, religion, and power all overthrown. Catherine, from the cabinet of the French kings, forthwith issued sentence of death on that inquiring spirit which threatened modern society—a sentence which Louis XIV finally carried out. The revocation of the Edict of Nantes was a measure that proved unfortunate, simply in consequence of the irritation Louis XIV had aroused in Europe. At any other time England, Holland, and the German Empire would not have encouraged on their territory French exiles and French rebels.

Why, in these days, refuse to recognize the greatness which the majestic adversary of that most barren heresy derived from the struggle itself? Calvinists have written strongly against Charles IX's stratagems; but travel through France: as you see the ruins of so many fine churches destroyed, and consider the vast breaches made by religious fanatics in the social body; when you learn the revenges they took, while deploring the mischief of individualism—the plague of France to-day, of which the germ lay in the questions of liberty of conscience which they stirred up—you will ask yourself on which side were the barbarians. There are always, as Catherine says "unluckily, in all ages, hypocritical writers ready to bewail two hundred scoundrels killed in due season." Cæsar, who tried to incite the senate to pity for Catiline's party, would very likely have conquered Cicero if he had had newspapers and an Opposition at his service.

Another consideration accounts for Catherine's historical and popular disfavor. In France the Opposition has always been Protestant, because its policy has never been anything but negative; it has inherited the theories of the Lutherans, the Calvinists, and the Protestants on the terrible texts of liberty, tolerance, progress, and philanthropy. The opponents of power spent two centuries in establishing the very doubtful doctrine of free-will. Two more were spent in working out the first corollary of free-will—liberty of conscience. Our age is striving to prove the second—political liberty.

Standing between the fields already traversed and the fields as yet untrodden, Catherine and the Church proclaimed the salutary principle of modern communities, *Una fides, unus Dominus,* but asserting their right of life and death over all innovators. Even if she had been conquered, succeeding times have shown that Catherine was right. The outcome of free-will, religious liberty, and political liberty (note, this does not mean *civil* liberty) is France as we now see it.

And what is France in 1840? A country exclusively absorbed in material interests, devoid of patriotism, devoid of conscience; where authority is powerless; where electoral rights, the fruit of free-will and political liberty, raise none but mediocrities; where brute force is necessary to oppose the violence of the populace; where discussion, brought to bear on the smallest matter, checks every action of the body politic; and where individualism—the odious result of the indefinite subdivision of property, which destroys family cohesion—will devour everything, even the nation, which sheer selfishness will some day lay open to invasion. Men will say, "Why not the Czar?" as they now say, "Why not the Duc d'Orléans?" We do not care for many things even now; fifty years hence we shall care for nothing.

Therefore, according to Catherine—and according to all who wish to see society soundly organized—man as a social unit, as a subject, has no free-will, has no right to accept the dogma of liberty of conscience, or to have political liberty. Still, as no community can subsist without some guarantee given to the subject against the sovereign, the subject derives from that certain liberties under restrictions. Liberty—no, but liberties—yes; well defined and circumscribed liberties. This is in the nature of things. For instance, it is beyond human power to fetter freedom of thought; and no sovereign may ever tamper with money.

The great politicians who have failed in this long contest—it has gone on for five centuries—have allowed their subjects wide liberties; but they never recognize their liberty to publish anti-social opinions, nor the unlimited freedom of the subject. To them the words *subject* and *free* are, politically speaking, a contradiction in terms; and, in the same way, the statement that all citizens are equal is pure nonsense, and contradicted by Nature every hour. To acknowledge the need for religion, the need for authority, and at the same time to leave all men at liberty to deny religion, to attack its services, to oppose the exercise of authority by the public and published expression of opinion, is an impossibility such as the Catholics of the sixteenth century would have nothing to say to. Alas! the triumph of Calvinism will cost France more yet than it has ever done; for the sects of to-day—religious, political, humanitarian, and levelling—are the train of Calvinism; and when we see the blunders of those in power, their contempt for intelligence, their devotion to those material interests in which they seek support, and which are the most delusive of all props, unless by the special aid of Providence the genius of destruction must certainly win the day from the genius of conservatism. The attacking forces, who have nothing to lose, and everything to win, are thoroughly in agreement; whereas their wealthy opponents refuse to make any sacrifice of money or of self-conceit to secure defenders.

Printing came to the aid of the resistance inaugurated by the Vaudois and the Albigenses. As soon as human thought —no longer condensed, as it had necessarily been in order to preserve the most communicable form—had assumed a multitude of garbs and become the very people, instead of remaining in some sense divinely axiomatic, there were two vast armies to contend with—that of ideas and that of men. Royal power perished in the struggle, and we, in France, at this day are looking on at its last coalition with elements which make it difficult, not to say impossible.

Power is action; the electoral principle is discussion. No political action is possible when discussion is permanently established. So we ought to regard the woman as truly great who foresaw that future, and fought it so bravely. The House of Bourbon was able to succeed to the House of Valois, and owed it to Catherine De Medici that it found that crown to wear. If the second Balafré had been alive it is very doubtful that the Béarnais, strong as he was, could have seized the throne, seeing how dearly it was sold by the Duc de Mayenne and the remnant of the Guise faction. The necessary steps taken by Catherine, who had the deaths of Francis II and Charles IX on her soul—both dying opportunely for her safety —are not, it must be noted, what the Calvinist and modern writers blame her for! Though there was no poisoning, as some serious authors have asserted, there were other not less criminal plots. It is beyond question that she hindered Paré from saving one, and murdered the other morally by inches.

But the swift death of Francis II and the skilfully contrived end of Charles IX did no injury to Calvinist interests. The causes of these two events concerned only the uppermost sphere, and were never suspected by writers or by the lower orders at the time; they were guessed only by De Thou, by L'Hôpital, by men of the highest talents, or the chiefs of the two parties who coveted and clung to the Crown, and who thought such means indispensable.

Though the executions at Amboise were attributed to Catherine, and the Calvinists made that able woman responsible for all the inevitable disasters of the struggle, she must be judged by posterity, like Robespierre at a future date.

And Catherine was cruelly punished for her preference for the Duc d'Anjou, which made her hold her two elder sons so cheap. Henri III having ceased, like all spoilt children, to care for his mother, rushed voluntarily into such debauchery as made him what the mother had made Charles IX, a childless husband, a king without an heir. Unhappily, Catherine's youngest son, the Duc d'Alençon, died—a natural death. The Queen-mother made every effort to control her son's passions, but she did not cure Henri III of his bad habits.

This great Queen's last words summed up her policy, which was indeed so governed by good sense that we see the Cabinets of every country putting it into practice in similar circumstances.

"Well cut, my son," said she, when Henri III came to her, on her death-bed, to announce that the enemy of the throne had been put to death. "Now you must sew up again."

She thus expressed her opinion that the sovereign must make friends with the House of Lorraine, and make it useful, as the only way to hinder the effects of the Guises' hatred, by giving them a hope of circumventing the King. But this indefatigable cunning of the Italian and the woman was incompatible with Henri III's life of debauchery. When once the great mother was dead, the mother of armies *(Mater castrorum)*, the policy of the Valois died too.

Before attempting to write this picture of manners in action, the author patiently and minutely studied the principal reigns of French history, the quarrels of the Burgundians and the Armagnacs, and those of the Guises and the Valois, each in the forefront of a century. His purpose was to write a picturesque history of France. Isabella of Bavaria, Catherine and Marie De Medici, each fills a conspicuous place, dominating from the fourteenth to the seventeenth centuries, and leading up to Louis XIV.

Of these three queens, Catherine was the most interesting and the most beautiful. Hers was a manly rule, while neither of the others had any political genius.

In the course of these studies and comparisons, the author became convinced of Catherine's greatness; by initiating himself into the peculiar difficulties of her position, he discerned how unjust historians, biassed by Protestantism, had been to this queen; and the outcome was three sketches, in which some erroneous opinions of her, of those who were about her, and of the aspect of the times, are combated.

The work is placed among my philosophical studies, because it illustrates the spirit of a period, and plainly shows the influence of opinions.

But before depicting the political arena on which Catherine comes into collision with the two great obstacles in her career, it is necessary to give a short account of her previous life from the point of view of an impartial critic, so that the reader may form a general idea of this large and royal life up to the time when the first part of this narrative opens.

Never at any period, in any country, or in any ruling family was there more contempt felt for legitimacy than by the famous race of the Medici (in French commonly written and pronounced Médicis). They held the same opinion of monarchy as is now professed in Russia: The ruler on whom the crown devolves is the real and legitimate monarch. Mirabeau was justified in saying, " There has been but one *mésalliance* in my family—that with the Medici "; for, notwithstanding the exertions of well-paid genealogists, it is certain that the Medici, till the time of Avérardo De Medici, gonfaloniere of Florence in 1314, were no more than Florentine merchants of great wealth. The first personage of the family who filled a conspicuous place in the history of the great Tuscan Republic was Salvestro De Medici, gonfaloniere in 1378. This Salvestro had two sons—Cosmo and Lorenzo De Medici.

From Cosmo descended Lorenzo the Magnificent, the Duc

de Nemours, the Duke of Urbino, Catherine's father, Pope Leo X, Pope Clement VII, and Alessandro, not indeed Duke of Florence, as he is sometimes called, but Duke *della città di Penna,* a title created by Pope Clement VII as a step towards that of Grand Duke of Tuscany.

Lorenzo's descendants were Lorenzino—the Brutus of Florence—who killed Duke Alessandro; Cosmo, the first Grand Duke, and all the rulers of Florence till 1737, when the family became extinct.

But neither of the two branches—that of Cosmo or that of Lorenzo—succeeded in a direct line, till the time when Marie De Medici's father subjugated Tuscany, and the Grand Dukes inherited in regular succession. Thus Alessandro De Medici, who assumed the title of Duke *della città di Penna,* and whom Lorenzino assassinated, was the son of the Duke of Urbino, Catherine's father, by a Moorish slave. Hence Lorenzino, the legitimate son of Lorenzo, had a double right to kill Alessandro, both as a usurper in the family and as an oppressor of the city. Some historians have indeed supposed that Alessandro was the son of Clement VII. The event that led to the recognition of this illegitimate son as head of the republic was his marriage with Margaret of Austria, the natural daughter of Charles V.

Francesco De Medici, the husband of Bianca Capello, recognized as his son a child of low birth bought by that notorious Venetian lady; and, strange to say, Fernando, succeeding Francesco, upheld the hypothetical rights of this boy. Indeed, this youth, known as Don Antonio De Medici, was recognized by the family during four ducal reigns; he won the affection of all, did them important service, and was universally regretted.

Almost all the early Medici had natural children, whose lot was in every case splendid. The Cardinal Giulio De Medici, Pope Clement VII, was the illegitimate son of Giuliano I. Cardinal Ippolito De Medici was also illegitimate, and he was within an ace of being pope and head of the family. Lorenzo De Medici, Catherine's father, had married, for the second time, in 1518, Madeleine de la Tour d'Auvergne, and died in 1519, a few days after his wife, who died in giving birth to Catherine. Catherine was thus fatherless and motherless as soon as she saw the light. Hence the strange events of her childhood, checkered by the violent struggles of the Florentines, in the attempt to recover their liberty, against the Medici who were determined to govern Florence, but who were so circumspect in their policy that Catherine's father took the title of Duke of Urbino.

At his death the legitimate head of the House of the Medici was Pope Leo X, who appointed Giuliano's illegitimate son, Giulio De Medici, then Cardinal, Governor of Florence. Leo X was Catherine's grand-uncle, and this Cardinal Giulio, afterwards Clement VII, was her *left-handed* uncle only.

During the siege by the Medici to regain possession of Florence, the Republican party, not satisfied with having shut up Catherine, then nine years old, in a convent, after stripping her of all her possessions, proposed to expose her to the fire of the artillery, between two battlements—the suggestion of a certain Battista Cei. Bernardo Castiglione went even further in a council held to determine on some conclusion to the business; he advised that, rather than surrender Catherine to the Pope who demanded it, she should be handed over to the tender mercies of the soldiers. All revolutions of the populace are alike. Catherine's policy, always in favor of royal authority, may have been fostered by such scenes, which an Italian girl of nine could not fail to understand.

Alessandro's promotion, to which Clement VII (himself illegitimate), largely contributed, was no doubt owing partly to the fact of Alessandro's illegitimacy, and to Charles V's affection for his famous natural daughter Margaret. Thus the Pope and the Emperor were moved by similar feelings. At this period Venice was mistress of the commerce of the world; Rome governed its morals; Italy was still supreme, by the poets, the generals, and the statesmen who were her sons. At no other time has any one country had so curious or so various a multitude of men of genius. There were so many that the smallest princelings were superior men. Italy was overflowing with talent, daring, science, poetry, wealth, and gallantry, though rent by constant internal wars, and at all times the arena on which conquerors met to fight for her fairest provinces.

When men are so great they are not afraid to confess their

weakness; hence, no doubt, this golden age for illegitimate sons. And it is but justice to declare that these illegitimate sons of the Medici were ardent for the glory and the advancement of the family, alike in possessions and in power. And as soon as the Duke *della città di Penna,* the Moorish slave's son, was established as Tyrant of Florence, he took up the interest shown by Pope Clement VII for Lorenzo II's daughter, now eleven years of age.

As we study the march of events and of men in that strange sixteenth century, we must never forget that the chief element of political conduct was unremitting craft, destroying in every nature the upright conduct, the squareness which imagination looks for in eminent men. In this, especially, lies Catherine's absolution. This observation, in fact, disposes of all the mean and foolish accusations brought against her by the writers of the reformed faith. It was indeed the golden age of this type of policy, of which Machiavelli and Spinoza formulated the code, and Hobbes and Montesquieu; for the dialogue of "Sylla and Eucrates" expresses Montesquieu's real mind, which he could not set forth in any other form, in consequence of his connection with the Encyclopædists. These principles are to this day the unconfessed morality of every Cabinet where schemes of vast dominion are worked out. In France we were severe on Napoleon when he exerted this Italian genius which was in his blood, and its plots did not always succeed; but Charles V, Catherine, Philip II, Giulio II, would have done just as he did in the affairs of Spain.

At the time when Catherine was born, history, if related from the point of view of honesty, would seem an impossible romance. Charles V, while forced to uphold the Catholic Church against the attacks of Luther, who by threatening the tiara threatened his throne, allowed Rome to be besieged, and kept Pope Clement VII in prison. This same Pope, who had no more bitter foe than Charles V, cringed to him that he might place Alessandro De Medici at Florence, and the Emperor gave his daughter in marriage to the bastard duke. No sooner was he firmly settled than Alessandro, in concert with the Pope, attempted to injure Charles V by an alliance, through Catherine De Medici, with Francis I, and both promised to assist the French king to conquer Italy.

Lorenzino De Medici became Alessandro's boon companion, and pandered to him to get an opportunity of killing him; and Filippo Strozzi, one of the loftiest spirits of that age, regarded this murder with such high esteem that he vowed that each of his sons should marry one of the assassin's daughters. The sons religiously fulfilled the father's pledge at a time when each of them, under Catherine's protection, could have made a splendid alliance; for one was Doria's rival, and the other Marshal of France.

Cosmo De Medici, Alessandro's successor, avenged the death of the Tyrant with great cruelty, and persistently for twelve years, during which his hatred never flagged against the people who had, after all, placed him in power. He was eighteen years of age when he succeeded to the government; his first act was to annul the rights of Alessandro's legitimate sons, at the time when he was avenging Alessandro! Charles V confirmed the dispossession of his grandson, and recognized Cosmo instead of Alessandro's son.

Cosmo, raised to the throne by Cardinal Cibo, at once sent the prelate into exile. Then Cardinal Cibo accused his creature, Cosmo, the first Grand Duke, of having tried to poison Alessandro's son. The Grand Duke, as jealous of his authority as Charles V was of his, abdicated, like the Emperor, in favor of his son Francesco, after ordering the death of Don Garcias, his other son, in revenge for that of Cardinal Giovanni De Medici, whom Garcias had assassinated.

Cosmo I and his son Francesco, who ought to have been devoted, soul and body, to the royal house of France, the only power able to lend them support, were the humble servants of Charles V and Philip II, and consequently the secret, perfidious, and cowardly foes of Catherine De Medici, one of the glories of their race.

Such are the more important features—contradictory and illogical indeed—the dishonest acts, the dark intrigues of the House of the Medici alone. From this sketch some idea may be formed of the other princes of Italy and Europe. Every envoy from Cosmo I to the Court of France had secret instructions to poison Strozzi, Queen Catherine's relation, when he should find him there. Charles V had three ambassadors from Francis I murdered.

It was early in October 1533 that the Duke *della città de Penna* left Florence for Leghorn, accompanied by Catherine De Medici, sole heiress of Lorenzo II. The Duke and the Princess of Florence, for this was the title borne by the girl, now fourteen years of age, left the city with a large following of servants, officials, and secretaries, preceded by men-at-arms, and escorted by a mounted guard. The young Princess as yet knew nothing of her fate, excepting that the Pope and Duke Alessandro were to have an interview at Leghorn; but her uncles, Filippo Strozzi, soon told her of the future that lay before her.

Flippo Strozzi had married Clarissa De Medici, whole sister to Lorenzo De Medici, Duke of Urbino, Catherine's father; but this union, arranged quite as much with a view to converting one of the stoutest champions of the popular cause to the support of Medici as to secure the recall of that then exiled family, never shook the tenets of the rough soldier who was persecuted by his party for having consented to it. In spite of some superficial change of conduct, somewhat overruled by this alliance, he remained faithful to the popular side, and declared against the Medici as soon as he perceived their scheme of subjugating Florence. This great man even refused the offer of a principality from Leo X. At that time Filippo Strozzi was a victim to the policy of the Medici, so shifty in its means, so unvarying in its aim.

After sharing the Pope's misfortunes and captivity, when, surprised by Colonna, he took refuge in the castle of Saint-Angelo, he was given up by Clement VII as a hostage and carried to Naples. As soon as the Pope was free he fell upon his foes, and Strozzi was then near being killed; he was forced to pay an enormous bribe to get out of the prison, where he was closely guarded. As soon as he was at liberty, with the natural trustfulness of an honest man, he was simple enough to appear before Clement VII, who perhaps had flattered himself that he was rid of him. The Pope had so much to be ashamed of that he received Strozzi very ungraciously. Thus Strozzi had very early begun his apprenticeship to the life of disaster, which is that of a man who is honest in politics, and whose conscience will not lend itself to the caprices of opportunity, whose actions are pleasing only to virtue, which is persecuted by all—by the populace, because it withstands their blind passions; by authority, because it resists its usurpations.

The life of these great citizens is a martyrdom, through which they have nothing to support them but the strong voice of conscience, and the sense of social duty, which in all cases dictate their conduct.

There were many such men in the republic of Florence, all as great as Strozzi and as masterly as their adversaries on the Medici side, though beaten by Florentine cunning. In the conspiracy of the Pazzi, what can be finer than the attitude of the head of that house? His trade was immense, and he settled all his accounts with Asia, the Levant, and Europe before carrying out that great plot, to the end that his correspondents should not be the losers if he should fail.

And the history of the rise of the Medici family in the fourteenth and fifteenth centuries is one of the finest that remains unwritten, though men of great genius have attempted it. It is not the history of a republic, or of any particular community or phase of civilization; it is the history of political man, and the eternal history of political developments, that of usurpers and conquerors.

On his return to Florence, Filippo Strozzi restored the ancient form of government, and banished Ippolito De Medici, another bastard, as well as Alessandro, with whom he was now acting. But he then was afraid of the inconstancy of the populace; and as he dreaded Pope Clement's vengeance, he went to take charge of a large commercial house he had at Lyons in correspondence with his bankers at Venice and Rome, in France, and in Spain. A strange fact! These men, who bore the burden of public affairs as well as that of a perennial struggle with the Medici, to say nothing of their squabbles with their own party, could also endure the cares of commerce and speculation, of banking with all its complications, which the vast multiplicity of coinages and frequent forgeries made far more difficult then than now. The word banker is derived from the bench on which they sat, and which served also to ring the gold and silver pieces on. Strozzi found in his adored wife's death a pretext to offer to the Republican party, whose police is always all the more terrible because everybody is a voluntary spy in the name of liberty, which justifies all things.

Filippo's return to Florence happened just at the time when the city was compelled to bow to Alessandro's yoke; but he had previously been to see Pope Clement, with whom matters were so promising that his feelings towards Strozzi had changed. In the moment of triumph the Medici so badly needed such a man as Strozzi, were it only to lend a grace to Alessandro's assumption of dignity, that Clement persuaded him to sit on Alessandro's council, which was about to take oppressive measures, and Filippo had accepted a diploma as senator. But for the last two years and a half—like Seneca and Burrhus with Nero—he had noted the beginnings of tyranny. He found himself the object of distrust to the populace, and so little in favor with the Medici, whom he opposed, that he foresaw a catastrophe. And as soon as he heard from Alessandro of the negotiations for the marriage of Catherine with a French prince, which were perhaps to be concluded at Leghorn, where the contracting powers had agreed to meet, he resolved to go to France and follow the fortunes of his niece, who would need a guardian. Alessandro, delighted to be quit of a man so difficult to manage in what concerned Florence, applauded this decision, which spared him a murder, and advised Strozzi to place himself at the head of Catherine's household.

In point of fact, to dazzle the French Court, the Medici had constituted a brilliant suite for the young girl whom they quite incorrectly styled the Princess of Florence, and who was also called the Duchess of Urbino. The procession, at the head of it Duke Alessandro, Catherine, and Strozzi, consisted of more than a thousand persons, exclusive of the escort and serving-men; and when the last of them were still at the gate of Florence, the foremost had already got beyond the first village outside the town—where straw plait for hats is now made.

It was beginning to be generally known that Catherine was to marry a son of Francis I, but as yet it was no more than a rumor which found confirmation in the country from this triumphant progress from Florence to Leghorn. From the preparations required, Catherine suspected that her marriage was in question, and her uncle revealed to her the abortive scheme of her ambitious family, who had aspired to the hand of the Dauphin. Duke Alessandro still hoped that the Duke of Albany might succeed in changing the determination of the French king, who, though anxious to secure the aid of the Medici in Italy, would only give them the Duc d'Orléans. This narrowness lost Italy to France, and did not hinder Catherine from being Queen.

This Duke of Albany, the son of Alexander Stuart, brother of James III of Scotland, had married Anne de la Tour de Boulogne, sister to Madeleine, Catherine's mother; he was thus her maternal uncle. It was through her mother that Catherine was so rich and connected with so many families; for, strangely enough, Diane de Poitiers, her rival, was also her cousin. Jean de Poitiers, Diane's father, was son of Jeanne de la Tour de Boulogne, the Duchess of Urbino's aunt. Catherine was also related to Mary Stuart, her daughter-in-law.

Catherine was now informed that her dower in money would amount to a hundred thousand ducats. The ducat was a gold piece as large as one of our old louis d'or, but only half as thick. Thus a hundred thousand ducats in those days represented, in consequence of the high value of gold, six millions of francs at the present time, the ducat being worth about twelve francs. The importance of the banking-house of Strozzi, at Lyons, may be imagined from this, as it was his factor there who paid over the twelve hundred thousand livres in gold. The counties of Auvergne and Lauraguais also formed part of Catherine's portion, and the Pope Clement VII made her a gift of a hundred thousand ducats more in jewels, precious stones, and other wedding gifts, to which Duke Alessandro contributed.

On reaching Leghorn, Catherine, still so young, must have been flattered by the extraordinary magnificence displayed by Pope Clement VII, her "left-handed uncle," then the head of the House of Medici, to crush the Court of France. He had arrived at the port in one of his galleys hung with crimson satin trimmed with gold fringe, and covered with an awning of cloth of gold. This barge, of which the decorations had cost nearly twenty thousand ducats, contained several rooms for the use of Henri de France's future bride, furnished with the choicest curiosities the Medici had been able to collect. The oarsmen, magnificently dressed, and the seamen were under the captaincy of a prior of the Order of the Knights of Rhodes. The Pope's household filled three more barges.

The Duke of Albany's galleys, moored by the side of the Pope's, formed, with these, a considerable flotilla.

Duke Alessandro presented the officers of Catherine's household to the Pope, with whom he held a secret conference, introducing to him, as seems probable, Count Sebastian Montecuculi, who had just left the Emperor's service—rather suddenly, it was said—and the two generals, Antonio de Leyva and Fernando Gonzaga. Was there a premeditated plan between these two bastards to make the Duc d'Orléans the Dauphin? What was the reward promised to Count Sebastian Montecuculi, who, before entering the service of Charles V, had studied medicine? History is silent on these points. We shall see indeed in what obscurity the subject is wrapped. It is so great that some serious and conscientious historians have recently recognized Montecuculi's innocence.

Catherine was now officially informed by the Pope himself of the alliance proposed for her. The Duke of Albany had had great difficulty in keeping the King of France to his promise of giving even his second son to Catherine De Medici; and Clement's impatience was so great, he was so much afraid of seeing his schemes upset either by some intrigue on the part of the Emperor, or by the haughtiness of France, where the great nobles cast an evil eye on this union, that he embarked forthwith and made for Marseilles. He arrived there at the end of October, 1533.

In spite of his splendor, the House of the Medici was eclipsed by the sovereign of France. To show to what a pitch these great bankers carried their magnificence, the dozen pieces given by the Pope in the bride's wedding purse consisted of gold medals of inestimable historical interest, for they were at that time unique. But Francis I, who loved festivity and display, distinguished himself on this occasion. The wedding feasts for Henri de Valois and Catherine went on for thirty-four days. It is useless to repeat here details which may be read in every history of Provençe and Marseilles as to this famous meeting between the Pope and the King of France, which was the occasion of a jest of the Duke of Albany's as to the duty of fasting; a retort recorded by Brantôme which vastly amused the Court, and shows the tone of manners at that time.

Though Henri de Valois was but three weeks older than Catherine, the Pope insisted on the immediate consummation of the marriage between these two children, so greatly did he dread the subterfuges of diplomacy and the trickery commonly practised at that period. Many facts show that the history of Catherine De Medici remains to be entirely rewritten; and that, as Napoleon very shrewdly remarked, the history of France should be in one volume only, or in a thousand.

When we compare the conduct of Charles V with that of the King of France during the Pope's stay at Marseilles, it is greatly to the advantage of Francis—as indeed in every instance. Here is a brief report of this meeting as given by a contemporary:

"His Holiness the Pope, having been conducted to the palace prepared for him, as I have said, outside the port, each one withdrew to his chamber until the morrow, when his said Holiness prepared to make his entry. Which was done with great sumptuousness and magnificence, he being set on a throne borne on the shoulders of two men in his pontifical habit, saving only the tiara, while before him went a white palfrey bearing the Holy Sacrament, the said palfrey being led by two men on foot in very fine raiment holding a bridle of white silk. After him came all the cardinals in their habit, riding their pontifical mules, and Madame the Duchess of Urbino in great magnificence, with a goodly company of ladies and gentlemen alike of France and of Italy. And the Pope, with all this company, being come to the place prepared where they should lodge, each one withdrew; and all this was ordered and done without any disorder or tumult. Now, while as the Pope was making his entry, the King crossed the water in his frigate and went to lodge there whence the Pope had come, to the end that on the morrow he might come from thence to pay homage to the Holy Father, as beseemed a most Christian King.

"The King being then ready, set forth to go to the palace where the Pope was, accompanied by the princes of his blood, Monseigneur the Duc de Vendosmois (father of the Vidame de Chartres), the Comte de Saint-Pol, Monsieur de Montmorency, and Monsieur de la Roche-sur-Yon, the Duc de Nemours (brother to the Duke of Savoy, who died at that place), the

Duke of Albany, and many others, counts, barons, and nobles, the Duc de Montmorency being at all times about the King's person. The King, being come to the palace, was received by the Pope and all the College of Cardinals assembled in consistory, with much civility *(fort humainement)*. This done, each one went to the place appointed to him, and the King took with him many cardinals to feast them, and among them Cardinal De Medici, the Pope's nephew, a very magnificent lord with a fine escort. On the morrow those deputed by his Holiness and by the King began to treat of those matters whereon they had met to agree. First of all, they treated of the question of faith, and a bull was read for the repression of heresy, and to hinder things from coming to a greater combustion *(une plus grande combustion)* than they are in already. Then was performed the marriage ceremony between the Duc d'Orléans, the King's second son, and Catherine De Medici, Duchess of Urbino, his Holiness's niece, under conditions the same, or nearly the same, as had been formerly proposed to the Duke of Albany. The said marriage was concluded with great magnificence, and our Holy Father married them.[2] This marriage being thus concluded, the Holy Father held a consistory, wherein he created four cardinals to wait on the King, to wit: Cardinal le Veneur, heretofore Bishop of Lisieux and High Almoner; Cardinal de Boulogne, of the family of La Chambre, half-brother on his mother's side to the Duke of Albany; Cardinal de Châtillon, of the family of Coligny, nephew to the Sire de Montmorency; and Cardinal de Givry."

When Strozzi paid down the marriage portion in the presence of the Court he observed some surprise on the part of the French nobles; they said pretty loudly that it was a small price for such a *mésalliance*—what would they say to-day? Cardinal Ippolito replied:

"Then you are not informed as to your King's secrets. His Holiness consents to bestow on France three pearls of inestimable price—Genoa, Milan, and Naples."

The Pope left Count Sebastian Montecuculi to present himself at the French Court, where he made an offer of his services, complaining of Antonio de Leyva and Fernando Gonzaga, for

[2] At that time in French, as in Italian, the words "marry" and "espouse" were used in a contrary sense to their present meaning. "Marier" was the fact of being married, "épouser" was the priestly function.

which reason he was accepted. Montecuculi was not one of Catherine's household, which was composed entirely of French ladies and gentlemen; for, by a law of the realm which the Pope was rejoiced to see carried out, Catherine was naturalized by letters patent before her marriage. Montecuculi was at first attached to the household of the Queen, Charles V's sister. Then, not long after, he entered the Dauphin's service in the capacity of cup-bearer.

The Duchesse d'Orléans found herself entirely swamped at the Court of Francis I. Her young husband was in love with Diane de Poitiers, who was certainly her equal in point of birth, and a far greater lady. The daughter of the Medici took rank below Queen Eleanor, Charles V's sister, and the Duchesse d'Etampes, whose marriage to the head of the family of De Brosse had given her one of the most powerful positions and highest titles in France. Her aunt, the Duchess of Albany, the Queen of Navarre, the Duchesse de Guise, the Duchesse de Vendôme, the wife of the Connétable, and many other women, by their birth and privileges as well as by their influence in the most sumptuous Court ever held by a French king—not excepting Louis XIV—wholly eclipsed the daughter of the Florentine merchants, who was indeed more illustrious and richer through the Tour de Boulogne family than through her descent from the Medici.

Filippo Strozzi, a republican at heart, regarded his niece's position as so critical and difficult that he felt himself incapable of directing her in the midst of conflicting interests, and deserted her at the end of a year, being indeed recalled to Italy by the death of Clement VII. Catherine's conduct, when we remember that she was but just fifteen, was a marvel of prudence. She very adroitly attached herself to the King, her father-in-law, leaving him as rarely as possible; she was with him on horseback, in hunting, and in war.

Her adoration of Francis I saved the House of Medici from all suspicion when the Dauphin died poisoned. At that time Catherine and the Duc d'Orléans were at the King's head-quarters in Provençe, for France had already been invaded by Charles V, the King's brother-in-law. The whole Court had remained on the scene of the wedding festivities, now the theatre of the most barbarous war. Just as Charles V, compelled to retreat, had fled, leaving the bones of his army in Provençe, the Dauphin was returning to Lyons by the Rhone. Stopping at Tournon for the night, to amuse himself, he went through some athletic exercises, such as formed almost the sole education he or his brother received, in consequence of their long detention as hostages. The Prince being very hot—it was in the month of August—was so rash as to ask for a glass of water, which was given to him, iced, by Montecuculi. The Dauphin died almost instantaneously.

The King idolized his son. The Dauphin was indeed, as historians are agreed, a very accomplished prince. His father, in despair, gave the utmost publicity to the proceedings against Montecuculi, and placed the matter in the hands of the most learned judges of the day.

After heroically enduring the first tests of torture without confessing anything, the Count made an avowal by which he fully implicated the Emperor and his two generals, Antonio de Leyva and Fernando Gonzaga. This, however, did not satisfy Francis I. Never was a case more solemnly thrashed out than this. An eye-witness gives the following account of what the King did:

" The King called all the princes of the blood, and all the knights of his order, and many other high personages of the realm, to meet at Lyons; the Pope's legate and nuncio, the cardinals who were of his Court, and the ambassadors of England, Scotland, Portugal, Venice, Ferrara, and others; together with all the princes and great nobles of foreign countries, both of Italy and of Germany, who were at that time residing at his Court, to wit: The Duke of Wittemberg, in Allemaigne; the Dukes of Somma, of Arianna, and of Atria; the Princes of Melphe [Malfi?] (who had desired to marry Catherine), and of Stilliano, Neapolitan; the Marquis di Vigevo, of the House of Trivulzio, Milanese; the Signor Giovanni Paolo di Ceri, Roman; the Signor Césare Fregose, Genoese; the Signor Annibale Gonzaga, Mantuan, and many more. Who being assembled, he caused to be read in their presence, from the beginning to the end, the trial of that wretched man who had poisoned his late Highness the Dauphin, with all the interrogations, confessions, confrontings, and other proceedings usual in criminal trials, not choosing that the sentence should be carried out until all those present had given their opinion on this monstrous and miserable matter."

Count Montecuculi's fidelity and devotion may seem extraordinary in our day of universal indiscretion, when everybody, and even ministers, talk over the most trivial incidents in which they have put a finger; but in those times princes could command devoted servants, or knew how to choose them. There were monarchical Moreys then, because there was faith. Never look for great things from self-interest: interests may change; but look for anything from feeling, from religious faith, monarchical faith, patriotic faith. These three beliefs alone can produce a Berthereau of Geneva, a Sydney or a Strafford in England, assassins to murder Thomas à Becket, or a Montecuculi; Jacques Cœur and Jeanne d'Arc, or Richelieu and Danton; a Bonchamp, a Talmont, or a Clément, a Chabot.

Charles V made use of the highest personages to carry out the murder of three ambassadors from Francis I. A year later Lorenzino, Catherine's cousin, assassinated Duke Alessandro after three years of dissimulation, and in circumstances which gained him the surname of the Florentine Brutus. The rank of the victim was so little a check on such undertakings that neither Leo X nor Clement VII seems to have died a natural death. Mariana, the historian of Philip II, almost jests in speaking of the death of the Queen of Spain, a princess of France, saying that " for the greater glory of the Spanish throne God suffered the blindness of the doctors who treated the Queen for dropsy." When King Henri II allowed himself to utter a scandal which deserved a sword-thrust, he could find La Châtaignerie willing to take it. At that time royal personages had their meals served to them in padlocked boxes of which they had the key. Hence the *droit de cadenas,* the right of the padlock, an honor which ceased to exist in the reign of Louis XIV

The Dauphin died of poison, the same perhaps as caused the death of Madame, under Louis XIV. Pope Clement had been dead two years; Duke Alessandro, steeped in debauchery, seemed to have no interest in the Duc d'Orléans's elevation. Catherine, now seventeen years old, was with her father-in-law, whom she devotedly admired; Charles V alone seemed to have an interest in the Dauphin's death, because Francis I intended his son to form an alliance which would have extended the power of France. Thus the Count's confession was very ingeniously based on the passions and policy of the day. Charles V had fled after seeing his troops overwhelmed in Provençe, and with them his good fortune, his reputation, and his hopes of aggrandizement. And note, that even if an innocent man had confessed under torture, the King afterwards gave him freedom of speech before an august assembly, and in the presence of men with whom innocence had a fair chance of a hearing. The King wanted the truth, and sought it in good faith.

In spite of her now brilliant prospects, Catherine's position at court was unchanged by the Dauphin's death; her childlessness made a divorce seem probable when her husband should become king. The Dauphin was now enslaved by Diane de Poitiers, who had dared to be the rival of Madame d'Etampes. Catherine was therefore doubly attentive and insinuating to her father-in-law, understanding that he was her sole mainstay.

Thus the first ten years of Catherine's married life were spent in the unceasing regrets caused by repeated disappointments when she hoped to have a child, and the vexations of her rivalry with Diane. Imagine what the life must be of a princess constantly spied on by a jealous mistress who was favored by the Catholic party, and by the strong support the Sénéchale had acquired through the marriage of her daughters—one to Robert de la Mark, Duc de Bouillon, Prince de Sédan; the other to Claude de Lorraine, Duc d'Aumale.

Swamped between the party of the Duchesse d'Etampes and that of the Sénéchale (the title borne by Diane de Poitiers during the reign of Francis I), who divided the Court and political feeling between the two mortal foes, Catherine tried to be the friend of both the Duchess and Diane de Poitiers. She, who was to become so great a queen, played the part of a subaltern. Thus she served her apprenticeship to the double-faced policy which afterwards was the secret clew to her life. At a later date the Queen found herself between the Catholics and the Calvinists, as the woman had been, for ten years, between Madame d'Etampes and Madame de Poitiers.

She studied the contradictions of French policy. Francis upheld Calvin and the Lutherans, to annoy Charles V. Then, after having covertly and patiently fostered the Reformation in

Germany, after tolerating Calvin's presence at the Court of Navarre, he turned against it with undisguised severity. So Catherine could see the Court and the women of the Court playing with the fire of heresy; Diane at the head of the Catholic party with the Guises, only because the Duchesse d'Etampes was on the side of Calvin and the Protestants.

This was Catherine's political education; and in the King's private circle she could study the mistakes made by the Medici. The Dauphin was antagonistic to his father on every point; he was a bad son. He forgot the hardest but the truest axiom of royalty, namely, that the throne is a responsible entity, and that a son who may oppose his father during his lifetime must carry out his policy on succeeding to the throne. Spinoza, who was as deep a politician as he was a great philosopher, says, in treating of the case of a king who has succeeded to another by a revolution or by treason: " If the new king hopes to secure his throne and protect his life, he must display so much zeal in avenging his predecessor's death that no one shall feel tempted to repeat such a crime. But to avenge him worthily it is not enough that he should shed the blood of his subjects; he must confirm the maxims of him whose place he fills, and walk in the same ways of government."

It was the application of this principle which gave the Medici to Florence. Cosmo I, Alessandro's successor, eleven years later instigated the murder, at Venice, of the Florentine Brutus, and, as has been said, persecuted the Strozzi without mercy. It was the neglect of this principle that overthrew Louis XVI. That king was false to every principle of government when he reinstated the Parlements suppressed by his grandfather. Louis XV had been clear-sighted; the Parlements, and especially that of Paris, were quite half to blame for the disorders that necessitated the assembling of the States-General. Louis XV's mistake was that when he threw down that barrier between the throne and the people, he did not erect a stronger one, that he did not substitute for the Parlements a strong constitutional rule in the provinces. There lay the remedy for the evils of the monarchy, the voting power for taxation and the incidence of the taxes, with consent gradually won to the reforms needed in the monarchical rule.

Henri II's first act was to give all his confidence to the Connétable de Montmorency, whom his father had desired him to leave in banishment. The Connétable de Montmorency, with Diane de Poitiers, to whom he was closely attached, was master of the kingdom. Hence Catherine was even less powerful and happy as Queen of France than she had been as the Dauphiness.

At first, from the year 1543, she had a child every year for ten years, and was fully taken up by her maternal functions during that time, which included the last years of Francis I's reign, and almost the whole of her husband's. Being thus kept out of the tide of affairs, this clever woman spent her time in observing all the interests of the persons at Court, and all the parties formed there. The Italians who had followed her excited violent suspicions. After the execution of Montecuculi, the Connétable de Montmorency, Diane, and most of the crafty politicians at Court were racked with doubts of the Medici; but Francis I always scouted them. Still the Gondi, the Biraguas, the Strozzi, the Ruggieri, the Sardini, in short, all who were classed as the Italians who had arrived in Catherine's wake, were compelled to exercise every faculty of wit, policy, and courage to enable them to remain at Court under the burden of disfavor that weighed on them. During the supremacy of Diane de Poitiers, Catherine's obligingness went so far that some clever folks have seen in it an evidence of the profound dissimulation to which she was compelled by men and circumstances, and by the conduct of Henri II. But it is going too far to say that she never asserted her rights as a wife and a queen. Her ten children (besides one dead born) were a sufficient explanation of the King's conduct, who was thus set free to spend his time with Diane de Poitiers. But the King certainly never fell short of what he owed to himself; he gave the Queen an entry worthy of any that had previously taken place, on the occasion of her coronation. The records of the Parlement and of the Exchequer prove that these two important bodies went to meet Catherine outside Paris, as far as Saint-Lazare. Here, indeed, is a passage from du Tillet's narrative:

"A scaffolding had been erected at Saint-Lazare, whereon was a throne (which du Tillet calls a chair of state, *chaire de parement*). Catherine seated herself on this, dressed in a surcoat, or sort of cape of ermine, covered with jewels; beneath it a bodice, with a court train, and on her head a crown of pearls and diamonds; she was supported by the Maréchale de la Mark, her lady of honor. Around her, standing, were the princes of the blood and other princes and noblemen richly dressed, with the Chancellor of France in a robe of cloth of gold in a pattern on a ground of red cramoisy.[3] In front of the Queen and on the same scaffolding were seated, in two rows, twelve duchesses and countesses, dressed in surcoats of ermine, stomachers, trains, and fillets, that is to say, coronets, whether duchesses or countesses. There were the Duchesses d'Estouteville, de Montpensier—the elder and the younger—the Princesse de la Roche-sur-Yon; the Duchesses de Guise, de Nivernois, d'Aumale, de Valentinois (Diane de Poitiers); the King's daughter Diane, who became Duchesse de Castro-Farnese, and afterwards Duchesse de Montmorency-Damville), Madame la Connétable, and Mademoiselle de Nemours, not to mention the other ladies who could find no room. The four capped Presidents (*à mortier*), with some other members of the Court and the chief clerk, Du Tillet, went up on to the platform and did their service, and the First President Lizet, kneeling on one knee, addressed the Queen. The Chancellor, likewise on one knee, made response. She made her entrance into Paris at about three in the afternoon, riding in an open litter, Madame Marguerite de France sitting opposite to her, and by the side of the litter came the Cardinals d'Amboise, de Châtillon, de Boulogne, and de Lenoncourt, in their rochets. She got out at the Church of Notre-Dame, and was received by the clergy. After she had made her prayer, she was carried along the Rue de la Calandre to the palace, where the royal supper was spread in the great hall. She sat there in the middle at a marble table, under a canopy of velvet powdered with gold fleurs-de-lys."

It will here be fitting to controvert a popular error which some persons have perpetuated, following Sauval in the mistake. It has been said that Henri II carried his oblivion of decency so far as to place Diane's initials even on the buildings which Catherine had advised him to undertake or to carry on at such lavish expense. But the cipher, which is to be seen at the Louvre, amply refutes those who have so little

---

[3] The old French word "cramoisi" did not mean merely a crimson red, but denoted a special excellence of the dye. (See Rabelais.)

comprehension as to lend credit to such nonsense, a gratuitous slur on the honor of our kings and queens. The H for Henri and the two C's, face to face, for Catherine seem indeed to make two D's for Diane; and this coincidence was no doubt pleasing to the King. But it is not the less certain that the royal cipher was officially constructed of the initials of the King and the Queen. And this is so true, that the same cipher is still to be seen on the corn-market in Paris which Catherine herself had built. It may also be found in the crypt of Saint-Denis on Catherine's tomb, which she caused to be constructed during her lifetime by the side of that of Henri II, and on which she is represented from life by the sculptor to whom she sat.

On a solemn occasion, when he was setting out on an expedition to Germany, Henri II proclaimed Catherine Regent during his absence, as also in the event of his death—on March 25, 1552. Catherine's bitterest enemy, the author of the "*Discours merveilleux sur les déportements de Catherine II,*" admits that she acquitted herself of these functions to the general approbation, and that the King was satisfied with her administration. Henri II had men and money at the right moment. And after the disastrous day of Saint-Quentin, Catherine obtained from the Parisians considerable sums, which she forwarded to Compiègne, whither the King had come.

In politics Catherine made immense efforts to acquire some little influence. She was clever enough to gain over to her interests the Connétable de Montmorency, who was all-powerful under Henri II. The King's terrible reply to Montmorency's insistency is well known. This answer was the result of the good advice given by Catherine in the rare moments when she was alone with the King, and could explain to him the policy of the Florentines, which was to set the magnates of a kingdom by the ears and build up the sovereign authority on the ruins —Louis XI's system, subsequently carried out by Richelieu. Henri II, who saw only through the eyes of Diane and the Connétable, was quite a feudal king, and on friendly terms with the great houses of the realm.

After an ineffectual effort in her favor made by the Connétable, probably in the year 1556, Catherine paid great court to the Guises, and schemed to detach them from Diane's party so as to set them in opposition to Montmorency. But, unfortunately, Diane and the Connétable were as virulent against the Protestants as the Guises were. Hence their antagonism lacked the virus which religious feeling would have given it. Besides, Diane boldly defied the Queen's plans by coquetting with the Guises and giving her daughter to the Duc d'Aumale.

The signs of grief and the ostentatious regret displayed by Catherine on the King's death cannot be regarded as genuine. The fact that Henri II had been so passionately and faithfully attached to Diane de Poitiers made it incumbent on Catherine that she should play the part of a neglected wife who idolized her husband; but, like every clever woman, she carried on her dissimulation, and never ceased to speak with tender regret of Henri II. Diane herself, it is well known, wore mourning all her life for her husband, Monsieur de Brézé. Her colors were black and white, and the King was wearing them at the tournament where he was fatally wounded. Catherine, in imitation no doubt of her rival, wore mourning for the King to the end of her life.

On the King's death the Duchesse de Valentinois was shamelessly deserted and dishonored by the Connétable de Montmorency, a man in every respect beneath his reputation. Diane sent to offer her estate and château of Chenonceaux to the Queen. Catherine then replied in the presence of witnesses, " I can never forget that she was all the joy of my dear Henri; I should be ashamed to accept, I will give her an estate in exchange. I would propose that of Chaumont-on-the-Loire." The deed of exchange was, in fact, signed at Blois in 1559. Diane, whose sons-in-law were the Duc d'Aumale and the Duc de Bouillon, kept her whole fortune and died peacefully in 1566 at the age of sixty-six. She was thus nineteen years older than Henri II. These dates, copied from the epitaph on her tomb by a historian who studied the question at the end of the last century, clear up many historical difficulties; for many writers have said she was forty when her father was sentenced in 1523, while others have said she was but sixteen. She was, in fact, four-and-twenty.

After reading everything both for and against her conduct with Francis I, at a time when the House of Poitiers was in the greatest danger, we can neither confirm nor deny anything. It is a passage of history that still remains obscure. We can see by what happens in our own day how history is falsified, as it were, in the making.

Catherine, who founded great hopes on her rival's age, several times made an attempt to overthrow her. On one occasion she was very near the accomplishment of her hopes. In 1554, Madame Diane, being ill, begged the King to go to Saint-Germain pending her recovery. This sovereign coquette would not be seen in the midst of the paraphernalia of doctors, nor bereft of the adjuncts of dress. To receive the King on his return, Catherine arranged a splendid ballet, in which five or six young ladies were to address him in verse. She selected for the purpose Miss Fleming, related to her uncle, the Duke of Albany, and one of the loveliest girls imaginable, fair and golden-haired; then a young connection of her own, Clarissa Strozzi, with magnificent black hair and rarely fine hands; Miss Lewiston, maid of honor to Mary Stuart; Mary Stuart herself; Madame Elisabeth de France, the unhappy Queen of Spain; and Madame Claude. Elisabeth was nine years old, Claude eight, and Mary Stuart twelve. Obviously, the Queen aimed at showing off Clarissa Strozzi and Miss Fleming without other rivals in the King's eyes. The King succumbed; he fell in love with Miss Fleming, and she bore him a son, Henri de Valois, Comte d'Angoulême, Grand Prior of France.

But Diane's influence and position remained unshaken. Like Madame de Pompadour later with Louis XV, the Duchesse de Valentinois was forgiving. But to what sort of love are we to ascribe this scheme on Catherine's part? Love of power or love of her husband? Women must decide.

A great deal is said in these days as to the license of the press; but it is difficult to imagine to what a pitch it was carried when printing was a new thing. Aretino, the Voltaire of his time, as is well known, made monarchs tremble, and foremost of them all Charles V. But few people know perhaps how far the audacity of pamphleteers could go. This château of Chenonceaux had been given to Diane, nay, she was entreated to accept it, to induce her to overlook one of the most horrible publications ever hurled at a woman, one which shows how violent was the animosity between her and Madame d'Etampes. In 1537, when she was eight-and-thirty, a poet of Champagne, named Jean Voûté, published a collection of Latin verses, and among them three epigrams aimed at her. We must conclude that the poet was under high patronage from the fact that his volume is introduced by a eulogium written by Simon Macrin, the King's first Gentleman of the Bed-Chamber.

This volume, printed by Simon de Colines, was dedicated "To a Bishop!"—To François Bohier, the brother of the man who, to save his credit at Court and atone for his crime, made an offering on the accession of Henri II of the château of Chenonceaux, built by his father, Thomas Bohier, Councillor of State under four kings: Louis XI, Charles VIII, Louis XII, and Francis I. What were the pamphlets published against Madame de Pompadour and Marie Antoinette in comparison with verses that might have been written by Martial! Voûté must have come to a bad end. Thus the estate and château of Chenonceaux cost Diane nothing but the forgiveness of an offence—a duty enjoined by the Gospel. Not being assessed by a jury, the penalties inflicted on the press were rather severer then than they are now.

The widowed Queens of France were required to remain for forty days in the King's bed-chamber, seeing no light but that of the tapers; they might not come out till after the funeral. This inviolable custom annoyed Catherine greatly; she was afraid of cabals. She found a way to evade it. The Cardinal de Lorraine walking one morning in the Rue Culture-Sainte-Catherine, was roughly handled by a party of roisterers. "Whereat his Holiness was much amazed," says Henri Estienne, "and gave it out that heretics were lying in wait for him." And on this account the Court moved from Paris to Saint-Germain. The Queen would not leave the King her son behind, but took him with her.

The accession of Francis II, the moment when Catherine proposed to seize the reins of power, was a disappointment that formed a cruel climax to the twenty-six years of endurance she had already spent at the French Court. The Guises, with incredible audacity, at once usurped the sovereign power. The Duc de Guise was placed in command of the army, and the Connétable de Montmorency was shelved. The Cardinal took the control of the finances and the clergy.

Catherine's political career opened with one of those dramas which, though it was less notorious than some others, was not the less horrible, and initiated her no doubt into the agitating shocks of her life. Whether it was that Catherine, after vainly trying the most violent remedies, had thought she might bring the King back to her through jealousy; whether on coming to her second youth she had felt it hard never to have known love, she had shown a warm interest in a gentleman of royal blood, François de Vendôme, son of Louis de Vendôme—the parent House of the Bourbons—the Vidame de Chartres, the name by which he is known to history. Catherine's covert hatred of Diane betrayed itself in many ways, which historians, studying only political developments, have failed to note with due attention. Catherine's attachment to the Vidame arose from an insult offered by the young man to the favorite. Diane looked for the most splendid matches for her daughters, who were indeed of the best blood in the kingdom. Above all, she was ambitious of an alliance with the royal family. And her second daughter, who became the Duchesse d'Aumale, was proposed in marriage to the Vidame, whom Francis I, with sage policy, kept in poverty. For, in fact, when the Vidame de Chartres and the Prince de Condé first came to Court, Francis I gave them appointments! What? the office of chamberlains in ordinary, with twelve hundred crowns a year, as much as he bestowed on the humblest of his gentlemen. And yet, though Diane offered him immense wealth, some high office under the Crown, and the King's personal favor, the Vidame refused. And then this Bourbon, factious as he was, married Jeanne, daughter of the Baron d'Estissac, by whom he had no children.

This proud demeanor naturally commended the Vidame to Catherine, who received him with marked favor, and made him her devoted friend. Historians have compared the last Duc de Montmorency, who was beheaded at Toulouse, with the Vidame de Chartres for his power of charming, his merits, and his talents.

Henri II was not jealous; he did not apparently think it possible that a Queen of France could fail in her duty, or that a Medici could forget the honor done her by a Valois. When the Queen was said to be flirting with the Vidame de Chartres, she had been almost deserted by the King since the birth of her last child. So this attempt came to nothing—as the King died wearing the colors of Diane de Poitiers.

Henri II's four sons nullified every pretension of the Bourbons, who were all miserably poor, and crushed under the scorn brought upon them by the Connétable de Montmorency's treason, in spite of the reasons which had led him to quit the country. The Vidame de Chartres, who was to the first Prince de Condé what Richelieu was to Mazarin, a father in politics, a model, and yet more a master in gallantry, hid the vast ambition of his family under a semblance of levity. Being unable to contend with the Guises, the Montmorencys, the Princes of Scotland, the Cardinals, and the Bouillons, he aimed at distinction by his gracious manners, his elegance, and his wit, which won him the favor of the most charming women, and the heart of many he never thought about. He was a man privileged by nature, whose fascinations were irresistible.

During the first twenty days of mourning for Henri II a sudden change came over the Vidame's prospects. Courted by the Queen-mother, and courting her as a man may court a queen, in the utmost secrecy, he seemed fated to play an important part; and Catherine, in fact, resolved to make him useful. The Prince received letters from her to the Prince de Condé, in which she pointed out the necessity for a coalition against the Guises. The Guises, informed of this intrigue, made their way into the Queen's chamber to compel her to sign an order consigning the Vidame to the Bastille, and Catherine found herself under the cruel necessity of submitting. The Vidame died after a few months' captivity, on the day when he came out of prison, a short time before the Amboise conspiracy.

This was the end of Catherine De Medici's first and only love-affair. Protestant writers declared that the Queen had him poisoned to bury the secret of her flirtation in the tomb.

Such was this woman's apprenticeship to the exercise of royal power.

CHOICE EXAMPLES OF EARLY PRINTING AND ENGRAVING.

Fac-similes from Rare and Curious Books.

EARLY VENETIAN PRINTING.

Page from Jenson's Bible.

This page is from the prologue or introduction to Jenson's Bible, printed at Venice before the close of the fifteenth century, and contains the letter which Jerome wrote to the Roman patrician lady, Paulina, on the historic books of the Old Testament. Nicholas Jenson, who printed it, was the successor of the German printers, Valdarfer, Spires, and others. He was afterwards excelled and his skill eclipsed by the work of the Aldi. The Aldine editions are still the delight of book collectors.

Incipit epl'a sancti Hieronymi ad Paulinu
pbr̃z. de oib' diuine hystorie libris Capl'z. I

Rater am
brosius tua mi
hi munuscula
pferens detulit
simul z suauissi
mas litteras; q̃
a pncipio ami
cicia; fide̅ pba
te ia̅ fidei z ve
teris amicicie no
ua pferebat. Ve
ra. n. illa necessitudo e̅ z chr̃i glutino co
pulata: qua no̅ vtilitas rei familiaris: non
pn̄tia tm̃ corporum non subdola z palpa̅s
adulatio: sed dei timor: z diuinar̲ scriptu
rar̲ studia co̅cıliant. Legımus i veteribus
historijs quosdam lustrasse puincias: ho
uos adijsse pplos: maria tra̅sisse: vt eos q̃s
ex libris nouerant: cora̅ quoq̃ viderent. Sic
pythagoras memphiticos vates: sic plato
egyptum z archyta tarentınum: eaq̃ ora̅
italie q̃ quondam magna grecia dicebat̃:
laboriosissime peragrauit: vt q̃ athenis ma
gıster erat z potens: cui' q̃ doctrinas aca
demie gymnasia psonabat: fieret peregrın'
atq̃ discipulus malens aliena verecunde
discere: q̃ sua ipuden̅ ıgerere. Deniq̃ cum
litteras quasi toto orbe fugientes psequit̃:
captus a piratis z venundatus tyranno
crudelissimo paruit: ductus captiu' victus
z seruus: tn̄ q̃a philosoph' maior emente se
fuit. Ad titum liuium lacteo eloquentie fo̅
te manantem de vltimıs hispanie gallıarz̃
q̃ finibus quosdam venisse nobiles legim'
z quos ad contemplationez sui roma non
traxerat: vnius hois fama pduxit. Habuit
illa etas inauditum oibus seculis: celebra̅
dumq̃ miraculum: vt vrbe̅ tata̅ ingressi ali
ud extra vrbem quererent. Apolloni' siue
ille magus vt vulgus loquitur: siue philo
sophus: vt pythagorici tradunt: itrauit psas
ptransiuit caucasu̅: albanos scythas mas
sagetas: opulentissima indie regna penetra
uit: z ad extremu̅ latissimo physon amne
transmisso puenit ad bragmanas: vt hıar
cha̅ in throno sedentem aureo z de tantali
fonte potantem inter paucos discipulos d̃
natura de moribus: ac de cursu dier̃ z sıde
rum audiret docentem. Inde p elamitas

baby lonios chaldeos medos assyrios par
thos syros phenices arabes palestinos re
uersus ad alexandria̅ perrexit ad ethiopia̅:
vt gymnosophistas z famosissimam solis
mensam videret in sabulo. Inuenit ille vir
vbiq̃ quod disceret: z semper pficiens sem
se melior fieret. Scripsit sup hoc plenissie
octo voluminıbus philostratus. II

Quid loquar de seculi hoibus: cum
aplus Paulus vas electionis z ma
gıster gentium; qui de p̃scientia ta̅
ti in se hospitis loquebatur dicens: an ex
perimentu̅ queritis eius q̃ in me loquitur
christus: post damascu̅ arabiaq̃ lustrata̅
ascendıt hierosolyma̅: vt videret petrum: z
mansit apud eum dieb' qndecim: Hoc enı
mysterio hebdoadis z ogdoadis futurus
gentium p̃dicator: instruendus erat. Rur
sumq̃ post annos quatuordecim assumpto
barnaba z tito exposuit cum aplis euan̅ge
lium: ne forte in vacuum curreret aut cu
currisset. Habet nescio quid latentis ener
gie viue vocis actus: et in aures discipuli d̃
auctoris ore transfusa fortius sonat. Vnde
z eschines cum thodi exularet z legeretur
illa demosthenis oratio: qua aduersus eu̅
habuerat: mirantibus cunctis atq̃ lauda̅
tibus suspıras ait. Quid si ipsa audissetis
bestias sua vba resonante̅. III

Hec hoc dico: q̃ sit aliq̃d in me tale:
q̃d vel possis a me audire vel velıs
discere sed quo ardor tuus z disce̅
di studıum et absq̃ nobis p se pbari debe
at. Ingenıum docıle z sine doctore laudabi
le e̅. No̅ quid inenias: sed q̃d q̃ras p̃sidera
mus. Mollis cera z ad formandu̅ facılis
et sı artificis z plaste cessent manus: tame̅
virtute totum est quıcq̃d esse potest. Pau
lus aplus ad pedes gamalielıs lege moysi
z pphetas didıcisse se gloriatur: vt arma
tus spualıb' telis: postea docet p̃fidens. Ar
ma. n. nr̃e milıtie no̅ carnalıa su̅t: sed pote̅
tia deo ad destructıone̅ munitıonu̅: z cogi
tationes destruentes z oem altıtudıne̅ extol
lente̅ se aduersus scıam dei: z captiuantes
oem intellectu̅ ad obedıendu̅ christo z para
ti subıugare oem ıobedıentıam. Timotheu̅
scribit ab ifantia sacrıs lı̃ıs erudıtu̅: z horta
tur ad studıu̅ lectıonıs: ne neglıgat gratıam
q̃ data sit ei p ipositıone̅ man' presbyterı.
Tıto precıpit: vt in̅ ceteras vtutes epı' q̃s
breui sermone depınxıt: scıam quoq̃ non

DON QUIXOTE

BY

HEINRICH HEINE

HEINRICH HEINE

1799—1856

Heinrich Heine was born of Hebrew parents at Düsseldorf on the Rhine, in 1799. His favorite books in childhood, he tells us, were "Gulliver's Travels," Sterne's "Sentimental Journey," and "Don Quixote." Later in life he made Don Quixote the subject of one of his most charming and characteristic essays. His parents desiring him to follow a business career, he was sent to Hamburg to serve an apprenticeship in the banking house of his uncle, Solomon Heine. This proving distasteful to him, he was enabled through pecuniary assistance from his uncle to study law at Bonn, Berlin, and Göttingen. He received his degree at Göttingen in 1825, after embracing Christianity. The first collection of his poems, "Gedichte," was published in 1822. This was followed by a volume of verse called "Buch des Lieder," in 1827, which received favorable notice from the critics, and was translated into English by Sir Walter Scott. "Neue Gedichte," which contains some of his finest lyrics, appeared in 1844. From 1826 to 1831 the four books of the "Reisebilder" were published. They were characterized at that time as "the most brilliant, the wittiest, the most entertaining, the most immoral, the coarsest, the most dangerous, the most revolutionary, the most atheistic books that any German author had ever printed." The work was interdicted in Germany, Austria, and other monarchical countries on account of its strong revolutionary sympathies, but was, nevertheless, widely circulated. While the "Reisebilder" greatly increased Heine's fame, the work also made for him a host of bitter enemies.

In 1831 Heine left Germany and settled in Paris. For sixteen years, he mingled with the society of authors and artists in that literary and artistic capital, met and finally married his "Mathilde," and did much literary work, both good and bad. His "History of Religion and Philosophy in Germany," and essays on the Romantic school, appeared during this period, in addition to the volume of poems referred to above.

In 1847 his uncle, Solomon Heine, died, and the heirs attempted to deprive Heine of the small annual allowance he had always received from his generous relative, and also of a legacy he had been promised. Their greed ultimately failed of its purpose, but the excitement broke down the poet's enfeebled constitution and brought on a terrible disease of the spine that made his last years a period of physical agony. Yet, during the eight years of suffering on his "mattress-grave," Heine's spirit never yielded, nor did his courage and gayety ever flag. From 1850 to 1851 he produced the wonderful series of poems entitled "Romanzero," and from 1852 to 1854 dictated his "Last Poems" and "Confessions." He died in 1856, and was buried in the cemetery of Montmarte, in accordance with his expressed wish.

Heine was pre-eminently a poet, his lyrics ranking with the best of Schiller and Goethe. His prose sparkles with wit and satire, and has, therefore, won enduring popularity. His style is lucid and incisive and marked by a purity and directness of diction unsurpassed in German literature.

DON QUIXOTE

THE first book that I read after I arrived at boyhood's years of discretion, and had tolerably mastered my letters, was "The Life and Deeds of the Sagacious Knight, Don Quixote de la Mancha," written by Miguel Cervantes de Saavedra.[1] Well do I remember the time, when, early in the morning, I stole away from home and hastened to the court-garden, that I might read " Don Quixote " without being disturbed. It was a beautiful day in May, the blooming spring lay basking in the silent morning light, listening to the compliments of that sweet flatterer, the nightingale, who sang so softly and caressingly, with such a melting fervor, that even the shyest of buds burst into blossom, and the lusty grasses and the fragrant sunshine kissed more rapturously, and the trees and flowers trembled from very ecstasy. But I seated myself on an old moss-covered stone bench in the so-called Avenue of Sighs, not far from the water-fall, and feasted my little heart with the thrilling adventures of the valiant knight. In my childish simplicity I took everything in sober earnest; no matter how ridiculous the mishaps which fate visited upon the poor hero, I thought it must be just so, and imagined that to be laughed at was as much a part of heroism as to be wounded; and the former vexed me just as sorely as the latter grieved my heart. I was a child, and knew nothing of the irony God has interwoven into the world, and which the great poet has imitated in his miniature world; and I wept most bitterly, when, for all his chivalry and generosity, the noble knight gained only ingratitude and cudgels. As I was unpractised in reading, I spoke every word aloud, and so the birds and the trees, the brooks and the flowers, could hear all I read, and as these innocent beings know as little as children of the irony of the world, they too took it all for sober earnest, and wept with me over the sor-

[1] [The admirable account of "Don Quixote" embodied in this essay was written by Heine in 1837, as the introduction to an edition de luxe of Cervantes's masterpiece.]

rows of the unfortunate knight; an old worn-out oak sobbed even; and the water-fall shook more vehemently his white beard, and seemed to scold at the wickedness of the world. We felt that the heroism of the knight was none the less worthy of admiration because the lion turned tail without fighting, and that if his body was weak and withered, his armor rusty, his steed a miserable jade, his deeds were all the more worthy of praise. We despised the vulgar rabble who beat the poor hero so barbarously, and still more the rabble of higher rank, who were decked in silk attire, gay courtly phrases, and grand titles, and jeered at the man who was so far their superior in powers of mind and nobility of soul. Dulcinea's knight rose ever higher in my esteem, and my love for him grew stronger and stronger the longer I read in that wonderful book, which I continued to do daily in that same garden, so that when autumn came I had reached the end of the story, and I shall never forget the day when I read the sorrowful combat, in which the knight came to so ignominious an end.

It was a gloomy day; dismal clouds swept over a leaden sky, the yellow leaves fell sorrowfully from the trees, heavy tear-drops hung on the last flowers that drooped down in a sad faded way their dying little heads, the nightingales had long since died away, from every side the image of transitoriness stared at me—and my heart was ready to break as I read how the noble knight lay on the ground, stunned and bruised, and through his closed visor said, in tones faint and feeble, as if he was speaking from the grave, "Dulcinea is the fairest lady in the world, and I the unhappiest knight on earth, but it is not meet that my weakness should disown this truth—strike with your lance, Sir Knight."

Ah me! that brilliant knight of the silver moon, who vanquished the bravest and noblest man in the world, was a disguised barber!

That was long ago. Many new springs have bloomed forth since then, yet their mightiest charm has always been wanting, for, alas! I no longer believe the sweet deceits of the nightingale, spring's flatterer; I know how soon his magnificence fades; and when I look at the youngest rosebuds I see them in spirit bloom to a sorrowful red, grow pale, and be scattered by the winds. Everywhere I see a disguised winter.

In my breast, however, still blooms that flaming love, which soared so ardently above the earth, to revel adventurously in the broad yawning spaces of heaven, and which, pushed back by the cold stars, and sinking home again to the little earth, was forced to confess, with sighing and triumph, that there is in all creation nothing fairer or better than the heart of man. This love is the inspiration that fills me, always divine, whether it does foolish or wise deeds. And so the tears the little boy shed over the sorrows of the silly knight were in nowise spent in vain, any more than the later tears of the youth, as on many a night he wept in the study over the deaths of the holy heroes of freedom—over King Agis of Sparta, over Caius and Tiberius Gracchus of Rome, over Jesus of Jerusalem, and over Robespierre and Saint-Just of Paris. Now that I have put on the *toga virilis,* and myself desire to be a man, the tears have come to an end, and it is necessary to act like a man, imitating my great predecessors; in the future, if God will, to be wept also by boys and youths. Yes, upon these one can still reckon in our cold age; for they can still be kindled by the breezes that blow to them from old books, and so they can comprehend the flaming hearts of the present. Youth is unselfish in its thoughts and feelings, and on that account it feels truth most deeply, and is not sparing, where a bold sympathy is wanted, with confession or deed. Older people are selfish and narrow-minded; they think more of the interest of their capital than of the interest of mankind; they let their little boat float quietly down the gutter of life, and trouble themselves little about the sailor who battles with the waves on the open sea; or they creep with clinging tenacity up to the heights of mayoralty or the presidency of their club, and shrug their shoulders over the heroic figures which the storm throws down from the columns of fame; and then they tell, perhaps, how they themselves also in their youth ran their heads against the wall, but that later on they reconciled themselves to the wall, for the wall was the absolute, existing by and for itself, which, because it was, was also reasonable, on which account he is unreasonable who will not endure a high, reasonable, inevitable, eternally ordained absolutism. Ah, these objectionable people, who wish to philosophize us into a gentle slavery, are yet more worthy of esteem than those depraved ones who do not even admit reasonable grounds for the defence of despotism, but being learned in history fight for it as a right of custom, to which men in the course of time have gradually accustomed themselves, and which has so become incontestably valid and lawful.

Ah, well! I will not, like Ham, lift up the garment of my fatherland's shame; but it is terrible how slavery has been made with us a matter for prating about, and how German philosophers and historians have tormented their brains to defend despotism, however silly or awkward, as reasonable and lawful. Silence is the honor of slaves, says Tacitus; these philosophers and historians maintain the contrary, and exhibit the badge of slavery in their button-holes.

Perhaps, after all, you are right, and I am only a Don Quixote, and the reading of all sorts of wonderful books has turned my head, as it was with the Knight of La Mancha, and Jean Jacques Rousseau was my Amadis of Gaul, Mirabeau my Roland or Agramante; and I have studied too much the heroic deeds of the French Paladins and the round-table of the National Convention. Indeed, my madness and the fixed ideas that I created out of books are of a quite opposite kind to the madness and the fixed ideas of him of La Mancha. He wished to establish again the expiring days of chivalry; I, on the contrary, wish to annihilate all that is yet remaining from that time, and so we work with altogether different views. My colleague saw windmills as giants; I, on the contrary, can see in our present giants only vaunting windmills. He took leather wine-skins for mighty enchanters, but I can see in the enchanters of to-day only leather wine-skins. He held beggarly pot-houses for castles, donkey-drivers for cavaliers, stable wenches for court ladies; I, on the contrary, hold our castles for beggarly pot-houses, our cavaliers for mere donkey-drivers, our court ladies for ordinary stable wenches. As he took a puppet-show for a state ceremony, so I hold our state ceremonies as sorry puppet-shows, yet as bravely as the brave Knight of La Mancha I strike out at the clumsy machinery. Alas! such heroic deeds often turn out as badly for me as for him, and like him I must suffer much for the honor of my lady. If I denied her from mere fear or base love of gain, I might live comfortably in this reasonably constructed world, and I should lead a fair Maritorna to the altar, and let myself be blessed by fat enchanters, and banquet with noble donkey-drivers, and engender harmless romances as well as other little slaves! Instead of that, wearing the three colors of my lady, I must strike through unspeakable opposition, and fight battles, every one of which costs me my heart's blood. Day and night I am in straits, for those enemies are so artful that many I struck to death still give themselves the appearance of being alive, changing themselves into all forms, and spoiling day and night for me. How many sorrows have I suffered by such fatal spectres! Where anything lovely bloomed for me then they crept in, those cunning ghosts, and broke even the most innocent buds. Everywhere, and when I should least suspect it, I discovered on the ground the traces of their silvery slime, and if I took no care, I might have a dangerous fall even in the house of my love. You may smile and hold such anxieties for idle fancies like those of Don Quixote. But fancied pains hurt all the same; and if one fancies that he has drunk hemlock he may get into a consumption, and he certainly will not get fat. And the report that I have got fat is a calumny; at least I have not yet received any fat sinecure, even if I possess the requisite talents. I fancy that everything has been done to keep me lean; when I was hungry they fed me with snakes, when I was thirsty they gave me wormwood to drink; they poured hell into my heart, so that I wept poison and sighed fire; they crouched near me even in my dreams; and I see horrible spectres, noble lackey faces with gnashing teeth and threatening noses, and deadly eyes glaring from cowls, and white ruffled hands with gleaming knives.

And even the old woman who lives near me in the next room considers me to be mad, and says that I talk the maddest nonsense in my sleep; and the other night she plainly heard me calling out—" Dulcinea is the fairest woman in the world, and I the unhappiest knight on earth; but it is not meet that my weakness should disown this truth. Strike with your lance, Sir Knight!"

. . . .

It is now eight years since I wrote the foregoing lines [2] for

[2] [Heine only quotes the first part of the passage from the "Reisebilder," which has here been given in full.]

the fourth part of the "Reisebilder," in which I described the impression which the reading of "Don Quixote" had made on my mind many years ago. Good Heavens! how swiftly time flies! It seems to me as if it were but yesterday that, in the Avenue of Sighs, in the court-garden at Düsseldorf, I finished reading the book, and my heart is still moved with admiration for the deeds and sufferings of the noble knight. Has my heart remained constant in this ever since, or has it, after passing through a wonderful cycle, returned to the emotions of childhood? The latter may well be the case, for I remember that during each lustrum of my life "Don Quixote" has made a different impression upon me. When I was blossoming into adolescence, and with inexperienced hands sought to pluck the roses of life, climbed the loftiest peaks in order to be nearer to the sun, and at night dreamed of naught else but eagles and chaste maidens, then "Don Quixote" was to me a very unsatisfactory book, and if it chanced to fall in my way I involuntarily shoved it aside. At a later period, when I had ripened into manhood, I became to a certain degree reconciled to Dulcinea's luckless champion, and I began to laugh at him. The fellow is a fool, said I. And yet, strange to say, the shadowy forms of the lean knight and his fat squire have ever followed me in all the journeyings of my life, particuarly when I came to any critical turning-point. Thus I recollect that while making the journey to France, one morning in the post-chaise I awakened from a half-feverish slumber, and saw in the early morning mist two well-known figures riding by my side. The one on my right was Don Quixote de la Mancha, mounted on his lean, abstract Rosinante, the other on my left was Sancho Panza, on his substantial, positive gray donkey. We had just reached the French frontier. The noble Manchean bowed his head reverently before the tri-colored flag, which fluttered towards us from the high post that marks the boundary line. Our good Sancho saluted with a somewhat less cordial nod the first French *gendarmes* whom we saw approaching near by. At last my two friends pushed on ahead, and I lost sight of them, only now and then I caught the sound of Rosinante's spirited neighing, and the donkey's responsive bray.

At that time I was of the opinion that the ridiculousness of Don Quixotism consisted in the fact that the noble knight endeavored to recall a long-perished past back to life, and his poor limbs and back came into painful contact with the harsh realities of the present. Alas! I have since learned that it is an equally ungrateful folly to endeavor to bring the future prematurely into the present, and that for such an assault upon the weighty interests of the day, one possesses but a very sorry steed, a brittle armor, and an equally frail body! And the wise man dubiously shakes his sage head at the one, as well as at the other, of these Quixotisms. But Dulcinea del Toboso is still the most beautiful woman in the world; although I lie stretched upon the earth, helpless and miserable, I will never take back that assertion, I cannot do otherwise—on with your lances, ye Knights of the Silver Moon, ye disguised barbers!

What leading idea guided Cervantes when he wrote his great book? Was his purpose merely the destruction of the romances of knight-errantry, the reading of which at that time was so much the rage in Spain that both clerical and secular ordinances against them were powerless? Or did he seek to hold up to ridicule all manifestations of human enthusiasm in general, military heroism in particular? Ostensibly he aimed only to satirize the romances above referred to, and through the exposition of their absurdities deliver them over to universal derision, and thus put an end to them. In this he succeeded most brilliantly; for that which neither the exhortations from the pulpit, nor the threats of the authorities could effect, that a poor writer accomplished with his pen. He destroyed the romances of chivalry so effectually that soon after the appearance of "Don Quixote" the taste for that class of literature wholly died out in Spain, and no more of that order were printed. But the pen of a man of genius is always greater than he himself; it extends far beyond his temporary purpose, and without being himself clearly conscious of it, Cervantes wrote the greatest satire against human enthusiasm. He had not the least presentiment of this, for he himself was a hero, who had spent the greater portion of his life in chivalrous conflicts, and who in his old age was wont to rejoice that he had participated in the battle of Lepanto, although he paid for this glory with the loss of his left hand.

The biographers can tell us but little concerning the person or private life of the poet who wrote "Don Quixote." We do not lose much by the omission of such details, which are generally picked up from the female gossips of the neighborhood. They see only the outer shell; but we see the man, his true, sincere, unslandered self.

He was a handsome, powerful man, Don Miguel Cervantes de Saavedra. He had a high forehead, and a large heart. His eyes possessed a wonderful magic; just as there are people who can look into the earth, and see the hidden treasures and the dead that lie buried there, so the eye of the great poet could penetrate the breasts of men, and see distinctly all what was concealed there. To the good his look was as a **ray of** sunlight gladdening and illuminating the heart; to the bad his glance was a sword, sharply piercing their souls. His searching eyes penetrated to the very soul of a person, and questioned it, and if it refused to answer, he put it to the torture, and the soul lay stretched bleeding on the rack, while perhaps the body assumed an air of condescending superiority. Is it to be wondered at that many formed a dislike for him, and gave him but scant assistance in his journey through life? He never achieved rank or position, and from all his toilsome pilgrimages he brought back no pearls, but only empty shells. It is said that he could not appreciate the value of money, but I assure you he fully appreciated its worth when he had no more. But he never prized it as highly as he did his honor. He had debts, and in one of his writings, in which Apollo is supposed to grant to the poets a charter of privileges, the first paragraph declares: When a poet says he has no money, his simple assurance shall suffice, and no oath shall be required of him. He loved music, flowers, and women, but in his love for the latter he sometimes fared very badly, particularly in his younger days. Did the consciousness of future greatness console him, when pert young roses stung him with their thorns? Once on a bright summer afternoon, while yet a young gallant, he walked along the banks of the Tagus in company with a pretty girl of sweet sixteen, who continually mocked at his tender speeches. The sun had not yet set, it still glowed with all its golden splendor, but high up in the heavens was the moon, pale and insignificant, like a little white cloud. " Seest thou," said the young poet to his sweetheart, " seest thou yonder small pale disc? The river by our side in which it mirrors itself seems to receive its pitiful reflex on its proud bosom merely out of compassion, and the curling billows at times cast it disdainfully aside, towards the shore. But wait until day fades into twilight; as soon as darkness descends, yonder pale orb will grow brighter and brighter, and will flood the whole stream with its silvery light, and the haughty billows that before were so scornful will then tremble with ecstasy at sight of the lovely moon, and roll rapturously towards it."

The history of poets must be sought for in their works, for there are to be found their most confidential confessions. In all his writings, in his dramas even more than in " Don Quixote," we see, as I have before mentioned, that Cervantes had long been a soldier. In fact, the Roman proverb, " Living means fighting," finds a double application in his case. He took part as a common soldier in most of those fierce games of war which King Philip II carried on in all countries for the honor of God and his own pleasure. The circumstance that Cervantes devoted his whole youth to the service of the greatest champion of Catholicism, and that he fought to advance Catholic interests, warrants the assumption that he had those interests at heart, and hence refutes the widely spread opinion that only the fear of the Inquisition withheld him from discussing in " Don Quixote " the great Protestant questions of the time. No, Cervantes was a faithful son of the Roman Church, and he not only bled physically in knightly combats for her blessed banner, but his whole soul suffered a most painful martyrdom during his many years of captivity among the unbelievers.

We are indebted to accident for most of the details of Cervantes's doings while in Algiers, and here we recognize in the great poet an equally great hero. The history of his captivity gives a most emphatic contradiction to the melodious lie of that polished man of the world, who made Augustus and the German pedants believe that he was a poet, and that poets are cowards. No, the true poet is also a true hero, and in his breast dwells that god-like patience, which, as the Spaniards say, is a second fount of courage. There is no more elevating spectacle than that of the noble Castilian who serves the Dey of Algiers as a slave, constantly meditating an escape, with unflagging energy preparing his bold plans, composedly facing all dangers, and when the enterprise miscarries, is ready to submit to torture and death rather than betray his accomplices. The bloodthirsty master of his body becomes disarmed by such grand magnanimity and virtue. The tiger spares the fettered lion, and trembles before the terrible "One-Arm," whom with but a single word he could despatch to his death. Cervantes is known in all Algiers as "One-Arm," and the Dey confesses that only when he knows that the one-armed Spaniard is in safe-keeping can he sleep soundly at night, assured of the safety of his city, his army, and his slaves.

I have referred to the fact that Cervantes was always a common soldier, but even in so subordinate a position he succeeded in distinguishing himself to such a degree as to attract the notice of the great general, Don John of Austria, and on his return from Italy to Spain he was furnished with the most complimentary letters of recommendation to the King, in which his advancement was most emphatically urged. When the Algerine corsairs, who captured him on the Mediterranean Sea, beheld these letters, they took him to be a person of the highest rank and importance, and hence demanded so large a ransom that notwithstanding all their efforts and sacrifices his family were not able to purchase his freedom, and the unfortunate poet's captivity was thereby prolonged and embittered. Thus the recognition of his merits became an additional source of misfortune, and thus to the very end of his days was he mocked by that cruel dame, the goddess Fortuna, who never forgives genius for having achieved fame and honor without her assistance.

But are the misfortunes of a man of genius always the work of blind chance, or do they necessarily follow from his inner nature and environment? Does his soul enter into strife with the world of reality, or do the coarse realities begin the unequal conflict with his noble soul?

Society is a republic. When an individual strives to rise, the collective masses press him back through ridicule and abuse. No one shall be wiser or better than the rest. But against him, who by the invincible power of genius towers above the vulgar masses, society launches its ostracism, and persecutes him so mercilessly with scoffing and slander, that he is finally compelled to withdraw into the solitude of his own thoughts.

Verily, society is republican in its very essence. Every sovereignty, intellectual as well as material, is hated by it. The latter oftener gives aid to the former than is generally imagined. We ourselves came to this conclusion soon after the revolution of July, when the spirit of republicanism manifested itself in all social relations. Our republicans hated the laurels of a great poet even as they hated the purple of a great king. They sought to level the intellectual inequalities of mankind, and inasmuch as they regarded all ideas that had been produced on the soil of the State as general property, nothing remained to be done but to decree an equality of style also. In sooth, a good style was decried as something aristocratic, and we heard manifold assertions: " A true democrat must write in the style of the people—sincere, natural, crude." Most of the party of action succeeded easily in doing this, but not everyone possesses the gift of writing badly, especially if one has previously formed the habit of writing well, and then it was at once said, " That is an aristocrat, a lover of style, a friend of art, an enemy of the people." They were surely honest in their views, like Saint Hieronymus, who considered his good style a sin, and gave himself sound scourgings for it.

Just as little as we find anti-Catholic, so also do we fail to discover anti-absolutist strains in " Don Quixote." The critics who think that they scent such sentiments therein are clearly in error. Cervantes was the son of a school which went so far as to poetically idealize the idea of unquestioning obedience to the sovereign. And that sovereign was the King of Spain at a time when its majesty dazzled the whole world. The common soldier felt himself a ray in that halo of glory, and willingly sacrificed his individual freedom to gratify the national pride of the Castilian.

The political grandeur of Spain at that time contributed not a little to exalt and enlarge the hearts of her poets. In the mind of a Spanish poet, as in the realm of Charles V, the sun never set. The fierce wars against the Moors were ended, and as after a storm the flowers are most fragrant, so poesy ever blooms most grandly after a civil war. We witness the same phenomenon in England at the time of Elizabeth, and at the same time as in Spain there arose a galaxy of poets, which invites the most remarkable parallelisms. There we see Shakespeare, here Cervantes, as the flower of the school.

Like the Spanish poets under the three Philips, so also the English poets under Elizabeth present a certain family likeness, and neither Shakespeare nor Cervantes has claim to originality in our sense of the word. They by no means differ from their contemporaries through peculiar modes of thought or feeling, or by an especial manner of portrayal, but only through greater depth, fervor, tenderness, and power. Their creations are more infused and penetrated with the divine spark of poetry.

But both poets were not only the flowers of their time, but they were also the germs of the future. As Shakespeare, by the influence of his works, particularly on Germany and the France of to-day, is to be regarded as the creator of the later dramatic art, so must we honor in Cervantes the author of the modern novel. I shall allow myself a few passing observations on the subject.

The older novels, the so-called romances of chivalry, sprang from the poetry of the Middle Ages. They were at first prose versions of those epic poems whose heroes are derived from the mythical traditions of Charlemagne and the Holy Grail. The subject was always knightly adventures. It was the romance of the nobility, and the personages that figured therein were either fabulous, fantastic beings, or knights with golden spurs; nowhere an allusion to the people. These romances of knighthood, which degenerated into the most ridiculous absurdities, Cervantes overthrew by his "Don Quixote." But while by his satire he destroyed the earlier romances, he also furnished a model for a new school of fiction, which we call the modern novel. Such is always the wont of great poets; while they tear down the old, they at the same time build up the new; they never destroy without replacing. Cervantes created the modern novel by introducing into his romances of knighthood a faithful description of the lower classes, by intermingling with it phases of folk-life. This partiality for describing the doings of the common rabble, of the vilest tatterdemalions, is not only found in Cervantes, but in all his literary contemporaries, and among the Spanish painters as well as among the poets of that period. A Murillo, who stole heaven's loveliest tints with which to paint his beautiful Madonnas, painted with the same love the filthiest creatures of this earth. It was perhaps the enthusiasm for art itself that made these noble Spaniards find as much pleasure in the faithful portrayal of a beggar lad scratching his head as in the representation of the Blessed Virgin. Or, perhaps, it was the charm of contrast that led noblemen of the highest rank, a dapper courtier like Quevedo, or a powerful minister like Mendoza, to fill their romances with ragged beggars and vagabonds. They perhaps sought to relieve the monotony of their lofty rank by putting themselves in imagination into a quite different sphere of life; as we find a similar tendency among some of our German authors, whose novels contain naught else but descriptions of the nobility, and who always make their heroes counts and barons. We do not find in Cervantes this one-sided tendency to portray the vulgar only; he intermingles the ideal and the common; one serves as light or as shade to the other, and the aristocratic element is as prominent in it as the popular. But this noble, chivalrous, aristocratic element disappears entirely from the novels of the English, who were the first to imitate Cervantes, and to this day always keep him in view as a model. These English novelists since Richardson's reign are prosaic natures; to the prudish spirit of their time even pithy descriptions of the life of the common people are repugnant, and we see on yonder side of the Channel those *bourgeois* novels arise, wherein the petty, humdrum life of the middle classes is depicted. The public was surfeited with this deplorable class of literature until recently, when appeared the great Scot, who effected a revolution, or rather a restoration, in novel-writing. As Cervantes introduced the democratic element into romance, at a time when one-sided knight-errantry ruled supreme, so Walter Scott restored the aristocratic element to romance when it had wholly disappeared, and only a prosaic *bourgeoisie* was to be found there. By an opposite course Walter Scott again restored to romance that beautiful symmetry which we admire in Cervantes's "Don Quixote."

I believe that the merits of England's second great poet have never in this respect been recognized. His Tory proclivities, his partiality for the past, were wholesome for literature, and for those masterpieces of his genius that everywhere found favor and imitators, and which drove into the darkest corners of the circulating libraries those ashen-gray, ghostly remains of the *bourgeoisie* romances. It is an error not to recognize Walter Scott as the founder of the so-called historical romance, and to endeavor to trace the latter to German initative. This error arises from the failure to perceive that the characteristic feature of the historical romance consists just in the harmony between the aristocratic and democratic elements, and that Walter Scott through the reintroduction of the aristocratic element, most beautifully restored that harmony which had been overthrown during the absolutism of the democratic element, whereas our German romanticists eliminated the democratic element entirely from their novels, and returned again to the ruts of those crazy romances of knight-errantry that flourished before Cervantes. Our De la Motte-Fouqué is only a straggler from the ranks of those poets who gave to the world " Amadis de Gaul," and similar extravagant absurdities. I admire not only the talent, but also the courage of the noble baron who, two centuries after the appearance of " Don Quixote," has written his romances of chivalry. It was a peculiar period in Germany when the latter appeared and found favor with the public. What was the significance in literature of that partiality for knight-errantry, and for those pictures of the old feudal times? I believe that the German people desired to bid an eternal farewell to the Middle Ages, but moved with emotion as we Germans are so apt to be, we took our leave with a kiss. For the last time we pressed our lips to the old tombstone. True, some of us behaved in a very silly manner on that occasion. Ludwig Tieck, the smallest boy in school, dug the dead ancestors out of their grave, rocked the coffin as if it were a cradle, and in childish, lisping accents sang, " Sleep, little grandsire, sleep."

I have called Walter Scott England's second great poet, and his novels masterpieces; but it is to his genius only that I would give the highest praise. His novels I can by no means place on an equality with the great romance of Cervantes. The latter surpasses him in epic spirit. Cervantes was, as I have already stated, a Catholic poet, and it is perhaps to this circumstance that he is indebted for that grand epic composure of soul, which, like a crystalline firmament, overarches those picturesque and poetical creations; nowhere is there a rift of scepticism. Added to this is the calm dignity which is the national characteristic of the Spaniard. But Walter Scott belongs to a Church which subjects even divine matters to a sharp examination; as an advocate and as a Scotchman he is accustomed to action and to debate, and we find the dramatic element most prominent in his novels, as well as in his life and his temperament. Hence his works can never be regarded as the pure model of that style of fiction which we denominate the romance. To the Spaniards is due the honor of having produced the best novel, as England is entitled to the credit of having achieved the highest rank in the drama.

And the Germans, what palm remains for them? Well, then, we are the best lyric poets on earth. No people possesses such beautiful songs as the Germans. At present the nations are too much occupied with political affairs, but when these are once laid aside, then let us Germans, English, Spaniards, French, Italians, all go out into the green forests and chant our lays, and the nightingale shall be umpire. I am convinced that in this tournament of minstrelsy the songs of Wolfgang Goethe will win the prize.

Cervantes, Shakespeare, and Goethe form the triumvirate of poets, who, in the three great divisions of poetry, epic, dramatic, and lyric, have achieved the greatest success. The writer of these pages is perhaps peculiarly fitted to sound the praises of our great countryman as the most perfect of lyric poets. Goethe stands midway between the two classes of song-writers, between those two schools, of which one, alas! is known by my own name, the other as the Suabian school. Both have their merits; they have indirectly promoted the welfare of German poetry. The first effected a wholesome reaction against the one-sided idealism of German poetry, it led the intellect back to stern realities, and uprooted that sentimental Petrarchism that has always seemed to us as a Quixotism in verse. The Suabian school also contributed indirectly to the weal of German poetry. If in northern Germany strong and healthy poetical productions came to light, thanks are perhaps due to the Suabian school, which attracted to itself all the sickly chlorotic, mawkishly-pious, clumsy votaries of the German muse. Stuttgart was the fontanel, as it were, for the German muse.

While I ascribe the highest achievements in drama, in romance, and in lyric poetry to this great triumvirate, far be it from me to depreciate the poetical merits of other great poets. Nothing is more foolish than the query, "Which poet is greater than the other?" Flame is flame, and its weight cannot be determined in pounds and ounces. Only a narrow shopkeeper mind will attempt to weigh genius in its miserable cheese scales. Not only the ancients, but some of the moderns, have written works in which the fire of poetry burns with a splendor equal to that of the masterpieces of Shakespeare, Cervantes, and Goethe. Nevertheless, these names hold together as if through some secret bond. A kindred spirit shines forth from their creations, an immortal tenderness exhales from them like the breath of God, the modesty of nature blooms in them. Goethe not only constantly reminds one of Shakespeare, but also of Cervantes, and he resembles the latter even in the details of style, and in that charming prose diction which is tinged with a vein of the sweetest and most harmless irony. Cervantes and Goethe resemble each other even in their faults, in diffusiveness of style, in those long sentences that we occasionally find in their writings, and which may be compared to a procession of royal equipages. Not infrequently but a single thought sits in one of those long, widespreading sentences that rolls majestically along like a great, gilded court-chariot, drawn by six plumed steeds. But that single idea is always something exalted, perhaps even royal.

My remarks concerning the genius of Cervantes and the influence of his book have been necessarily scant. Concerning the true value of his romance from an artistic standpoint, I must express myself still more briefly, as otherwise questions might arise which would lead to wide digressions into the sphere of æsthetics. I may only call attention in a general way to the form of the romance, and to the two figures that constitute its central point. The form is that of a description of travels which has ever been the most natural for this class of writings. I am reminded of "The Golden Ass" of Apuleius, the first romance of antiquity. Later poets sought to relieve the monotony of this form through what we to-day call *fabliaux.* But on account of poverty of invention the majority of romance writers have borrowed each other's fables; at least, part have always used the same tales, making but slight variations. Hence, through the resulting sameness of characters, situations, and complications, the public became at last somewhat wearied of romance-reading. To escape from the tediousness of hackneyed tales and fables, they sought refuge in the ancient, original form of narratives of travels. But this form will again be wholly supplanted just as soon as some creative genius shall arise with a new and original style of romance. In literature, as well as in politics, all things are subject to the law of action and reaction.

As regards the two figures that are called Don Quixote and Sancho Panza, that so constantly burlesque, and yet so wonderfully complement each other, so that together they form the one true hero of the romance—these two figures give evidence equally of the poet's artistic taste and of his intellectual profundity. If other authors, in whose romances the hero journeys solitary and alone through the world, are compelled to have recourse to monologues, letters, or diaries in order to communicate the thoughts and emotions of their heroes, Cervantes can always let a natural dialogue arise; and, inasmuch as the one figure always parodies the other, the author's purpose is the more clearly shown. Manifold have been the imitations of this double figure which lends to the romance of Cervantes such an artistic naturalness, and out of which, as from a single seed, has grown the whole novel, with all its wild foliage, its fragrant blossoms, its glowing fruits, its apes and marvellous birds that cluster amid its branches, resembling one of those giant trees of India.

But it would be unjust to charge all this to a servile imitation; on the surface, as it were, lay the introduction of two such figures as Don Quixote and Sancho Panza, of which the one, the poetical nature, seeks adventures, and the other, half out of affection, half out of selfish motives, follows through sunshine and rain, as we often meet them in real life. In order to recognize this couple anywhere, under the most varied disguises, in art as well as in life, one must keep in view only the essential, the spiritual characteristics, not the incidental or external. I could offer innumerable instances of this. Do we not find Don Quixote and Sancho Panza clearly repeated in Don Juan and Leperello, and to a certain degree also in the persons of Lord Byron and his servant Fletcher? Do we not recognize these two types and their changed relations in the figures of the Knight von Waldsee and his Caspar Larifari, as also in the form of many an author and his publisher? The latter clearly discerns his author's follies, but in order to reap pecuniary profit out of them, faithfully accompanies him in all his ideal vagaries. And Master Publisher Sancho, even if at times he gains only buffets in the transaction, yet always remains fat, while the noble knight grows daily more and more emaciated. But not only among men, but also among women, have I often met the counterparts of Don Quixote and his henchman. I particularly remember a beautiful English lady, an impulsive, enthusiastic blonde, who, accompanied by her friend, had run away from a London boarding-school, to roam the wide world over in search of a noble, true-hearted lover, such as she had dreamed of on soft moonlight nights. Her friend, a short, plump brunette, also hoped through this opportunity to gain, if not so rare and high an ideal, at least a husband of good appearance. Still do I see her, with her slender figure, and blue, love-longing eyes, standing on the beach at Brighton, casting wistful glances over the billowy sea towards the French coast; meanwhile her companion cracked hazel-nuts, munched the sweet kernels with relish, and threw the shells into the water.

And yet neither in the masterpieces of other artists, nor in nature herself, do we find these two types in their varying relations so minutely elaborated as in Cervantes. Every trait in the character and appearance of the one answers to a contrasting, and yet kindred, trait in the other. Here every detail has a burlesque signification; yes, even between Rosinante and Sancho's gray donkey there exists the same ironic parallelism as between the squire and the knight, and the two beasts are made to convey symbolically the same idea. As in their modes of thought, so also in their speech, do master and servant reveal a most marvellous contrast, and I cannot here omit to refer to the difficulties with which the translator has had to contend in order to reproduce in German the homely gnarled dialect of our good Sancho. Through his blunt, frequently vulgar speeches, and his fondness for proverbializing, our good Sancho reminds us of King Solomon's fool, and of Marculfe, who, also, in opposition to a somewhat pathetic idealism, expresses in short and pithy sayings the practical wisdom of the common people. Don Quixote, on the contrary, speaks the language of culture, of the higher classes, and in the solemn gravity of his well-rounded periods, he fairly represents the highborn hidalgo. At times his sentences are spun out too broadly, and the knight's language resembles a haughty court dame, attired in a much bepuffed silken robe, with a long rustling train. But the graces, disguised as pages, laughingly carry the tips of this train, and the long sentences end with the most charming turns.

The character of Don Quixote's language and that of Sancho Panza may be briefly summarized in the words: the former, when he speaks, seems always mounted on his high horse; the latter, as if seated on his humble donkey.

It is remarkable that a book which is so rich as "Don Quixote" in picturesque matter has as yet found no painter who has taken from it subjects for a series of independent art works. Is the spirit of the book so volatile and fanciful that the variegated colors elude the artist's skill? I do not think so, for "Don Quixote," light and fanciful as it is, is still based on rude, earthly realities, as must necessarily be the case to make it a book of the people. Is it, perhaps, because behind the figures brought before us by the poet, deeper ideas lie hidden, which the artist cannot produce again, so that he can give only the outward features, salient though they be, but fails to grasp and reproduce the deeper meaning?

FUNERAL OF NAPOLEON

BY
VICTOR HUGO

VICTOR MARIE HUGO
1802—1885

Victor Marie Hugo was born at Besançon in 1802. His father was a general of some note in the Napoleonic wars. Some years of the poet's childhood were passed in Spain, where his father held an important command, and some in Italy. His early education was superintended by his mother. While a mere boy Victor Hugo showed a precocious talent for poetry. He began serious literary work at the age of seventeen by contributions to the "Conservateur Litteraire," a literary publication founded by himself. In 1822 "Odes et poésies diverses" appeared. This collection was received with considerable favor and secured for him a pension from Louis XVIII which he deemed sufficient to justify him to assume the responsibilities of matrimonial life. Other volumes of poetry, chiefly lyrical, followed in rapid succession, the most notable being "Odes et ballades" in 1826 and "Les orientales" in 1829. The first of Hugo's romances was "Han d'islande" in 1823, followed by "Bug-Jargal" three years later. "Notre Dame de Paris" appeared in 1831. During the next ten years four new volumes of verse appeared and six dramas, among the latter "Hernani," "Le roi s'amuse," and "Ruy Blas." In 1841 Hugo was elected a member of the Academy, and four years later he became a peer. In 1848 he served as a deputy from Paris, his sympathies being ardently republican. The empire and the hostility of Napoleon drove him into years of exile, spent first at Brussels, then in Jersey, and finally in Guernsey.

During this period appeared the bitter attack on Napoleon III, entitled "Les châtiments," and another notable book of lyrics, "Les contemplations." The long romance of "Les misérables" was also written at this time and published in 1862. Although of uneven merit in its parts, this is without doubt Victor Hugo's greatest prose work. In 1866 the exquisite tale "Les travailleurs de la mer" appeared. With the fall of Napoleon his exile came to an end. Victor Hugo returned to France and was elected to the National Assembly. He resigned his seat, however, not long after his election, and again spent some time in Brussels. On his return to France in 1876 he was elected senator for life. His later years were spent quietly in Paris. His eightieth birthday was celebrated all over the world. His death occurred three years later, and his body was laid to rest in the Pantheon with great pomp and ceremony.

As a lyrical poet Victor Hugo ranks as one of the greatest of all ages. His prose writings alone would entitle him to rank as one of the beacon lights in the annals of the world's literature. In America and England he is undoubtedly better known as a writer of fiction than of verse, perhaps because his prose is susceptible of adequate translation, while his poetry, like most French poetry, is not. Of Hugo's style it is difficult to speak in a few words. As a vehicle of thought—now delicate, now profound—as a means for expressing emotion—now calm and peaceful, now tempestuous—his style is always dignified and natural. Victor Hugo has no superior in adaptability and force of expression. The selection given here, "The Funeral of Napoleon," is a characteristic example of his prose.

FUNERAL OF NAPOLEON

Notes taken on the spot, December 15, 1840

I HAVE heard the drums beat to arms in the streets since half-past six o'clock in the morning. I go out at eleven.

The streets are deserted, the shops shut; no passer-by is to be seen, save, perhaps, an old woman here and there. It is evident that all Paris has poured forth towards one side of the city like fluid in a slanting vessel. It is very cold; a bright sun, slight mists overhead. The gutters are frozen. As I reach the Louis-Philippe bridge a cloud descends, and a few snow-flakes, driven by the northerly wind, lash me in the face. Passing near Notre-Dame I notice that the great bell does not ring.

In the Rue Saint-André-des-Arts the fevered commotion of the *fête* begins to manifest itself. Ay, it is a *fête,* the *fête* of an exiled coffin returning in triumph. Three men of the lower classes, of those poor workmen in rags who are cold and hungry the whole winter-time, walk in front of me rejoicing. One of them jumps about, dances, and goes through a thousand absurd antics, crying, "*Vive l'Empereur!*" Pretty *grisettes,* smartly dressed, pass by, led by their student companions. Hired carriages are making rapidly in the direction of the Invalides. In the Rue du Four the snow thickens. The sky becomes black. The snow-flakes are interspersed with white tear-drops. Heaven itself seems to wish to hang out signs of mourning.

The storm, however, lasts but a short time. A pale streak of light illumines the angle of the Rue de Grenelle and the Rue du Bac, and there the municipal guards stop the vehicles. I pass by. Two great empty wagons conducted by artillerymen come from behind me, and return to their quarters at the end of the Rue de Grenelle just as I come out on the Place des Invalides. Here I fear at first that all is over, and that the Emperor has passed by, so many are the passers-by coming towards me who appear to be returning. It is only the crowd flowing back, driven by a cordon of municipal guards on foot. I show my ticket for the first platform on the left, and pass the barrier.

These platforms are immense wooden structures, covering, from the quay to the dome-shaped building, all the grass-plots of the esplanade. There are three of these on each side.

At the moment of my arrival the side of the platforms on the right as yet hides the square from my view. I hear a formidable and dismal noise. It seems like innumerable hammers beating time upon the boarding. It is the hundred thousand spectators crowded upon the platforms, who, being frozen by the northerly wind, are stamping to keep themselves warm until such time as the procession shall arrive. I climb up on the platform. The spectacle is no less strange. The women, nearly all of them wearing heavy boots, and veiled like the female ballad-singers of the Pont-Neuf, are hidden beneath great heaps of furs and cloaks; the men display neckerchiefs of extraordinary size.

The decoration of the square, good and bad. Shabbiness surmounting magnificence. On the two sides of the avenue two rows of figures, heroic, colossal, pale in this cold sunlight, producing rather a fine impression. They appear to be of white marble; but this marble is of plaster. At the extremity opposite the building the statue of the Emperor in bronze; this bronze is also of plaster. In each gap between the statues a pillar of painted cloth, and gilded in rather bad taste, surmounted by a brazier, just now filled with snow. Behind the statues the platforms and the crowd; between the statues a straggling file of the National Guard; above the platforms masts, on top of which grandly fluttered sixty long tricolored pennants.

It appears that there has been no time to finish the decoration of the principal entrance to the building. Above the railings has been roughly constructed a sort of funeral triumphal arch of painted cloth and crape, with which the wind plays as with old linen clothes hung out from the garret of a hovel. A row of poles, plain and bare, rise above the cannon, and from a distance look like those small sticks which little children plant in the sand. Clothes and rags, which are supposed to be black drapery with silver spangles, flutter and flap together feebly between these poles. At the end the dome, with its flag and

FUNERAL OF NAPOLEON

mourning drapery, sparkling with a metallic lustre, subdued by the mist in a brilliant sky, has a sombre and splendid appearance.

It is mid-day.

The cannon at the building is fired at quarter-hour intervals. The crowd stamp their feet. Gendarmes disguised in plain clothes, but betraying themselves by their spurs and the stocks of their uniforms, walk hither and thither. In front of me a ray of light shows up vividly a rather poor statue of Joan of Arc, who holds in her hand a palm-branch, which she appears to use as a shade, as though the sun affected her eyes.

At a few steps from the statue a fire, at which a number of men of the National Guard warm their feet, is alight in a heap of sand.

From time to time military bandsmen invade an orchestra, raised between the two platforms on the opposite side, perform a funeral flourish, then come down again hastily and disappear in the crowd, only to reappear the moment after. They leave the music for the wine-shop.

A hawker passes along the platform selling dirges at a half-penny each, and accounts of the ceremony. I buy two of these documents.

All eyes are fixed upon the corner of the Quai d'Orsay, whence the procession is to come out. The cold adds to the feeling of impatience. Black and white lines of vapor ascend here and there through the thick mist of the Champs-Elysées, and detonations are heard in the distance.

Of a sudden the National Guards hasten to arms. An orderly officer crosses the avenue at a gallop. A line is formed. Workmen place ladders against the pillars and begin to light the braziers. A salvo of heavy artillery explodes loudly at the east corner of the Invalides; a dense yellow smoke, mingled with golden flashes, fills this whole corner. From the position in which I am placed the firing of the guns can be seen. They are two fine old engraved cannon of the seventeenth century, which one hears from the noise are of bronze. The procession approaches.

It is half-past twelve.

At the far end of the esplanade, near the river, a double row of mounted grenadiers, with yellow shoulder-belts, solemnly debouch. This is the *gendarmerie* of the Seine. It is the head of the procession. At this moment the sun does its duty, and appears in its glory. It is the month of Austerlitz.

After the bear-skins of the *gendarmerie* of the Seine, the brass helmets of the Paris municipal guard, then the tricolored pennants of the lancers, fluttering in the air in charming fashion. Flourishes of trumpets and beating of drums.

A man in a blue blouse climbs over the outside wood-work, at the risk of breaking his neck, on the platform in front of me. No one assists him. A spectator in white gloves looks at him as he does so, and does not hold out a hand to him. The man, however, reaches his destination.

The procession, including generals and marshals, has an admirable effect. The sun, striking the cuirasses of the carabineers, lights up the breast of each of them with a dazzling star. The three military schools pass by with erect and solemn bearing, then the artillery and infantry, as though going into action. The ammunition wagons have the spare wheel at the rear, the soldiers carry their knapsacks upon their backs. A short distance off, a great statue of Louis XIV, of ample dimensions and tolerably good design, gilded by the sun, seems to view with amazement all this splendor.

The mounted National Guard appear. Uproar in the crowd. It is sufficiently well disciplined notwithstanding, but it is an inglorious regiment, and this detracts from the effect of a procession of this kind. People laugh. I hear this conversation: "Just look at that fat colonel! How strangely he holds his sword!" "Who is that fellow?" "That is Montalivet."

Interminable legions of the infantry of the National Guard now march past, with arms reversed, like the line regiments, beneath the shadow of this gray sky. A mounted National Guard who lets fall his shako, and so gallops bareheaded for some time, although successful in catching it, causes much amusement to the gallery, that is to say, to a hundred thousand people.

From time to time the procession halts, then continues on its way. The lighting of the braziers is completed, and they smoke between the statues like great bowls of punch.

Expectation rises higher. Here is the black carriage with silver ornamentation of the chaplain of the Belle-Poule, in the inside of which is seen a priest in mourning; then the great black velvet coach with mirror panels of the St. Helena Commission, four horses to each of these two carriages.

Suddenly the cannon are discharged simultaneously from three different points on the horizon. This triple sound hems in the ear in a sort of triangle, formidable and superb. Drums beat a salute in the distance. The funeral carriage of the Emperor appears. The sun, obscured until this moment, reappears at the same time. The effect is prodigious.

In the distance is seen, in the mist and sunlight, against the gray and russet background of the trees in the Champs-Elysées, beyond the great white phantom-like statues, a kind of golden mountain slowly moving. All that can be distinguished of it as yet is a sort of luminous glistening, which makes now stars, now lightning sparkle over the whole surface of the car. A mighty roar follows this apparition. It would seem as though this draws after it the acclamation of the whole city, as a torch draws after it its smoke.

As it turns in the avenue of the esplanade it remains for a few moments at a stand-still, through some contingency, before a statue which stands at the corner of the avenue and of the quay. I have since ascertained that this statue was that of Marshal Ney.

At the moment when the funeral car appeared it was half-past one.

The procession resumes its progress. The car advances slowly. The shape begins to display itself.

Here are the saddle-horses of the marshals and generals who hold the cords of the imperial pall. Here are the eighty-six subaltern legionaries bearing the banners of the eighty-six departments. Nothing prettier to be conceived than this square, above which flutters a forest of flags. It might be supposed that a gigantic field of dahlias is on the march.

Here comes a white horse covered from head to foot with a violet pall, accompanied by a chamberlain in pale blue, embroidered with silver, and led by two footmen, dressed in green, with gold lace. It is the Emperor's livery. A shudder goes through the crowd. It is Napoleon's charger! The majority firmly believed it. Had the horse been ridden only for two years by the Emperor, he would be thirty years old, which is a good age for a horse.

The fact is that this palfrey is a good old supernumerary horse, who has filled for some ten years the office of charger in all the military burials over which the Funeral Administration presides. This charger of straw carries on his back the genuine saddle of Bonaparte at Marengo: a crimson velvet saddle with a double row of gold lace, tolerably well worn.

After the horse come, in close and regular formation, the five hundred sailors of the Belle-Poule, youthful faces for the most part, dressed for action, with round jackets, round varnished hats, each with his pistol in his belt, his boarding axe in hand, and at his side a sword, a cutlass with a large handle of polished iron.

The salvoes continue. At this moment the story goes the round of the crowd that the first discharge of cannon at the Invalides has cut off the legs of a municipal guard at the thighs. By an oversight the gun had not been unloaded. It is added that a man has fallen down in the Place Louis XV under the wheels of the cars, and has been crushed to death.

The car is now very near. It is almost immediately preceded by the officers of the Belle-Poule, under the command of the Prince de Joinville, on horseback. The Prince de Joinville's face is covered with a beard (fair), which appears to me contrary to the rules of the naval forces. He wears for the first time the grand ribbon of the Legion of Honor. Hitherto he figured upon the roll of the Legion only as a plain knight.

Arriving immediately in front of me, a slightly momentary interruption, I know not from what cause, takes place; the car halts. It remains stationary for a few minutes between the statue of Joan of Arc and the statue of Charles V.

I can survey it at leisure. The effect, as a whole, is not wanting in grandeur. It is an enormous mass, gilt all over, of which the tiers rise pyramid-like above the four great gilt wheels which bear it. Under the violet pall, studded with bees, which covers it from top to bottom, some tolerably fine details may be observed; the wild-looking eagles of the base, the fourteen Victories of the top-piece bearing upon a golden support the representation of a coffin. The real coffin is invisible. It has been deposited inside the basement, which detracts from the sensational effect. That is the grave defect of this car. It conceals what one would wish to see, what France has demanded, what the people expect, what every eye seeks—the coffin of Napoleon.

Upon the sham sarcophagus have been deposited the insignia of the Emperor—the crown, the sword, the sceptre, and the robe. In the gilded orifice which divides the Victories on the summit from the eagles at the base can be distinctly seen, in spite of the gilding already partly chipped off, the joints in the deal planks. Another defect. This gold is merely imitation. Deal and pasteboard, that is the reality. I could have wished for the Emperor's funeral car a splendor of a genuine character.

Nevertheless, the greater part of this sculptural composition has some boldness and artistic merit, although the conception of the design and the ornamentation hesitate between the Renaissance and the rococo.

Two immense bundles of flags, conquered from all the nations of Europe, rise in glorious splendor from the front and rear of the car.

The car, with all its load, weighs twenty-six thousand pounds. The coffin alone weighs five thousand pounds.

Nothing more surprising and more superb could be imagined than the set of sixteen horses which draw the car. They are terrific creatures, adorned with white plumes flowing down to the haunches, and covered from head to foot with a splendid caparison of gold cloth, leaving only their eyes visible, which gives them an indescribable air of phantom steeds.

Valets in the imperial livery lead this imposing cavalcade.

On the other hand, the worthy and venerable generals who hold the cords of the pall have an appearance as far removed from the fantastic as could well be conceived. At the head two marshals—the Duke de Reggio,[1] diminutive and blind in one eye, to the right; to the left Count Molitor; in the rear, on the right, an admiral, Baron Duperre, a stout and jovial sailor;

---

[1] The Duke de Reggio is not really blind in one eye. A few years ago, as the result of a cold, the marshal had an attack of local paralysis which affected the right cheek and pupil. Since that time he cannot open the right eye. However, throughout this ceremony he displayed wonderful courage. Covered with wounds, and seventy-five years of age, he remained in the open air, in a temperature of fourteen degrees, from eight o'clock in the morning until two o'clock in the afternoon, in full uniform, and without a cloak, out of respect for his general. He made the journey from Courbevoie to the Invalides on foot, on his three broken legs, as the Duchess de Reggio wittily said to me. The marshal, in fact, having suffered two fractures of the right leg and one of the left, has really had three legs broken. After all, it is remarkable that, out of so many veterans exposed for so great a length of time to this severe cold, no mishap should have happened to any one of them. Strange to say, this funeral did not bury anybody.

on the left a lieutenant-general, Count Bertrand—old, exhausted, broken-down, a noble and illustrious figure. All four wear the red ribbon.

The car, let it be said, by the way, was not intended to be drawn by more than eight horses. Eight horses is a symbolical number which has a significance in the ceremonial. Seven horses, nine horses, are a wagoner's team; sixteen horses are for a stone-mason's dray; eight horses are for an Emperor.[2]

The spectators upon the platforms have continued without intermission to stamp with the soles of their boots, except at the moment when the catafalque passed before them. Then only are the feet silent. One can tell that a great thought flashes through the crowd.

The car has resumed its progress, the drums beat a salute, the firing of the cannon is more rapid. Napoleon is at the gates of the Invalides. It is ten minutes to two.

Behind the bier come in civilian dress all the survivors of the Emperor's household, then all the survivors of the soldiers of the Guard, clad in their glorious uniforms, already unfamiliar to us.

The remainder of the procession, made up of regiments of the regular army and the National Guard, occupies, it is said, the Quai d'Orsay, the Louis XVI bridge, the Place de la Concorde, and the Avenue des Champs-Elysées as far as the Arc de l'Étoile.

The car does not enter the court-yard of the Invalides; the railings planted by Louis XIV are too low. It turns off to the right; sailors are seen to enter into the basement and issue forth again with the coffin, then disappear beneath the porch erected at the entrance to the enclosure. They are in the court-yard.

---

[2] December 29, 1840.—It has since been ascertained that the magnificent saddle-cloths of gold brocade which caparisoned the sixteen horses were of spun glass. An unworthy saving. An unseemly deception. This singular announcement now appears in the newspapers: "A large number of persons who came to the spun-glass warehouse at No. 97 Rue de Charonne, to see the mantle which adorned the sides of the funeral car of Napoleon, wished to keep a souvenir of the great ceremony by buying a few eagles from this mantle. The manager of the establishment, who, in obedience to the command of the government, was obliged to refuse them, is now in a position to accede to their request." So we have a bronze statue in plaster, solid gold Victories in pasteboard, an imperial mantle in spun glass, and—a fortnight after the ceremony—eagles for sale.

All is over for the spectators outside. They descend very noisily and hurriedly from the platforms. Knots of people stop at short distances apart before some posters stuck to the boards, and running thus: "Leroy, refreshment contractor, Rue de la Serpe, near the Invalides. Choice wines and hot pastry."

I can now examine the decoration of the avenue. Nearly all these statues in plaster are bad. Some are ridiculous. The Louis XIV, which at a distance had solidity, is grotesque at near sight. Macdonald is a good likeness. Mortier the same. Ney would be so if he had not had so high a forehead given to him. In fact, the sculptor has made it exaggerated and ridiculous in the attempt to be melancholy. The head is too large. In reference to this, it is said that in the hurry of improvising the statues the measurements have been given incorrectly. On the day when they had to be delivered, the statuary sent in a Marshal Ney a foot too tall. What did the people of the Fine Arts department do? They sawed out of the statue a slice of the stomach twelve inches wide, and stuck the two pieces together again as well as they were able.

The bronze-colored plaster of the statue of the Emperor is stained and covered with spots, which make the imperial robe look like a patchwork of old green baize.

This reminds me, for the generation of ideas is a strange mystery, that this summer, at the residence of M. Thiers, I heard Marchand, the Emperor's *valet-de-chambre,* say how Napoleon loved old coats and old hats. I understand and share this taste. For a brain which works the pressure of a new hat is insupportable.

The Emperor, said Marchand, took away with him when he quitted France three coats, two surtouts, and two hats; he got through his six years at St. Helena with this wardrobe; he did not wear any uniform.

Marchand added other curious details. The Emperor, at the Tuileries, often appeared to rapidly change his attire. In reality this was not so. The Emperor usually wore civilian dress, that is to say, breeches of white kerseymere, white silk stockings, shoes with buckles. But there was always in the next apartment a pair of riding-boots, lined with white silk up to the knees. When anything happened which made it necessary for the Emperor to mount on horseback, he took off his slippers, put on his boots, got into his uniform, and was transformed into a soldier. Then he returned home, took off his boots, put on his slippers again, and became once more a civilian. The white breeches, the stockings, and the shoes were never worn more than one day. On the morrow these imperial cast-off clothes belonged to the *valet-de-chambre.*

It is three o'clock. A salvo of artillery announces that the ceremony at the Invalides is at an end. I meet B——. He has just come out. The sight of the coffin has produced an ineffable impression.

The words which were spoken were simple and grand. The Prince de Joinville said to the King, " Sire, I present to you the body of the Emperor Napoleon." The King replied, " I receive it in the name of France." Then he said to Bertrand, " General, place upon the coffin the glorious sword of the Emperor." And to Gourgaud, " General, place upon the coffin the hat of the Emperor."

Mozart's " Requiem " had but little effect. Beautiful music already faded with age. Music too, alas, becomes faded with age!

The catafalque was only finished one hour before the arrival of the coffin. B—— was in the church at eight o'clock in the morning. It was as yet only half draped, and ladders, tools, and workmen encumbered it. The crowd were coming in during this time. Large gilt palms of five or six feet in height were tried on the four corners of the catafalque; but after being put in position they were seen to produce but a poor effect. They were removed.[3]

The Prince de Joinville, who had not seen his family for six months, went up and kissed the hand of the Queen, and heartily shook hands with his brothers and sisters. The Queen received him in stately fashion, without demonstration, as a Queen rather than as a mother.

During this time the archbishops, *curés,* and priests sang the *Requiescat in pace* around the coffin of Napoleon.

---

[3] December 23d.—Since the transfer of the coffin the church of the Invalides is open to the crowd who visit it. There pass through it daily a hundred thousand persons, from ten o'clock in the morning until four o'clock in the evening. The lighting of the chapel costs the State 350 francs a day. M. Duchatel, Minister of the Interior (who, it may be stated, by the way, is said to be a son of the Emperor), groans aloud at this expense.

The procession was fine, but too exclusively military, sufficing for Bonaparte, not for Napoleon. All the bodies in the State should have figured in it, at least by deputy. The fact is, the thoughtlessness of the government has been extreme. It was in haste to be done with the affair. Philippe de Ségur, who followed the car as a former aide-de-camp of the Emperor, told me how at Courbevoie, on the banks of the river, in an atmosphere of fourteen degrees, this morning, there was not even a waiting-room with a fire in it. These two hundred veterans of the Emperor's household had to wait for an hour and a half in a kind of Greek temple, exposed to the wind from all quarters of the compass.

The same neglect was shown with respect to the steamboats which took the body from Havre to Paris, a journey remarkable, nevertheless, for the earnest and solemn demeanor of the riverside populations. None of these boats was suitably fitted up. Victuals were wanting. No beds. Orders given that no one should land. The Prince de Joinville was obliged to sleep, one of a party of twenty, in a common room upon a table. Others slept underneath. The men slept on the ground, and the more fortunate upon benches or chairs. It seemed as though those in authority were in ill-humor. The Prince complained openly of it, and said, " In this affair all that emanates from the people is great, all that emanates from the government is paltry."

Wishing to reach the Champs-Elysées, I crossed the suspension-bridge, where I paid my half-penny. A real act of generosity, for the mob which crowds the bridge neglects to pay.

The legions and regiments are in battle array in the Avenue de Neuilly. The avenue is decorated, or rather dishonored, along its entire length by fearful statues in plaster representing figures of Fame, and triumphal columns crowned with golden eagles and placed in a blank space upon gray marble pedestals. The street-boys amuse themselves by making holes in this marble, which is made of cloth.

Upon each column are seen, between two bundles of tricolored flags, the name and the date of one of the victories of Bonaparte.

An inferior theatrical-looking group occupies the top of the Arc de Triomphe: the Emperor erect upon a car surrounded by figures of Fame, having on his right Glory, and on his left Grandeur. What is the meaning of a statue of grandeur? How can grandeur be expressed by means of a statue? Is it in making it larger than the others? This is monumental nonsense.

This scenic effect, poorly gilt, is turned towards Paris. By going to the other side of the Arc one can see the back of it. It is a regular theatrical set piece. On the side looking towards Neuilly, the Emperor, the Glories, and the Fames become simply pieces of framework clumsily shaped.

With regard to this matter, the figures in the Avenue des Invalides have been strangely chosen, be it said by the way. The published list gives bold and singular conjunctions of names. Here is one: Lobau, Charlemagne, Hugues Capet.

A few months ago I was taking a walk in these same Champs-Elysées with Thiers, then Prime Minister. He would, without doubt, have managed the ceremony with greater success. He would have put his heart into it. He had ideas. He loves and appreciates Napoleon. He told me some anecdotes of the Emperor. M. de Rémusat allowed him to see the unpublished memoirs of his mother. There are in them a hundred details. The Emperor was good-natured, and loved to tease people. To tease is the malice of good men. Caroline, his sister, wanted to be a Queen. He made her a Queen—Queen of Naples. But the poor woman had many troubles from the moment she had a throne, and became, as she sat on it, somewhat careworn and faded. One day Talma was breakfasting with Napoleon—etiquette permitted Talma to come only to breakfast. Hereupon Queen Caroline, just arrived from Naples, pale and fatigued, calls upon the Emperor. He looks at her, then turns towards Talma, much embarrassed between these two majesties. "My dear Talma," he said, "they all want to be Queens; they lose their beauty in consequence. Look at Caroline. She is a Queen; she is ugly."

As I pass, the demolition is just being finished of the innumerable stands, draped with black, and filled with seats, which have been erected by speculators at the entrance to the Avenue de Neuilly. Upon one of them, facing the Beaujon garden, I read this inscription: "Seats to let. Austerlitz grand stand. Apply to M. Berthellemot, confectioner."

On the other side of the avenue, upon a showman's booth adorned with frightful pictorial signs representing, one of them the death of the Emperor, the other the encounter at Mazagran, I read another inscription: "Napoleon in his coffin. Three half-pence."

Men of the lower classes pass by and sing, "Long live my great Napoleon!" "Long live old Napoleon!" Hawkers make their way through the crowd, shouting tobacco and cigars! Others offer to the passers-by some kind of hot and steaming liquor out of a copper tea-urn covered with a black cloth. An old woman at a stall coolly puts on an undergarment in the midst of the hurly-burly. Towards five o'clock the funeral car, now empty, returns by way of the Avenue des Champs-Elysées, to be put up under the Arc de Triomphe. This is a capital idea. But the magnificent spectre-horses are tired. They walk with difficulty, and slowly, notwithstanding all the efforts of the drivers. Nothing stranger can be imagined than the shouts of *hu-ho* and *dia-hu* lavished upon this imperial, but at the same time fantastic, team.

I return home by the boulevards. The crowd there is immense; suddenly it falls back and looks round with a certain air of respect. A man passes proudly by in its midst. He is an old hussar of the Imperial Guard, a veteran of great height and lusty appearance. He is in full uniform, with tight-fitting red trousers, a white waistcoat with gold braid, a sky-blue pelisse, a busby with a grenade and plaited loop, his sword at his side, his sabre-tache beating upon his thighs, an eagle upon his satchel. All round him the little children cry, "*Vive l'Empéreur!*"

It is certain that all this ceremony has been curiously like a juggle. The government appeared to fear the phantom which it had raised. It seemed as though the object was both to show and to hide Napoleon. Everything which would have been too grand or too touching was left out of sight. The real and the grandiose were concealed beneath more or less splendid coverings, the imperial procession was juggled into the military procession, the army was juggled into the National Guard, the Chambers were juggled into the Invalides, the coffin was juggled into the cenotaph.

What was wanted, on the contrary, was that Napoleon should be taken up, frankly honored, treated royally and popularly as Emperor, and then strength would have been found just where a failure almost took place.

To-day, the eighth of May, I return to the Invalides to see the St. Jérôme chapel, where the Emperor is temporarily placed. All traces of the ceremony of the fifteenth of December have disappeared from the esplanade. The quincunxes have been cut out afresh; the grass, however, has not yet grown again. There was some sunshine, accompanied now and then by clouds and rain. The trees were green and lusty. The poor old pensioners were talking quietly to a group of youngsters, and walking in their little gardens full of bouquets. It is that delightful period of the year when the late lilacs have shed their petals, when the early laburnums are in bloom. The great shadows of the clouds pass rapidly across the forecourt, where stands under an archivault on the first floor a plaster equestrian statue of Napoleon, a rather pitiful counterpart to the equestrian Louis XIV, boldly chiselled in stone over the great portal.

All round the court, below the eaves of the building, are still stuck up, as the last vestiges of the funeral, the long narrow strips of black cloth upon which had been painted in golden letters, three by three, the names of the generals of the Revolution and the Empire. The wind begins, however, to tear them down here and there. On one of these strips, of which the torn end floated in mid-air, I read these three names:

Sauret—Chambure—Hug—

The end of the third name had been torn and carried off by the wind. Was it Hugo or Huguet?

Some young soldiers were entering the church. I followed these *tourlourous,* as the phrase goes nowadays. For in time of war the soldier calls the citizen a *pékin;* in time of peace the citizen calls the soldier a *tourlourou.*

The church was bare and cold, almost deserted. At the end a large gray cloth covering, stretched from top to bottom, hid the enormous archivault of the dome. Behind this covering could be heard the muffled and almost funereal sound of hammers.

I walked about for an instant or two, reading upon the pillars the names of all the warriors buried there.

All along the nave above our heads the flags conquered from the enemy, that accumulation of splendid tatters, were gently wafted near the roof. In the intervals between the blows of the hammers I heard a muttering in a corner of the church. It was an old woman at confession.

The soldiers went out, and myself behind them. They turned to the right along the Metz corridor, and we mixed with a tolerably large and very well-dressed crowd going in that direction. The corridor leads to the inner court in which the minor entrance to the dome is situated.

There I found three more statues, of lead, taken I know not where from, which I remember to have seen on this same spot as a little child in 1815, at the time of the mutilation of buildings, dynasties, and nations, which took place at that period. These three statues, in the worst style of the Empire, cold as allegory, gloomy as mediocrity, stand alongside the wall there, on the grass, amid a mass of architectural capitals, with an indescribable suggestion of tragedies which have been damned. One of them leads a lion by a chain, and represents Might. Nothing can appear so much out of place as a statue standing upon the ground without a pedestal; it looks like a horse without a rider, or a king without a throne. There are but two alternatives for the soldier—battle or death; there are but two for the king—empire or the tomb; there are but two for the statue—to stand erect against the sky or to lie flat upon the ground. A statue on foot puzzles the mind and bothers the eye. One forgets that it is of plaster or bronze, and that bronze does not walk any more than plaster; and one is tempted to say to this poor creature with a human face so awkward and wretched-looking in its ostentatious attitude: " Now then, go on, be off with you, march, keep going, move yourself! The ground is beneath your feet. What stops you? Who hinders you? " The pedestal, at least, explains the want of motion. For statues as for men a pedestal is a small space, narrow and respectable, with four precipices around it.

After having passed by the statues I turned to the right and entered the church by the great door at the rear, facing the boulevard. Several young women pass through the doorway at the same time as myself, laughing and calling to each other. The sentry allowed us to pass. He was a bent and melancholy-looking old soldier, sword in hand, perhaps an old grenadier of the Imperial Guard, silent and motionless in the shadow, and resting the end of his worn wooden leg upon a marble fleur-de-lis, half chipped out of the stone.

To get to the chapel where Napoleon is one has to walk over a pavement tessellated with fleurs-de-lis. The crowd, women and soldiers, were in haste. I entered the church with slow steps.

A light from above, wan and pale, the light of a workshop rather than of a church, illuminated the interior of the dome. Immediately under the cupola, at the spot where the altar was and the tomb will be, stood, covered on the side of the aisle by the mass of black drapery, the immense scaffolding used in pulling down the baldachin erected under Louis XIV. No trace of this baldachin remained save the shafts of six great wooden columns supporting the head. These columns, destitute of capital or abacus, were still supported vertically by six shaped logs which had been put in place of the pedestals. The gold foliage, the spirals of which gave them a certain appearance of twisted columns, had already disappeared, leaving a black mark upon the six gilt shafts. The workmen perched up here and there inside the scaffolding looked like great birds in an enormous cage.

Others, below, were tearing up the stone floor. Others again passed up and down the church, carrying their ladders, whistling and chatting.

On my right the chapel of Saint-Augustin was full of *débris*. Huge blocks, broken and in heaps, of that splendid mosaic work in which Louis XIV had set his fleurs-de-lis and sun-flowers concealed the feet of Saint Monica and Saint Alipa, looking wonder-stricken and shocked in their niches. The statue of Religion, by Girardon, erect between the two windows, looked gravely down upon this confusion.

Beyond the chapel of Saint-Augustin some large marble slabs which had formed the covering of the dome, placed vertically against each other, half hid a white, war-like, recumbent figure of a warrior beneath a rather high pyramid of black marble fixed in the wall. Underneath this figure, in a gap between the flagstones, could be read the three letters

U B A

It was the tomb of V*auba*n.

On the opposite side of the church, in front of the tomb of Vauban, was the tomb of Turenne. The latter had been treated with greater respect than the other. No accumulation of ruins rested against that great sculptural design, more pompous than funereal, made for the stage rather than the church, in harmony with the frigid and exalted etiquette which ruled the art of Louis XIV. No palisade, no mound of rubbish prevented the passer-by from seeing Turenne, attired as a Roman Emperor, dying of an Austrian bullet above the bronze bas-relief of the battle of Turckheim, or from deciphering this memorable date, 1675—the year in which Turenne died, the Duke de Saint-Simon was born, and Louis XIV laid the foundation-stone of the Hôtel des Invalides.

On the right, against the scaffolding of the dome and the tomb of Turenne, between the silence of this sepulchre and the noise of the workmen, in a little barricaded and deserted chapel, I could discern behind a railing, through the opening of a white arch, a group of gilt statues, placed there pell-mell, and doubtless torn from the baldachin, conversing apparently in whispers on the subject of all this devastation. There were six of them— six-winged and luminous angels, six golden phantoms, gloomily illuminated by a pale stream of sunlight. One of these statues indicated to the others with uplifted finger the chapel of Saint-Jérôme, gloomy, and in mourning drapery, and seemed to utter with consternation the word Napoleon. Above these six spectres, upon the cornice of the little roof of the chapel, a great angel in gilt wood was playing upon a violoncello, with eyes upturned to heaven, almost in the attitude which Veronese ascribes to Tintoretto in the "Marriage at Cana."

By this time I had arrived at the threshold of the chapel of Saint-Jérôme.

A great archivault, with a lofty door-curtain of rather paltry violet cloth, stamped with a fretwork pattern, and with golden palm-leaves; at the top of the door-curtain the imperial escutcheon in painted wood; on the left two bundles of tricolored flags, surmounted with eagles looking like cocks touched up for the occasion; pensioners, wearing the Legion of Honor, carrying pikes; the crowd, silent and reverential, entering under the archway; at the extremity, eight or ten paces distant, an iron gate-way, bronzed; upon the gate-way, which is of a heavy and feeble style of ornamentation, lions' heads, gilt N's with a tinsel-like appearance, the arms of the empire, the *main-de-justice* and sceptre, the latter surmounted by a seated miniature of Charlemagne, crowned, and globe in hand; beyond the gate-way the interior of the chapel, a something indescribably august, formidable, and striking: a swinging lamp alight, a golden eagle with wide-spread wings, the stomach glistening in the gloomy reflection of the lamplight, and the wings in the reflection of the sunlight; under the eagle, beneath a vast and dazzling bundle of enemies' flags, the coffin, the ebony supports and brass handles of which were visible; upon the coffin the great imperial crown, like that of Charlemagne, the gold laurel diadem, like that of Cæsar, the violet velvet pall studded with bees; in front of the coffin, upon a credence-table, the hat of St. Helena and the sword of Eylau; upon the wall, to the right of the coffin, in the centre of a silver shield, the word Wagram; on the left, in the centre of another shield, another word—Austerlitz; all round upon the wall a hanging of violet velvet, embroidered with bees and eagles; at the top, on the spandrel of the nave, above the lamp, the eagle, the crown, the sword, and the coffin, a fresco, and in this fresco the angel of judgment sounding the trumpet over Saint-Jérôme asleep—that is what I saw at a glance, and that is what a minute sufficed to engrave upon my memory for life.

The hat, low-crowned, wide-brimmed, but little worn, trimmed with a black ribbon, out of which appeared a small tricolored cockade, was placed upon the sword, of which the chased gold hilt was turned towards the entrance to the chapel and the point towards the coffin.

There was some admixture of meanness amid all this grandeur. It was mean on account of the violet cloth, which was stamped and not embroidered; of the pasteboard painted to look like stone; of the hollow iron made to look like bronze; of that wooden escutcheon; of those N's in tinsel; of that canvas Roman column, painted to look like granite; of those eagles almost like cocks. The grandeur was in the spot, in the man, in the reality, in the sword, in the hat, in that eagle, in those soldiers, in that assemblage of people, in that ebony coffin, in that ray of sunlight.

The people were there as before an altar in which the Supreme Being should be visible. But in leaving the chapel, after having gone a hundred steps, they entered to see the kitchen and the great saucepan. Such is the nature of the people.

It was with profound emotion that I contemplated that coffin. I remembered that, less than a twelvemonth previously, in the month of July, a M.—— presented himself at my house, and after having told me that he was in business as a cabinetmaker in the Rue des Tourelles, and a neighbor of mine, begged me to give him my advice respecting an important and precious article which he was commissioned to make just then. As I am greatly interested in the improvement of that small internal architecture which is called furniture, I responded favorably to the request, and accompanied M. —— to the Rue des Tourelles. There, after having made me pass through several large, well-filled rooms, and shown me an immense quantity of oak and mahogany furniture, Gothic chairs, writing-tables with carved rails, tables with twisted legs, among which I admired a genuine old sideboard of the Renaissance, inlaid with mother-of-pearl and marble, very dilapidated and very charming, the cabinetmaker showed me into a great workshop full of activity, bustle, and noise, where some twenty workmen were at work upon some kind or other of pieces of black wood which they had in their hands. I saw in a corner of the workshop a kind of large black ebony box, about eight feet long and three feet wide, ornamented at each end with big brass rings. I went towards it. "That is precisely," said the employer, "what I wanted to show to you." This black box was the coffin of the Emperor. I saw it then, I saw it again to-day. I saw it empty, hollow, wide open. I saw it once more full, tenanted by a great souvenir, forever closed.

I remember that I contemplated the inside for a long time. I looked especially at a long pale streak in the ebony which formed the left-hand side, and I said to myself, "In a few months the lid will be closed upon this coffin, and my eyes will perhaps have been closed for three or four thousand years before it will be given to any other human eyes to see what I see at this moment—the inside of the coffin of Napoleon."

I then took all the pieces of the coffin which were not yet fastened. I raised them and weighed them in my hands. The ebony was very fine and very heavy. The head of the establishment, in order to give me an idea of the general effect, had the lid put on the coffin by six men. I did not like the commonplace shape given to the coffin, a shape given nowadays to all coffins, to all altars, and to all wedding caskets. I should have preferred that Napoleon should have slept in an Egyptian tomb like Sesostris, or in a Roman sarcophagus like Merovée. That which is simple is also imposing.

Upon the lid shone in tolerably large characters the name Napoleon. "What metal are these letters made of?" I asked the man. He replied, "In copper, but they will be gilded." "These letters," I rejoined, "must be in gold. In less than a hundred years copper letters will have become oxydized, and will have eaten into the wood-work of the coffin. How much would gold letters cost the State?" "About twenty thousand francs, sir." The same evening I called on M. Thiers, who was then President of the Council, and I explained the matter to him. "You are right," said M. Thiers, "the letters shall be of gold; I will go and give the necessary order for them." Three days afterwards the treaty of the fifteenth of July burst upon us; I do not know whether M. Thiers gave the order, whether it was executed, or whether the letters on the coffin are gold letters.

I left the chapel of Saint-Jérôme as four o'clock was striking, and I said to myself as I left, "To all appearance, here is a tinsel N which smashes, eclipses, and supersedes the marble L's, with their crowns and fleurs-de-lis, of Louis XIV; but in reality it is not so. If this dome is narrow, history is wide. A day will come when Louis XIV will have his dome restored to him, and a sepulchre will be given to Napoleon. The great King and the great Emperor will each be at home, in peace the one with the other, both venerated, both illustratious—the one because he personifies royalty in the eyes of Europe, the other because he represents France in the eyes of the world."

To-day, March 11, 1841, three months afterwards, I saw once more the Esplanade of the Invalides.

I went to see an old officer who was ill. The weather was the finest imaginable; the sun was warm and young; it was a day for the end rather than the beginning of spring.

The whole esplanade is in confusion. It is encumbered with the ruins of the funeral. The scaffolding of the platforms has been removed. The squares of grass which they covered have reappeared, hideously cut up by the deep ruts of the builder's wagons. Of the statues which lined the triumphal avenue, two only remain standing—Marceau and Duguesclin. Here and there heaps of stone, the remains of the pedestals. Soldiers, pensioners, apple-women, wander about amid this fallen poetry.

A merry crowd was passing rapidly in front of the Invalides, going to see the artesian well. In a silent corner of the esplanade stood two omnibuses, painted a chocolate color (*Béarnaises*), bearing this inscription in large letters:

Puits de l'Abattoir de Grenelle.

Three months ago they bore this one:

Funeral of Napoleon at the Invalides.

In the court-yard of the building the sun cheered and warmed a crowd of youngsters and old men, the most charming sight imaginable. It was public visiting-day. The curious presented themselves in great numbers. Gardeners were clipping the hedges. The lilacs were bursting into bud in the little gardens of the pensioners. A little boy of fourteen years of age was singing at the top of his voice while sitting up on the carriage of the last cannon on the right, the same one which killed a gendarme in firing the first funeral salvo on the fifteenth of December.

I may mention, by the way, that during the last three months these excellent sixteenth and seventeenth century pieces have been perched upon hideous little cast-iron carriages, producing a most mean and wretched effect. The old wooden carriages, enormous, squat, massive, worthily supported these gigantic and magnificent bronzes. A bevy of children, languidly looked after by their nurses, each of whom was leaning against her soldier, were playing among the twenty-four great culverins brought from Constantine and Algiers.

These gigantic engines, at least, have been spared the affront of uniform carriages. They lie flat on the ground on the two sides of the gate-way. Time has painted the bronze a light and pretty green color, and they are covered with arabesques on large plates. Some of them, the least handsome, it must be admitted, are of French manufacture. Upon the breech is the inscription: "François Durand, metal-founder to the King of France, Algiers."

While I copied the inscription, a tiny little girl, pretty and fresh-colored, dressed all in white, amused herself by filling with sand, with her ruddy little fingers, the touchhole of one of these great Turkish cannon. A pensioner, with bare sword, standing upon two wooden legs, and no doubt guarding this artillery, looked at her as she did so, and smiled.

Just as I was leaving the esplanade, towards three o'clock, a little group walked slowly across it. It was composed of a man dressed in black, with a band of crape on his arm and hat, followed by three others, of whom one, clad in a blue blouse, held a little boy by the hand. The man with the crape had under his arm a kind of box of a lightish color, half hidden under a black cloth, which he carried as a musician carries the case in which his instrument is kept. I approached them. The black man was an undertaker's mute; the box was a child's coffin.

The course taken by the little procession, parallel with the front of the Invalides, intersected at a right angle that which, three months ago, had been followed by the hearse of Napoleon.

ALFRED DE MUSSET

—

RABELAIS

—

BALZAC

—

MONTAIGNE

—

BY

CHARLES AUGUSTIN SAINTE-BEUVE

CHARLES AUGUSTIN SAINTE-BEUVE
1804—1869

The great literary critic of France, Charles Augustin Sainte-Beuve, was born at Boulogne in 1804. He began the study of medicine, but soon turned to literature as a pursuit more congenial to his tastes. His first book, published in 1827, was entitled "Tableau de la poésie française au seizième siècle." During this period he also wrote some creditable poetry. He, however, soon devoted himself entirely to literary criticism, contributing weekly articles to the "Constitution," the "Moniteur," and other periodicals. His *feuilletons* were published every Monday and came to be regarded as an important weekly literary event. He continued this series of *feuilletons* to the time of his death, which took place in 1869.

Sainte-Beuve's system of work was extremely methodical. "Assisted by his secretary," says one of his biographers, "he began each Monday to prepare the article for the following week. Having selected his subject, he dictated a rough outline of the article, filling in blanks and making corrections with his own hand. This first draft was then copied, revised, and sometimes rewritten. For twelve hours daily this continued, until Thursday, when the manuscript was sent to the printer. The proof was then subjected to a revision as minute and thorough as that which the manuscript had undergone before everything was pronounced ready for publication on Monday. When it did appear, the accuracy and aptness of every quotation, the correctness of every name and date, were as noteworthy as its general finish and effect as a whole." These articles formed a series of literary monographs covering the widest possible range, from the classic writers of antiquity to the writers of his own day. They have been republished under the various titles of "Critiques et portraits litteraires," "Portraits contemporains," "Causeries de lundi," and "Nouveaux lundis." The essays on "Alfred de Musset," "Rabelais," "Balzac," and "Montaigne," given here, are characteristic examples of Saint-Beuve's literary style and method. In 1845 he was elected a member of the Academy, and in 1865 became a senator of the second empire.

Sainte-Beuve's style is a model of French prose, being clear, dignified, and precise. His work, not only on account of its volume and scope, but because of its sound insight and discriminating judgment, entitles Sainte-Beuve to rank as one of the greatest critics in all literature.

ALFRED DE MUSSET

IN a few days a collection of new poems, written by M. Alfred de Musset, from 1840 to 1849, will appear; his former delightful collection contained only the poems composed before 1840. A number of lyrics and others (songs, sonnets, epistles) have been published since that date in the " Revue des Deux Mondes " and elsewhere: they are those which have just been collected, with the addition of a few unpublished pieces. Thus I have a pretext of which, after all, there is scarcely any need for speaking of M. Alfred de Musset, and for forming a general opinion of the character of his talent, and of his place and influence in our poetry.

About ten years ago M. de Musset addressed a " Letter," in verse, to M. de Lamartine, in which he turned for the first time to the prince of the poets of the age, and made him the public and direct declaration that the singer of Elvire had for a long time been accustomed to receive from anyone entering on the career of poet, but which M. de Musset, in defiance of etiquette, had delayed longer than most to make him. The poet of " Namouna " and " Rolla " told him in very fine lines that after doubting, denying, and blaspheming, a sudden light manifested itself within him. " I write, O poet! to tell you of my love—A ray of light has penetrated my soul—And at a time of grief and supreme sorrow—The tears I shed brought thought of thee to me."

In the midst of his passion and suffering, a sentiment of divine elevation, an idea of immortality, was, he said, awakened in his soul; the " angels of sorrow " spoke to him, and he naturally thought first of him who revealed the sacred sources of inspiration in French poetry. M. de Musset opportunely recalled the lines which the young Lamartine had addressed to Lord Byron when he was on the point of setting out for Greece; and without aspiring to an ambitious comparison, he asked Lamartine to welcome him and his offering now, as he had formerly been received by the " Great Byron."

A journal has just published the reply in verse which M. de Lamartine made to M. de Musset, a reply bearing the date 1840. Its appearance now has almost an air of injustice, for it is many a long day since M. de Musset was the mere beginner that M. de Lamartine was pleased to see in him. He evidently took M. de Musset's modesty too literally. He forgot that in 1840 the "fair-haired child," the "youth with heart of wax," as he calls him, had written the "May Night" and the "October Night," poems that will survive as long as the "Lake," and that are equally passionate, and almost as pure. M. de Lamartine's criticisms on poetry are superficial; I remember his early criticisms of Petrarch and of André Chénier. In the poem to M. de Musset he stopped at the Musset of the songs, of the "Marquise," and the "Andalouse." He tells him things disagreeable to hear when spoken by any other than one's self. In the "Confession of a Child of the Century," and in many other places, M. de Musset made confessions that poetry in our age sanctions and defends. M. de Lamartine turns them into a moral lesson; he quotes himself as an example, and ends, according to custom, by insensibly suggesting himself as a model. This is to what we expose ourselves in addressing our homage to the illustrious men in whose footprints we tread. M. de Lamartine himself was not so cordially received by Byron as M. de Musset seems to think. In his "Memoirs," Byron speaks of the fine epistle "On Man" very lightly, of the early "Meditations" as the work of someone who thought fit to compare him to the devil, and to call him the "singer of hell." In fact, it is useless to demand justice and attention from illustrious predecessors when we are ourselves of their race; they are too full of themselves. How, I ask you, would Byron have welcomed advances from Keats, from the young wounded eagle who fell so soon, and whom he always treats so cavalierly—from the heights of his pity or contempt? How would M. de Chateaubriand himself, who so cleverly kept up appearances, have criticised the underlying principle of M. de Lamartine, the poet, if not as a man of great talent and melody who had had success with women and in drawing-rooms? Poets, go straight to the people for your diploma, and among them, to those who feel, whose minds and hearts are free, to the youths or to men who were youths yesterday and are old to-day, to those who read and sing you, to those, too, who read you again. It is among them that you will find faithful and sincere friends who will love you for your fine qualities and not for your faults; who will not admire you because it is the fashion, and who, when it shall change, will defend you against the fashion.

M. de Musset came before the public when scarcely twenty years old, and from the very first wished to mark emphatically his unlikeness to the other poets then famous. In order that there should be no mistake he assumed from the first a mask, a fantastic costume, a manner; he disguised himself as a Spaniard and an Italian, although he had not yet seen Spain and Italy: hence ensued disadvantages which were not easily thrown off. I am certain that, endowed as he was with original power and an individual genius, even if he had begun more simply and without taking so much pains to make himself singular, he would soon have been distinguished from the poets whose society he disclaimed and whose sentimental and melancholy, solemn and serious temperaments were so different from his. He possessed a feeling for raillery which the others lacked, and a need of true passion they felt but rarely. " My first verses are those of a child, my second those of a youth," he said, criticising himself. M. de Musset wrote his juvenile poems, but with a brilliance, an insolence of animation (as Regnier says), with a more than virile audacity, with a page's charm and effrontery: he was Cherubino at a masked ball, playing the part of Don Juan. The early manner, in which we note a vein of affectation and traces of reminiscences, is crowned by two poems (if we may call poems things not composed as such), by two wondrous divagations, " Namouna " and " Rolla," in which, under the pretext of relating a story he always forgets, the poet breathed forth his dreams and fancies, and abandoned himself to unrestrained freedom. Wit, nudities and crudities, lyrical power, a charm and refinement at times adorable, the highest poetry for no reason, debauch along with the ideal, sudden whiffs of lilac that bring back freshness, here and there a scrap of *chic* (to speak the language of the studio), all these things mingled and compounded, produced the strangest and certainly the most astonishing thing that French poetry, the virtuous girl who, already elderly, had formerly espoused M. de Malherbe, had yet furnished. It may be said that in " Namouna " we find the faults and fine qualities of Alfred de Musset, the poet. But the latter are so great and of such a high order that they compensate for everything.

Byron wrote to his publisher, Murray: " You say that a half of ' Don Juan ' is very fine: you are mistaken, for if it was true it would be the most beautiful poem that exists. Where is the poem of which a half is of worth? " Byron was right in speaking thus about himself and his contemporaries; but opposite and above is the school of Vergil, the poet who wanted to burn his poem because he did not find it perfect enough as a whole. It was the same Byron who wrote: " I am like the tiger (in poetry): if I fail at the first leap I go back muttering to my cave." As a rule, modern French poets, Béranger excepted, have only aspired to making the first leap in poetry, and what they did not reach then they never attained.

I need not then hesitate to say that in the poems of " Rolla " and of " Namouna " there is a good half that does not correspond with the other. The fine part of " Namouna," the part in which the poet reveals himself with full power, is the second canto. It is there that M. de Musset unfolds his theory of Don Juan, and contrasts the two sorts of libertines who, according to him, share the stage of the world: the heartless libertine, ideal, full of egoism and vanity, finding it difficult to get pleasure out of anything, and only desirous of inspiring love without returning it, Lovelace, in fact; and the other type of libertine, amiable and loving, almost innocent, passing through all phases of inconstancy in order to reach an ideal that eludes him, believing he loves, the dupe of none but himself in his seductions, and changing only because he ceases to love. There, according to M. de Musset, is the real poetical Don Juan, " whom no one succeeded in drawing, whom Mozart dreamed of, whom Hoffmann saw pass before him to the sound of music—In a divine lightning flash on one of his fantastic nights—An excellent portrait he never finished—And which in our time a Shakespeare might have painted." And M. de Musset attempts to paint him in the brightest and most charming colors, in colors which remind me (Heaven forgive me!) of those used by Milton when painting his happy couple in Eden. He shows him to us, handsome, twenty years of age, sitting by a meadow-side near his sleeping mistress, and watching over her slumber like an angel. "There he is, young and handsome, under the sky of France . . . Bringing to nature a heart full of hope—Loving, loved by all, open as a flower; So candid and fresh that the angel of innocence—Would kiss on his brow the beauty of his heart—There he is, look at him, divine his life for him—What fate can be predicted for that child of heaven?—Love, in approaching him, swears to be everlasting! Fortune thinks of him. . . ." And all that follows. From a poetical point of view nothing could be more delightful, better imagined, and better carried out. Nevertheless, in vain has the poet created, in vain has he desired to draw for us an unique Don Juan, a contradiction as he makes him, living almost innocent in the midst of his crimes; the "innocent corrupter" does not exist. He succeeded in evoking him, in giving momentary life by his magic to an impossible abstraction. It is said that words do no harm on paper. Such a combination and contrast of virtues and vices in the same being is all very well to write about, and especially to celebrate in verse, but it is true neither according to humanity nor nature. And then, why put us to the absolute alternative of choosing between the two sorts of libertines? Would poetry suffer, O poet! if there were no libertines? In the divine company of Vergil's Elysian Fields, in which the greatest of mortals hold a place, there is room in the first rank for the virtuous poets, for the poets who were entirely human, who uttered with emotion and tenderness the large accents of nature:

"*Quique pii vates et Phœbo digna locuti.*"

How distant such subtleties were from those lofty and wholesome thoughts!

So much for my reservations. There are, however, in "Namouna" two or three hundred consecutive lines quite beyond comparison. Be incredulous, and turn them about in every sense; apply the surgeon's knife; cavil at your pleasure; a few stains, a little loud coloring may be discovered; but if you possess true poetic feeling, and if you are sincere, you will recognize the strength and power of the inspiration; the god —or if you prefer it, the devil—has touched it.

Young men, who in such a matter are scarcely ever mistaken, were the first to recognize it. When the poems of " Namouna " and " Rolla " had only appeared in the reviews, and before they were collected in a volume, law students and medical students knew them by heart from beginning to end, and recited them to their friends, the new arrivals. Many of them still know the splendid exordium of " Rolla," the apostrophe to Christ, the other apostrophe to Voltaire (for there are many apostrophes), especially the enchanting slumber of the fifteen-year-old girl: " Oh! the flower of Eden, why hast thou let it fade—Careless child, beautiful fair-haired Eve? . . ." I speak of young men as they were ten years ago. Then the whole of these youthful poems were recited; now, perhaps, a selection is already beginning to be made.

After " Namouna " and " Rolla," there remained one step for M. de Musset to take. He had gone as far as was possible in the attempt and anticipation of passion without being touched by passion itself. But by means of talking of it, by attributing to himself the desire and torment of it, patience! it will come. In spite of his insults and blasphemies, his heart was worthy of it. He who had described in burning stanzas the odious and selfish Lovelace, and had made a show of libertine pretensions, had at base the heart of an honest man and of a poet. For, observe carefully, that even with the author of " Namouna," coxcombry (if I dare say it) is only on the surface: he throws it off as soon as the flame of his poetry is kindled.

At length M. de Musset loved. He told and repeated it so often in his verse, his passion has made so much noise, and has been so loudly proclaimed on both sides and in all tones, that we commit no indiscretion in stating it here in simple prose. Besides, it is never a dishonor for a woman to have been loved and sung by a true poet, even when afterwards she seems to be cursed for it. The malediction is a supreme homage. A far-sighted confidant could say: " Take care, you love her still."

That love was the great event of M. de Musset's life, I mean of his poetic life. His talent was suddenly purified and ennobled; the sacred flame seemed on a sudden to reject all impure alloy. In the poems composed under that powerful star almost all the faults disappeared; his finer qualities, till then, as it were, scattered and fragmentary, were combined, assembled, and grouped in a powerful although sad harmony. The four poems M. de Musset called " Nights " are short, complex, meditative poems, marking the loftiest height of his lyrical genius. The " May Night " and the " October Night " are the finest for the flow and the inexhaustible vein of the poetry, for the expression of violent and unmasked passion. But the " December Night " and the " August Night " are also delightful—the latter for action and sentiment, the former for grace and flexibility of expression. The four, taken together, make one work, animated by the same sentiment, possessing harmony and skilfully contrived relations.

Parallel with De Musset's " Nights " I read over again the famous poems of Milton's youth, " L'Allegro," and especially " Il Penseroso." But in those compositions of supreme and somewhat cold beauty the poet was passionless; he waited for an impulse from without; he received his impressions successively from nature; he carried to it a grave, noble, sensible temperament, but calm like a mirror slightly ruffled. The " Penseroso " is the masterpiece of meditative and contemplative poems; it resembles a magnificent oratorio, in which by degrees prayer slowly ascends to the Eternal. The contrast to the subject in hand is very noticeable. I am not instituting a comparison. Let us not displace august names from their proper sphere. All that is fine in Milton is beyond comparison; it reveals the calm habitude of high regions and a continuity of power. However, in the more terrestrial, and at the same time more human, " Nights " of M. de Musset, it is from within that the inspiration, the passion that paints and the breeze that makes nature fragrant, springs; or, rather, the charm consists in the combination and alliance of the two sources of impressions—that is to say, of a deep sorrow and of a soul still open to vivid impressions. The poet, wounded to the heart, shedding real tears, is conscious of a renewal of youth, and is almost intoxicated by the spring. He is more sensitive than before to the innumerable beauties of the universe, to the verdure and the flowers, to the morning sunlight, to the birds' songs, and fresh as at the age of fifteen, he brings us his poesy of lilies and eglantine. M. de Musset's muse will always, even at the least happy moments, be conscious of such renewals; but in no other place will the natural freshness be so happily wedded, as in this case, to bleeding passion and sincere grief. Poetry, chaste consoler, was there treated almost with adoration and affection.

Which of the poets of this age will survive? Rash would be the man who should at the present time take upon himself the task of assigning lots and making a division. But in our day time runs on so swiftly that even now we can recognize its different effects on works which at their birth seemed equally likely to live. Consider the works that were at first most warmly greeted and applauded: how many places are already empty, how many colors already pale and faded! One of the poets most certain to survive, Béranger, said to me one day: " You all began too young, and before you arrived at maturity." He might easily speak thus. It is not every man's good fortune to meet obstacles which restrain and keep him back until the right moment—the moment at which the fruit as well as the flowers can be produced. Béranger (he or his good fairy) had the sense to let the poetry of the Empire die away before his came into being; had he planned his life himself, he could not have had a greater success. The others, a little sooner, a little later, all very young, some still children, entered the lists pell-mell entirely at hazard. What may be stated with certainty is that a rich lyrical poetry, richer than France until then had suspected, but an unequal and motley poetry, resulted during several seasons from that assemblage of talent. The greater number of the poets abandoned themselves without curb or bridle to all the instincts of their nature, and moreover to all the pretensions of their pride and the foolishness of their vanity. Faults and fine qualities came out in all their freedom, and posterity will have to do the sorting. We feel it has begun already. Which among the poems written between 1819 and 1830 are read now with emotion and pleasure? I merely state the proposition, and have no intention of solving it, nor of following closely the faint yet visible line that, among illustrious men most sure of themselves, already divides the quick from the dead. Poets of to-day, there are three or four of you who will claim the sceptre, who believe that each is the first! Who knows which is he, who with our indifferent descendants will have the last word? Some of your accents will surely reach posterity, and therein lies your honor; it will cover the rest of them in a kindly oblivion. Nothing complete of the poets of the time will survive. M. de Musset will not escape that fate, and on that score he has perhaps little reason to complain; for his accents will reach much farther, and we may believe will pierce time the better, because they will have been thus purified. His accents are accents of pure passion, and it is in the " Nights " that they are specially to be found.

M. de Musset has quite a small school of imitators. What do they imitate in him? That which imitators usually copy, form, surface, the smart tone, the sprightly gesture, the dashing faults, everything that he knew how to carry off with a certain charm and ease, they religiously set to work to copy. They imitated his vocabulary in the names of gallants, " Manon, Ninon, Marion," his jingle of courtesans and marquises. They imitated his weak lines and his affectations of carelessness. They took the form and the bad habit; but the fire, the passion, the elevation, and the lyrical power they did not care, and for good reasons, to borrow from him.

Sometimes the French public criticises poetry in strange fashion. I mentioned above those who in the young generation were the first to admire M. de Musset with sincerity and candor. A piquant chapter concerning manners might be written, taking as a text the fine ladies and gentlemen and the enthusiasts who, following the rest, have fully adopted him, the same who five-and-twenty years ago would have admired Alexandrines, because they believed them to be cast in the mould of Racine, and who now extol the slightest trifles of the brilliant poet equally with his best and really good work. It was not when he was at his best that he became the fashion and the vogue; as usually happens, it came later, but is now a fact. He is the favorite poet of the day; the boudoir outdoes the inns of court. When we are young, and new to the world, it is by Musset we prefer to attack modern poetry. Mothers do not advise their daughters to read it; husbands read it to their young wives from the first year of marriage. I believe I once saw a volume of his poems slipped among the wedding presents, an amusing circumstance, and not altogether displeasing to the poet. He should hasten to enjoy it, and should not rely on it.

The lyrics produced by M. de Musset since the " Nights," and which have just been collected, contain some remarkable poems. I point out one called " A Lost Evening," where he charmingly mingles a motive of André Chénier with a thought of Molière, a satire " On Idleness," in which the poet was influenced by reading Regnier; a pretty tale, " Simone," savoring of Boccaccio and La Fontaine; but especially a " Recollection," full of charm and feeling, where the inspiration came from himself alone. The poet once again revisited places dear to him, some forest, Fontainebleau maybe, where he had spent happy days. His friends feared the effect of the pilgrimage and of the awakening of his memories. There is no greater woe, says Dante, than the remembrance of past happy days in misery. But M. de Musset experienced the contrary; and he tells us how he found the awakening of the past that was feared for him, and that he himself feared, consoling and sweet. To be frank, that is the kind of poem I like in M. de Musset, and by no means the little verses " On Three Steps of Rose-colored Marble," and other gew-gaws which savor of their source.

M. de Musset's taste has reached maturity, and it would be best henceforth for his talent to obey his taste and not to allow itself any more weaknesses. After so many varied attempts and experiences, after trying to love many things in order to discover the only and supreme one worthy of love, that is to say simple truth clothed at the same time with beauty, it is not wonderful that when we return to it and recognize it, we find ourselves less animated and more fatigued in its presence than we were in the presence of the idols. However, his genius possesses power of renewal, sources of youth of which he has more than once shown that he knew the secret, and which he has not yet exhausted. For a few years his genius has exhibited itself to the public in a new form, and the poet has triumphed in a somewhat hazardous experiment. The delicate sketches, charming proverbs that he did not intend for the stage, suddenly became delightful little comedies that arose and walked before us. The success of his " Caprice " did honor, I do not fear to say it, to the public, and proves that for him who can awaken it, it still possesses delicate literary feeling. He has seen the circle of his admirers extend as if by magic. Many minds that would never have dreamed of seeking him out for his lyrical talent learned to appreciate him in his easy and graceful proverbs. He had more than ever the suffrages of men of the world, and of young women; he made eccentric and inelegant critics angry; nothing wanted to his success. For all that, I cannot say I am mad for his " Louison "; it is only a style. M. de Musset as a dramatic poet has still much to learn. On the stage a happy situation, ingenious dialogue are not enough; invention, fertility, development, above all, action, are necessary to consummate, as it has been said, the work of the devil. But it is time to conclude, and without asking too much, without making more ceremony than M. de Musset himself, I shall end with a line of his own that puts a stop to argument:

" What do I say! Such as he is, the world loves him still."

RABELAIS

A WRITER, as yet little known, who, judging from his ideas, must be young, has just published a pleasant little book on Rabelais, whom he places in a sort of gallery of French legends. The word legend sufficiently indicates that the young author has not attempted to give an accurate, exact, and critical biography of Rabelais, and has welcomed the Rabelais of tradition, such as popular imagination has transformed him. Later on, when I have talked for a space with the master, and tried to refresh my memory of him, I shall say a word of the spirit in which the little pamphlet is written.

If only it could be accomplished, what would we not give to talk with Rabelais, to come for an instant into contact with him in his habit as he lived, to hear him? Everyone has his ideal in the past. I believe the nature and bent of each mind would be best shown in the choice of the person first sought if we went back to a bygone age. Some, I know, would have no particular choice, but would wander indifferently from one to the other, or would not even go at all. Let us leave minds like those, wanting in love, passion, and desire; they are lukewarm spirits who lack the sacred fire of literature. I know others who would rush to many at one time, and, in their eagerness and affection, would embrace a crowd of favorite authors without knowing by whom to commence. Those minds are not indifferent like the others, they are not lukewarm; they are volatile, unsettled, and I fear we critics have something in common with them. But the wise and praiseworthy minds are those who have a decided taste in the past, an avowed preference; who would, for example, make straight for Molière without stopping even at Bossuet. They are those, in fact, who have the courage of their passion, and do not seek to disguise their highly placed affection. At that price, were it possible to spend a whole day in the sixteenth century, and to talk every man with his author, to whom would you go?

Calvin, Rabelais, Amyot, and Montaigne are the four great prose writers of the sixteenth century; Rabelais and Montaigne might rather be called two poets. I do not here include a number of secondary writers, worthy to be mentioned and saluted at their side. On the day which I suppose we might spend in the sixteenth century with our chosen author, I scarcely think at the present time Calvin would find many friends. Good Amyot, with his kindly old man's smile and his somewhat languid charms, would have some attraction for us. But all would flock to Montaigne—all except a numerous and decided company who, while regretting the necessity of choosing between the two, would elect to pay their respects to Rabelais.

In the taste of certain persons for Rabelais and their worship of him, there is more even than admiration, there is the alert curiosity which belongs to a spice of the unknown and mysterious. We almost know in advance what Montaigne would be like; we picture him almost as he would appear at first view; but Rabelais, who knows him? Rabelais's life and true character have been much discussed. I believe, and every thoughtful reader will believe with me, that those who expected to find in him exactly the man of his book, a sort of jovial priest-physician, a half-drunken buffoon living like a fighting-cock, would be vastly disappointed. Rabelais's debauches were held entirely in his imagination and humor; they were studious debauches, debauches of a very learned man, full of good sense, who, pen in hand, gave himself up to them without restraint. I am none the less convinced, however, that after a very short time passed in intercourse with him, in associating with the man of science and the student—doubtless very good company for his time—the inimitable jester would as a matter of fact be very quickly discovered. It was impossible that the natural flow of such a vein could be restrained and not allowed to come out. The man's person, however noble in bearing, and however venerable its first aspect, would at times grow animated and rejoice in the thousand sallies of the inner genius, the irresistible good humor which frolics in his romance or rather in his drama. I say that of Rabelais as of Molière. The latter was not always gay and amusing, quite the contrary; he was called "the contemplative man"; when he was alone, he was even sad and melancholy. But it is certain that excited and urged to converse, he would again become the Molière we know. So doubtless would it be with Rabelais. There is a charming piece of Latin verse on Rabelais, physician and anatomist, by Étienne Dolet, the man who was burnt alive for the crime of heresy. In it Dolet makes a criminal, who had the honor of being dissected after his execution in the public amphitheatre of Lyons, by Rabelais himself, and at any rate furnished the subject of a good lesson in anatomy, speak: "In vain did an adverse fortune desire to cover me with outrage and shame," said the criminal in Dolet's lines; "it was otherwise decreed. If I died in a disgraceful manner, there was a moment in which I gained more than anyone would have dared to hope from great Jove's favor. Exposed in a public theatre, I was dissected: a learned physician describing me, explained to all how nature formed the human body with beauty, art, and perfect harmony. A numerous company surrounded me and contemplated all my parts, and, while listening to him, admired the wonders of the human structure." Truly, when Rabelais gave that public lecture on anatomy in the Lyons amphitheatre, he must, like Vesalius, have had the doctor's and master's venerable aspect of which some of his contemporaries have spoken, and must have worthily represented the dignity of science.

Son of a tavern-keeper or apothecary of Chinon, it is known that he began life as a monk and a Franciscan. The seriousness and elevation of his tastes, the natural and generous liberty of his inclinations soon rendered him, in that age of decadence, an unsuitable subject for a monastery of that order. He left, tried the Benedictines, a less contemptible order, but fared no better there; then he put off the regular monastical habit, and donned the costume of a secular priest. As we say, he threw his gown to the dogs, and went to study medicine at Montpellier. The little known with certainty of his actual and not legendary biography has been well put together and set forth in the thirty-second volume of Niceron's "Memoirs." If the honest biographer represents Rabelais with slightly austere, or at any rate serious characteristics, and with much sobriety, he has the advantage of saying nothing problematical, and of being free from prejudice. There, the bulls Rabelais was clever enough to obtain from the Holy See during one of his voyages to Rome in Cardinal du Bellay's suite, by which he prudently set himself right with his enemies in France, may be seen. In a bull dated January 12, 1536, it is stated that he was permitted to practise the art of medicine everywhere, gratuitously, however, and excluding the application of the knife and caustic; those sort of operations were forbidden to priests. But nothing was said of the pantagruelic books he had already written and was going to write; and never did Rabelais think it incumbent on him to forbid them to himself.

Nothing is less easy than to hit on the right way of speaking of those books, for Rabelais takes licenses peculiarly his own, of which the most enthusiastic critic cannot take the responsibility. When we want to read Rabelais aloud, even before men (before women it is impossible), we are always in the position of a man wishing to cross a vast open space full of mud and filth: every moment it is necessary to take a long stride, and to walk without getting rather dirty is difficult. Once a lady reproached Sterne for the nudities of his " Tristram Shandy." At the moment a three-year-old child was playing on the floor and exhibiting himself in complete innocence. "Look," said Sterne, " my book is that three-year-old child who is rolling on the carpet." But with Rabelais the child has grown up; he is a man, a monk, a giant Gargantua, Pantagruel, or at any rate Panurge, and he still conceals nothing. Here there is no possibility of saying to the ladies: Look! And even when we are speaking in the company of men only, and are perfectly cool-headed, it is necessary to make a choice. I, too, shall choose. In M. Rabelais's first book, " Gargantua," not perhaps the first according to date, but which is the most consistent, the most complete in itself, with a beginning, a middle, and an end, some admirable chapters are to be found, neither too serious nor too comic, where Rabelais's great powers of good sense are to be seen. I intend to speak of the chapters dealing with Gargantua's education. After all the extravagance of the beginning, the birth of Gargantua by the left ear, the marvellous description of his *layette,* the first signs he gives of his intelligence, and a certain very nonsensical answer he gives his father, in which he recognizes with admiration his son's marvellous wit, a master is given him, a sophist in Latin learning. Then follows a very clever and striking satire on the bad education of that time. Gargantua was supposed to have been born in the latter half of the fifteenth century, and was first subjected to the scholastic and pedantic education, full of laborious and complicated puerilities, an education which seemed to be formed expressly for corrupting good and noble minds. However, his father Grandgousier perceived that his son studied hard, and yet grew more stupid every day. He was greatly astonished to learn from one of his friends, the viceroy of some neighboring country, that any young man who had only studied for two years under a good master, by means of a new method only just discovered, would know more than all the little prodigies of olden times, given to the care of masters " whose knowledge was nothing but brutishness." Gargantua is brought into the company of the young Endemon, a child of twelve, who addresses him with charm, politeness, and a noble modesty that in no way injures his facility. Gargantua found nothing to reply to all the young page so amiably and encouragingly said to him, " but all the countenance he kept was that he fell to crying like a cow, and cast down his face, hiding it with his cap." The father was grievously vexed. In his rage he would have killed Maître Jobelin, the pedant who had furnished such a wretched education, but he contented himself with kicking him out of doors, and intrusting Gargantua to the charge of the tutor who had brought up Endemon so successfully, and whose name was Ponocrates.

Here we touch on one of the parts of Rabelais's book which contains much good sense, and up to a certain point a serious meaning. But I speak with reserve; because, while recognizing the serious parts, it is necessary to be careful not to imagine and create them, as so many commentators have done—a proceeding that must give Rabelais plenty to laugh at, if he takes any heed of us in the shades. But in the present instance the meaning is not to be doubted. We saw the young Gargantua given up to the pedagogues of the old school, and the sad results of the wretched, methodical, pedantic, and brutalizing education, the last legacy of the expiring Middle Ages. Ponocrates, on the contrary, is an innovation, a modern man, in accord with the true renaissance. He accepts the pupil, takes him away with him to Paris, and sets himself to form his manners and character.

And what merry tricks as they go along, what adventures by the way, and on entering Paris! What a welcome Gargantua receives from the Parisians, over curious and always loafing! Then in return he has to pay his footing! Read all those things, those miraculous, mischievous students' tricks, which make excellent scenes of comedy; I take refuge in the semi-serious parts.

Ponocrates begins by examining his pupil; he employs in advance Montaigne's method, who advises that " you should first trot out " the young mind before you, to judge its pace. For some time Ponocrates allows the young Gargantua to do as he had been accustomed, and Rabelais describes the routine of idleness, gluttony, and sloth, the result of a wrongly directed early education. Let me briefly sum up the system. The young Gargantua already conducts himself like one of the most ignorant and gluttonous monks of that time, commencing his day late, sleeping far into the morning, taking a plentiful breakfast, hearing a number of masses which scarcely fatigue him, entirely given up to good living, sleep, and idleness. In reading the description, we thoroughly understand Rabelais's disgust for that ignoble life when he was a Franciscan!

It was high time to reform the vicious education; but Ponocrates, like a wise man, did not make the change too sudden, " considering that nature does not endure sudden changes without great violence." The twenty-third and twenty-fourth chapters of the first book are truly admirable, and present the soundest and most far-reaching system of education imaginable, a better contrived system than that of the " Emile," Montaigne-like, practical, formed for use, for developing the whole man, the physical as well as the mental faculties. At every turn we recognize the enlightened physician, physiologist, and philosopher.

Gargantua rises at about four in the morning; during his early toilet some chapter of the Holy Scriptures was read to him, aloud and clearly, in such a way as to direct his mind to the works and judgments of God from the morning. A few hygienic details follow, for the physician in Rabelais forgets nothing. Afterwards the tutor takes his pupil out, and they consider the face of the sky, if it was such as they had observed it the night before. He is made to note the difference of position, the changes of the constellations and stars, for with Rabelais the astronomer who had published almanacs was not less clever than the doctor, and he considered no science, no human or physical knowledge, irrelevant to his purpose.

In regard to physical knowledge of the heavens, education has advanced little since Rabelais. Although Newton came, and Arago led the way in his lectures at the observatory, ordinary instruction has not improved. We, who should be ashamed not to know geography and its chief divisions, need only lift our eyes to the sky to perceive that we scarcely know anything of the sublime cosmography. A few evenings with a professor would suffice to teach us. Ponocrates would have been ashamed for his pupil to be ignorant of so majestic and ordinary a spectacle.

After the lesson in the open air came lessons indoors, " three good hours of reading;" then games, ball, tennis, all that might be useful in " gallantly exercising their bodies, as before they had done their minds." According to Rabelais, such combination and accurate balance was what characterized real and complete education: in every prescription you find in him the physician, the man who understands the relation of the physical to the moral world, and who in everything consults nature.

At table, at what was then called dinner (and what we call luncheon), he only allowed his pupil to eat what was necessary to appease " the demands of the appetite;" he desired dinner, the early meal, to be " sober and frugal," reserving him a more extensive and plentiful supper. During the morning meal, in reference to the dishes, conversation turned on the virtue, propriety, and nature of the objects, the viands, herbs, and roots. Passages on these subjects from the ancients were talked of; at need books were fetched; without knowing it, the pupil becomes as learned as Pliny, " that in that time there was not a physician that knew half so much as he did."

After the repast came cards, to learn under that novel pretext a thousand pretty new tricks and inventions, all grounded upon arithmetic and numbers. Thus the young Gargantua, so to say, takes his mathematical instruction while amusing himself.

Digestion finished, after certain hygienic tasks I pass over in silence, but which Rabelais never left to the imagination, they recommence study for the second time, and seriously " for three hours or more." Afterwards, about two or three hours after midday, they leave the house in company of Squire Gymnast, and practise the art of riding and gymnastics. Under so accomplished a master, Gargantua profited boldly and usefully. He did not amuse himself by breaking his lance, " for it is the greatest foolishness in the world," observes Rabelais, " to say: ' I have broken ten lances at tilts or in fight;' a carpenter can do even as much; but it is a glorious and praiseworthy action with one lance to break and overthrow ten of his enemies." Do you not already perceive how good-sense is substituted for a false point of honor, and how Rabelais, who does not believe in vainglory and swaggering, wants to reform the last of the Bayards? They were only too well reformed.

In describing the various exercises of riding, hunting, wrestling, and swimming, Rabelais amused himself. Master Gymnast's feats of strength became, under his pen, feats of strength of language. French prose also performed gymnastics, and the style became astounding in its copiousness, freedom, suppleness, suitability, and animation. Never before had language had such a glorious time of it.

It is, in fact, an admirable picture of an ideal education, and, reduced to proportions rather less than those of the giant Gargantua, almost all of it is serious. There is excess, exaggeration, assuredly, in the whole; but it is an exaggeration easily reduced to the truth and the correct sense of human nature. The new character of the education lies in the combination of play and study, in learning things by making use of them, in putting books and the things of life side by side, theory and practice, body and mind, gymnastics and music, as with the Greeks, without, however, modelling ourselves on the past, but having regard continually to the present and future.

If the weather was rainy, the employment of the time was different, and the diet also varied. Taking less exercise in the open air on those days, he feeds more soberly. On those days the workshops and factories of different artificers, lapidaries, goldsmiths, alchemists, money-coiners, watchmakers, printers, not omitting the casting of great ordnance, then quite new, are more particularly visited, and everywhere they give them wine; they learn the different industries. It is to be remarked that Rabelais wants his royal pupil to examine and become acquainted with all useful arts, every modern invention, so that he may never find himself hindered or at a loss, like so many poor learned men who know nothing but books. An education *à la Ponocrates* reconciled the ancient and modern system. Perrault, Colbert's worthy clerk, would find nothing further to desire there, and Madame Dacier, the worshipper of Homer, would discover there all she liked best.

In the young Gargantua's course of education and study we have the first plan of what Montaigne, Charron, in places and parts the Port Royal School, the Christian school which did not recognize itself so strong in the same path as Rabelais, strange precursor! set forth with greater seriousness, but not with more good sense. We have in advance at one glance, and with brilliant genius, what Rousseau will expound later in "Emile," reducing it to a system, and Bernardin de Saint-Pierre in his "Studies of Nature," rendering it vapid.

Bernardin de Saint-Pierre, melancholy and a dreamer by choice, whose chaste and ideal genius seems to have little in common with Rabelais's mind, comprehended him marvellously on the serious side we have been describing, and in a memorable passage, not altogether chimerical, although giving a too uniform explanation, and too much embellished, said:

"It was all up with the happiness of nations, and even of religion, when two men of letters, Rabelais and Miguel Cervantes, arose, one in France, the other in Spain, and shook the power of the monasteries and of chivalry. To overturn the two giants, they made use of no arms, but ridicule, the natural antithesis to human terror. [What more exact and happy explanation could you have?] Like children, the people laughed, and were reassured. The only incentives to happiness they possessed were those their princes liked to give them, had their princes been capable of giving them any. 'Telemachus' appeared, and the book reminded Europe of the harmonies of nature. It produced a great revolution in politics. . . ."

I do not dare to accept altogether the fashion of explaining modern history by ascribing its chief results to two or three names, to two or three books. In the intervals of "Gargantua," "Don Quixote," and "Telemachus" more things than seem to be dreamed of in Bernardin de Saint-Pierre's philosophy happened. There is truth, however, in regarding Rabelais, the untrammelled jester, as having, at the end of the terrors of the Middle Ages and the labyrinth of scholasticism, consoled and reassured the human race.

The system of education I admire in Rabelais, Montaigne, Charron, and some of their followers, had a great opportunity, when it was a question of emancipating the young, of freeing them from servile and oppressive methods, and of leading their minds into natural paths.

To realize that programme, even after three centuries, much progress has yet to be made. We should, however, bear in mind the new and, above all, pleasant modes of imparting knowledge to children was by means of a preceptor or tutor for each, and took no account of the inherent difficulties of public education nor of those difficulties which depend on the condition of society. Then, and in proportion as we advance in life, what fatigues, struggles, and pains we have to endure! It is no bad thing to have become early accustomed to them by education, and to have felt the consequences of things while young. An eighteenth century philosopher, wiser than Rousseau (Galiani), recommends two particular aims in education: to teach children to support injustice, and to endure *ennui*.

But Rabelais's purpose was merely to advance certain sensible and appropriate notions in a jest: do not demand more of him. His book contains everything, and each admirer can pride himself on discovering in it what best suits his own mind. But he also finds many comic, unreservedly diverting parts to justify to all Rabelais's renown and glory. The rest is disputable, equivocal, liable to controversy and commentary. To those parts candid readers will confess they find a difficulty in paying attention and in taking pleasure in them. What is indisputably admirable is the form of the language, the fulness and richness of the expressions, the abundant and inexhaustible flow of the eloquence. His French, in spite of his scoffs at the " latinizings " and " græcizings " of the time, is full of, almost crammed with, the ancient languages; but it is so from a kind of interior nourishment; it does not seem strange in him, and in his mouth everything has the ease of naturalness, familiarity, and genius. With him, as with Aristophanes, although more rarely, pure, charming, lucid, and truly poetic passages may be distinguished. Here, for example, is one of those passages, full of grace and beauty. There is talk of studies and of the Muses who turn aside from love. In a dialogue between Venus and Cupid, Lucian made the goddess ask her son why he so greatly respected the Muses, and the boy replied much as Rabelais summed it up, expanded and embellished it in the following words:

"I remember reading that Cupid, when asked sometimes by his mother why he did not attack the Muses, replied that he found them so beautiful, so innocent, so virtuous, so modest, and continually employed, one in contemplating the stars, another in reckoning numbers, another in measuring geometrical bodies, another in rhetorical invention, another in poetical composition, another in the disposition of music, that, approaching them, he unbent his bow, closed his case of arrows, and extinguished his torch for shame and fear of harming them. Then he tore the bandage from his eyes, in order to see them more easily and to listen to their charming songs and poetic odes. It gave him the greatest pleasure in the world. So much so he was often conscious of feeling quite enchanted by their beauty and grace, and was lulled to sleep by the sweet sounds of their harmony."

That is Rabelais when he remembered Lucian, or rather Plato.

No author is more admired than Rabelais; but he is worshipped in two ways, and by two races, as it were, very different in intelligence and conduct. Some admire him less than they enjoy him; they read him, understand him where they can, and console themselves for what they do not understand with the exquisite pieces they extract like marrow from a bone and take delight in. That is Montaigne's way of admiring Rabelais, who ranks him among books " merely amusing "; it is the way of the whole of the seventeenth century, of Racine and La Fontaine, who naïvely asked a doctor who was speaking to him of St. Augustine if that great saint had as much wit as Rabelais. Another method of admiring Rabelais is in desiring to be a man of his party, of his set, to draw him to one side, to prove him, as Ginguené did in a pamphlet, one of the harbingers and apostles of the revolution of 1789, and of those which are still to come. The latter way, which prides itself on being more philosophical and logical, seems to me much less Rabelaisian.

The young author of the pamphlet I mentioned at the beginning, M. Eugène Noël, somewhat favors the latter method, applying it, however, according to the ideas and views of our time—that is to say, in still further exaggerating it. He thus systematically spoils an otherwise valuable study, which implies a great deal of reading, and a fairly intimate knowledge of his subject. M. Michelet, carrying on at a distance of three centuries the war against mediæval times, a period, in his belief, still fraught with danger to us, once began one of his lectures at the Collège de France in these words: "God resembles a mother who wishes her children to be strong and proud, and to oppose her; his favorites also are the strong, indomitable natures which wrestle with him like Jacob, the strongest and most cunning of shepherds. Voltaire and Rabelais are his chosen elect." M. Michelet's Rabelais, who wrestles with God to give him pleasure, is a little like M. Eugène Noël's Rabelais. "He rescued," says the biographer, "the men of his time from the darkness and terrible fasts of the old world. . . . His book, almost paternal, answers the cry of universal thirst of the sixteenth century: 'Drink for the people!' . . . The great river of the papal church of which the Middle Ages had drunk for so long was exhausted: Drink! drink! was the universal cry; that was also Gargantua's first word." That is an allegorical thirst for a new explanation of which commentators have not yet thought. Every age has its hobby; and his, which does not jest, has the humanitarian craze, and thinks to do great honor to Rabelais by attributing it to him.

I fancy when we try to explain Rabelais according to our own ideas, he permits it merely to have a laugh over it. He might well be astonished to find that under legendary form he is an apostle, saint, what shall I say? a future Christ of the Evangel. Speaking of the manner in which he performed his duties as priest at Meudon, and persisting in the symbolical mode of explanation, the new biographer writes:

"How I should have liked to hear him! How I should have liked on a fine Easter day to assist him at his mass, to contemplate his majestic and serene face, while, hearing sung around him, '*Quemadmodum desiderat cervus ad fontes aquarum,*' he remembered with a divine smile of satisfaction the infinite thirst of his Pantagruel!"

In concluding, let us return to common sense and moderation; Voltaire will help us. When young he cared very little for Rabelais. He relates how one day the regent, the Duc d'Orléans, leaving the opera in conversation with him, began a great eulogy of Rabelais. "I took him for a prince in bad company," he said, "whose taste was spoiled. At that time I had a supreme contempt for Rabelais." In his "Philosophical Letters" he spoke very slightingly of him, putting him below Swift, which is not just. "He is a drunken philosopher," he concluded, "who only wrote when he was drunk." But five-and-twenty years later, in writing to Madame du Deffand, he made him reparation.

"After Clarissa Harlowe, I read over again some chapters of Rabelais, such as the fight of Friar John des Entommeures and Picrochole's council of war. I know them, indeed, almost by heart, but I read them with the greatest pleasure, because they are the most vivid descriptions in the world. It is not that I regard Rabelais as equal to Horace. . . . Rabelais, when he is in good humor, is the best of good buffoons: two of the craft are not wanted in a nation, but there must be one. I repent that I formerly spoke ill of him."

Yes, Rabelais is a buffoon, but a unique buffoon, a Homeric buffoon! Voltaire's latest opinion will remain that of all men of sense and taste, of those who do not possess a decided inclination and particular predilection for Rabelais. But for the rest, for the true amateur, for the real pantagruelist devotees, Rabelais is something very different. At the bottom of Master François's cask, even in the dregs, there is a flavor not to be explained, that they prefer to everything. If we are permitted to have an opinion on so serious a subject, we believe that what we most enjoy in him in his best places with a certain mystery of debauch, is to be found in the same quality and without concealment in Molière.

I have sometimes asked myself what Molière, learned, a physician, enveloped in Greek and Latin, would have been like. Molière, physician (imagine such a miracle) and priest after having been a monk; Molière, born at a period when every independent thinker had to preserve himself from the stakes of Geneva as from those of the Sorbonne; Molière, without a theatre, and forced to hide his splendid comedy in torrents of absurdities, burlesque rhapsodies, and drunken gossip, to safeguard, at every hour, the jest which touches society to the quick, by laughing without cause, and it seems to me we should get something very like Rabelais. However, he will always possess in himself the singular attraction which attaches us to a difficulty overcome, to a freemasonry both bacchic and learned, of which, in loving him, we feel ourselves a part. In a word, there is in pure pantagruelism an air of initiation which always pleases us.

BALZAC

A CAREFUL study of the famous novelist who has just been taken from us, and whose sudden loss has excited universal interest, would require a whole work, and the time for that, I think, has not yet come. Those sorts of moral autopsies cannot be made over a freshly dug grave, especially when he who has been laid in it was full of strength and fertility, and seemed still full of future works and days. All that is possible and fitting in respect of a great contemporary renown at the moment death lays it low, is to point out by means of a few clear-cut lines the merits, the varied skill, the delicate and powerful attraction, by which it charmed its epoch and acquired influence over it. I shall attempt to do this in respect to Balzac, with a feeling free from all personal recollection,[1] and in a spirit where criticism only reserves to itself some few rights.

Balzac was a painter of the manners of this age, and he was the most original, the most individual and penetrating of them all. From the first he regarded the nineteenth century as his subject and material, he eagerly threw himself into it, and never left it. Society is like a woman—she desires a painter, a painter all to herself: he was this; no tradition was in his painting of it; he applied the methods and artifices of the brush to the use of the ambitious and coquettish society, anxious only to date from itself, and to resemble no other; for that reason it has had much more affection for him. Born in 1799, he had fifteen years to the fall of the Empire; he knew and felt the imperial age with the clear-sightedness and quick penetration belonging to childhood; reflection will perfect it later on, but nothing will equal its youthful lucidity. Someone of the

---

[1] See in M. de Balzac's "Revue Parisienne" of August 25, 1840, the article which concerns me. If I have forgotten it, it is certain I do not doubt that others remember it. Such opinions only reflect in the future on those who held them.

same period as himself said: " From my childhood I saw into things with a sensibility that pierced my heart like a sharp blade at every moment." He might have said the same himself. The impressions of childhood, put later into criticisms and pictures, make themselves felt by a strange depth of emotion, and are precisely what give delicacy and life. A young man under the Restoration, he passed through it; he saw it wholly from what is perhaps the best position for an observing artist to see things, from below, in the crowd, in suffering and struggle, with the immense covetousness of genius and nature, which causes forbidden things to be divined, imagined, and penetrated a thousand times before they are obtained and known; he felt the Restoration like a lover. He began to acquire reputation at the same time as the new *régime*, set on foot in July, 1830, was established. That *régime* he saw from the same plane and even from a little above it; he criticized it frankly, he painted it enchantingly in its most striking types and commonplace forms. Thus the three very diverse epochs of physiognomy which form the century, now in its middle, were all known and lived through by Balzac, and up to a certain point his work is the reflection of them. Who, for instance, has described better than he the old men and the beautiful women of the Empire? Who has more delightfully hit off the duchesses and countesses of the end of the Restoration, the women of thirty, who, already on the spot, were awaiting their painter with a vague anxiety, so that when he and they met there was a sort of magnetic thrill of recognition? Who, in fact, has better understood and described in all its fulness the lower middle class triumphant under the dynasty of July, the class ever immortal and already gone, alas! of the Birotteaus and Crevels?

There was a vast field, and it must be said M. Balzac soon made it his own in all its extent; he traversed and penetrated it in every sense, and found it too narrow for his valor and ardor. Not content with observing and guessing, he very often invented and dreamed. However it may be with his dreams, it was at first by his delicate and keen observation that he won the heart of the aristocratic society to which he aspired. The first picked troops he introduced into the fortress were "The Woman of Thirty," "The Deserted Woman,"

"The Grenadier," and he was soon master of the citadel. The woman of thirty is not altogether an unexpected creation. Since civilized society has existed, women of that age have held a large, perhaps the chief place in it. In the eighteenth century, which had time to subtilize everything, a ball was given at court on Shrove Tuesday, 1763, a ball which was called "The Mothers' Ball"; the young girls, to speak the truth, were lookers-on, and only women of thirty danced. A pretty song was composed on the subject, of which the refrain was, "Girls of fifteen, let your mothers dance!" It is seen how the eighteenth century was doing something towards the real rehabilitation of this matter which lasted only one evening. But the nineteenth century was to improve on it, and the theory of the woman of thirty, with all her advantages, superiority, and definite perfection, only dates from the present time. Balzac is the inventor of it, and it is one of his most real discoveries in the order of familiar novels. The key of his enormous success was wholly in that early little masterpiece.[2] Afterwards women forgave him many things and always believed his word, because he had guessed so correctly the first time.

However rapid and great was Balzac's success in France, it was perhaps even greater and less contested in Europe. The details that could be given in respect of it would seem fabulous, and yet would be only true. Yes, Balzac described the manners of his time, and his success is one of the most curious pictures of it. It was already more than two centuries since, in 1642, Honoré d'Urfé (the author of the famous novel of "Astrée"), who lived in Piedmont, received a most serious letter addressed to him by twenty-nine princes and princesses and nineteen noblemen and noble ladies of Germany. Those persons informed him that they had assumed the names of the heroes and heroines of "Astrée," and had formed themselves into an "Academy of true lovers;" they earnestly entreated him to continue the work. What happened to D'Urfé occurred in exactly the same manner to Balzac. There was a time when, at Venice for instance, the society gathered there thought of assuming the names of his chief characters and of

[2] Only read it, I beg of you, in the early editions. The author spoiled it for me in enlarging it afterwards.

playing their parts. During the whole of one season only Rastignacs, Duchesses of Langeais and Manfrigneuse, were seen; and we are assured that more than one among the actors and actresses in that comedy of society were anxious actually to go through with their parts. Such is usually the case with the reciprocal influences between the painter and his models: the novelist begins, depicts it to the life; exaggerates it a little; society make it a point of honor and carries it out; and it is thus that what at first appeared an exaggeration ends by being only the truth.

What I said of Venice occurred in different degrees in other places. In Hungary, Poland, Russia, Balzac's novels became the law. At this distance, the slightly fantastic portions mingled with reality which, seen close, prevented a perfect success with difficult minds, have disappeared, and form an extra attraction. For instance, the costly and strange furniture where he heaped up the masterpieces of twenty countries and twenty epochs became afterwards a reality; what seemed to us the dream of an artistic millionaire was copied exactly. People furnished *à la Balzac*. How could the artist remain insensible and deaf to the thousand echoes of celebrity, and not hear in it the accents of fame?

He believed in it, and the sentiment of a certainly lofty ambition made him draw from his strong and fertile organization all the resources and productions it contained. Balzac had the body of an athlete and the soul of an artist in love with fame; less would not have sufficed for his great task. It is only in our time that we have seen vigorous and herculean organizations lay themselves in some sense under the necessity of deriving from themselves all they could produce, and carry on the difficult wager for twenty years. When we read Racine, Voltaire, Montesquieu, it does not particularly occur to us to inquire if they were robust or not in frame, and of strong physical organization. Buffon was an athlete, but his style does not show it. The authors of the more or less classical ages only wrote with their thought, with their higher and intellectual part, with the essence of their being. Now, as a consequence of the enormous work the writer imposes on himself, and which society imposes on him at short date, as a consequence of the necessity in which he finds himself of striking rapidly and forcibly, he has not time to be platonic and delicate. The writer's person and whole organization are enlisted and stand confessed in his works; he does not write them only with his pure thought, but with his blood and muscle. A writer's physiology and hygiene have become one of the indispensable chapters in making an analysis of his genius.

Balzac prided himself on being a physiologist, and he certainly was one, although with less rigor and exactness than he imagined; but physical nature, his and that of others, plays a great part, and continually reveals itself in his descriptions of morals. I do not reproach him; it is a feature which affects and characterizes all the descriptive literature of the present time. One day M. Villemain, then very young, read to Sieyès his "Eulogy of Montaigne," the delightful eulogy, the first he wrote, full of charm and sweetness. When in his reading he reached the passage where he said—" but I feared in reading Rousseau, to let my eyes rest too long on those guilty weaknesses from which we ought always to keep our distance.'—Sieyès interrupted him, saying, " But no, it is better to approach them in order to study them at closer quarters." The physiologist, curious in everything, comes in the way of the man of letters who desires taste above all. Shall I confess it? I am like Sieyès.

That is also saying I am a little like Balzac. But I hold back, however. I dwell on two points. I like his style in the finer parts—the efflorescence (I cannot find another word) by which he gives the feeling of life to everything, and makes the page itself thrill. But I cannot accept, under the cover of physiology, the continual abuse of that quality, the style so often unsteady and dissolvent, enervated, rosy and streaked with all colors, the style of a delicious corruption; Asiatic, as our masters said; in places more interrupted and more softened than the body of an ancient mime. From the midst of the scenes he describes does not Petronius somewhere regret what he calls *oratio pudica,* the modest style which does not abandon itself to the fluidity of every movement?

Another point on which I dwell in Balzac as physiologist and anatomist, is that he at least imagined as much as he observed. A fine anatomist morally, he certainly discovered new veins; he found, and as it were injected, lymph ducts, till then unperceived, and he also invented them. There is a point in his analysis when the real and actual plexus ends and the illusory plexus begins, and he does not distinguish between the two. The greater part of his readers, especially of his lady readers, confused them as he did. This is not the place to insist on those points of separation. But it is known that Balzac had an avowed weakness for the Swedenborgs, Van Helmonts, Mesmers, Saint-Germains, and Cagliostros of all sorts—that is to say, he was subject to illusion. In short, to carry out my physical and anatomical metaphor, I shall say, when he holds the carotid artery of his subject, he injects it at bottom with firmness and vigor; but when he is at fault he injects all the same, and always produces, creating, without quite perceiving it, an imaginary net-work.

Balzac pretended to knowledge, but what he really possessed was a sort of physiological intuition. M. Chasles said excellently: "It has been repeated to excess that Balzac was an observer, an analyst; he was for good and all a seer." What he did not see at a first glance he generally lacked; reflection did not give it him. But what things he could see and take in at a single glance! He came, he talked with you; he, so wrapped up in his work, and apparently so full of himself, knew how to ask questions to advantage, how to listen; but even when he had not listened, when he seemed to have been full only of himself and his own idea, he ended by carrying away, absorbing all he wanted to know, and he astonished you later by describing it.

I said that he was as it were wrapped up in his work; in truth, from his youth, he never came out of it, he lived in it. The society he had partly observed, partly created in every sense, the characters of every class and kind that he had endowed with life were confused by him with real society and people who were scarcely more than a weak copy of his own. He saw them, talked to them, quoted them like people both you and he were familiar with; he had so powerfully and clearly formed them of flesh and blood that, once realized, both they and he were never more parted: all the characters surrounded him, and in moments of enthusiasm began to circle round him and to hurry him into the immense rounds of the human comedy; it makes us a little giddy even to look at in passing, and made its author so before us.

Balzac's particular power requires definition; it was that of a rich, copious, opulent nature, full of ideas, types, and inventions; a nature that repeats unceasingly and is never tired. It was that power he possessed, and not the other, which is doubtless the true strength; power that governs and rules a work, and acts so that the artist is above it as he is above his creation. It might be said of him that he was the prey of his work, and his talent often carries him along like a chariot drawn by four horses. I do not ask that a man should be exactly like Goethe, and should always lift his marble brow above the fiery cloud, but Balzac (and he has said so) desired the artist to precipitate himself headlong into his work, like Curtius into the gulf. A genius of that sort affords much animation and passion, but also danger and a great deal of smoke.

To set forth his real literary theory we need only borrow his own words; if, for instance, I take " The Poor Relation," his last and one of his most powerful novels, published in this paper,[3] I find, in the instance of the Polish artist, Wenceslas Steinbock, the favorite ideas and all the secrets—if he could be said to have secrets—of the author. According to him, " a great artist nowadays is a prince without a title; he is fame and fortune." But the fame is not gained either by amusing one's self or by dreaming; it is the reward of persevering labor and unceasing ardor. " You have ideas in your brain? A fine thing! I also have ideas. . . . But where's the use of what may be in our minds if we derive no advantage from it?" That is what he thought, and he never spared himself in the relentless labor of execution. " To imagine," he said, " is to enjoy, to smoke enchanted cigarettes; but without execution everything vanishes as a dream, as smoke." " Constant labor," he said again, " is a law of art, as of life; for art is idealized creation. Great artists, poets, want neither for orders nor customers; they labor to-day, to-morrow, always. From it results the habit of work, the ever-present knowledge of the difficulties which keep artists *en concubinage* with the Muse, with her creative strength. Canova lived in his studio, like Voltaire lived in his study; Homer and Phidias must have lived in the same way." I wanted particularly to quote that passage, because, side by side with the good qualities of cour-

[3] " Poor Relations " first appeared as a feuilleton in the " Constitutional."

age and hard work shown in it, qualities that do Balzac honor, we grasp his modern side—the strange inadvertence by which he disparages and outrages the beauty he pretends to follow. No, neither Homer nor Phidias lived *en concubinage* with the Muse. They always received and knew her chaste and severe.

M. de Bonald said " Beauty is always severe." I need a few words of such authority; they are unchangeable sacred columns that I am anxious to point to in the distance, so that even our admiration and our meed of regret for a man of marvellous genius may not be carried beyond lawful bounds.

Balzac speaks somewhere of the artists who had " a prodigious success, a success likely to crush men whose backs were not broad enough to support it "; which, he adds parenthetically, often happens. Indeed, the day after victory is for the artist a more terrible trial than the great battle he must sooner or later fight. To uphold his victory, to carry on his reputation, neither to be frightened nor discouraged, neither to sink nor fall under the blow, as Leopold Robert did, it is necessary to possess a real strength, and to be conscious of reaching only one's level. Balzac has proved that he had that sort of strength.

When people spoke of fame to him, he accepted the word as well as the omen; he sometimes spoke jestingly of it himself. " Fame," he said one day; " to whom are you speaking? I have known it, seen it. I was travelling with some friends in Russia, night was coming on, we demanded hospitality at a castle. On our arrival the *châtelaine* and her ladies-in-waiting bustled about; one of the latter left the room immediately to fetch refreshments. In the interval my name was mentioned to the mistress of the house; we entered into conversation. When the lady returned, with a tray in her hands, she suddenly heard the words: ' Well, M. de Balzac, you think, then . . .' In an impulse of surprise and joy she let the tray fall, and everything was broken. Was not that fame? "

We smiled, he smiled himself, and yet he enjoyed it. The feeling supported and encouraged him in his work. The wittiest and most to be regretted of his disciples, Charles de Bernard, dead but a short time since, lacked that incentive; he suspected everything with irony and even with taste, and his remarkable work is a witness of it. Balzac's work gained in animation and ardor from the artist's excitement. An exquisite delicacy insinuated itself into the excitement.

All Europe was to him a park, in which he had only to take a walk in order to meet friends, admirers, cordial and sumptuous hospitality. The little flower he showed you, scarcely dry, he gathered the other morning returning from the Villa-Diodati; the picture he described to you he had seen yesterday in the palace of a Roman prince. It seemed to him that from one capital to another, from a Roman villa or from Isola-Bella to a Polish or Bohemian castle was but a step. A stroke of the wand transported him there. It cannot be said that it was a dream to him, for a devoted woman, one of those he deified in passing, fortunately realized for him what for a long while seemed the poet's dream and illusion.

All the artists of the time were his friends, and he placed them almost magnificently in his works. He possessed excellent taste and had a great love of works of art, painting, sculpture, antique furniture. When he had leisure (and he often found means of getting it, giving up his days to imagination, spending his nights in work), he liked to go on a hunt for what he called fine pieces. In this way he knew all the *bric-à-brac* shops of Europe, and he expatiated on them admirably. When he afterwards put into a novel masses of objects, which, in the hands of another writer, would have resembled an inventory, it was with color and life, and with love. The furniture he describes possesses a sort of life; the tapestries rustle. He describes too much, but usually the light falls in the right place. Even when the result does not correspond to the care he seems to have taken, the reader retains the impression of having been moved. Balzac has the gift of color and massing. By it he attracted painters who recognized in him one of themselves transplanted and strayed into literature.

He paid scant attention to criticism; he had cut his way into the world almost in spite of it, and his enthusiasm was not, I think, of the sort that could be moderated or guided. He said somewhere of a disheartened sculptor, fallen into idleness: " Become again an artist *in partibus;* he had great success in drawing-rooms, he was consulted by many amateurs, he turned critic, like all weak men who do not fulfil their early promise." The last characteristic may be true of a sculptor or painter who, instead of working, spends his time in discoursing and arguing; but in the order of ideas, Balzac's saying, often repeated by a whole school of young men of letters, is (I ask their pardon) at once an injustice and an error. However, as it is always a delicate matter to prove to people in what they are or are not weak, let us pass on.

A true, sincere, intelligent Aristarchus, if he could have tolerated him, would have been useful to Balzac; for his rich and luxurious nature was lavish, and did not control itself. In a novel three things are to be considered: the characters, the action, the style. Balzac excels in the disposing of his characters; he makes them live, he chisels them in an indelible manner. There is exaggeration and minuteness, what does it matter? The characters have in them something enduring. With him we make refined, charming, coquettish, and merry acquaintances, at other times very unpleasant ones; but once made, we are sure of never forgetting either the one or the other. He is not contented with drawing his characters well, he names them after some strange, happy fashion, and so fixes them forever in the memory. He attaches the greatest importance to baptizing his men and women; like Sterne, he attributed a certain occult power to proper names in harmony or in irony with the characters. The Marneffes, Bixious, Birotteaus, Crevels are thus named by him in virtue of some indescribable onomatopœia which makes the man and the name resemble each other. After the characters comes the action; with Balzac it is often weak, it wanders about, it is exaggerated. He is less successful in that than in the creation of the characters. His style is delicate, subtle, fluent, picturesque, owing nothing to tradition. I have sometimes wondered what effect a novel of Balzac would produce on an honest mind brought up on good ordinary French prose in all its frugality, on a mind of which there are no more, a mind formed by reading Nicole, Bourdaloue, by the simple, serious, and scrupulous style which goes far, as La Bruyère said; such a mind would be giddy for a month. La Bruyère said that for every thought there is only one right expression, and it must be found. Balzac in writing ignores La Bruyère's saying. He has series of animated, unsatisfied, capricious, never definite expressions, attempts at expressions, which ever seek. His printers knew it well. In the course of the printing of his books he altered, he rewrote each proof in never-ending fashion. With him the mould itself was always at boiling heat, and the metal did not set. He had found the desired form, and sought it still.

Would the most friendly criticism, that of a friend, a companion as he was of Louis Lambert, have ever induced him to accept ideas of relative moderation, and to introduce them into the torrent of his genius, so that he might have restrained and regulated it a little? Without desiring to lose anything of his fertile manner, I wish there had been present to his mind a few axioms that are, I consider, essential to every art, to all literature:

" Clearness is the varnish of masters."—Vauvenargues.

" A work of art ought only to express what elevates the soul, nobly rejoices it, and nothing more. The artist's feeling ought only to be directed to that, all the rest is false."—Bettine to Goethe's mother.

" Good sense and genius are of the same family; wit is only a collateral."—Bonald.

In fact I wish that he who so much admired Napoleon, whom that great example, transported and reflected into literature, dazzled as it dazzled so many besides, had left aside the similes, the foolish emulations fit only for children, and that, if he felt absolutely obliged to seek his ideal of power in military matters, he had sometimes asked himself the question, eminently fitted to find a place in every good French treatise on rhetoric: " Which is finer, an Asiatic conqueror dragging countless hordes behind him, or Turenne defending the Rhine at the head of thirty thousand men?"

Do not let us force nature, and since death has closed his career, let us accept of the genius that is gone the rich and complex inheritance it has left us. The author of " Eugénie Grandet " will live. The father—I was going to say the lover of Madame de Vieuménil—of Madame de Beauséant will retain his place on the small tables of the most retired and select boudoirs. Those who seek joy, gayety, expansion of heart, the satirical and frank vein of the Rabelaisian Tourangeau cannot despise the admirable Gaudissart, the excellent Birotteau, and all their race. There is something, it seems, for everyone. If I had the space, I should like to speak of Balzac's last novel, in my opinion one of his most remarkable books, although not the most flattering to society. " Poor Relations " shows us Balzac's vigorous genius in its ripest maturity, in its widest scope. He is over-abundant, he swims, he seems completely in his element. Never was the topsy-turvydom of human worthlessness better displayed or put into motion. The first part of the novel (Cousin Bette) presents characters of much truth side by side with the exaggeration inseparable from this author. Bette, who lends her name to the novel, is one of the exaggerations; it does not seem that the poor creature who appears first as a simple Vosges peasant, ill-clothed, badly dressed, rough, a little envious, but neither wicked nor a rogue, could be the same who, at a given moment, is transformed into an almost beautiful woman of society, and extremely obstinate and wicked, a female Iago or Richard III! Things do not happen thus in real life; that woman is of the race of Ferragus and Treize. Our degenerate and vitiated society does not admit of those atrocious hatreds and vengeances. Our sins are certainly not small; our crimes, however, are less great. But other characters of the novel are true, profoundly true, and especially that of Baron Hulot, with his immoderate love of women that step by step leads the honorable man to dishonor and the old man to degradation; and Crevel, excellent all round, in tone, in gesture, in humor, all the vices of the bourgeois clearly showing in his bearing and his self-importance. For note we are not here confronted only with caprice, eccentricity, nor even with human folly: vice is the mainspring, social depravity is the subject of the novel. The author plunges into it; to see his animation we might even say that in parts he enjoys it. A few lofty, pathetic scenes move us to tears; but the horrible scenes predominate, the sap of impurity overflows, the infamous Marneffe infects everything. The remarkable novel, studied by itself, would give rise to reflections which would affect not only Balzac but all of us, the more or less secret or avowed children of a sensual literature. Some men, sons of René, hide and envelop their sensualism in mysticism, while others frankly strip off the mask.

Balzac often thought of Walter Scott, and he says the genius of the great Scotch novelist roused his keenest interest. But in the midst of the vast work of the delightful wizard, did he not recognize, according to Lamartine's happy expression: "The noble sentiments rising from the pages—like the perfume of odoriferous shores"? Did he not breathe the universal charm of purity and health, salubrious breezes that blow even athwart the conflict of human passions? After reading "Poor Relations," we feel the need of new vigor, of throwing ourselves into some healthful and limpid book, of plunging into some song of Milton in lucid streams, as the poet says.

In a more complete work, and if we were free to give ourselves full play, it would be interesting to establish and graduate the true relation of the genius of Balzac to that of his most celebrated contemporaries—Madame Sand, Eugène Sue, Alexandre Dumas. Of an entirely different style, but with a view of human nature neither more favorable nor more flattering, Merimée might be taken as a contrast in tone and manner.

Merimée has not perhaps a better opinion of human nature than Balzac, and if it has been slandered it is certainly not he who will reinstate it. But he is a man of taste, of nice discernment, of exact and rigorous sense, who even in the excess of the idea preserves a prudence and discretion of manner. He possesses the personal feeling for ridicule as much as Balzac lacked it, and in him, in the midst of the clearness, vigor of line, and precision of burin that we admire, we cannot help missing a little of the animation the other possessed in too high a degree. It might be said of him that the accomplished man of the world, the gentleman, as it was formerly said, held the artist in check.

Is it necessary to recall to mind that Madame Sand is a greater, surer, and stronger writer than Balzac? She never hesitates in expresssion. She is a greater painter of nature and landscape. As a novelist her characters in the beginning are often well conceived, well designed; but they soon turn to a Rousseau-like ideal which becomes almost a system. Her characters are not entirely alive; at a certain point they become types. She never calumniates human nature, neither does she adorn it; she tries to enrich it, but in aiming at enlarging it, she forces and distends it. She lays the blame on society, and disparages whole classes, and desires in any and every case to bring into notice, individuals, who are, notwithstanding, half abstract. In short, the masterly precision which she puts into expression and description is not found in an equal degree in the realization of her characters. This is said, however, with all the reservation due to so many charming and natural situations and scenes. Her style, however, is a gift of the first quality, and of the finest stamp.

M. Eugène Sue (let us turn from the socialist and speak only of the novelist) is perhaps Balzac's equal in invention, fertility, and composition. He constructs wonderfully big frames; his characters live, and we remember them against our will; above all, he possesses action and dramatic machinery of which he thoroughly understands the manipulation. But the details are often weak; they are numerous and varied enough, but less delicate, of less research, showing less original and fresh observation than in Balzac. He also possesses gayety, and seizes happy and natural types; but in addition he loves and affects eccentricities, and takes too much pleasure in describing them. With one, as with the other, we must set no store by wholesome nature; they prefer to work on what is corrupt or artificial. Eugène Sue cannot write so much, nor so badly, nor so subtly in regard to evil, as Balzac. He was wrong in not entirely abandoning himself to the instincts of his own nature, and in consulting the systems in vogue and in setting them forth in his later novels—a thing Balzac never did. He at least only obeyed his instincts, his favorite inspirations, and abandoned himself to them more and more as an artist who never makes compromises. As regards the stream, Balzac has never followed any but his own.

Everybody knows M. Dumas's immense animation, high spirits, happy set scenes, and witty and always living dialogue. His graceful narrative runs on without stopping, and can remove obstacles and even space without becoming weak. He covers enormous canvases, and neither his brush nor his reader grows weary. He is amusing; he charms our imagination, but does not take tight hold of it like Balzac.

Of the three last, Balzac lays hold of things most closely, and sounds them most deeply.

The Revolution of February struck Balzac a keen blow. The whole edifice of refined civilization, such as he had always dreamed of it, seemed ruined. For a moment, Europe, his own Europe, was to fail him like France. However, he soon took heart again, and meditated describing at close quarters the new society in the fourth dress in which it presented itself to him. I could sketch in his next novel, his last projected novel, of which he spoke with ardor. But of what use is one dream the more? He died of heart disease, as so many men who have worked too ardently in life die nowadays. Scarcely three years ago Frédéric Soulié succumbed to the same malady, a man it would be unjust to forget in grouping together the gods of that literature.

Perhaps, the place to repeat that that literature created its school and served its time, is over the grave of one of the most fertile of them, assuredly of the most inventive; the school gave us its most vigorous, almost gigantic talents; for good or bad it may be thought now that the best of its sap is exhausted. Let it at least cry truce and rest; let it also leave society time to recruit its strength after its excesses, to compose itself into some sort of order, and to present new pictures to painters of a fresher inspiration. There was latterly a terrible rivalry and a keen competition between the strongest men of that active, devouring, inflammatory literature. The mode of publication in *feuilletons*, which necessitated in each new chapter a striking situation that should impress itself on the reader, drove the effects and tones of the novel to an extreme pitch, discouraging and no longer tolerable. Let us compose ourselves a little. While admitting the advantage derived by men whose talent lacked the conditions necessary for a better development, let us desire for the future of our society, pictures, not less vast, but more satisfying, more consoling, and let us hope for those who paint them a quieter life, and an inspiration not more delicate, but more calm, more soundly natural and serene.

MONTAIGNE

WHILE the good ship France is taking a somewhat haphazard course, getting into unknown seas, and preparing to double what the pilots (if there is a pilot) call the Stormy Cape, while the look-out at the mast-head thinks he sees the spectre of the giant Adamastor rising on the horizon, many honorable and peaceable men continue their work and studies all the same, and follow out to the end, or as far as they can, their favorite hobbies. I know, at the present time, a learned man who is collating more carefully than has ever yet been done the different early editions of Rabelais—editions, mark you, of which only one copy remains, of which a second is not to be found: from the careful collation of the texts some literary and maybe philosophical result will be derived with regard to the genius of the French Lucian-Aristophanes. I know another scholar whose devotion and worship is given to a very different man—to Bossuet: he is preparing a complete, exact, detailed history of the life and works of the great bishop. And as tastes differ, and " human fancy is cut into a thousand shapes " (Montaigne said that), Montaigne also has his devotees, he who, himself, was so little of one: a sect is formed round him. In his lifetime he had Mademoiselle de Gournay, his daughter of *alliance,* who was solemnly devoted to him; and his disciple, Charron, followed him closely, step by step, only striving to arrange his thoughts with more order and method. In our time amateurs, intelligent men, practise the religion under another form: they devote themselves to collecting the smallest traces of the author of the " Essays," to gathering up the slightest relics, and Dr. Payen may be justly placed at the head of the group. For years he has been preparing a book on Montaigne, of which the title will be—

" Michel de Montaigne: a collection of unedited or little

known facts about the author of the 'Essays,' his book, and his other writings, about his family, his friends, his admirers, his detractors."

While awaiting the conclusion of the book, the occupation and amusement of a lifetime, Dr. Payen keeps us informed in short pamphlets of the various works and discoveries made about Montaigne.

If we separate the discoveries made during the last five or six years from the jumble of quarrels, disputes, cavilling, quackery, and law-suits (for there have been all those), they consist in this—

In 1846 M. Macé found in the (then) Royal Library, amongst the " Collection Du Puys," a letter of Montaigne, addressed to the King, Henri IV, September 2, 1590.

In 1847 M. Payen printed a letter, or a fragment of a letter, of Montaigne of February 16, 1588, a letter corrupt and incomplete, coming from the collection of the Comtesse Boni de Castellane.

But most important of all, in 1848, M. Horace de Viel-Castel found in London, at the British Museum, a remarkable letter of Montaigne, May 22, 1585, when Mayor of Bordeaux, addressed to M. de Matignon, the King's lieutenant in the town. The great interest of the letter is that it shows Montaigne for the first time in the full discharge of his office with all the energy and vigilance of which he was capable. The pretended idler was at need much more active than he was ready to own.

M. Detcheverry, keeper of the records to the mayoralty of Bordeaux, found and published (1850) a letter of Montaigne, while mayor, to the *Jurats*, or aldermen of the town, July 30, 1585.

M. Achille Jubinal found among the manuscripts of the National Library, and published (1850), a long, remarkable letter from Montaigne to the King, Henri IV, January 18, 1590, which happily coincides with that already found by M. Macé.

Lastly, to omit nothing and to do justice to all, in a " Visit to Montaigne's Château in Périgord," of which the account appeared in 1850, M. Bertrand de Saint-Germain described the place and pointed out the various Greek and Latin inscriptions that may still be read in Montaigne's tower in the third-story chamber (the ground floor counting as the first), which the philosopher made his library and study.

M. Payen, collecting together and criticising in his last pamphlet the various notices and discoveries, not all of equal importance, allowed himself to be drawn into some little exaggeration of praise; but we cannot blame him. Admiration, when applied to such noble, perfectly innocent and disinterested subjects, is truly a spark of the sacred fire: it produces research that a less ardent zeal would quickly leave aside, and sometimes leads to valuable results. However, it would be well for those who, following M. Payen's example, intelligently understand and greatly admire Montaigne, to remember, even in their ardor, the advice of the wise man and the master.

"There is more to do," said he, speaking of the commentators of his time, "in interpreting the interpretations than in interpreting the things themselves; and more books about books than on any other subject. We do nothing but everything swarms with commentators; of authors there is a great rarity." Authors are of great price and very scarce at all times—that is to say, authors who really increase the sum of human knowledge. I should like all who write on Montaigne, and give us the details of their researches and discoveries, to imagine one thing—Montaigne himself reading and criticising them. "What would he think of me and of the manner in which I am going to speak of him to the public?" If such a question was put, how greatly it would suppress useless phrases and shorten idle discussions! M. Payen's last pamphlet was dedicated to a man who deserves equally well of Montaigne—M. Gustave Brunet, of Bordeaux. He, speaking of M. Payen, in a work in which he pointed out interesting and various corrections of Montaigne's text, said: "May he soon decide to publish the fruits of his researches: he will have left nothing for future Montaignologues." Montaignologues! Great Heaven! what would Montaigne say of such a word coined in his honor? You who occupy yourselves so meritoriously with him, but who have, I think, no claim to appropriate him to yourselves, in the name of him whom you love, and whom we all love by a greater or lesser title, never, I beg of you, use such words; they smack of the brotherhood and the sect, of pedantry and of the chatter of the schools—things utterly repugnant to Montaigne.

Montaigne had a simple, natural, affable mind, and a very happy disposition. Sprung from an excellent father, who, though of no great education, entered with real enthusiasm into the movement of the Renaissance and all the liberal novelties of his time, the son corrected the excessive enthusiasm, vivacity, and tenderness he inherited by a great refinement and justness of reflection; but he did not abjure the original groundwork. It is scarcely more than thirty years ago that whenever the sixteenth century was mentioned it was spoken of as a barbarous epoch, Montaigne only excepted: therein lay error and ignorance. The sixteenth century was a great century, fertile, powerful, learned, refined in parts, although in some aspects it was rough, violent, and seemingly coarse. What it particularly lacked was taste, if by taste is meant the faculty of clear and perfect selection, the extrication of the elements of the beautiful. But in the succeeding centuries taste quickly became distaste. If, however, in literature it was crude, in the arts properly so called, in those of the hand and the chisel, the sixteenth century, even in France, is, in the quality of taste, far greater than the two succeeding centuries: it is neither meagre nor massive, heavy nor distorted. In art its taste is rich and of fine quality—at once unrestrained and complex, ancient and modern, special to itself and original. In the region of morals it is unequal and mixed. It was an age of contrasts, of contrasts in all their crudity, an age of philosophy and fanaticism, of scepticism and strong faith. Everything was at strife and in collision; nothing was blended and united. Everything was in ferment; it was a period of chaos; every ray of light caused a storm. It was not a gentle age, or one we can call an age of light, but an age of struggle and combat. What distinguished Montaigne and made a phenomenon of him was, that in such an age he should have possessed moderation, caution, and order.

Born on the last day of February, 1533, taught the ancient languages as a game while still a child, waked even in his cradle by the sound of musical instruments, he seemed less fitted for a rude and violent epoch than for the commerce and sanctuary of the muses. His rare good sense corrected what was too ideal and poetical in his early education; but he preserved the happy faculty of saying everything with freshness and wit. Married, when past thirty, to an estimable woman who was his companion for twenty-eight years, he seems to have put passion only into friendship. He immortalized his love for Étienne de la Boëtie, whom he lost after four years of the sweetest and closest intimacy. For some time counsellor in the Parliament of Bordeaux, Montaigne, before he was forty, retired from public life and flung away ambition to live in his tower of Montaigne, enjoying his own society and his own intellect, entirely given up to his own observations and thoughts, and to the busy idleness of which we know all the sports and fancies. The first edition of the "Essays" appeared in 1580, consisting of only two books, and in a form representing only the first rough draft of what we have in the later editions. The same year Montaigne set out on a voyage to Switzerland and Italy. It was during that voyage that the aldermen of Bordeaux elected him mayor of their town. At first he refused and excused himself, but warned that it would be well to accept, and enjoined by the King, he took the office, "the more beautiful," he said, "that there was neither remuneration nor gain other than the honor of its performance." He filled the office for four years, from July, 1582, to July, 1586, being re-elected after the first two years. Thus Montaigne, at the age of fifty, and a little against his will, re-entered public life when the country was on the eve of civil disturbances which, quieted and lulled to sleep for a while, broke out more violently at the cry of the League. Although, as a rule, lessons serve for nothing, since the art of wisdom and happiness cannot be taught, let us not deny ourselves the pleasure of listening to Montaigne; let us look on his wisdom and happiness; let him speak of public affairs, of revolutions and disturbances, and of his way of conducting himself with regard to them. We do not put forward a model, but we offer our readers an agreeable recreation.

Although Montaigne lived in so agitated and stormy a time, a period that a man who had lived through the Terror (M. Daunou) called the most tragic century in all history, he by no means regarded his age as the worst of ages. He was not of those prejudiced and afflicted persons, who, measuring everything by their visual horizon, valuing everything according to their present sensations, always declare that the disease they suffer from is worse than any ever before experienced by a human being. He was like Socrates, who did not consider himself a citizen of one city but of the world; with his broad and full imagination he embraced the universality of countries and of ages; he even judged more equitably the very evils of which he was witness and victim. "Who is it," he said, " that, seeing the bloody havoc of these civil wars of ours, does not cry out that the machine of the world is near dissolution, and that the day of judgment is at hand, without considering that many worse revolutions have been seen, and that, in the mean time, people are being merry in a thousand other parts of the earth for all this? For my part, considering the license and impunity that always attend such commotions, I admire they are so moderate, and that there is not more mischief done. To him who feels the hailstones patter about his ears, the whole hemisphere appears to be in storm and tempest." And raising his thoughts higher and higher, reducing his own suffering to what it was in the immensity of nature, seeing there not only himself, but whole kingdoms as mere specks in the infinite, he added in words which foreshadowed Pascal, in words whose outline and salient points Pascal did not disdain to borrow: " But whoever shall represent to his fancy, as in a picture, that great image of our mother nature, portrayed in her full majesty and lustre, whoever in her face shall read so general and so constant a variety, whoever shall observe himself in that figure, and not himself but a whole kingdom, no bigger than the least touch or prick of a pencil in comparison of the whole, that man alone is able to value things according to their true estimate and grandeur."

Thus Montaigne gives us a lesson, a useless lesson, but I state it all the same, because among the many unprofitable ones that have been written down, it is perhaps of greater worth than most. I do not mean to underrate the gravity of the circumstances in which France is just now involved, for I believe there is pressing need to bring together all the energy, prudence, and courage she possesses in order that the country may come out with honor.[1] However, let us reflect, and re-

---
[1] This essay appeared April 28, 1851.

member that, leaving aside the Empire, which as regards internal affairs was a period of calm, and before 1812 of prosperity, we who utter such loud complaints, lived in peace from 1815 to 1830, fifteen long years; that the three days of July only inaugurated another order of things that for eighteen years guaranteed peace and industrial prosperity; in all, thirty-two years of repose. Stormy days came; tempests burst, and will doubtless burst again. Let us learn how to live through them, but do not let us cry out every day, as we are disposed to do, that never under the sun were such storms known as we are enduring. To get away from the present state of feeling, to restore lucidity and proportion to our judgments, let us read every evening a page of Montaigne.

A criticism of Montaigne on the men of his day struck me, and it bears equally well on those of ours. Our philosopher says somewhere that he knows a fair number of men possessing various good qualities—one, intelligence; another, heart; another, address, conscience or knowledge, or skill in languages, each has his share: " but of a great man as a whole, having so many good qualities together, or one with such a degree of excellence that we ought to admire him, or compare him with those we honor in the past, my fortune has never shown me one." He afterwards made an exception in favor of his friend Étienne de la Boëtie, but he belonged to the company of great men dead before attaining maturity, and showing promise without having time to fulfil it. Montaigne's criticism called up a smile. He did not see a true and wholly great man in his time, the age of L'Hôpital, Coligny, and the Guises. Well! how does ours seem to you? We have as many great men as in Montaigne's time, one distinguished for his intellect, another for his heart, a third for skill, some (a rare thing) for conscience, many for knowledge and language. But we too lack the perfect man, and he is greatly to be desired. One of the most intelligent observers of our day recognized and proclaimed it some years ago: " Our age," said M. de Rémusat, " is wanting in great men." [2]

How did Montaigne conduct himself in his duties as first magistrate of a great city? If we take him literally and on a hasty first glance, we should believe he discharged them

---

[2] " Essais de Philosophie," vol. i. p. 22.

slackly and languidly. Did not Horace, doing the honors to himself, say that in war he one day let his shield fall *(relicta non bene parmula)*? We must not be in too great a hurry to take too literally the men of taste who have a horror of over-estimating themselves. Minds of a fine quality are more given to vigilance and to action than they are apt to confess. The man who boasts and makes a great noise, will, I am almost sure, be less brave in the combat than Horace, and less vigilant at the council board than Montaigne.

On entering office Montaigne was careful to warn the aldermen of Bordeaux not to expect to find in him more than there really was; he presented himself to them without affectation. " I represented to them faithfully and conscientiously all that I felt myself to be—a man without memory, without vigilance, without experience, and without energy; but also, without hate, without ambition, without avarice, and without violence." He should be sorry, while taking the affairs of the town in hand, that his feelings should be so strongly affected as those of his worthy father had been, who in the end had lost his place and health. The eager and ardent pledge to satisfy an impetuous desire was not his method. His opinion was " that you must lend yourself to others, and only give yourself to yourself." And repeating his thought, according to his custom in all kinds of metaphors and picturesque forms, he said again that if he sometimes allowed himself to be urged to the management of other men's affairs, he promised to take them in hand, not " into my lungs and liver." We are thus forewarned, we know what to expect. The mayor and Montaigne were two distinct persons; under his *rôle* and office he reserved to himself a certain freedom and secret security. He continued to judge things in his own fashion and impartially, although acting loyally for the cause confided to him. He was far from approving or even excusing all he saw in his party, and he could judge his adversaries and say of them: " He did that thing wickedly, and this virtuously." " I would have," he added, " matters go well on our side; but if they do not, I shall not run mad. I am heartily for the right party; but I do not affect to be taken notice of for an especial enemy to others." And he entered into some details and applications which at that time were piquant. Let us remark, however, in order to explain and justify his somewhat extensive profession of impartiality, that the chiefs of the party then in evidence, the three Henris, were famous and considérable men on several counts: Henri, Duke of Guise, head of the League; Henri, King of Navarre, leader of the Opposition; and the King Henri III, in whose name Montaigne was mayor, who wavered between the two. When parties have neither chief nor head, when they are known by the body only, that is to say in their hideous and brutal reality, it is more difficult and also more hazardous to be just towards them and to assign to each its share of action.

The principle which guided him in his administration was to look only at the fact, at the result, and to grant nothing to noise and outward show: " How much more a good effect makes a noise, so much I abate of the goodness of it." For it is always to be feared that it was more performed for the sake of the noise than upon the account of goodness: " Being exposed upon the stall, 'tis half sold." That was not Montaigne's way: he made no show; he managed men and affairs as quietly as he could; he employed in a manner useful to all alike the gifts of sincerity and conciliation; the personal attraction with which nature endowed him was a quality of the highest value in the management of men. He preferred to warn men of evil rather than to take on himself the honor of repressing it: " Is there any one who desires to be sick that he may see his physician's practice? And would not that physician deserve to be whipped who should wish the plague amongst us that he might put his art into practice? " Far from desiring that trouble and disorder in the affairs of the city should rouse and honor his government, he had ever willingly, he said, contributed all he could to their tranquillity and ease. He is not of those whom municipal honors intoxicate and elate, those " dignities of office " as he called them, and of which all the noise " goes from one cross-road to another." If he was a man desirous of fame, he recognized that it was of a kind greater than that. I do not know, however, if even in a vaster field he would have changed his method and manner of proceeding. To do good for the public imperceptibly would always seem to him the ideal of skill and the culminating point of happiness. " He who will not thank me," he said, " for the order and quiet calm that have accompanied my administration, cannot, however, deprive me of the share that belongs to me by the title of my good fortune." And he is inexhaustible in describing in lively and graceful expressions the kinds of effective and imperceptible services he believed he had rendered —services greatly superior to noisy and glorious deeds: " Actions which come from the workman's hand carelessly and noiselessly have most charm, that some honest man chooses later and brings from their obscurity to thrust them into the light for their own sake." Thus fortune served Montaigne to perfection, and even in his administration of affairs, in difficult conjunctures, he never had to belie his maxim, nor to step very far out of the way of life he had planned: " For my part I commend a gliding, solitary, and silent life." He reached the end of his magistracy almost satisfied with himself, having accomplished what he had promised himself, and much more than he had promised others.

The letter lately discovered by M. Horace de Viel-Castel corroborates the chapter in which Montaigne exhibits and criticises himself in the period of his public life. " That letter," says M. Payen, " is entirely on affairs. Montaigne is mayor; Bordeaux, lately disturbed, seems threatened by fresh agitations; the King's lieutenant is away. It is Wednesday, May 22, 1585; it is night, Montaigne is wakeful, and writes to the governor of the province." The letter, which is of too special and local an interest to be inserted here, may be summed up in these words: Montaigne regretted the absence of Marshal de Matignon, and feared the consequences of its prolongation; he was keeping, and would continue to keep, him acquainted with all that was going on, and begged him to return as soon as his circumstances would permit. " We are looking after our gates and guards, and a little more carefully in your absence. . . . If anything important and fresh occurs, I shall send you a messenger immediately, so that if you hear no news from me, you may consider that nothing has happened." He begs M. de Matignon to remember, however, that he might not have time to warn him, " entreating you to consider that such movements are usually so sudden, that if they do occur they will take me by the throat without any warning." Besides, he will do everything to ascertain the march of events beforehand. "I will do what I can to hear news from all parts, and to that end shall visit and observe the inclinations of all sorts of men." Lastly, after keeping the marshal informed of everything, of the least rumors abroad in the city, he pressed him to return, assuring him "that we spare neither our care, nor, if need be, our lives to preserve everything in obedience to the King." Montaigne was never prodigal of protestations and praises, and what with others was a mere form of speech was with him a real undertaking and the truth.

Things, however, became worse and worse: civil war broke out; friendly or hostile parties (the difference was not great) infested the country. Montaigne, who went to his country house as often as he could, whenever the duties of his office, which was drawing near its term, did not oblige him to be in Bordeaux, was exposed to every sort of insult and outrage. "I underwent," he said, "the inconveniences that moderation brings along with it in such a disease. I was pitied on all hands; to the Ghibelline I was a Guelph, and to the Guelph a Ghibelline." In the midst of his personal grievances he could disengage and raise his thoughts to reflections on the public misfortunes and on the degradation of men's characters. Considering closely the disorder of parties, and all the abject and wretched things which developed so quickly, he was ashamed to see leaders of renown stoop and debase themselves by cowardly complacency; for in those circumstances we know, like him, "that in the word of command to march, draw up, wheel, and the like, we obey him indeed; but all the rest is dissolute and free." "It pleases me," said Montaigne ironically, "to observe how much pusillanimity and cowardice there is in ambition; by how abject and servile ways it must arrive at its end." Despising ambition as he did, he was not sorry to see it unmasked by such practices and degraded in his sight. However, his goodness of heart overcoming his pride and contempt, he adds sadly, "it displeases me to see good and generous natures, and that are capable of justice, every day corrupted in the management and command of this confusion. . . . We had ill-contrived souls enough without spoiling those that were generous and good." He rather sought in that misfortune an opportunity and motive for fortifying and strengthening himself. Attacked one by one by many disagreeables and evils, which he would have endured more cheerfully in a heap—that is to say, all at once—pursued by war, disease, by all the plagues (July, 1585), in the course things were taking, he already asked himself to whom he and his could have recourse, of whom he could ask shelter and subsistence for his old age; and having looked and searched thoroughly all around, he found himself actually destitute and ruined. For, " to let a man's self fall plumb down, and from so great a height, it ought to be in the arms of a solid, vigorous, and fortunate friendship. They are very rare, if there be any." Speaking in such a manner, we perceive that La Boëtie had been some time dead. Then he felt that he must after all rely on himself in his distress, and must gain strength; now or never was the time to put into practice the lofty lessons he spent his life in collecting from the books of the philosophers. He took heart again, and attained all the height of his virtue: " In an ordinary and quiet time, a man prepares himself for moderate and common accidents; but in the confusion wherein we have been for these thirty years, every Frenchman, whether in particular or in general, sees himself every hour upon the point of the total ruin and overthrow of his fortune." And far from being discouraged and cursing fate for causing him to be born in so stormy an age, he suddenly congratulated himself: " Let us thank fortune that has not made us live in an effeminate, idle, and languishing age." Since the curiosity of wise men seeks the past for disturbances in States in order to learn the secrets of history, and, as we should say, the whole physiology of the body social, " so does my curiosity," he declares, " make me in some sort please myself with seeing with my own eyes this notable spectacle of our public death, its forms and symptoms; and, seeing I could not hinder it, am content to be destined to assist in it, and thereby to instruct myself." I shall not suggest a consolation of that sort to most people; the greater part of mankind does not possess the heroic and eager curiosity of Empedocles and the elder Pliny, the two intrepid men who went straight to the volcanoes and the disturbances of nature to examine them at close quarters, at the risk of destruction and death. But to a man of Montaigne's nature, the thought of that stoical observation gave him consolation even amid real evils. Considering the condition of false peace and doubtful truce, the *régime* of dull and profound corruption which had preceded the last disturbances, he almost congratulated himself on seeing their cessation; for "it was," he said of the *régime* of Henri III, "a universal juncture of particular members, rotten to emulation of one another, and the most of them with inveterate ulcers, that neither required nor admitted of any cure. This conclusion therefore did really more animate than depress me." Note that his health, usually delicate, is here raised to the level of his morality, although what it had suffered through the various disturbances might have been enough to undermine it. He had the satisfaction of feeling that he had some hold against fortune, and that it would take a greater shock still to crush him.

Another consideration, humbler and more humane, upheld him in his troubles, the consolation arising from a common misfortune, a misfortune shared by all, and the sight of the courage of others. The people, especially the real people, they who are victims and not robbers, the peasants of his district, moved him by the manner in which they endured the same, or even worse, troubles than his. The disease or plague which raged at that time in the country pressed chiefly on the poor; Montaigne learned from them resignation and the practice of philosophy. "Let us look down upon the poor people that we see scattered upon the face of the earth, prone and intent upon their business, that neither know Aristotle nor Cato, example nor precept. Even from these does nature every day extract effects of constancy and patience, more pure and manly than those we so inquisitively study in the schools." And he goes on to describe them working to the bitter end, even in their grief, even in disease, until their strength failed them. "He that is now digging in my garden has this morning buried his father, or his son. . . . They never keep their beds but to die." The whole chapter is fine, pathetic, to the point, evincing noble, stoical elevation of mind, and also the cheerful and affable disposition which Montaigne said, with truth, was his by inheritance, and in which he had been nourished. There could be nothing better as regards "consolation in public calamities," except a chapter of some not more human, but of some truly divine book, in which the hand of God should be everywhere visible, not perfunctorily, as with Montaigne, but actually and lovingly present. In fact, the consolation Montaigne gives himself and others is perhaps as lofty and beautiful as human consolation without prayer can be.

He wrote the chapter, the twelfth of the third book, in the midst of the evils he described, and before they were ended. He concluded it in his graceful and poetical way with a collection of examples, "a heap of foreign flowers," to which he furnished only the thread for fastening them together.

There is Montaigne to the life; no matter how seriously he spoke, it was always with the utmost charm. To form an opinion on his style you have only to open him indifferently at any page and listen to his talk on any subject; there is none that he did not enliven and make suggestive. In the chapter "Of Liars," for instance, after enlarging on his lack of memory and giving a list of reasons by which he might console himself, he suddenly added this fresh and delightful reason, that, thanks to his faculty for forgetting, "the places I revisit, and the books I read over again, always smile upon me with a fresh novelty." It is thus that on every subject he touched he was continually new, and created sources of freshness.

Montesquieu, in a memorable exclamation, said: "The four great poets, Plato, Malebranche, Shaftesbury, Montaigne!" How true it is of Montaigne! No French writer, including the poets proper, had so lofty an idea of poetry as he had. "From my earliest childhood," he said, "poetry had power over me to transport and transpierce me." He considered, and therein shows penetration, that "we have more poets than judges and interpreters of poetry. It is easier to write than to understand." In itself and its pure beauty his poetry defies definition; whoever desired to recognize it at a glance and discern of what it actually consisted would see no more than "the brilliance of a flash of lightning." In the constitution and continuity of his style, Montaigne is a writer very rich in animated, bold similes, naturally fertile in metaphors that are never detached from the thought, but that seize it in its very centre, in its interior, that join and bind it. In that respect, fully obeying his own genius, he has gone beyond and sometimes exceeded the genius of language. His concise, vigorous, and always forcible style, by its poignancy, emphasizes and repeats the meaning. It may be said of his style that it is a continual epigram, or an ever-renewed metaphor, a style that has only been successfully employed by the French once, by Montaigne himself. If we wanted to imitate him, supposing we had the power and were naturally fitted for it—if we desired to write with his severity, exact proportion, and diverse continuity of figures and turns—it would be necessary to force our language to be more powerful, and poetically more complete, than is usually our custom. Style *à la* Montaigne, consistent, varied in the series and assortment of the metaphors, exacts the creation of a portion of the tissue itself to hold them. It is absolutely necessary that in places the woof should be enlarged and extended, in order to weave into it the metaphor; but in defining him I come almost to write like him. The French language, French prose, which in fact always savors more or less of conversation, does not, naturally, possess the resources and the extent of canvas necessary for a continued picture: by the side of an animated metaphor it will often exhibit a sudden lacuna and some weak places. In filling this by boldness and invention as Montaigne did, in creating, in imagining the expression and locution that is wanting, our prose should appear equally finished. Style *à la* Montaigne would, in many respects, be openly at war with that of Voltaire. It could only come into being and flourish in the full freedom of the sixteenth century, in a frank, ingenious, jovial, keen, brave, and refined mind, of a unique stamp, that even for that time, seemed free and somewhat licentious, and that was inspired and emboldened, but not intoxicated by the pure and direct spirit of ancient sources.

Such as he is, Montaigne is the French Horace; he is Horatian in the groundwork, often in the form and expression, although in that he sometimes approaches Seneca. His book is a treasure-house of moral observations and of experience; at whatever page it is opened, and in whatever condition of mind, some wise thought expressed in a striking and enduring fashion is certain to be found. It will at once detach itself and engrave itself on the mind, a beautiful meaning in full and forcible words, in one vigorous line, familiar or great. The whole of his book, said Étienne Pasquier, is a real seminary of beautiful and remarkable sentences, and they come in so much the better that they run and hasten on without thrusting themselves into notice. There is something for every age, for every hour of life: you cannot read in it for any time without having the mind filled and lined as it were, or, to put it better, fully armed and clothed. We have just seen how much useful counsel and actual consolation it contains for an honorable man, born for private life, and fallen on times of disturbance and revolution. To this I shall add the counsel he gave those who, like myself and many men of my acquaintance, suffer from political disturbances without in any way provoking them, or believing ourselves capable of averting them. Montaigne, as Horace would have done, counsels them, while apprehending everything from afar off, not to be too much preoccupied with such matters in advance; to take advantage to the end of pleasant moments and bright intervals. Stroke on stroke come his piquant and wise similes, and he concludes, to my thinking, with the most delightful one of all, and one, besides, entirely appropriate and seasonable: it is folly and fret, he said, "to take out your furred gown at Saint John because you will want it at Christmas."

BYRON AND GOETHE

BY
GIUSEPPE MAZZINI

GIUSEPPE MAZZINI

1805—1872

The life of Giuseppe Mazzini was devoted primarily to the cause of Italian liberation, and only secondarily to literature, but he achieved a great reputation in both fields of activity. He was born in Genoa in 1805, and from his earliest childhood he was filled with a longing to see Italy become something more than "a geographical expression," and his countrymen free. While a student at the University of Genoa he gathered around him a group of ardent young men whom he fired with his own enthusiasm. In 1827 Mazzini joined the Carbonari, and soon became a prominent member of this famous secret society. In 1830 he was arrested for conspiracy and confined in the fortress of Savona, the governor of Genoa informing his father that "the Government was not fond of young men of talent, the subject of whose musings is unknown to it." He was finally acquitted of the charges brought against him by the Senate at Turin, but while in his cell he conceived the plan of organizing the new association of "Young Italy." This organization became at once vigorously active, its headquarters being established at Marseilles. In 1831 he issued the journal of "Young Italy," to which he was the principal contributor. He published at this time numerous essays and appeals on the subject of Italian liberty. In 1832 Mazzini was exiled from France, but remained another year at Marseilles in disguise, planning a rising in Piedmont, which proved abortive and resulted in the death of most of those implicated. In 1834 another attempt at insurrection was made, the insurrectionists entering Italy from Switzerland. This, too, failed completely. Mazzini remained two years longer in Switzerland, but was finally expelled from that country and forced to flee to London, where he lived for a long time in the most abject poverty, often subsisting on loans at usurious rates of interest. It was during this period that several of the most important of his essays were written, those on "Lamennais" and on "Byron and Goethe" in 1839, the two on Carlyle in 1843, and that on the minor works of Dante in 1844.

In 1848, "the year of revolutions," Mazzini hastened to Italy. In 1849 the Republic was proclaimed, with Mazzini as the guiding spirit of the revolt. After the battle of Novara Mazzini became the chief of a triumvirate, and distinguished himself during the siege of Rome by the French. In 1857 he participated in another abortive insurrection. He then returned to England, where he had many friends and was assured of a comfortable living by his pen. His health had been shattered by his violent efforts during the siege of Rome, but his mind remained clear and active, and he wrote during this period many notable papers, chiefly political. His "Duties of Man" and "Thoughts upon Democracy in Europe" were written at this time. In 1870 he took part in an insurrection at Palermo, during which he was captured. He was released, however, by a general amnesty, but banished by the Italian Government after the occupation of Rome. He died in 1872 at Pisa, and the honors paid him at his funeral assumed the nature of a national demonstration.

BYRON AND GOETHE

I STOOD one day in a Swiss village at the foot of the Jura, and watched the coming of a storm. Heavy black clouds, their edges purpled by the setting sun, were rapidly covering the loveliest sky in Europe, save that of Italy. Thunder growled in the distance, and gusts of biting wind were driving huge drops of rain over the thirsty plain. Looking upwards, I beheld a large Alpine falcon, now rising, now sinking, as he floated bravely in the very midst of the storm and I could almost fancy that he strove to battle with it. At every fresh peal of thunder, the noble bird bounded higher aloft, as if in answering defiance. I followed him with my eyes for a long time, until he disappeared in the east. On the ground, about fifty paces beneath me, stood a stork; perfectly tranquil and impassive in the midst of the warring elements. Twice or thrice she turned her head towards the quarter from whence the wind came, with an indescribable air of half indifferent curiosity; but at length she drew up one of her long sinewy legs, hid her head beneath her wing, and calmly composed herself to sleep.

I thought of Byron and Goethe; of the stormy sky that overhung both; of the tempest-tossed existence, the life-long struggle, of the one, and the calm of the other; and of the two mighty sources of poetry exhausted and closed by them.

Byron and Goethe—the two names that predominate, and, come what may, ever will predominate, over our every recollection of the fifty years that have passed away. They rule; the master-minds, I might almost say the tyrants, of a whole period of poetry; brilliant, yet sad; glorious in youth and daring, yet cankered by the worm i' the bud, despair. They are the two representative poets of two great schools; and around them we are compelled to group all the lesser minds which contributed to render the era illustrious. The qualities which adorn and distinguish their works are to be found, although more thinly scattered, in other poets their contemporaries; still theirs are the names that involuntarily rise to our lips whenever we seek to characterize the tendencies of the age in which they lived. Their genius pursued different, even opposite routes; and yet very rarely do our thoughts turn to either without evoking the image of the other, as a sort of necessary complement to the first. The eyes of Europe were fixed upon the pair, as the spectators gaze on two mighty wrestlers in the same arena; and they, like noble and generous adversaries, admired, praised, and held out the hand to each other. Many poets have followed in their footsteps; none have been so popular. Others have found judges and critics who have appreciated them calmly and impartially; not so they: for them there have been only enthusiasts or enemies, wreaths or stones; and when they vanished into the vast night that envelops and transforms alike men and things—silence reigned around their tombs. Little by little, poetry had passed away from our world, and it seemed as if their last sigh had extinguished the sacred flame.

A reaction has now commenced; good, in so far as it reveals a desire for and promise of new life; evil, in so far as it betrays narrow views, a tendency to injustice towards departed genius, and the absence of any fixed rule or principle to guide our appreciation of the past. Human judgment, like Luther's drunken peasant, when saved from falling on one side, too often topples over on the other. The reaction against Goethe, in his own country especially, which was courageously and justly begun by Menzel during his lifetime, has been carried to exaggeration since his death. Certain social opinions, to which I myself belong, but which, although founded on a sacred principle, should not be allowed to interfere with the impartiality of our judgment, have weighed heavily in the balance; and many young, ardent, and enthusiastic minds of our day have reiterated with Bönne that Goethe is the worst of despots; the cancer of the German body.

The English reaction against Byron—I do not speak of that mixture of cant and stupidity which denies the poet his place in Westminster Abbey, but of literary reaction—has shown itself still more unreasoning. I have met with adorers of Shelley who denied the poetic genius of Byron; others who seriously compared his poems with those of Sir Walter Scott. One very much overrated critic writes that " Byron makes man after his own image, and woman after his own heart; the one is a capricious tyrant, the other a yielding slave." The first forgot the verses in which their favorite hailed

" The pilgrim of eternity, whose fame
Over his living head like Heaven is bent; "[1]

the second, that after the appearance of " The Giaour " and " Childe Harold," Sir Walter Scott renounced writing poetry.[2] The last forgot that while he was quietly writing criticisms, Byron was dying for new-born liberty in Greece. All judged, too many in each country still judge, the two poets, Byron and Goethe, after an absolute type of the beautiful, the true, or the false, which they had formed in their own minds; without regard to the state of social relations as they were or are; without any true conception of the destiny or mission of poetry, or of the law by which it, and every other artistic manifestation of human life, is governed.

There is no absolute type on earth: the absolute exists in the Divine Idea alone; the gradual comprehension of which man is destined to attain; although its complete realization is impossible on earth; earthly life being but one stage of the eternal evolution of life, manifested in thought and action; strengthened by all the achievements of the past, and advancing from age to age towards a less imperfect expression of that idea. Our earthly life is one phase of the eternal aspiration of the soul towards progress, which is our law; ascending in increasing power and purity from the finite towards the infinite; from the real towards the ideal; from that which is, towards that which is to come. In the immense storehouse of the past evolutions of life constituted by universal tradition, and in the prophetic instinct brooding in the depths of the human soul, does poetry seek inspiration. It changes with the times, for it is their expression; it is transformed with society, for—consciously or unconsciously—it sings the lay of Humanity; although, according to the individual bias or circumstances of the singer, it assumes the hues of the present,

[1] Adonais. [2] Lockhart.

or of the future in course of elaboration, and foreseen by the inspiration of genius. It sings now a dirge and now a cradle song; it initiates or sums up.

Byron and Goethe summed up. This is at once the philo- No; it was the law of the times, and yet society at the present day, twenty years after they have ceased to sing, assumes to condemn them for having been born too soon. Happy indeed are the poets whom God raises up at the commencement of an era, under the rays of the rising sun. A series of generations will lovingly repeat their verses, and attribute to them the new life which they did but foresee in the germ.

Byron and Goethe summed up. This is at once the philosophical explanation of their works, and the secret of their popularity. The spirit of an entire epoch of the European world became incarnate in them ere its decease, even as—in the political sphere—the spirit of Greece and Rome became incarnate before death in Cæsar and Alexander. They were the poetic expression of that principle, of which England was the economic, France the political, and Germany the philosophic expression: the last formula, effort, and result of a society founded on the principle of individuality. That epoch, the mission of which had been, first through the labors of Greek philosophy, and afterwards through Christianity, to rehabilitate, emancipate, and develop individual man—appears to have concentrated in them, in Fichte, in Adam Smith, and in the French school *des droits de l'homme*, its whole energy and power, in order fully to represent and express all that it had achieved for mankind. It was much; but it was not the whole; and therefore it was doomed to pass away. The epoch of individuality was deemed near the goal; when lo! immense horizons were revealed; vast unknown lands in whose untrodden forests the principle of individuality was an insufficient guide. By the long and painful labors of that epoch the human unknown quantity had been disengaged from the various quantities of different nature by which it had been surrounded; but only to be left weak, isolated, and recoiling in terror from the solitude in which it stood. The political schools of the epoch had proclaimed the sole basis of civil organization to be the right to liberty and equality (liberty for all), but they had encountered social anarchy by the way. The philosophy of the epoch had asserted the sovereignty of the human *Ego*, and had ended in the mere adoration of *fact*, in Hegelian immobility. The economy of the epoch imagined it had organized free competition, while it had but organized the oppression of the weak by the strong; of labor by capital; of poverty by wealth. The poetry of the epoch had represented individuality in its every phase; had translated in sentiment what science had theoretically demonstrated; and it had encountered the void. But as society at last discovered that the destinies of the race were not contained in a mere problem of liberty, but rather in the harmonization of liberty with association—so did poetry discover that the life it had hitherto drawn from individuality alone was doomed to perish for want of aliment; and that its future existence depended on enlarging and transforming its sphere. Both society and poetry uttered a cry of despair: the death-agony of a form of society produced the agitation we have seen constantly increasing in Europe since 1815: the death-agony of a form of poetry evoked Byron and Goethe. I believe this point of view to be the only one that can lead us to a useful and impartial appreciation of these two great spirits.

There are two forms of individuality; the expressions of its internal and external, or—as the Germans would say—of its subjective and objective life. Byron was the poet of the first, Goethe of the last. In Byron the *Ego* is revealed in all its pride of power, freedom, and desire, in the uncontrolled plenitude of all its faculties; inhaling existence at every pore, eager to seize " the life of life." The world around him neither rules nor tempers him. The Byronian *Ego* aspires to rule it; but solely for dominion's sake, to exercise upon it the Titanic force of his will. Accurately speaking, he cannot be said to derive from it either color, tone, or image; for it is he who colors; he who sings; he whose image is everywhere reflected and reproduced. His poetry emanates from his own soul; to be thence diffused upon things external; he holds his state in the centre of the universe, and from thence projects the light radiating from the depths of his own mind; as scorching and intense as the concentrated solar ray. Hence that terrible unity which only the superficial reader could mistake for monotony.

Byron appears at the close of one epoch, and before the dawn of the other; in the midst of a community based upon an aristocracy which has outlived the vigor of its prime; surrounded by a Europe containing nothing grand, unless it be Napoleon one one side and Pitt on the other, genius degraded to minister to egotism; intellect bound to the service of the past. No seer exists to foretell the future: belief is extinct; there is only its pretence: prayer is no more; there is only a movement of the lips at a fixed day or hour, for the sake of the family, or what is called the people; love is no more; desire has taken its place; the holy warfare of ideas is abandoned; the conflict is that of interests. The worship of great thoughts has passed away. That which *is*, raises the tattered banner of some corpse-like traditions; that which *would be*, hoists only the standard of physical wants, of material appetites: around him are ruins, beyond him the desert; the horizon is a blank. A long cry of suffering and indignation bursts from the heart of Byron: he is answered by anathemas. He departs; he hurries through Europe in search of an ideal to adore; he traverses it distracted, palpitating, like Mazeppa on the wild horse; borne onwards by a fierce desire; the wolves of envy and calumny follow in pursuit. He visits Greece; he visits Italy; if anywhere a lingering spark of the sacred fire, a ray of divine poetry, is preserved, it must be there. Nothing. A glorious past, a degraded present; none of life's poetry; no movement, save that of the sufferer turning on his couch to relieve his pain. Byron, from the solitude of his exile, turns his eyes again towards England; he sings. What does he sing? What springs from the mysterious and unique conception which rules, one would say in spite of himself, over all that escapes him in his sleepless vigil? The funeral hymn, the death-song, the epitaph of the aristocratic idea; we discovered it, we Continentalists; not his own countrymen. He takes his types from amongst those privileged by strength, beauty, and individual power. They are grand, poetical, heroic, but solitary; they hold no communion with the world around them, unless it be to rule over it; they defy alike the good and evil principle; they "will bend to neither." In life and in death "they stand upon their strength;" they resist every power, for their own is all their own; it was purchased by

"Superior science—penance—daring—
And length of watching—strength of mind—and skill
In knowledge of our fathers."

Each of them is the personification, slightly modified, of a single type, a single idea—the individual; free, but nothing more than free; such as the epoch now closing has made him; Faust, but without the compact which submits him to the enemy; for the heroes of Byron make no such compact. Cain kneels not to Arimanes; and Manfred, about to die, exclaims:

> " The mind, which is immortal, makes itself
> Requital for its good and evil thoughts—
> Is its own origin of ill, and end—
> And its own place and time, its innate sense,
> When stripped of this mortality, derives
> No color from the fleeting things without,
> But is absorbed in sufferance or in joy;
> Born from the knowledge of its own desert."

They have no kindred: they live from their own life only; they repulse humanity, and regard the crowd with disdain. Each of them says: " I have faith in myself "; never, " I have faith in ourselves." They all aspire to power or to happiness. The one and the other alike escape them; for they bear within them, untold, unacknowledged even to themselves, the presentiment of a life that mere liberty can never give them. Free they are; iron souls in iron frames, they climb the Alps of the physical world as well as the Alps of thought; still is their visage stamped with a gloomy and ineffaceable sadness; still is their soul—whether, as in Cain and Manfred, it plunge into the abyss of the infinite, " intoxicated with eternity," or scour the vast plain and boundless ocean with the Corsair and Giaour—haunted by a secret and sleepless dread. It seems as if they were doomed to drag the broken links of the chain they have burst asunder, riveted to their feet. Not only in the petty society against which they rebel does their soul feel fettered and restrained; but even in the world of the spirit. Neither is it to the enmity of society that they succumb; but under the assaults of this nameless anguish; under the corroding action of potent faculties " inferior still to their desires and their conceptions; " under the deception that comes from within. What can they do with the liberty so painfully won? On whom, on what, expend the exuberant vitality within them? They are alone; this is the secret of their wretchedness and impotence. They " thirst for good "—Cain has said it for them all—but cannot achieve it; for they have no mission, no belief, no comprehension even of the world around them. They have never realized the conception of humanity in the multitudes that have preceded, surround, and will follow after them; never thought on their own place between the past and future; on the continuity of labor that unites all the generations into one whole; on the common end and aim, only to be realized by the common effort; on the spiritual post-sepulchral life even on earth of the individual, through the thoughts he transmits to his fellows; and, it may be—when he lives devoted and dies in faith—through the guardian agency he is allowed to exercise over the loved ones left on earth.

Gifted with a liberty they know not how to use; with a power and energy they know not how to apply; with a life whose purpose and aim they comprehend not; they drag through their useless and convulsed existence. Byron destroys them one after the other, as if he were the executioner of a sentence decreed in heaven. They fall unwept, like a withered leaf into the stream of time.

" Nor earth nor sky shall yield a single tear,
Nor cloud shall gather more, nor leaf shall fall,
Nor gale breathe forth one sigh for thee, for all."

They die, as they have lived, alone; and a popular malediction hovers round their solitary tombs.

This, for those who can read with the soul's eyes, is what Byron sings; or rather what humanity sings through him. The emptiness of the life and death of solitary individuality has never been so powerfully and efficaciously summed up as in the pages of Byron. The crowd do not comprehend him: they listen; fascinated for an instant; then repent, and avenge their momentary transport by calumniating and insulting the poet. His intuition of the death of a form of society they call wounded self-love; his sorrow for *all* is misinterpreted as cowardly egotism. They credit not the traces of profound suffering revealed by his lineaments; they credit not the presentiment of a new life which from time to time escapes his trembling lips; they believe not in the despairing embrace in which he grasps the material universe—stars, lakes, alps, and sea—and identifies himself with it, and through it with God, of whom—to him at least—it is a symbol. They do, however, take careful count of some unhappy moments, in which, wearied out by the emptiness of life, he has raised—with remorse I am sure—the cup of ignoble pleasures to his lips, believing he might find forgetfulness there. How many times have not his accusers drained this cup, without redeeming the sin by a single virtue; without—I will not say bearing—but without having even the capacity of appreciating the burden which weighed on Byron! And did he not himself dash into fragments the ignoble cup, so soon as he beheld something worthy the devotion of his life?

Goethe—individuality in its objective life—having, like Byron, a sense of the falsehood and evil of the world round him—followed exactly the opposite path. After having—he, too, in his youth—uttered a cry of anguish in his Werther; after having laid bare the problem of the epoch in all its terrific nudity, in Faust; he thought he had done enough, and refused to occupy himself with its solution. It is possible that the impulse of rebellion against social wrong and evil which burst forth for an instant in Werther may long have held his soul in secret travail; but that he despaired of the task of reforming it as beyond his powers. He himself remarked in his later years, when commenting on the exclamation made by a Frenchman on first seeing him: " That is the face of a man who has suffered much;" that he should rather have said: " That is the face of a man who has struggled energetically;" but of this there remains no trace in his works. Whilst Byron writhed and suffered under the sense of the wrong and evil around him, he attained the calm—I cannot say of victory—but of indifference. In Byron the man always ruled, and even at times overcame the artist: the man was completely lost in the artist in Goethe. In him there was no subjective life; no unity springing either from heart or head. Goethe is an intelligence that receives, elaborates, and reproduces the poetry affluent to him from all external objects: from all points of the circumference; to him as centre. He dwells aloft alone; a mighty watcher in the midst of creation. His curious scrutiny investigates, with equal penetration and equal interest, the depths of the ocean and the calyx of the floweret. Whether he studies the rose exhaling its Eastern perfume to the sky, or the ocean casting its countless wrecks upon the shore, the brow of the poet remains equally calm: to him they are but two forms of the beautiful; two subjects for art.

Goethe has been called a pantheist. I know not in what sense critics apply this vague and often ill-understood word to him. There is a materialistic pantheism and a spiritual pantheism; the pantheism of Spinoza and that of Giordano Bruno; of St. Paul; and of many others—all different. But there is no poetic pantheism possible, save on the condition of embracing the whole world of phenomena in one unique conception: of feeling and comprehending the life of the universe in its divine unity. There is nothing of this in Goethe. There is pantheism in some parts of Wordsworth; in the third canto of "Childe Harold," and in much of Shelley; but there is none in the most admirable compositions of Goethe; wherein life, though admirably comprehended and reproduced in each of its successive manifestations, is never understood as a whole. Goethe is the poet of details, not of unity; of analysis, not of synthesis. None so able to investigate details; to set off and embellish minute and apparently trifling points; none throw so beautiful a light on separate parts; but the connecting link escapes him. His works resemble a magnificent encyclopædia, unclassified. He has felt everything; but he has never felt the whole. Happy in detecting a ray of the beautiful upon the humblest blade of grass gemmed with dew; happy in seizing the poetic elements of an incident the most prosaic in appearance—he was incapable of tracing all to a common source, and recomposing the grand ascending scale in which, to quote a beautiful expression of Herder's, "every creature is a numerator of the grand denominator, Nature." How, indeed, should he comprehend these things, he who had no place in his works or in his poet's heart for humanity, by the light of which conception only can the true worth of sublunary things be determined? "Religion and politics,"[3] said he, "are a troubled element for art. I have always kept myself aloof from them as much as possible." Questions of life and death for the millions were agitated around him; Germany re-echoed to the war-songs of Körner; Fichte, at the close of one of his lectures,

[3] "Goethe and his Contemporaries."

seized his musket, and joined the volunteers who were hastening (alas! what have not the Kings made of that magnificent outburst of nationality!) to fight the battles of their fatherland. The ancient soil of Germany thrilled beneath their tread; he, an artist, looked on unmoved; his heart knew no responsive throb to the emotion that shook his country; his genius, utterly passive, drew apart from the current that swept away entire races. He witnessed the French Revolution in all its terrible grandeur, and saw the old world crumble beneath its strokes; and while all the best and purest spirits of Germany, who had mistaken the death-agony of the old world for the birth-throes of a new, were wringing their hands at the spectacle of dissolution, he saw in it only the subject of a farce. He beheld the glory and the fall of Napoleon; he witnessed the reaction of down-trodden nationalities—sublime prologue of the grand epopee of the peoples destined sooner or later to be unfolded—and remained a cold spectator. He had neither learned to esteem men, to better them, nor even to suffer with them. If we except the beautiful type of Berlichingen, a poetic inspiration of his youth, man, as the creature of thought and action; the artificer of the future, so nobly sketched by Schiller in his dramas, has no representative in his works. He has carried something of this nonchalance even into the manner in which his heroes conceive love. Goethe's altar is spread with the choicest flowers, the most exquisite perfumes, the first-fruits of nature; but the priest is wanting. In his work of second creation—for it cannot be denied that such it was—he has gone through the vast circle of living and visible things; but stopped short before the seventh day. God withdrew from him before that time; and the creatures the poet has evoked wander within the circle, dumb and prayerless; awaiting until the man shall come to give them a name, and appoint them to a destination.

No, Goethe is not the poet of pantheism; he is a polytheist in his method as an artist; the pagan poet of modern times. His world is, above all things, the world of forms: a multiplied Olympus. The Mosaic heaven and the Christian are veiled to him. Like the pagans, he parcels out Nature into fragments, and makes of each a divinity; like them, he worships the sensuous rather than the ideal; he looks, touches, and listens far more than he feels. And what care and labor are bestowed upon the plastic portion of his art! what importance is given—I will not say to the objects themselves—but to the external representation of objects! Has he not somewhere said that " the beautiful is the result of happy position " ? [4]

Under this definition is concealed an entire system of poetic materialism, substituted for the worship of the ideal; involving a whole series of consequences, the logical result of which was to lead Goethe to indifference, that moral suicide of some of the noblest energies of genius. The absolute concentration of every faculty of observation on each of the objects to be represented, without relation to the *ensemble;* the entire avoidance of every influence likely to modify the view taken of that object, became in his hands one of the most effective means of art. The poet, in his eyes, was neither the rushing stream, a hundred times broken on its course, that it may carry fertility to the surrounding country; nor the brilliant flame, consuming itself in the light it sheds around while ascending to heaven; but rather the placid lake, reflecting alike the tranquil landscape and the thunder-cloud; its own surface the while unruffled even by the lightest breeze. A serene and passive calm, with the absolute clearness and distinctness of successive impressions, in each of which he was for the time wholly absorbed, are the peculiar characteristics of Goethe. " I allow the objects I desire to comprehend, to act tranquilly upon me," said he; " I then observe the impression I have received from them, and I endeavor to render it faithfully." Goethe has here portrayed his every feature to perfection. He was in life such as Madame Von Armin proposed to represent him after death; a venerable old man, with a serene, almost radiant countenance; clothed in an antique robe, holding a lyre resting on his knees, and listening to the harmonies drawn from it either by the hand of a genius, or the breath of the winds. The last chords wafted his soul to the East; to the land of inactive contemplation. It was time: Europe had become too agitated for him.

Such were Byron and Goethe in their general characteristics; both great poets; very different, and yet, complete as is the contrast between them, and widely apart as are the paths

[4] In the " Kunst und Alterthum," I think.

they pursue, arriving at the same point. Life and death, character and poetry, everything is unlike in the two, and yet the one is the complement of the other. Both are the children of fatality—for it is especially at the close of epochs that the providential law which directs the generations assumes towards individuals the semblance of fatality—and compelled by it unconsciously to work out a great mission. Goethe contemplates the world in parts, and delivers the impressions they make upon him, one by one, as occasion presents them. Byron looks upon the world from a single comprehensive point of view; from the height of which he modifies in his own soul the impressions produced by external objects, as they pass before him. Goethe successively absorbs his own individuality in each of the objects he reproduces. Byron stamps every object he portrays with his own individuality. To Goethe, nature is the symphony; to Byron it is the prelude. She furnishes to the one the entire subject; to the other the occasion only of his verse. The one executes her harmonies; the other composes on the theme she has suggested. Goethe better expresses lives; Byron life. The one is more vast; the other more deep. The first searches everywhere for the beautiful, and loves, above all things, harmony and repose; the other seeks the sublime, and adores action and force. Characters, such as Coriolanus or Luther, disturbed Goethe. I know not if, in his numerous pieces of criticism, he has ever spoken of Dante; but assuredly he must have shared the antipathy felt for him by Sir Walter Scott; and although he would undoubtedly have sufficiently respected his genius to admit him into his Pantheon, yet he would certainly have drawn a veil between his mental eye and the grand but sombre figure of the exiled seer, who dreamed of the future empire of the world for his country, and of the world's harmonious development under her guidance. Byron loved and drew inspiration from Dante. He also loved Washington and Franklin, and followed, with all the sympathies of a soul athirst for action, the meteor-like career of the greatest genius of action our age has produced, Napoleon; feeling indignant—perhaps mistakenly—that he did not die in the struggle.

When travelling in that second fatherland of all poetic souls —Italy—the poets still pursued divergent routes; the one experienced sensations; the other emotions; the one occupied himself especially with nature; the other with the greatness dead, the living wrongs, the human memories.[5]

And yet, notwithstanding all the contrasts, which I have only hinted at, but which might be far more elaborately displayed by extracts from their works; they arrived—Goethe, the poet of individuality in its objective life—at the egotism of indifference; Byron—the poet of individuality in its subjective life—at the egotism (I say it with regret, but *it*, too, is egotism) of despair: a double sentence upon the epoch which it was their mission to represent and to close!

Both of them—I am not speaking of their purely literary merits, incontestable and universally acknowledged—the one by the spirit of resistance that breathes through all his creations; the other by the spirit of sceptical irony that pervades his works, and by the independent sovereignty attributed to art over all social relations—greatly aided the cause of intellectual emancipation, and awakened in men's minds the sentiment of liberty. Both of them—the one, directly, by the implacable war he waged against the vices and absurdities of the privileged classes, and indirectly, by investing his heroes with all the most brilliant qualities of the despot, and then dashing them to pieces as if in anger;—the other, by the poetic rehabilitation of forms the most modest, and objects the most insig-

---

[5] The contrast between the two poets is nowhere more strikingly displayed than by the manner in which they were affected by the sight of Rome. In Goethe's "Elegies" and in his "Travels in Italy" we find the impressions of the artist only. He did not understand Rome. The eternal synthesis that, from the heights of the Capitol and St. Peter, is gradually unfolded in ever-widening circles, embracing first a nation and then Europe, as it will ultimately embrace humanity, remained unrevealed to him; he saw only the inner circle of paganism; the least prolific, as well as least indigenous. One might fancy that he caught a glimpse of it for an instant, when he wrote: "History is read here far otherwise than in any other spot in the universe; elsewhere we read it from without to within; here one seems to read it from within to without;" but if so, he soon lost sight of it again, and became absorbed in external nature. "Whether we halt or advance, we discover a landscape ever renewing itself in a thousand fashions. We have palaces and ruins; gardens and solitudes; the horizon lengthens in the distance, or suddenly contracts; huts and stables, columns and triumphal arches, all lie pell-mell, and often so close that we might find room for all on the same sheet of paper."

At Rome Byron forgot passions, sorrows, his own individuality, all, in the presence of a great idea; witness this utterance of a soul born for devotedness:—

"O Rome! my country! city of the soul!
The orphans of the heart must turn to thee,
Lone mother of dead empires! and control
In their shut breasts their petty misery."

When at last he came to a recollection of himself and his position, it was with a hope for the world (stanza 98) and a pardon for his enemies. From the fourth canto of "Childe Harold," the daughter of Byron might learn more of the true spirit of her father than from all the reports she may have heard, and all the many volumes that have been written upon him.

nificant, as well as by the importance attributed to details—combated aristocratic prejudices, and developed in men's minds the sentiment of equality. And having by their artistic excellence exhausted both forms of the poetry of individuality, they have completed the cycle of its poets; thereby reducing all followers in the same sphere to the subaltern position of imitators, and creating the necessity of a new order of poetry; teaching us to recognize a want where before we felt only a desire. Together they have laid an era in the tomb; covering it with a pall that none may lift; and, as if to proclaim its death to the young generation, the poetry of Goethe has written its history, while that of Byron has graven its epitaph.

And now farewell to Goethe; farewell to Byron! farewell to the sorrows that crush but sanctify not—to the poetic flame that illumines but warms not—to the ironical philosophy that dissects without reconstructing—to all poetry which, in an age where there is so much to do, teaches us inactive contemplation; or which, in a world where there is so much need of devotedness, would instil despair. Farewell to all types of power without an aim; to all personifications of the solitary individuality which seeks an aim to find it not, and knows not how to apply the life stirring within it; to all egotistic joys and griefs:

> " Bastards of the soul;
> O'erweening slips of idleness: weeds—no more—
> Self-springing here and there from the rank soil;
> O'erflowings of the lust of that same mind
> Whose proper issue and determinate end,
> When wedded to the love of things divine,
> Is peace, complacency, and happiness."

Farewell, a long farewell to the past! The dawn of the future is announced to such as can read its signs, and we owe ourselves wholly to it.

The duality of the Middle Ages, after having struggled for centuries under the banners of emperor and pope; after having left its trace and borne its fruit in every branch of intellectual development; has reascended to heaven—its mission accomplished—in the twin flames of poesy called Goethe and Byron. Two hitherto distinct formulæ of life became incarnate in these two men. Byron is isolated man, representing only the internal aspect of life; Goethe isolated man, representing only the external.

Higher than these two incomplete existences; at the point of intersection between the two aspirations towards a heaven they were unable to reach, will be revealed the poetry of the future; of humanity; potent in new harmony, unity, and life.

But because, in our own day, we are beginning, though vaguely, to foresee this new social poetry, which will soothe the suffering soul by teaching it to rise towards God through humanity; because we now stand on the threshold of a new epoch, which, but for them, we should not have reached; shall we decry those who were unable to do more for us than cast their giant forms into the gulf that held us all doubting and dismayed on the other side? From the earliest times has genius been made the scapegoat of the generations. Society has never lacked men who have contented themselves with reproaching the Chattertons of their day with not being patterns of self-devotion, instead of physical or moral suicides; without ever asking themselves whether they had, during their lifetime, endeavored to place aught within the reach of such but doubt and destitution. I feel the necessity of protesting earnestly against the reaction set on foot by certain thinkers against the mighty-souled, which serves as a cloak for the cavilling spirit of mediocrity. There is something hard, repulsive, and ungrateful in the destructive instinct which so often forgets what has been done by the great men who preceded us, to demand of them merely an account of what more might have been done. Is the pillow of scepticism so soft to genius as to justify the conclusion that it is from egotism only that at times it rests its fevered brow thereon? Are we so free from the evil reflected in their verse as to have a right to condemn their memory? That evil was not introduced into the world by them. They saw it, felt it, respired it; it was around, about, on every side of them, and they were its greatest victims. How could they avoid reproducing it in their works? It is not by deposing Goethe or Byron that we shall destroy either sceptical or anarchical indifference amongst us. It is by becoming believers and organizers ourselves. If we are such, we need fear nothing. As is the public, so will be the poet. If we revere enthusiasm, the fatherland, and humanity;

if our hearts are pure, and our souls steadfast and patient, the genius inspired to interpret our aspirations, and bear to heaven our ideas and our sufferings, will not be wanting. Let these statues stand. The noble monuments of feudal times create no desire to return to the days of serfdom.

But I shall be told, there are imitators. I know it too well; but what lasting influence can be exerted on social life by those who have no real life of their own? They will but flutter in the void, so long as void there be. On the day when the living shall arise to take the place of the dead, they will vanish like ghosts at cock-crow. Shall we never be sufficiently firm in our own faith to dare to show fitting reverence for the grand typical figures of an anterior age? It would be idle to speak of social art at all, or of the comprehension of humanity, if we could not raise altars to the new gods, without overthrowing the old. Those only should dare to utter the sacred name of progress, whose souls possess intelligence enough to comprehend the past, and whose hearts possess sufficient poetic religion to reverence its greatness. The temple of the true believer is not the chapel of a sect; it is a vast Pantheon, in which the glorious images of Goethe and Byron will hold their honored place, long after Goetheism and Byronism shall have ceased to be.

When, purified alike from imitation and distrust, men learn to pay righteous reverence to the mighty fallen, I know not whether Goethe will obtain more of their admiration as an artist, but I am certain that Byron will inspire them with more love, both as man and poet—a love increased even by the fact of the great injustice hitherto shown to him. While Goethe held himself aloof from us, and from the height of his Olympian calm seemed to smile with disdain at our desires, our struggles, and our sufferings—Byron wandered through the world, sad, gloomy, and unquiet; wounded, and bearing the arrow in the wound. Solitary and unfortunate in his infancy; unfortunate in his first love, and still more terribly so in his ill-advised marriage; attacked and calumniated both in his acts and intentions, without inquiry or defence; harassed by pecuniary difficulties; forced to quit his country, home, and child; friendless—we have seen it too clearly since his death—pursued even on the Continent by a thousand absurd and infamous falsehoods, and by the cold malignity of a world that twisted even his sorrows into a crime; he yet, in the midst of inevitable reaction, preserved his love for his sister and his Ada; his compassion for misfortune; his fidelity to the affections of his childhood and youth, from Lord Clare to his old servant Murray, and his nurse Mary Gray. He was generous with his money to all whom he could help or serve, from his literary friends down to the wretched libeller Ashe. Though impelled by the temper of his genius, by the period in which he lived, and by that fatality of his mission to which I have alluded, towards a poetic individualism, the inevitable incompleteness of which I have endeavored to explain, he by no means set it up as a standard. That he presaged the future with the prevision of genius is proved by his definition of poetry in his journal—a definition hitherto misunderstood, but yet the best I know: "Poetry is the feeling of a former world and of a future." Poet as he was, he preferred activity for good, to all that his art could do. Surrounded by slaves and their oppressors; a traveller in countries where even remembrance seemed extinct; never did he desert the cause of the peoples; never was he false to human sympathies. A witness of the progress of the Restoration, and the triumph of the principles of the Holy Alliance, he never swerved from his courageous opposition; he preserved and publicly proclaimed his faith in the rights of the peoples and in the final [6] triumph of liberty. The following passage from his journal is the very abstract of the law governing the efforts of the true party of progress at the present day: "Onwards! it is now the time to act; and what signifies self, if a single spark of that which would be worthy of the past [7] can be bequeathed unquenchably to the future? It is not one man, nor a million, but the spirit of liberty which must be spread. The waves which dash on the shore are, one by one, broken; but yet the ocean conquers nevertheless. It overwhelms the armada; it wears the rock; and if

[6] "Yet, Freedom! yet, thy banner torn, but flying,
Streams, like the thunder-storm, against the wind:
Thy trumpet voice, though broken now and dying,
The loudest still the tempest leaves behind.
The tree hath lost its blossoms, and the rind,
Chopped by the axe, looks rough and little worth,
But the sap lasts—and still the seed we find
Sown deep, even in the bosom of the North,
So shall a better spring less bitter fruit bring forth."

[7] Written in Italy.

the Neptunians are to be believed, it has not only destroyed but made a world." At Naples, in the Romagna, wherever he saw a spark of noble life stirring, he was ready for any exertion; or danger, to blow it into a flame. He stigmatized baseness, hypocrisy, and injustice, whencesoever they sprang.

Thus lived Byron, ceaselessly tempest-tossed between the ills of the present and his yearnings after the future; often unequal; sometimes sceptical; but always suffering—often most so when he seemed to laugh;[8] and always loving, even when he seemed to curse.

Never did "the eternal spirit of the chainless mind" make a brighter apparition amongst us. He seems at times a transformation of that immortal Prometheus, of whom he has written so nobly; whose cry of agony, yet of futurity, sounded above the cradle of the European world; and whose grand and mysterious form, transfigured by time, reappears from age to age, between the entombment of one epoch and the accession of another; to wail forth the lament of genius, tortured by the presentiment of things it will not see realized in its time. Byron, too, had the "firm will" and the "deep sense;" he, too, made of his "death a victory." When he heard the cry of nationality and liberty burst forth in the land he had loved and sung in early youth, he broke his harp and set forth. While the Christian Powers were protocolizing or worse—while the Christian nations were doling forth the alms of a few piles of ball in aid of the Cross struggling with the Crescent; he, the poet, and pretended sceptic, hastened to throw his fortune, his genius, and his life at the feet of the first people that had arisen in the name of the nationality and liberty he loved.

I know no more beautiful symbol of the future destiny and mission of art than the death of Byron in Greece. The holy alliance of poetry with the cause of the peoples; the union—still so rare—of thought and action—which alone completes the human Word, and is destined to emancipate the world; the grand solidarity of all nations in the conquest of the rights ordained by God for all his children, and in the accomplishment of that mission for which alone such rights exist—all that is now the religion and the hope of the party of progress through-

---

[8] "And if I laugh at any mortal thing,
'Tis that I may not weep."

out Europe, is gloriously typified in this image, which we, barbarians that we are, have already forgotten.

The day will come when democracy will remember all that it owes to Byron. England, too, will, I hope, one day remember the mission—so entirely English, yet hitherto overlooked by her—which Byron fulfilled on the Continent; the European *rôle* given by him to English literature, and the appreciation and sympathy for England which he awakened amongst us.

Before he came, all that was known of English literature was the French translation of Shakespeare, and the anathema hurled by Voltaire against the "intoxicated barbarian." It is since Byron that we Continentalists have learned to study Shakespeare and other English writers. From him dates the sympathy of all the true-hearted amongst us for this land of liberty, whose true vocation he so worthily represented among the oppressed. He led the genius of Britain on a pilgrimage throughout all Europe.

England will one day feel how ill it is—not for Byron but for herself—that the foreigner who lands upon her shores should search in vain in that temple which should be her national Pantheon, for the poet beloved and admired by all the nations of Europe, and for whose death Greece and Italy wept as it had been that of the noblest of their own sons.

In these few pages—unfortunately very hasty—my aim has been, not so much to criticise either Goethe or Byron, for which both time and space are wanting, as to suggest, and if possible lead, English criticism upon a broader, more impartial, and more useful path than the one generally followed. Certain travellers of the eleventh century relate that they saw at Teneriffe a prodigiously lofty tree, which, from its immense extent of foliage, collected all the vapors of the atmosphere; to discharge them, when its branches were shaken, in a shower of pure and refreshing water. Genius is like this tree, and the mission of criticism should be to shake the branches. At the present day it more resembles a savage striving to hew down the noble tree to the roots.

THE POETRY OF THE CELTIC RACES
—
BY
JOSEPH ERNEST RENAN

JOSEPH ERNEST RENAN

1823—1892

Joseph Ernest Renan was born at Tréguier, a little town in Brittany, in 1823. His father was a Breton seafaring man, and all his life Renan retained a deep and abiding love for the life, legends, and poetry of Brittany. The essay on "The Poetry of the Celtic Races" shows Renan at his best, for in it he describes the poetry of his own race, the legends learned during his own childhood. Until the age of fifteen Renan attended the convent school of his native village. His proficiency attracted the attention of the Abbé Dupanloup, and he was given a free scholarship in the Parisian preparatory school of St. Nicholas du Chardonnet. Subsequently he entered the theological seminary of St. Sulpice, but decided, after long meditation, that his religious views would not permit him to enter the priesthood, and he accordingly, in 1845, took a position as tutor. Two years later he wrote an essay on the "General History of the Semitic Languages" that won the Volney prize at the Institute of France. In 1851 he accepted a position in the Bibliothèque Nationale, and in 1856 he became a member of the Académie des Inscriptions et Belles-Lettres. About this time he wrote numerous essays of great learning and power on topics ranging from philosophy, theology, and history, to literary criticism. These were soon gathered together and published in the volumes "Etudes d'histoire religieuse" and "Essais de morale et de critique." In 1863 appeared his "La vie de Jésus." This book aroused a storm of criticism and protest. The clamors resulted in Renan's removal from the chair of Hebrew which he had occupied in the Collège de France since 1862. In "Les apôtres," which appeared in 1866, Renan applied, with similar results, the same critical and historical method to the study of the lives of the apostles that had previously created so much sensation in his "Life of Jesus." The remaining volumes of Renan's celebrated "Histoire des origines du christianisme" were "St. Paul" (1867), "L'Antechrist" (1873), "Les évangiles" (1877), "L'Église chrétienne" (1879), and "Marc Aurele" (1880).

In 1870 Renan resumed his professorship at the College of France, and was soon placed at the head of the institution, a position he held until his death. In 1878 he was elected a member of the French Academy. His last great work was the "Histoire du peuple d'Israël." He died at Paris in 1892.

Renan was one of the masters of modern French prose. In his expository passages no writer could be more clear, in his descriptive work none more vivid. He was the acknowledged leader of the school of critical philosophy in France, and fills an important place both in French literature and in the history of the development of human thought.

THE POETRY OF THE CELTIC RACES

EVERYONE who travels through the Armorican peninsula experiences a change of the most abrupt description as soon as he leaves behind the district most closely bordering upon the Continent, in which the cheerful but commonplace type of face of Normandy and Maine is continually in evidence, and passes into the true Brittany, that which merits its name by language and race. A cold wind arises full of a vague sadness, and carries the soul to other thoughts; the tree-tops are bare and twisted; the heath with its monotony of tint stretches away into the distance; at every step the granite protrudes from a soil too scanty to cover it; a sea that is almost always sombre girdles the horizon with eternal moaning. The same contrast is manifest in the people: to Norman vulgarity, to a plump and prosperous population, happy to live, full of its own interests, egoistical as are all those who make a habit of enjoyment, succeeds a timid and reserved race living altogether within itself, heavy in appearance but capable of profound feeling, and of an adorable delicacy in its religious instincts. A like change is apparent, I am told, in passing from England into Wales, from the Lowlands of Scotland, English by language and manners, into the Gaelic Highlands; and, too, though with a perceptible difference, when one buries one's self in the districts of Ireland where the race has remained pure from all admixture of alien blood. It seems like entering on the subterranean strata of another world, and one experiences in some measure the impression given us by Dante, when he leads us from one circle of his Inferno to another.

Sufficient attention is not given to the peculiarity of this fact of an ancient race living, until our days and almost under our eyes, its own life in some obscure islands and peninsulas in the West, more and more affected, it is true, by external influences, but still faithful to its own tongue, to its own memories, to its own customs, and to its own genius. Especially is it forgotten that this little people, now concentrated on the very confines of the world, in the midst of rocks and mountains whence its enemies have been powerless to force it, is in possession of a literature which, in the Middle Ages, exercised an immense influence, changed the current of European civilization, and imposed its poetical motives on nearly the whole of Christendom. Yet it is only necessary to open the authentic monuments of the Gaelic genius to be convinced that the race which created them has had its own original manner of feeling and thinking, that nowhere has the eternal illusion clad itself in more seductive hues, and that in the great chorus of humanity no race equals this for penetrative notes that go to the very heart. Alas! it, too, is doomed to disappear, this emerald set in the Western seas. Arthur will return no more from his isle of faery, and St. Patrick was right when he said to Ossian, " The heroes that thou weepest are dead; can they be born again?" It is high time to note, before they shall have passed away, the divine tones thus expiring on the horizon before the growing tumult of uniform civilization. Were criticism to set itself the task of calling back these distant echoes, and of giving a voice to races that are no more, would not that suffice to absolve it from the reproach, unreasonably and too frequently brought against it, of being only negative?

Good works now exist which facilitate the task of him who undertakes the study of these interesting literatures. Wales, above all, is distinguished by scientific and literary activity, not always accompanied, it is true, by a very rigorous critical spirit, but deserving the highest praise. There, researches which would bring honor to the most active centres of learning in Europe are the work of enthusiastic amateurs. A peasant called Owen Jones published in 1801-7, under the name of the " Myvyrian Archaiology of Wales," the precious collection which is to this day the arsenal of Cymric antiquities. A number of erudite and zealous workers, Aneurin Owen, Thomas Price of Crickhowell, William Rees, and John Jones, following in the footsteps of the Myvyrian peasant, set themselves to finish his work, and to profit from the treasures which he had collected. A woman of distinction, Lady Charlotte Guest, charged herself with the task of acquainting Europe with the collection of the *Mabinogion*,[1] the pearl of Gaelic literature, the completest expression of the Cymric genius. This magnificent work, executed in twelve years with the luxury that the wealthy English amateur knows how to use in his publications, will one day attest how full of life the consciousness of the Celtic races remained in the present century. Only indeed the sincerest patriotism could inspire a woman to undertake and achieve so vast a literary monument. Scotland and Ireland have in like measure been enriched by a host of studies of their ancient history. Lastly, our own Brittany, though all too rarely studied with the philological and critical rigor now exacted in works of erudition, has furnished Celtic antiquities with her share of worthy research. Does it not suffice to cite M. de la Villemarqué, whose name will be henceforth associated among us with these studies, and whose services are so incontestable, that criticism need have no fear of depreciating him in the eyes of a public which has accepted him with so much warmth and sympathy?

I

If the excellence of races is to be appreciated by the purity of their blood and the inviolability of their national character, it must needs be admitted that none can vie in nobility with the still surviving remains of the Celtic race.[2] Never has a human family lived more apart from the world, and been purer from all alien admixture. Confined by conquest within forgotten islands and peninsulas, it has reared an impassable barrier against external influences; it has drawn all from itself;

---

[1] "The Mabinogion, from the Llyfr Coch O Hergest and other ancient Welsh Manuscripts, with an English Translation and Notes." By Lady Charlotte Guest. London and Llandovery, 1837-49. The word Mabinogi (in the plural Mabinogion) designates a form of romantic narrative peculiar to Wales. The origin and primitive meaning of this word are very uncertain, and Lady Guest's right to apply it to the whole of the narratives which she has published is open to doubt.

[2] To avoid all misunderstanding, I ought to point out that by the word Celtic I designate here, not the whole of the great race which, at a remote epoch, formed the population of nearly the whole of Western Europe, but simply the four groups which, in our days, still merit this name, as opposed to the Teutons and to the Neo-Latin peoples. These four groups are: (1) The inhabitants of Wales or Cambria, and the peninsula of Cornwall, bearing even now the ancient name of Cymry; (2) the Bretons bretonnants, or dwellers in French Brittany speaking Bas-Breton, who represent an emigration of the Cymry from Wales; (3) the Gaels of the North of Scotland speaking Gaelic; (4) the Irish, although a very profound line of demarcation separates Ireland from the rest of the Celtic family. [It is also necessary to point out that Renan in this essay applies the name Breton both to the Bretons proper, i.e. the inhabitants of Brittany, and to the British members of the Celtic race.]

it has lived solely on its own capital. From this ensues that powerful individuality, that hatred of the foreigner, which even in our own days has formed the essential feature of the Celtic peoples. Roman civilization scarcely reached them, and left among them but few traces. The Teutonic invasion drove them back, but did not penetrate them. At the present hour they are still constant in resistance to an invasion dangerous in an altogether different way—that of modern civilization, destructive as it is of local variations and national types. Ireland in particular (and herein we perhaps have the secret of her irremediable weakness) is the only country in Europe where the native can produce the titles of his descent, and designate with certainty, even in the darkness of prehistoric ages, the race from which he has sprung.

It is in this secluded life, in this defiance of all that comes from without, that we must search for the explanation of the chief features of the Celtic character. It has all the failings, and all the good qualities, of the solitary man; at once proud and timid, strong in feeling and feeble in action, at home free and unreserved, to the outside world awkward and embarrassed. It distrusts the foreigner, because it sees in him a being more refined than itself, who abuses its simplicity. Indifferent to the admiration of others, it asks only one thing, that it should be left to itself. It is before all else a domestic race, fitted for family life and fireside joys. In no other race has the bond of blood been stronger, or has it created more duties, or attached man to his fellow with so much breadth and depth. Every social institution of the Celtic peoples was in the beginning only an extension of the family. A common tradition attests, to this very day, that nowhere has the trace of this great institution of relationship been better preserved than in Brittany. There is a widely-spread belief in that country, that blood speaks, and that two relatives, unknown one to the other, in any part of the world wheresoever it may be, recognize each other by the secret and mysterious emotion which they feel in each other's presence. Respect for the dead rests on the same principle. Nowhere has reverence for the dead been greater than among the Breton peoples; nowhere have so many memories and prayers clustered about the tomb. This is because life is not for these people a personal adventure, undertaken by each man on his own account, and at his own risks and perils; it is a link in a long chain, a gift received and handed on, a debt paid and a duty done.

It is easily discernible how little fitted were natures so strongly concentrated to furnish one of those brilliant developments, which imposes the momentary ascendancy of a people on the world; and that, no doubt, is why the part played externally by the Cymric race has always been a secondary one. Destitute of the means of expansion, alien to all idea of aggression and conquest, little desirous of making its thought prevail outside itself, it has only known how to retire so far as space has permitted, and then, at bay in its last place of retreat, to make an invincible resistance to its enemies. Its very fidelity has been a useless devotion. Stubborn of submission and ever behind the age, it is faithful to its conquerors when its conquerors are no longer faithful to themselves. It was the last to defend its religious independence against Rome—and it has become the staunchest stronghold of Catholicism; it was the last in France to defend its political independence against the King—and it has given to the world the last royalists.

Thus the Celtic race has worn itself out in resistance to its time, and in the defence of desperate causes. It does not seem as though in any epoch it had any aptitude for political life. The spirit of family stifled within it all attempts at more extended organization. Moreover, it does not appear that the peoples which form it are by themselves susceptible of progress. To them life appears as a fixed condition, which man has no power to alter. Endowed with little initiative, too much inclined to look upon themselves as minors and in tutelage, they are quick to believe in destiny and resign themselves to it. Seeing how little audacious they are against God, one would scarcely believe this race to be the daughter of Japhet.

Thence ensues its sadness. Take the songs of its bards of the sixth century; they weep more defeats than they sing victories. Its history is itself only one long lament; it still recalls its exiles, its flights across the seas. If at times it seems to be cheerful, a tear is not slow to glisten behind its smile; it does not know that strange forgetfulness of human conditions and destinies which is called gayety. Its songs of joy end as elegies; there is nothing to equal the delicious sadness of its national melodies. One might call them emanations from on high which, falling drop by drop upon the soul, pass through it like memories of another world. Never have men feasted so long upon these solitary delights of the spirit, these poetic memories which simultaneously intercross all the sensations of life, so vague, so deep, so penetrative, that one might die from them, without being able to say whether it was from bitterness or sweetness.

The infinite delicacy of feeling which characterizes the Celtic race is closely allied to its need of concentration. Natures that are little capable of expansion are nearly always those that feel most deeply, for the deeper the feeling, the less it tends to express itself. Thence we have that charming shamefastness, that veiled and exquisite sobriety, equally far removed from the sentimental rhetoric too familiar to the Latin races, and the reflective simplicity of Germany, which are so admirably displayed in the ballads published by M. de la Villemarqué. The apparent reserve of the Celtic peoples, often taken for coldness, is due to this inward timidity which makes them believe that a feeling loses half its value if it be expressed; and that the heart ought to have no other spectator than itself.

If it be permitted us to assign sex to nations as to individuals, we should have to say without hesitation that the Celtic race, especially with regard to its Cymric or Breton branch, is an essentially feminine race. No human family, I believe, has carried so much mystery into love. No other has conceived with more delicacy the ideal of woman, or been more fully dominated by it. It is a sort of intoxication, a madness, a vertigo. Read the strange " Mabinogi of Peredur," or its French imitation " Parceval le Gallois "; its pages are, as it were, dewy with feminine sentiment. Woman appears therein as a kind of vague vision, an intermediary between man and the supernatural world. I am acquainted with no literature that offers anything analogous to this. Compare Guinevere or Iseult with those Scandinavian furies Gudrun and Chrimhilde, and you will avow that woman such as chivalry conceived her, an ideal of sweetness and loveliness set up as the supreme end of life, is a creation neither classical, nor Christian, nor Teutonic, but in reality Celtic.

Imaginative power is nearly always proportionate to concentration of feeling, and lack of the external development of life. The limited nature of Greek and Italian imagination is due to the easy expansiveness of the peoples of the South, with whom the soul, wholly spread abroad, reflects but little within itself. Compared with the classical imagination, the Celtic imagination is indeed the infinite contrasted with the finite. In the fine *Mabinogi* of the " Dream of Maxem Wledig," the Emperor Maximus beholds in a dream a young maiden so beautiful that on waking he declares he cannot live without her. For several years his envoys scour the world in search of her; at last she is discovered in Brittany. So is it with the Celtic race; it has worn itself out in taking dreams for realities, and in pursuing its splendid visions. The essential element in the Celt's poetic life is the adventure—that is to say, the pursuit of the unknown, an endless quest after an object ever flying from desire. It was of this that St. Brandan dreamed, that Peredur sought with his mystic chivalry, that Knight Owen asked of his subterranean journeyings. This race desires the infinite, it thirsts for it, and pursues it at all costs, beyond the tomb, beyond hell itself. The characteristic failing of the Breton peoples, the tendency to drunkenness—a failing which, according to the traditions of the sixth century, was the cause of their disasters—is due to this invincible need of illusion. Do not say that it is an appetite for gross enjoyment; never has there been a people more sober and more alien to all sensuality. No, the Bretons sought in mead what Owen, St. Brandan, and Peredur sought in their own way—the vision of the invisible world. To this day in Ireland drunkenness forms a part of all Saint's Day festivals—that is to say, the festivals which best have retained their national and popular aspect.

Thence arises the profound sense of the future and of the eternal destinies of his race, which has ever borne up the Cymry, and kept him young still beside his conquerors who have grown old. Thence that dogma of the resurrection of the heroes, which appears to have been one of those that Christianity found most difficulty in rooting out. Thence Celtic Messianism, that belief in a future avenger who shall restore Cambria, and deliver her out of the hands of her oppressors, like the mysterious Leminok promised by Merlin, the Lez-Breiz of the Armoricans, the Arthur of the Welsh.[3] The hand that arose from the

---

[3] M. Augustin Thierry (" Histoire de la Conquête d'Angleterre ") has finely remarked that the renown attaching to Welsh prophecies in the Middle Ages was due to their steadfastness in affirming the future of their race.

mere, when the sword of Arthur fell therein, that seized it, and brandished it thrice, is the hope of the Celtic races. It is thus that little peoples dowered with imagination revenge themselves on their conquerors. Feeling themselves to be strong inwardly and weak outwardly, they protest, they exult; and such a strife unloosing their might, renders them capable of miracles. Nearly all great appeals to the supernatural are due to peoples hoping against all hope. Who shall say what in our own times has fermented in the bosom of the most stubborn, the most powerless of nationalities—Poland? Israel in humiliation dreamed of the spiritual conquest of the world, and the dream has come to pass.

II

At a first glance the literature of Wales is divided into three perfectly distinct branches: the bardic or lyric, which shines forth in splendor in the sixth century by the works of Taliessin, of Aneurin, and of Liwarc'h Hên, and continues through an uninterrupted series of imitations up to modern times; the *Mabinogion,* or literature of romance, fixed towards the twelfth century, but linking themselves in the groundwork of their ideas with the remotest ages of the Celtic genius; finally, an ecclesiastical and legendary literature, impressed with a distinct stamp of its own. These three literatures seem to have existed side by side, almost without knowledge of one another. The bards, proud of their solemn rhetoric, held in disdain the popular tales, the form of which they considered careless; on the other hand, both bards and romancers appear to have had few relations with the clergy; and one at times might be tempted to suppose that they ignored the existence of Christianity. To our thinking it is in the *Mabinogion* that the true expression of the Celtic genius is to be sought; and it is surprising that so curious a literature, the source of nearly all the romantic creations of Europe, should have remained unknown until our own days. The cause is doubtless to be ascribed to the dispersed state of the Welsh manuscripts, pursued till last century by the English as seditious books compromising those who possessed them. Often too they fell into the hands of ignorant owners, whose caprice or ill-will sufficed to keep them from critical research.

The *Mabinogion* have been preserved for us in two principal documents—one of the thirteenth century from the library of Hengurt, belonging to the Vaughan family; the other dating from the fourteenth century, known under the name of the "Red Book of Hergest," and now in Jesus College, Oxford. No doubt it was some such collection that charmed the weary hours of the hapless Leolin in the Tower of London, and was burned after his condemnation, with the other Welsh books which had been the companions of his captivity. Lady Charlotte Guest has based her edition on the Oxford manuscript; it cannot be sufficiently regretted that paltry considerations have caused her to be refused the use of the earlier manuscript, of which the later appears to be only a copy. Regrets are redoubled when one knows that several Welsh texts, which were seen and copied fifty years ago, have now disappeared. It is in the presence of facts such as these that one comes to believe that revolutions—in general so destructive of the works of the past—are favorable to the preservation of literary monuments, by compelling their concentration in great centres, where their existence, as well as their publicity, is assured.

The general tone of the *Mabinogion* is rather romantic than epic. Life is treated naïvely and not too emphatically. The hero's individuality is limitless. We have free and noble natures acting in all their spontaneity. Each man appears as a kind of demi-god characterized by a supernatural gift. This gift is nearly always connected with some miraculous object, which in some measure is the personal seal of him who possesses it. The inferior classes, which this people of heroes necessarily supposes beneath it, scarcely show themselves, except in the exercise of some trade, for practising which they are held in high esteem. The somewhat complicated products of human industry are regarded as living beings, and in their manner endowed with magical properties. A multiplicity of celebrated objects have proper names, such as the drinking-cup, the lance, the sword, and the shield of Arthur; the chess-board of Gwendolen, on which the black pieces played of their own accord against the white; the horn of Bran Galed, where one found whatever liquor one desired; the chariot of Morgan, which directed itself to the place to which one wished to go; the pot of Tyrnog, which would not cook when meat for a coward was put into it; the grindstone of Tudwal, which would only sharpen brave men's swords; the coat of Padarn, which none save a noble could don; and the mantle of Tegan, which no woman could put upon herself were she not above reproach.[4] The animal is conceived in a still more individual way; it has a proper name, personal qualities, and a rôle which it develops at its own will and with full consciousness. The same hero appears as at once man and animal, without it being possible to trace the line of demarcation between the two natures.

The tale of "Kilhwch and Olwen," the most extraordinary of the *Mabinogion,* deals with Arthur's struggle against the wild-boar King Twrch Trwyth, who with his seven cubs holds in check all the heroes of the Round Table. The adventures of the three hundred ravens of Kerverhenn similarly form the subject of the " Dream of Rhonabwy." The idea of moral merit and demerit is almost wholly absent from all these compositions. There are wicked beings who insult ladies, who tyrannize over their neighbors, who only find pleasure in evil because such is their nature; but it does not appear that they incur wrath on that account. Arthur's knights pursue them, not as criminals, but as mischievous fellows. All other beings are perfectly good and just, but more or less richly gifted. This is the dream of an amiable and gentle race which looks upon evil as being the work of destiny, and not a product of the human conscience. All nature is enchanted, and fruitful as imagination itself in indefinitely varied creations. Christianity rarely discloses itself; although at times its proximity can be felt, it alters in no respect the purely natural surroundings in which everything takes place. A bishop figures at table beside Arthur, but his function is strictly limited to blessing the dishes. The Irish saints, who at one time present themselves to give their benediction to Arthur and receive favors at his hands, are portrayed as a race of men vaguely known and difficult to understand. No mediæval literature held itself further removed from all monastic influence. We evidently must suppose that the Welsh bards and story-tellers lived in a state of great isolation from the clergy, and had their culture and traditions quite apart.

[4] Here may be recognized the origin of trial by court mantle, one of the most interesting episodes in "Lancelot of the Lake."

The charm of the *Mabinogion* principally resides in the amiable serenity of the Celtic mind, neither sad nor gay, ever in suspense between a smile and a tear. We have in them the simple recital of a child, unwitting of any distinction between the noble and the common; there is something of that softly animated world, of that calm and tranquil ideal to which Ariosto's stanzas transport us. The chatter of the later mediæval French and German imitators can give no idea of this charming manner of narration. The skilful Chrétien de Troyes himself remains in this respect far below the Welsh story-tellers, and as for Wolfram of Eschenbach, it must be avowed that the joy of the first discovery has carried German critics too far in the exaggeration of his merits. He loses himself in interminable descriptions, and almost completely ignores the art of his recital.

What strikes one at a first glance in the imaginative compositions of the Celtic races, above all when they are contrasted with those of the Teutonic races, is the extreme mildness of manners pervading them. There are none of those frightful vengeances which fill the "Edda" and the "Niebelungen." Compare the Teutonic with the Gaelic hero—Beowulf with Peredur, for example. What a difference there is! In the one all the horror of disgusting and blood-embrued barbarism, the drunkenness of carnage, the disinterested taste, if I may say so, for destruction and death; in the other a profound sense of justice, a great height of personal pride, it is true, but also a great capacity for devotion, an exquisite loyalty. The tyrannical man, the monster, the Black Man, find a place here, like the Lestrigons and the Cyclops of Homer, only to inspire horror by contrast with softer manners; they are almost what the wicked man is in the naïve imagination of a child brought up by a mother in the ideas of a gentle and pious morality. The primitive man of Teutonism is revolting by his purposeless brutality, by a love of evil that only gives him skill and strength in the service of hatred and injury. The Cymric hero on the other hand, even in his wildest flights, seems possessed by habits of kindness and a warm sympathy with the weak. Sympathy indeed is one of the deepest feelings among the Celtic peoples. Even Judas is not denied a share of their pity. St. Brandan found him upon a rock in the midst of the Polar seas; once a week he passes a day there to refresh himself from the fires of hell. A cloak that he had given to a beggar is hung before him, and tempers his sufferings.

If Wales has a right to be proud of her *Mabinogion,* she has not less to felicitate herself in having found a translator truly worthy of interpreting them. For the proper understanding of these original beauties there was needed a delicate appreciation of Welsh narration, and an intelligence of the naïve order, qualities of which an erudite translator would with difficulty have been capable. To render these gracious imaginings of a people so eminently dowered with feminine tact, the pen of a woman was necessary. Simple, animated, without effort and without vulgarity, Lady Guest's translation is the faithful mirror of the original Cymric. Even supposing that, as regards philology, the labors of this noble Welsh lady be destined to receive improvement, that does not prevent her book from forever remaining a work of erudition and highly distinguished taste.[5]

The *Mabinogion,* or at least the writings which Lady Guest thought she ought to include under this common name, divide themselves into two perfectly distinct classes—some connected exclusively with the two peninsulas of Wales and Cornwall, and relating to the heroic personality of Arthur; the others alien to Arthur, having for their scene not only the parts of England that have remained Cymric, but the whole of Great Britain, and leading us back by the persons and traditions mentioned in them to the later years of the Roman occupation. The second class, of greater antiquity than the first, at least on the ground of subject, is also distinguished by a much more mythological character, a bolder use of the miraculous, an enigmatical form, a style full of alliteration and plays upon words. Of this number are the tales of "Pwyll," of "Branwen," of "Manawyddan," of "Math the son of Mathonwy," the "Dream of the Emperor Maximus," the story of "Llud and Llewelys," and the legend of Taliessin. To the Arthurian cycle belong the narratives of "Owen," of "Geraint," of "Peredur," of "Kilhwch and Olwen," and the "Dream of Rhonabwy." It is also to be remarked that the two last-named narratives have a particularly antique character. In them Arthur dwells in Cornwall, and

---

[5] M. de la Villemarqué published in 1842 under the title of "Contes populaires des anciens Bretons," a French translation of the narratives that Lady Guest had already presented in English at that time.

not as in the others at Caerleon on the Usk. In them he appears with an individual character, hunting and taking a personal part in warfare, while in the more modern tales he is only an emperor all-powerful and impassive, a truly sluggard hero, around whom a pleiad of active heroes groups itself. The *Mabinogi* of "Kilhwch and Olwen," by its entirely primitive aspect, by the part played in it by the wild-boar in conformity to the spirit of Celtic mythology, by the wholly supernatural and magical character of the narration, by innumerable allusions the sense of which escapes us, forms a cycle by itself. It represents for us the Cymric conception in all its purity, before it had been modified by the introduction of any foreign element. Without attempting here to analyze this curious poem, I should like by some extracts to make its antique aspect and high originality apparent.

Kilhwch, son of Kilydd, prince of Kelyddon, having heard some one mention the name of Olwen, daughter of Yspaddaden Penkawr, falls violently in love, without having ever seen her. He goes to find Arthur, that he may ask for his aid in the difficult undertaking which he meditates; in point of fact, he does not know in what country the fair one of his affection dwells. Yspaddaden is besides a frightful tyrant who suffers no man to go from his castle alive, and whose death is linked by destiny to the marriage of his daughter.[6] Arthur grants Kilhwch some of his most valiant comrades in arms to assist him in this enterprise. After wonderful adventures the knights arrive at the castle of Yspaddaden, and succeed in seeing the young maiden of Kilhwch's dream. Only after three days of persistent struggle do they manage to obtain a response from Olwen's father, who attaches his daughter's hand to conditions apparently impossible of realization. The performance of these trials makes a long chain of adventures, the framework of a veritable romantic epic which has come to us in a very fragmentary form. Of the thirty-eight adventures imposed on Kilhwch the manuscript used by Lady Guest only relates seven or eight. I choose at random one of these narratives, which appears to me fitted to give an idea of the whole composition. It deals with the find-

---

[6] The idea of making the death of the father the condition of possession of the daughter is to be found in several romances of the Breton cycle, in "Lancelot" for example.

ing of Mabon the son of Modron, who was carried away from his mother three days after his birth, and whose deliverance is one of the labors exacted of Kilhwch.

"His followers said unto Arthur, 'Lord, go thou home; thou canst not proceed with thy host in quest of such small adventures as these.' Then said Arthur, 'It were well for thee, Gwrhyr Gwalstawd Ieithoedd, to go upon this quest, for thou knowest all languages, and art familiar with those of the birds and the beasts. Thou, Eidoel, oughtest likewise to go with my men in search of thy cousin. And as for you, Kai and Bedwyr, I have hope of whatever adventure ye are in quest of, that ye will achieve it. Achieve ye this adventure for me.'"

They went forward until they came to the Ousel of Cilgwri. And Gwrhyr adjured her for the sake of Heaven, saying, "Tell me if thou knowest aught of Mabon the son of Modron, who was taken when three nights old from between his mother and the wall." And the Ousel answered, "When I first came here there was a smith's anvil in this place, and I was then a young bird; and from that time no work has been done upon it, save the pecking of my beak every evening, and now there is not so much as the size of a nut remaining thereof; yet all the vengeance of Heaven be upon me, if during all that time I have ever heard of the man for whom you inquire. Nevertheless I will do that which is right, and that which it is fitting I should do for an embassy from Arthur. There is a race of animals who were formed before me, and I will be your guide to them."

So they proceeded to the place where was the Stag of Redynvre. "Stag of Redynvre, behold we are come to thee, an embassy from Arthur, for we have not heard of any animal older than thou. Say, knowest thou aught of Mabon the son of Modron, who was taken from his mother when three nights old?" The Stag said, "When first I came hither there was a plain all around me, without any trees save one oak sapling, which grew up to be an oak with a hundred branches. And that oak has since perished, so that now nothing remains of it but the withered stump; and from that day to this I have been here, yet have I never heard of the man for whom you inquire. Nevertheless, being an embassy from Arthur, I will be your guide to the place where there is an animal which was formed before I was."

So they proceeded to the place where was the Owl of Cwm Cawlwyd. "Owl of Cwm Cawlwyd, here is an embassy from Arthur; knowest thou aught of Mabon the son of Modron, who was taken after three nights from his mother?" "If I knew I would tell you. When first I came hither, the wide valley you see was a wooded glen. And a race of men came and rooted it up. And there grew there a second wood; and this wood is the third. My wings, are they not withered stumps? Yet all this time, even until to-day, I have never heard of the man for whom you inquire. Nevertheless I will be the guide of Arthur's embassy until you come to the place where is the oldest animal in the world, and the one that has travelled most, the Eagle of Gwern Abwy."

Gwrhyr said, "Eagle of Gwern Abwy, we have come to thee an embassy from Arthur, to ask thee if thou knowest aught of Mabon the son of Modron, who was taken from his mother when he was three nights old." The Eagle said, "I have been here for a great space of time, and when I first came hither there was a rock here, from the top of which I pecked at the stars every evening; and now it is not so much as a span high. From that day to this I have been here, and I have never heard of the man for whom you inquire, except once when I went in search of food as far as Llyn Llyw. And when I came there, I struck my talons into a salmon, thinking he would serve me as food for a long time. But he drew me into the deep, and I was scarcely able to escape from him. After that I went with my whole kindred to attack him, and to try to destroy him, but he sent messengers, and made peace with me; and came and besought me to take fifty fish spears out of his back. Unless he know something of him whom you seek, I cannot tell who may. However, I will guide you to the place where he is."

So they went thither; and the Eagle said, "Salmon of Llyn Llyw, I have come to thee with an embassy from Arthur, to ask thee if thou knowest aught concerning Mabon the son of Modron, who was taken away at three nights old from his mother." "As much as I know I will tell thee. With every tide I go along the river upwards, until I come near to the walls of Gloucester, and there have I found such wrong as I never found elsewhere; and to the end that ye may give credence thereto, let one of you go thither upon each of my two shoulders." So Kai and Gwrhyr Gwalstawd Ieithoedd went upon the shoulders of the salmon, and they proceeded until they came unto the wall of the prison, and they heard a great wailing and lamenting from the dungeon. Said Gwrhyr, "Who is it that laments in this house of stone?" "Alas there is reason enough for whoever is here to lament. It is Mabon the son of Modron who is here imprisoned; and no imprisonment was ever so grievous as mine, neither that of Lludd Llaw Ereint, nor that of Greid the son of Eri." "Hast thou hope of being released for gold or for silver, or for any gifts of wealth, or through battle and fighting?" "By fighting will whatever I may gain be obtained."

We shall not follow the Cymric hero through trials the result of which can be foreseen. What, above all else, is striking in these strange legends is the part played by animals, transformed by the Welsh imagination into intelligent beings. No race conversed so intimately as did the Celtic race with the lower creation, and accorded it so large a share of moral life.[7] The close association of man and animal, the fictions so dear to mediæval poetry of the Knight of the Lion, the Knight of the Falcon, the Knight of the Swan, the vows consecrated by the presence of birds of noble repute, are equally Breton imaginings. Ecclesiastical literature itself presents analogous features; gentleness towards animals informs all the legends of the saints of Brittany and Ireland. One day St. Kevin fell asleep while he was praying at his window with outstretched arms; and a swallow perceiving the open hand of the venerable monk, considered it an excellent place wherein to make her nest. The saint on awaking saw the mother sitting upon her eggs, and, loath to disturb her, waited for the little ones to be hatched before he arose from his knees.

This touching sympathy was derived from the singular vivacity with which the Celtic races have inspired their feeling for nature. Their mythology is nothing more than a transparent naturalism, not that anthropomorphic naturalism of Greece and India, in which the forces of the universe, viewed as living beings and endowed with consciousness, tend more and more to detach themselves from physical phenomena, and

[7] See especially the narratives of Nennius, and of Giraldus Cambrensis. In them animals have at least as important a part as men.

to become moral beings; but in some measure a realistic naturalism, the love of nature for herself, the vivid impression of her magic, accompanied by the sorrowful feeling that man knows, when, face to face with her, he believes that he hears her commune with him concerning his origin and his destiny. The legend of Merlin mirrors this feeling. Seduced by a fairy of the woods, he flies with her and becomes a savage. Arthur's messengers come upon him as he is singing by the side of a fountain; he is led back again to court; but the charm carries him away. He returns to his forests, and this time forever. Under a thicket of hawthorn Vivien has built him a magical prison. There he prophesies the future of the Celtic races; he speaks of a maiden of the woods, now visible and now unseen, who holds him captive by her spells. Several Arthurian legends are impressed with the same character. Arthur himself in popular belief became, as it were, a woodland spirit. " The foresters on their nightly round by the light of the moon," says Gervais of Tilbury, " often hear a great sound as of horns, and meet bands of huntsmen; when they are asked whence they come, these huntsmen make reply that they are of King Arthur's following." [8] Even the French imitators of the Breton romances keep an impression—although a rather insipid one —of the attraction exercised by nature on the Celtic imagination. Elaine, the heroine of Lancelot, the ideal of Breton perfection, passes her life with her companions in a garden, in the midst of flowers which she tends. Every flower culled by her hands is at the instant restored to life; and the worshippers of her memory are under an obligation, when they cut a flower, to sow another in its place.

The worship of forest, and fountain, and stone is to be explained by this primitive naturalism, which all the councils of the Church held in Brittany united to proscribe. The stone, in truth, seems the natural symbol of the Celtic races. It is an immutable witness that has no death. The animal, the plant, above all the human figure, only express the divine life under a determinate form; the stone on the contrary, adapted to re-

[8] This manner of explaining all the unknown noises of the wood by "Arthur's hunting" is still to be found in several districts. To understand properly the cult of nature, and, if I may say so, of landscape among the Celts, see Gildas and Nennius, pp. 131, 136, 137, etc. (Edit. San Marte, Berlin, 1844.)

ceive all forms, has been the fetich of peoples in their childhood. Pausanias saw, still standing erect, the thirty square stones of Pharæ, each bearing the name of a divinity. The *men-hir* to be met with over the whole surface of the ancient world, what is it but the monument of primitive humanity, a living witness of its faith in Heaven? [9]

It has frequently been observed that the majority of popular beliefs still extant in our different provinces are of Celtic origin. A not less remarkable fact is the strong tinge of naturalism dominant in these beliefs. Nay more, every time that the old Celtic spirit appears in our history, there is to be seen, re-born with it, faith in nature and her magic influences. One of the most characteristic of these manifestations seems to me to be that of Joan of Arc. That indomitable hope, that tenacity in the affirmation of the future, that belief that the salvation of the kingdom will come from a woman—all those features, far removed as they are from the taste of antiquity, and from Teutonic taste, are in many respects Celtic. The memory of the ancient cult perpetuated itself at Domremy, as in so many other places, under the form of popular superstition. The cottage of the family of Arc was shaded by a beech tree, famed in the country and reputed to be the abode of fairies. In her childhood Joan used to go and hang upon its branches garlands of leaves and flowers, which, so it was said, disappeared during the night. The terms of her accusation speak with horror of this innocent custom, as of a crime against the faith; and indeed they were not altogether deceived, those unpitying theologians who judged the holy maid. Although she knew it not, she was more Celtic than Christian. She has been foretold by Merlin; she knows of neither Pope nor Church—she only believes the voice that speaks in her own heart. This voice she hears in the fields, in the sough of the wind among the trees, when measured and distant sounds fall upon her ears. During her trial, worn out with questions and scholastic subtleties, she is asked whether she still hears her voices. "Take me to the woods," she says, "and I shall hear them clearly." Her legend

---

[9] It is, however, doubtful whether the monuments known in France as Celtic (men-hir, dol-men, etc.) are the work of the Celts. With M. Worsaae and the Copenhagen archæologists, I am inclined to think that these monuments belong to a more ancient humanity. Never, in fact, has any branch of the Indo-European race built in this fashion. (See two articles by M. Mérimée in "L'Athenæum français," Sept. 11, 1852, and April 25, 1853.)

is tinged with the same colors; nature loved her, the wolves never touched the sheep of her flock. When she was a little girl, the birds used to come and eat bread from her lap as though they were tame.[10]

III

The *Mabinogion* do not recommend themselves to our study, only as a manifestation of the romantic genius of the Breton races. It was through them that the Welsh imagination exercised its influence upon the Continent, that it transformed, in the twelfth century, the poetic art of Europe, and realized this miracle—that the creations of a half-conquered race have become the universal feast of imagination for mankind.

Few heroes owe less to reality than Arthur. Neither Gildas nor Aneurin, his contemporaries, speak of him; Bede did not even know his name; Taliessin and Liwarc'h Hên gave him only a secondary place. In Nennius, on the other hand, who lived about 850, the legend has fully unfolded. Arthur is already the exterminator of the Saxons; he has never experienced defeat; he is the suzerain of an army of kings. Finally, in Geoffrey of Monmouth, the epic creation culminates. Arthur reigns over the whole earth; he conquers Ireland, Norway, Gascony, and France. At Caerleon he holds a tournament at which all the monarchs of the world are present; there he puts upon his head thirty crowns, and exacts recognition as the sovereign lord of the universe. So incredible is it that a petty king of the sixth century, scarcely remarked by his contemporaries, should have taken in posterity such colossal proportions, that several critics have supposed that the legendary Arthur and the obscure chieftain who bore that name have nothing in common, the one with the other, and that the son of Uther Pendragon is a wholly ideal hero, a survivor of the old Cymric mythology. As a matter of fact, in the symbols of Neo-Druidism—that is

---

[10] Since the first publication of these views, on which I should not like more emphasis to be put than what belongs to a passing impression, similar considerations have been developed, in terms that appear a little too positive, by M. H. Martin ("History of France," vol. vi., 1856). The objections raised to it are, for the most part, due to the fact that very few people are capable of delicately appreciating questions of this kind, relative to the genius of races. It frequently happens that the resurrection of an old national genius takes place under a very different form from that which one would have expected, and by means of individuals who have no idea of the ethnographical part which they play.

to say, of that secret doctrine, the outcome of Druidism, which prolonged its existence even to the Middle Ages under the form of Freemasonry—we again find Arthur transformed into a divine personage, and playing a purely mythological part. It must at least be allowed that, if behind the fable some reality lies hidden, history offers us no means of attaining it. It cannot be doubted that the discovery of Arthur's tomb in the Isle of Avalon in 1189 was an invention of Norman policy, just as in 1283, the very year in which Edward I was engaged in crushing out the last vestiges of Welsh independence, Arthur's crown was very conveniently found, and forthwith united to the other crown jewels of England.

We naturally expect Arthur, now become the representative of Welsh nationality, to sustain in the *Mabinogion* a character analogous to this rôle, and therein, as in Nennius, to serve the hatred of the vanquished against the Saxons. But such is not the case. Arthur, in the *Mabinogion*, exhibits no characteristics of patriotic resistance; his part is limited to uniting heroes around him, to maintaining the retainers of his palace, and to enforcing the laws of his order of chivalry. He is too strong for anyone to dream of attacking him. He is the Charlemagne of the Carlovingian romances, the Agamemnon of Homer—one of those neutral personalities that serve but to give unity to the poem. The idea of warfare against the alien, hatred towards the Saxon, does not appear in a single instance. The heroes of the *Mabinogion* have no fatherland; each fights to show his personal excellence, and satisfy his taste for adventure, but not to defend a national cause. Britain is the universe; no one suspects that beyond the Cymry there may be other nations and other races.

It was by this ideal and representative character that the Arthurian legend had such an astonishing prestige throughout the whole world. Had Arthur been only a provincial hero, the more or less happy defender of a little country, all peoples would not have adopted him, any more than they have adopted the Marco of the Serbs, or the Robin Hood of the Saxons. The Arthur who has charmed the world is the head of an order of equality, in which all sit at the same table, in which a man's worth depends upon his valor and his natural gifts. What mattered to the world the fate of an unknown peninsula, and the strife waged on its behalf? What enchanted it was the ideal court presided over by Gwenhwyvar (Guinevere), where around the monarchical unity the flower of heroes was gathered together, where ladies, as chaste as they were beautiful, loved according to the laws of chivalry, and where the time was passed in listening to stories, and learning civility and beautiful manners.

This is the secret of the magic of that Round Table, about which the Middle Ages grouped all their ideas of heroism, of beauty, of modesty, and of love. We need not stop to inquire whether the ideal of a gentle and polished society in the midst of the barbarian world is, in all its features, a purely Breton creation, whether the spirit of the courts of the Continent has not in some measure furnished the model, and whether the *Mabinogion* themselves have not felt the reaction of the French imitations;[11] it suffices for us that the new order of sentiments which we have just indicated was, throughout the whole of the Middle Ages, persistently attached to the groundwork of the Cymric romances. Such an association could not be fortuitous; if the imitations are all so glaring in color, it is evidently because in the original this same color is to be found united to particularly strong character. How otherwise shall we explain why a forgotten tribe on the very confines of the world should have imposed its heroes upon Europe, and, in the domain of imagination, accomplished one of the most singular revolutions known to the historian of letters?

If, in fact, one compares European literature before the introduction of the Cymric romances with what it became when the *trouvères* set themselves to draw from Breton sources, one recognizes readily that with the Breton narratives a new element entered into the poetic conception of the Christian peoples, and modified it profoundly. The Carlovingian poem, both by its structure and by the means which it employs, does not depart from classical ideas. The motives of man's action are the same as in the Greek epic. The essentially romantic element, the life of forests and mysterious adventure, the feeling for nature,

---

[11] The surviving version of the "Mabinogion" has a later date than these imitations, and the Red Book includes several tales borrowed from the French trouvères. But it is out of the question to maintain that the really Welsh narratives have been borrowed in a like manner, since among them are some unknown to the trouvères, which could only possess interest for Breton countries.

and that impulse of imagination which makes the Breton warrior unceasingly pursue the unknown—nothing of all this is as yet to be observed. Roland differs from the heroes of Homer only by his armor; in heart he is the brother of Ajax or Achilles. Perceval, on the contrary, belongs to another world, separated by a great gulf from that in which the heroes of antiquity live and act.

It was above all by the creation of woman's character, by introducing into mediæval poetry, hitherto hard and austere, the *nuances* of love, that the Breton romances brought about this curious metamorphosis. It was like an electric spark; in a few years European taste was changed. Nearly all the types of womankind known to the Middle Ages, Guinevere, Iseult, Enid, are derived from Arthur's court. In the Carlovingian poems woman is a nonentity without character or individuality; in them love is either brutal, as in the romance of " Ferebras," or scarcely indicated, as in the " Song of Roland." In the *Mabinogion,* on the other hand, the principal part always belongs to the women. Chivalrous gallantry, which makes the warrior's happiness to consist in serving a woman and meriting her esteem, the belief that the noblest use of strength is to succor and avenge weakness, results, I know, from a turn of imagination which possessed nearly all European peoples in the twelfth century; but it cannot be doubted that this turn of imagination first found literary expression among the Breton peoples. One of the most surprising features in the *Mabinogion* is the delicacy of the feminine feeling breathed in them; an impropriety or a gross word is never to be met with. It would be necessary to quote at length the two romances of " Peredur " and "Geraint " to demonstrate an innocence such as this; but the naïve simplicity of these charming compositions forbids us to see in this innocence any underlying meaning. The zeal of the knight in the defence of ladies' honor became a satirical euphemism only in the French imitators, who transformed the virginal modesty of the Breton romances into a shameless gallantry—so far indeed that these compositions, chaste as they are in the original, became the scandal of the Middle Ages, provoked censures, and were the occasion of the ideas of immorality which, for religious people, still cluster about the name of romance.

Certainly chivalry is too complex a fact for us to be permitted to assign it to any single origin. Let us say however that in the idea of envisaging the esteem of a woman as the highest object of human activity, and setting up love as the supreme principle of morality, there is nothing of the antique spirit, or indeed of the Teutonic. Is it in the " Edda " or in the " Niebelungen " that we shall find the germ of this spirit of pure love, of exalted devotion, which forms the very soul of chivalry? As to following the suggestion of some critics and seeking among the Arabs for the beginnings of this institution, surely of all literary paradoxes ever mooted, this is one of the most singular. The idea of conquering woman in a land where she is bought and sold, of seeking her esteem in a land where she is scarcely considered capable of moral merit! I shall oppose the partisans of this hypothesis with one single fact—the surprise experienced by the Arabs of Algeria when, by a somewhat unfortunate recollection of mediæval tournaments, the ladies were intrusted with the presentation of prizes at the Beiram races. What to the knight appeared an unparalleled honor seemed to the Arabs a humiliation and almost an insult.

The introduction of the Breton romances into the current of European literature worked a not less profound revolution in the manner of conceiving and employing the marvellous. In the Carlovingian poems the marvellous is timid, and conforms to the Christian faith; the supernatural is produced directly by God or his envoys. Among the Cymry, on the contrary, the principle of the marvel is in nature herself, in her hidden forces, in her inexhaustible fecundity. There is a mysterious swan, a prophetic bird, a suddenly appearing hand, a giant, a black tyrant, a magic mist, a dragon, a cry that causes the hearer to die of terror, an object with extraordinary properties. There is no trace of the monotheistic conception, in which the marvellous is only a miracle, a derogation of eternal laws. Nor are there any of those personifications of the life of nature which form the essential part of the Greek and Indian mythologies. Here we have perfect naturalism, an unlimited faith in the possible, belief in the existence of independent beings bearing within themselves the principle of their strength—an idea quite opposed to Christianity, which in such beings necessarily sees either angels or fiends. And besides, these strange beings are always presented as being outside the pale of the Church; and when the knight of the Round Table has conquered them he forces them to go and pay homage to Guinevere, and have themselves baptized.

Now, if in poetry there is a marvellous element that we might accept, surely it is this. Classical mythology, taken in its first simplicity, is too bold, taken as a mere figure of rhetoric, too insipid, to give us satisfaction. As to the marvellous element in Christianity, Boileau is right: no fiction is compatible with such a dogmatism. There remains then the purely naturalistic marvellous, nature interesting herself in action and acting herself, the great mystery of fatality unveiling itself by the secret conspiring of all beings, as in Shakespeare and Ariosto. It would be curious to ascertain how much of the Celt there is in the former of these poets; as for Ariosto he is the Breton poet *par excellence.* All his machinery, all his means of interest, all his fine shades of sentiment, all his types of women, all his adventures, are borrowed from the Breton romances.

Do we now understand the intellectual rôle of that little race which gave to the world Arthur, Guinevere, Lancelot, Perceval, Merlin, St. Brandan, St. Patrick, and almost all the poetical cycles of the Middle Ages? What a striking destiny some nations have, in alone possessing the right to cause the acceptance of their heroes, as though for that were necessary a quite peculiar degree of authority, seriousness, and faith! And it is a strange thing that it is to the Normans, of all peoples the one least sympathetically inclined towards the Bretons, that we owe the renown of the Breton fables. Brilliant and imitative, the Norman everywhere became the pre-eminent representative of the nation on which he had at first imposed himself by force. French in France, English in England, Italian in Italy, Russian at Novgorod, he forgot his own language to speak that of the race which he had conquered, and to become the interpreter of its genius. The deeply suggestive character of the Welsh romances could not fail to impress men so prompt to seize and assimilate the ideas of the foreigner. The first revelation of the Breton fables, the "Latin Chronicle" of Geoffrey of Monmouth, appeared about the year 1137, under the auspices of Robert of Gloucester, natural son of Henry I. Henry II acquired a taste for the same narratives, and at his request Robert Wace, in 1155, wrote in French the first history of Arthur, thus opening the path in which walked after him a host of poets or imitators of all nationalities, French, Provençal, Italian, Spanish, English, Scandinavian, Greek, and Georgian. We need not belittle the glory of the first *trouvères* who put into a language, then read and understood from one end of Europe to the other, fictions which, but for them, would have doubtless remained forever unknown. It is however difficult to attribute to them an inventive faculty, such as would permit them to merit the title of creators. The numerous passages in which one feels that they do not fully understand the original which they imitate, and in which they attempt to give a natural significance to circumstances of which the mythological bearing escaped them, suffice to prove that, as a rule, they were satisfied to make a fairly faithful copy of the work before their eyes.

What part has Armorican Brittany played in the creation or propagation of the legends of the Round Table? It is impossible to say with any degree of precision; and in truth such a question becomes a matter of secondary import, once we form a just idea of the close bonds of fraternity which did not cease until the twelfth century to unite the two branches of the Breton peoples. That the heroic traditions of Wales long continued to live in the branch of the Cymric family which came and settled in Armorica cannot be doubted when we find Geraint, Urien, and other heroes become saints in Lower Brittany;[12] and above all when we see one of the most essential episodes of the Arthurian cycle, that of the Forest of Brocéliande, placed in the same country. A large number of facts collected by M. de la Villemarqué[13] prove, on the other hand, that these same traditions produced a true poetic cycle in Brittany, and even that at certain epochs they must have recrossed the Channel, as though to give new life to the mother country's memories. The fact that Gauthier Calenius, Archdeacon of Oxford, brought back from Brittany to England (about 1125) the very text of the

---

[12] I shall only cite a single proof; it is a law of Edward the Confessor: "Britones vero Armorici quum venerint in regno isto, suscipi debent et in regno protegi sicut probi cives de corpore regni hujus; exierunt quondam de sanguine Britonum regni hujus."— Wilkins, "Leges Anglo-Saxonicæ," p. 206.

[13] "Les Romans de la Table-Ronde et les contes des anciens Bretons" (Paris, 1859), pp. 20 et seq. In the "Contes populaires des anciens Bretons," of which the above may be considered as a new edition, the learned author had somewhat exaggerated the influence of French Brittany. In the present article, when first published, I had, on the other hand, depreciated it too much.

legends which were translated into Latin ten years afterwards by Geoffrey of Monmouth, is here decisive. I know that to readers of the *Mabinogion* such an opinion will appear surprising at a first glance. All is Welsh in these fables, the places, the genealogies, the customs; in them Armorica is only represented by Hoel, an important personage no doubt, but one who has not achieved the fame of the other heroes of Arthur's court. Again, if Armorica saw the birth of the Arthurian cycle, how is it that we fail to find there any traces of that brilliant nativity?[14]

These objections, I avow, long barred my way, but I no longer find them insoluble. And first of all there is a class of *Mabinogion,* including those of Owen, Geraint, and Peredur, stories which possess no very precise geographical localization. In the second place, national written literature being less successfully defended in Brittany than in Wales against the invasion of foreign culture, it may be conceived that the memory of the old epics should be there more obliterated. The literary share of the two countries thus remains sufficiently distinct. The glory of French Brittany is in her popular songs; but it is only in Wales that the genius of the Breton people has succeeded in establishing itself in authentic books and achieved creations.

IV

In comparing the Breton cycle as the French *trouvères* knew it, and the same cycle as it is to be found in the text of the *Mabinogion,* one might be tempted to believe that the European imagination, enthralled by these brilliant fables, added to them some poetical themes unknown to the Welsh. Two of the most celebrated heroes of the Continental Breton romances, Lancelot and Tristan, do not figure in the *Mabinogion;* on the other hand, the characteristics of the Holy Grail are presented in a totally different way from that which we find in the French and German poets. A more attentive study shows that these elements, apparently added by the French poets, are in reality of

---

[14] M. de la Villemarqué makes appeal to the popular songs still extant in Brittany, in which Arthur's deeds are celebrated. In fact, in his " Chants populaires de la Bretagne " two poems are to be found in which that hero's name figures.

Cymric origin. And first of all, M. de la Villemarqué has demonstrated to perfection that the name of Lancelot is only a translation of that of the Welsh hero Maël, who in point of fact exhibits the fullest analogy with the Lancelot of the French romances.[15] The context, the proper names, all the details of the romance of Lancelot also present the most pronounced Breton aspect. As much must be said of the romance of Tristan. It is even to be hoped that this curious legend will be discovered complete in some Welsh manuscript. Dr. Owen states that he has seen one of which he was unable to obtain a copy. As to the Holy Grail, it must be avowed that the mystic cup, the object after which the French Parceval and the German Parsifal go in search, has not nearly the same importance among the Welsh. In the romance of "Peredur" it only figures in an episodical fashion, and without a well-defined religious intention.

"Then Peredur and his uncle discoursed together, and he beheld two youths enter the hall, and proceed up to the chamber, bearing a spear of mighty size, with three streams of blood flowing from the point to the ground. And when all the company saw this, they began wailing and lamenting. But for all that, the man did not break off his discourse with Peredur. And as he did not tell Peredur the meaning of what he saw, he forbore to ask him concerning it. And when the clamor had a little subsided, behold two maidens entered, with a large salver between them, in which was a man's head, surrounded by a profusion of blood. And thereupon the company of the court made so great an outcry, that it was irksome to be in the same hall with them. But at length they were silent." This strange and wondrous circumstance remains an enigma to the end of the narrative. Then a mysterious young man appears to Peredur, apprises him that the lance from which the blood was dropping is that with which his uncle was wounded, that the vessel contains the blood and the head of one of his cousins, slain by the witches of Kerloiou, and that it is predestined that he, Peredur, should be their avenger. In point of fact, Peredur goes and

---

[15] Ancelot is the diminutive of Ancel, and means servant, page, or esquire. To this day in the Cymric dialects Maël has the same signification. The surname of Poursigant, which we find borne by some Welshmen in the French service in the early part of the fourteenth century, is also no doubt a translation of Maël.

convokes the Round Table; Arthur and his knights come and put the witches of Kerloiou to death.

If we now pass to the French romance of "Parceval," we find that all this phantasmagoria clothes a very different significance. The lance is that with which Longus pierced Christ's side, the Grail or basin is that in which Joseph of Arimathea caught the divine blood. This miraculous vase procures all the good things of heaven and earth; it heals wounds, and is filled at the owner's pleasure with the most exquisite food. To approach it one must be in a state of grace; only a priest can tell of its marvels. To find these sacred relics after the passage of a thousand trials—such is the object of Peredur's chivalry, at once worldly and mystical. In the end he becomes a priest; he takes the Grail and the lance into his hermitage; on the day of his death an angel bears them up to Heaven. Let us add that many traits prove that in the mind of the French *trouvère* the Grail is confounded with the eucharist. In the miniatures which occasionally accompany the romance of "Parceval," the Grail is in the form of a pyx, appearing at all the solemn moments of the poem as a miraculous source of succor.

Is this strange myth, differing as it does from the simple narrative presented in the Welsh legend of Peredur, really Cymric, or ought we rather to see in it an original creation of the *trouvères,* based upon a Breton foundation? With M. de la Villemarqué [16] we believe that this curious fable is essentially Cymric. In the eighth century a Breton hermit had a vision of Joseph of Arimathea bearing the chalice of the Last Supper, and wrote the history called the "Gradal." The whole Celtic mythology is full of the marvels of a magic caldron under which nine fairies blow silently, a mysterious vase which inspires poetic genius, gives wisdom, reveals the future, and unveils the secrets of the world. One day as Bran the Blessed was hunting in Ireland upon the shore of a lake, he saw come forth from it a black man bearing upon his back an enormous caldron, followed by a witch and a dwarf. This caldron was the instrument of the supernatural power of a family of giants. It cured all ills, and gave back life to the dead, but without restoring to them the use of speech—an allusion to the secret of the bardic

[16] See the excellent discussion of this interesting problem in the introduction to "Contes populaires des anciens Bretons" (pp. 181 et seq.).

initiation. In the same way Perceval's wariness forms the whole plot of the quest of the Holy Grail. The Grail thus appears to us in its primitive meaning as the pass-word of a kind of freemasonry which survived in Wales long after the preaching of the Gospel, and of which we find deep traces in the legend of Taliessin. Christianity grafted its legend upon the mythological data, and a like transformation was doubtless made by the Cymric race itself. If the Welsh narrative of Peredur does not offer the same developments as the French romance of "Parceval," it is because the "Red Book of Hergest" gives us an earlier version than that which served as a model for Chrétien de Troyes. It is also to be remarked that, even in "Parceval," the mystical idea is not as yet completely developed, that the *trouvère* seems to treat this strange theme as a narrative which he has found already complete, and the meaning of which he can scarcely guess. The motive that sets Parceval a-field in the French romance, as well as in the Welsh version, is a family motive; he seeks the Holy Grail as a talisman to cure his uncle the Fisherman-King, in such a way that the religious idea is still subordinated to the profane intention. In the German version, on the other hand, full as it is of mysticism and theology, the Grail has a temple and priests. Parsifal, who has become a purely ecclesiastical hero, reaches the dignity of King of the Grail by his religious enthusiasm and his chastity.[17] Finally, the prose versions, more modern still, sharply distinguish the two chivalries, the one earthly, the other mystical. In them Parceval becomes the model of the devout knight. This was the last of the metamorphoses which that all-powerful enchantress called the human imagination made him undergo; and it was only right that, after having gone through so many dangers, he should don a monkish frock, wherein to take his rest after his life of adventure.

V

When we seek to determine the precise moment in the history of the Celtic races at which we ought to place ourselves in order

---

[17] It is indeed remarkable that all the Breton heroes in their last transformation are at once gallant and devout. One of the most celebrated ladies of Arthur's court, Luned, becomes a saint and a martyr for her chastity, her festival being celebrated on August 1st. She it is who figures in the French romances under the name of Lunette. See Lady Guest, vol. i. pp. 113, 114.

to appreciate their genius in its entirety, we find ourselves led back to the sixth century of our era. Races have nearly always a predestined hour at which, passing from simplicity to reflection, they bring forth to the light of day, for the first time, all the treasures of their nature. For the Celtic races the poetic moment of awakening and primal activity was the sixth century. Christianity, still young amongst them, has not completely stifled the national cult; the religion of the Druids defends itself in its schools and holy places; warfare against the foreigner, without which a people never achieves a full consciousness of itself, attains its highest degree of spirit. It is the epoch of all the heroes of enduring fame, of all the characteristic saints of the Breton Church; finally, it is the great age of bardic literature, illustrious by the names of Taliessin, of Aneurin, of Liwarc'h Hên.

To such as would view critically the historical use of these half-fabulous names, and would hesitate to accept as authentic, poems that have come down to us through so long a series of ages, we reply that the objections raised to the antiquity of the bardic literature—objections of which W. Schlegel made himself the interpreter in opposition to M. Fauriel—have completely disappeared under the investigations of an enlightened and impartial criticism.[18] By a rare exception sceptical opinion has for once been found in the wrong. The sixth century is in fact for the Breton peoples a perfectly historical century. We touch this epoch of their history as closely and with as much certainty as Greek or Roman antiquity. It is indeed known that, up to a somewhat late period, the bards continued to compose pieces under the names—which had become popular—of Aneurin, Taliessin, and Liwarc'h Hên; but no confusion can be made between these insipid rhetorical exercises and the really ancient fragments which bear the names of the poets cited—fragments full of personal traits, local circumstances, and individual passions and feelings.

Such is the literature of which M. de la Villemarqué has attempted to unite the most ancient and authentic monuments in

---

[18] This evidently does not apply to the language of the poems in question. It is well known that mediæval scribes, alien as they were to all ideas of archæology, modernized the texts, in measure as they copied them; and that a manuscript in the vulgar tongue, as a rule, only attests the language of him who transcribed it.

his " Breton Bards of the Sixth Century." Wales has recognized the service that our learned compatriot has thus rendered to Celtic studies. We confess, however, to much preferring to the " Bards " the " Popular Songs of Brittany." It is in the latter that M. de la Villemarqué has best served Celtic studies, by revealing to us a delightful literature, in which, more clearly than anywhere else, are apparent these features of gentleness, fidelity, resignation, and timid reserve which form the character of the Breton peoples.[19]

The theme of the poetry of the bards of the sixth century is simple and exclusively heroic; it ever deals with the great motives of patriotism and glory. There is a total absence of all tender feeling, no trace of love, no well-marked religious idea, but only a vague and naturalistic mysticism—a survival of Druidic teaching—and a moral philosophy wholly expressed in Triads, similar to that taught in the half-bardic, half-Christian schools of St. Cadoc and St. Iltud. The singularly artificial and highly wrought form of the style suggests the existence of a system of learned instruction possessing long traditions. A more pronounced shade, and there would be a danger of falling into a pedantic and mannered rhetoric. The bardic literature, by its lengthened existence through the whole of the Middle Ages, did not escape this danger. It ended by being no more than a somewhat insipid collection of unoriginalities in style, and conventional metaphors.[20]

The opposition between bardism and Christianity reveals itself in the pieces translated by M. de la Villemarqué by many features of original and pathetic interest. The strife which rent

---

[19] This interesting collection ought not, however, to be accepted unreservedly; and the absolute confidence with which it has been quoted is not without its inconveniences. We believe that when M. de la Villemarqué comments on the fragments which, to his eternal honor, he has been the first to bring to light, his criticism is far from being proof against all reproach, and that several of the historical allusions which he considers that he finds in them are hypotheses more ingenious than solid. The past is too great, and has come down to us in too fragmentary a manner, for such coincidences to be probable. Popular celebrities are rarely those of history, and when the rumors of distant centuries come to us by two channels, one popular, the other historical, it is a rare thing for these two forms of tradition to be fully in accord with one another. M. de la Villemarqué is also too ready to suppose that the people repeats for centuries songs that it only half understands. When a song ceases to be intelligible it is nearly always altered by the people, with the end of approximating it to the sounds familiar and significant to their ears. Is it not also to be feared that in this case the editor, in entire good faith, may lend some slight inflection to the text, so as to find in it the sense that he desires, or has in his mind?

[20] A Welsh scholar, Mr. Stephens, in his " History of Cymric Literature " (Llandovery, 1849), has demonstrated these successive transformations very well.

the soul of the old poets, their antipathy to the gray men of the monastery, their sad and painful conversion, are to be found in their songs. The sweetness and tenacity of the Breton character can alone explain how a heterodoxy so openly avowed as this maintained its position in face of the dominant Christianity, and how holy men, Kolumkill for example, took upon themselves the defence of the bards against the kings who desired to stamp them out. The strife was the longer in its duration, in that Christianity among the Celtic peoples never employed force against rival religions, and, at the worst, left to the vanquished the liberty of ill humor. Belief in prophets, indestructible among these peoples, created, in despite of faith, the Anti-Christian type of Merlin, and caused his acceptance by the whole of Europe. Gildas and the orthodox Bretons were ceaseless in their thunderings against the prophets, and opposed to them Elias and Samuel, two bards who only foretold good; even in the twelfth century Giraldus Cambrensis saw a prophet in the town of Caerleon.

Thanks to this toleration bardism lasted into the heart of the Middle Ages, under the form of a secret doctrine, with a conventional language, and symbols almost wholly borrowed from the solar divinity of Arthur. This may be termed Neo-Druidism, a kind of Druidism subtilized and reformed on the model of Christianity, which may be seen growing more and more obscure and mysterious, until the moment of its total disappearance. A curious fragment belonging to this school, the dialogue between Arthur and Eliwlod, has transmitted to us the latest sighs of this latest protestation of expiring naturalism. Under the form of an eagle Eliwlod introduces the divinity to the sentiments of resignation, of subjection, and of humility, with which Christianity combated pagan pride. Hero-worship recoils step by step before the great formula, which Christianity ceases not to repeat to the Celtic races to sever them from their memories: There is none greater than God. Arthur allows himself to be persuaded to abdicate from his divinity, and ends by reciting the *Pater*.

I know of no more curious spectacle than this revolt of the manly sentiments of hero-worship against the feminine feeling which flowed so largely into the new faith. What, in fact, exasperates the old representatives of Celtic society are the exclusive triumph of the pacific spirit and the men, clad in linen and chanting psalms, whose voice is sad, who preach asceticism, and know the heroes no more.[21] We know the use that Ireland has made of this theme, in the dialogues which she loves to imagine between the representatives of her profane and religious life, Ossian and St. Patrick.[22] Ossian regrets the adventures, the chase, the blast of the horn, and the kings of old time. "If they were here," he says to St. Patrick, "thou shouldst not thus be scouring the country with thy psalm-singing flock." Patrick seeks to calm him by soft words, and sometimes carries his condescension so far as to listen to his long histories, which appear to interest the saint but slightly. "Thou has heard my story," says the old bard in conclusion; "albeit my memory groweth weak, and I am devoured with care, yet I desire to continue still to sing the deeds of yore, and to live upon ancient glories. Now am I stricken with years, my life is frozen within me, and all my joys are fleeting away. No more can my hand grasp the sword, nor mine arm hold the lance in rest. Among priests my last sad hour lengthened out, and psalms take now the place of songs of victory." "Let thy songs rest," says Patrick, "and dare not to compare thy Finn to the King of kings, whose might knoweth no bounds: bend thy knees before Him, and know Him for thy Lord." I was indeed necessary to surrender, and the legend relates how the old bard ended his days in the cloister, among the priests whom he had so often used rudely, in the midst of these chants that he knew not. Ossian was too good an Irishman for anyone to make up his mind to damn him utterly. Merlin himself had to cede to the new spell. He was, it is said, converted by St. Columba; and the popular voice in the ballads repeats to him unceasingly this sweet and touching appeal: "Merlin, Merlin, be converted; there is no divinity save that of God."

[21] The antipathy to Christianity attributed by the Armorican people to the dwarfs and korigans belongs in like measure to traditions of the opposition encountered by the Gospel in its beginnings. The korigans in fact are, for the Breton peasant, great princesses who would not accept Christianity when the apostles came to Brittany. They hate the clergy and the churches, the bells of which make them take to flight. The Virgin above all is their great enemy; she it is who has hounded them forth from their fountains, and on Saturday, the day consecrated to her, whosoever beholds them combing their hair or counting their treasures is sure to perish. (Villemarqué, "Chants populaires," Introduction.)

[22] See Miss Brooke's "Reliques of Irish Poetry," Dublin, 1789, pp. 37 et seq., pp. 75 et seq.

VI

We should form an altogether inadequate idea of the physiognomy of the Celtic races were we not to study them under what is perhaps the most singular aspect of their development —that is to say, their ecclesiastical antiquities and their saints. Leaving on one side the temporary repulsion which Christian mildness had to conquer in the classes of society which saw their influence diminished by the new order of things, it can be truly said that the gentleness of manners and the exquisite sensibility of the Celtic races, in conjunction with the absence of a formerly existing religion of strong organization, predestined them to Christianity. Christianity in fact, addressing itself by preference to the more humble feelings in human nature, met here with admirably prepared disciples; no race has so delicately understood the charm of littleness, none has placed the simple creature, the innocent, nearer God. The ease with which the new religion took possession of these peoples is also remarkable. Brittany and Ireland between them scarce count two or three martyrs; they are reduced to venerating as such those of their compatriots who were slain in the Anglo-Saxon and Danish invasions. Here comes to light the profound difference dividing the Celtic from the Teutonic race. The Teutons only received Christianity tardily and in spite of themselves, by scheming or by force, after a sanguinary resistance, and with terrible throes. Christianity was in fact on several sides repugnant to their nature; and one understands the regrets of pure Teutonists who, to this day, reproach the new faith with having corrupted their sturdy ancestors.

Such was not the case with the Celtic peoples; that gentle little race was naturally Christian. Far from changing them, and taking away some of their qualities, Christianity finished and perfected them. Compare the legends relating to the introduction of Christianity into the two countries, the " Kristni Saga " for instance, and the delightful legends of Lucius and St. Patrick. What a difference we find! In Iceland the first apostles are pirates, converted by some chance, now saying mass, now massacring their enemies, now resuming their former profession of sea-rovers; everything is done in accord with expediency, and without any serious faith. In Ireland and Brittany grace operates through women, by I know not what charm of purity and sweetness. The revolt of the Teutons was never effectually stifled; never did they forget the forced baptisms, and the sword-supported Carlovingian missionaries, until the day when Teutonism took its revenge, and Luther through seven centuries gave answer to Witikind. On the other hand, the Celts were, even in the third century, perfect Christians. To the Teutons Christianity was for long nothing but a Roman institution, imposed from without. They entered the Church only to trouble it; and it was not without very great difficulty that they succeeded in forming a national clergy. To the Celts, on the contrary, Christianity did not come from Rome; they had their native clergy, their own peculiar usages, their faith at first hand. It cannot, in fact, be doubted that in apostolic times Christianity was preached in Brittany; and several historians, not without justification, have considered that it was borne there by Judaistic Christians, or by disciples of the school of St. John. Everywhere else Christianity found, as a first substratum, Greek or Roman civilization. Here it found a virgin soil of a nature analogous to its own, and naturally prepared to receive it.

Few forms of Christianity have offered an ideal of Christian perfection so pure as the Celtic Church of the sixth, seventh, and eighth centuries. Nowhere, perhaps, has God been better worshipped in spirit than in those great monastic communities of Hy, or of Iona, of Bangor, of Clonard, or of Lindisfarne. One of the most distinguished developments of Christianity—doubtless too distinguished for the popular and practical mission which the Church had to undertake—Pelagianism, arose from it. The true and refined morality, the simplicity, and the wealth of invention which give distinction to the legends of the Breton and Irish saints, are indeed admirable. No race adopted Christianity with so much originality, or, while subjecting itself to the common faith, kept its national characteristics more persistently. In religion, as in all else, the Bretons sought isolation, and did not willingly fraternize with the rest of the world. Strong in their moral superiority, persuaded that they possessed the veritable canon of faith and religion, having received their Christianity from an apostolic and wholly primitive preaching, they experienced no need of feeling themselves in communion with Christian societies less noble than their own. Thence arose that long struggle of the Breton churches against Roman pretensions, which is so admirably narrated by M. Augustin Thierry,[23] thence those inflexible characters of Columba and the monks of Iona, defending their usages and institutions against the whole Church, thence finally the false position of the Celtic peoples in Catholicism, when that mighty force, grown more and more aggressive, had drawn them together from all quarters, and compelled their absorption in itself. Having no Catholic past, they found themselves unclassed on their entrance into the great family, and were never able to succeed in creating for themselves an archbishopric. All their efforts and all their innocent deceits to attribute that title to the churches of Dol and St. Davids were wrecked on the overwhelming divergence of their past; their bishops had to resign themselves to being obscure suffragans of Tours and Canterbury.

It remains to be said that, even in our own days, the powerful originality of Celtic Christianity is far from being effaced. The Bretons of France, although they have felt the consequences of the revolutions undergone by Catholicism on the Continent, are, at the present hour, one of the populations in which religious feeling has retained most independence. The new devotions find no favor with it; the people are faithful to the old beliefs and the old saints; the psalms of religion have for them an ineffable harmony. In the same way, Ireland keeps, in her more remote districts, quite unique forms of worship from those of the rest of the world, to which nothing in other parts of Christendom can be compared. The influence of modern Catholicism, elsewhere so destructive of national usages, has had here a wholly contrary effect, the clergy having found it incumbent on them to seek a vantage ground against Protestantism, in attachment to local practices and the customs of the past.

It is the picture of these Christian institutions, quite distinct from those of the remainder of the West, of this sometimes strange worship, of these legends of the saints marked with so distinct a seal of nationality, that lends an interest to the

---

[23] In his "History of the Conquest." The objections raised by M. Varin and some other scholars to M. Thierry's narrative only affect some secondary details, which were rectified in the edition published after the illustrious historian's death.

ecclesiastical antiquities of Ireland, of Wales, and of Armorican Brittany. No hagiology has remained more exclusively natural than that of the Celtic peoples; until the twelfth century those peoples admitted very few alien saints into their martyrology. None, too, includes so many naturalistic elements. Celtic Paganism offered so little resistance to the new religion that the Church did not hold itself constrained to put in force against it the rigor with which elsewhere it pursued the slightest traces of mythology. The conscientious essay by W. Rees on the " Saints of Wales," and that by the Rev. John Williams, an extremely learned ecclesiastic of the diocese of St. Asaph, on the " Ecclesiastical Antiquities of the Cymry," suffice to make one understand the immense value which a complete and intelligent history of the Celtic churches, before their absorption in the Roman Church, would possess. To these might be added the learned work of Dom Lobineau on the " Saints of Brittany," reissued in our days by the Abbé Tresvaux, had not the half-criticism of the Benedictine, much worse than a total absence of criticism, altered those naïve legends and cut away from them, under the pretext of good sense and religious reverence, that which to us gives them interest and charm.

Ireland above all would offer a religious physiognomy quite peculiar to itself, which would appear singularly original, were history in a position to reveal it in its entirety. When we consider the legions of Irish saints who in the sixth, seventh, and eighth centuries inundated the Continent, and arrived from their isle bearing with them their stubborn spirit, their attachment to their own usages, their subtle and realistic turn of mind, and see the Scots (such was the name given to the Irish) doing duty, until the twelfth century, as instructors in grammar and literature to all the West, we cannot doubt that Ireland, in the first half of the Middle Ages, was the scene of a singular religious movement. Studious philologists and daring philosophers, the Hibernian monks were above all indefatigable copyists; and it was in part owing to them that the work of the pen became a holy task. Columba, secretly warned that his last hour is at hand, finishes the page of the psalter which he has commenced, writes at the foot that he bequeaths the continuation to his successor, and then goes into the church to die. Nowhere was monastic life to find such docile subjects. Credulous as a child, timid, indolent, inclined to submit and obey, the Irishman alone was capable of lending himself to that complete self-abdication in the hands of the abbot, which we find so deeply marked in the historical and legendary memorials of the Irish Church. One easily recognizes the land where, in our own days, the priest, without provoking the slightest scandal, can, on a Sunday before quitting the altar, give the orders for his dinner in a very audible manner, and announce the farm where he intends to go and dine, and where he will hear his flock in confession. In the presence of a people which lived by imagination and the senses alone, the Church did not consider itself under the necessity of dealing severely with the caprices of religious fantasy. It permitted the free action of the popular instinct; and from this freedom emerged what is perhaps of all cults the most mythological and most analogous to the mysteries of antiquity, presented in Christian annals, a cult attached to certain places, and almost exclusively consisting in certain acts held to be sacramental.

Without contradiction the legend of St. Brandan is the most singular product of this combination of Celtic naturalism with Christian spiritualism. The taste of the Hibernian monks for making maritime pilgrimages through the archipelago of the Scottish and Irish seas, everywhere dotted with monasteries,[24] and the memory of yet more distant voyages in Polar seas, furnished the framework of this curious composition, so rich in local impressions. From Pliny (IV. xxx. 3) we learn that, even in his time, the Bretons loved to venture their lives upon the high seas, in search of unknown isles. M. Letronne has proved that in 795, sixty-five years consequently before the Danes, Irish monks landed in Iceland and established themselves on the coast. In this island the Danes found Irish books and bells; and the names of certain localities still bear witness to the sojourn of those monks, who were known by the name of *Papæ* (fathers). In the Faröe Isles, in the Orkneys, and the Shetlands, indeed in all parts of the Northern seas, the Scandinavians found themselves preceded by those *Papæ*, whose habits con-

---

[24] The Irish saints literally covered the Western seas. A very considerable number of the saints of Brittany, St. Tenenan, St. Renan, for example, were emigrants from Ireland. The Breton legends of St. Malo, St. David, and of St. Pol of Léon are replete with similar stories of voyages to the distant isles of the West.

trasted so strangely with their own.[5] Did they not have a glimpse too of that great land, the vague memory of which seems to pursue them, and which Columbus was to discover, following the traces of their dreams? It is only known that the existence of an island, traversed by a great river and situated to the west of Ireland, was, on the faith of the Irish, a dogma for mediæval geographers.

The story went that, towards the middle of the sixth century, a monk called Barontus, on his return from voyaging upon the sea, came and craved hospitality at the monastery of Clonfert. Brandan the abbot besought him to give pleasure to the brothers by narrating the marvels of God that he had seen on the high seas. Barontus revealed to them the existence of an island surrounded by fogs, where he had left his disciple Mernoc; it is the Land of Promise that God keeps for his saints. Brandan with seventeen of his monks desired to go in quest of this mysterious land. They set forth in a leather boat, bearing with them as their sole provision a utensil of butter, wherewith to grease the hides of their craft. For seven years they lived thus in their boat, abandoning to God sail and rudder, and only stopping on their course to celebrate the feasts of Christmas and Easter on the back of the king of fishes, Jasconius. Every step of this monastic Odyssey is a miracle, on every isle is a monastery, where the wonders of a fantastical universe respond to the extravagances of a wholly ideal life. Here is the Isle of Sheep, where these animals govern themselves according to their own laws; elsewhere the Paradise of Birds, where the winged race lives after the fashion of monks, singing matins and lauds at the canonical hours. Brandan and his companions celebrate mass here with the birds, and remain with them for fifty days, nourishing themselves with nothing but the singing of their hosts. Elsewhere there is the Isle of Delight, the ideal of monastic life in the midst of the seas. Here no material necessity makes itself felt; the lamps light of themselves for the offices of religion, and never burn out, for they shine with a spiritual light. An absolute stillness reigns in the island; everyone knows precisely the hour of his death; one feels neither cold, nor heat, nor sadness, nor sickness of body or soul. All

[25] On this point see the careful researches of Humboldt in his "History of the Geography of the New Continent," vol. ii.

this has endured since the days of St. Patrick, who so ordained it. The Land of Promise is more marvellous still; there an eternal day reigns; all the plants have flowers, all the trees bear fruits. Some privileged men alone have visited it. On their return a perfume is perceived to come from them, which their garments keep for forty days.

In the midst of these dreams there appears with a surprising fidelity to truth the feeling for the picturesque in Polar voyages —the transparency of the sea, the aspect of bergs and islands of ice melting in the sun, the volcanic phenomena of Iceland, the sporting of whales, the characteristic appearance of the Norwegian fiords, the sudden fogs, the sea calm as milk, the green isles crowned with grass which grows down to the very verge of the waves. This fantastical nature created expressly for another humanity, this strange topography at once glowing with fiction and speaking of truth, make the poem of St. Brandan one of the most extraordinary creations of the human mind, and perhaps the completest expression of the Celtic ideal. All is lovely, pure, and innocent; never has a gaze so benevolent and so gentle been cast upon the earth; there is not a single cruel idea, not a trace of frailty or repentance. It is the world seen through the crystal of a stainless conscience, one might almost say a human nature, as Pelagius wished it, that has never sinned. The very animals participate in this universal mildness. Evil appears under the form of monsters wandering on the deep, or of Cyclops confined in volcanic islands; but God causes them to destroy one another, and does not permit them to do hurt to the good.

We have just seen how, around the legend of a monk, the Irish imagination grouped a whole cycle of physical and maritime myths. The Purgatory of St. Patrick became the framework of another series of fables, embodying the Celtic ideas concerning the other life and its different conditions.[26] Perhaps the profoundest instinct of the Celtic peoples is their desire to penetrate the unknown. With the sea before them, they wish to know what lies beyond; they dream of a Promised Land. In the face of the unknown that lies beyond the tomb, they dream of that great journey which the pen of Dante has cele-

[26] See Thomas Wright's excellent dissertation, "St. Patrick's Purgatory" (London, 1844), and Calderon's "The Well of St. Patrick."

brated. The legend tells how while St. Patrick was preaching about Paradise and Hell to the Irish, they confessed that they would feel more assured of the reality of these places if he would allow one of them to descend there, and then come back with information. St. Patrick consented. A pit was dug, by which an Irishman set out upon the subterranean journey. Others wished to attempt the journey after him. With the consent of the abbot of the neighboring monastery, they descended into the shaft, they passed through the torments of Hell and Purgatory, and then each told of what he had seen. Some did not emerge again; those who did laughed no more, and were henceforth unable to join in any gayety. Knight Owen made a descent in 1153, and gave a narrative of his travels which had a prodigious success.

Other legends related that when St. Patrick drove the goblins out of Ireland he was greatly tormented in this place for forty days by legions of black birds. The Irish betook themselves to the spot, and experienced the same assaults which gave them an immunity from purgatory. According to the narrative of Giraldus Cambrensis, the isle which served as the theatre of this strange superstition was divided into two parts. One belonged to the monks, the other was occupied by evil spirits, who celebrated religious rites in their own manner, with an infernal uproar. Some people, for the expiation of their sins, voluntarily exposed themselves to the fury of those demons. There were nine ditches in which they lay for a night, tormented in a thousand different ways. To make the descent it was necessary to obtain the permission of the bishop. His duty it was to dissuade the penitent from attempting the adventure, and to point out to him how many people had gone in who had never come out again. If the devotee persisted, he was ceremoniously conducted to the shaft. He was lowered down by means of a rope, with a loaf and a vessel of water to strengthen him in the combat against the fiend which he proposed to wage. On the following morning the sacristan offered the rope anew to the sufferer. If he mounted to the surface again, they brought him back to the church, bearing the cross and chanting psalms. If he were not to be found, the sacristan closed the door and departed. In more modern times pilgrims to the sacred isles spent nine days there. They passed over to them in a boat hollowed out of the trunk of a tree. Once a day they drank of the water of the lake; processions and stations were performed in the beds or cells of the saints. Upon the ninth day the penitents entered into the shaft. Sermons were preached to them warning them of the danger they were about to run, and they were told of terrible examples. They forgave their enemies and took farewell of one another, as though they were at their last agony. According to contemporary accounts, the shaft was a low and narrow kiln, into which nine entered at a time, and in which the penitents passed a day and a night, huddled and tighty pressed against one another. Popular belief imagined an abyss underneath, to swallow up the unworthy and the unbelieving. On emerging from the pit they went and bathed in the lake, and so their purgatory was accomplished. It would appear from the accounts of eye-witnesses that, to this day, things happen very nearly after the same fashion.

The immense reputation of the purgatory of St. Patrick filled the whole of the Middle Ages. Preachers made appeal to the public notoriety of this great fact, to controvert those who had their doubts regarding purgatory. In the year 1358 Edward III gave to a Hungarian of noble birth, who had come from Hungary expressly to visit the sacred well, letters patent attesting that he had undergone his purgatory. Narratives of those travels beyond the tomb became a very fashionable form of literature; and it is important for us to remark the wholly mythological, and as wholly Celtic, characteristics dominant in them. It is in fact evident that we are dealing with a mystery or local cult, anterior to Christianity, and probably based upon the physical appearance of the country. The idea of purgatory, in its final and concrete form, fared specially well amongst the Bretons and the Irish. Bede is one of the first to speak of it in a descriptive manner, and the learned Mr. Wright very justly observes that nearly all the descriptions of purgatory come from Irishmen, or from Anglo-Saxons who have resided in Ireland, such as St. Fursey, Tundale, the Northumbrian Dryhthelm, and Knight Owen. It is likewise a remarkable thing that only the Irish were able to behold the marvels of their purgatory. A canon from Hemstede in Holland, who descended in 1494, saw nothing at all. Evidently this idea of travels in the other world and its infernal categories, as the Middle Ages accepted it, is

Celtic. The belief in the three circles of existence is again to be found in the " Triads," [27] under an aspect which does not permit one to see any Christian interpolation.

The soul's peregrinations after death are also the favorite theme of the most ancient Armorican poetry. Among the features by which the Celtic races most impressed the Romans were the precision of their ideas upon the future life, their inclination to suicide, and the loans and contracts which they signed with the other world in view. The more frivolous peoples of the South saw with awe in this assurance the fact of a mysterious race, having an understanding of the future and the secret of death. Through the whole of classical antiquity runs the tradition of an Isle of Shadows, situated on the confines of Brittany, and of a folk devoted to the passage of souls, which lives upon the neighboring coast. In the night they hear dead men prowling about their cabin, and knocking at the door. Then they rise up; their craft is laden with invisible beings; on their return it is lighter. Several of these features reproduced by Plutarch, Claudian, Procopius, and Tzetzes would incline one to believe that the renown of the Irish myths made its way into classical antiquity about the first or second century. Plutarch, for example, relates, concerning the Cronian Sea, fables identical with those which fill the legend of St. Malo. Procopius, describing the sacred island of Brittia, which consists of two parts separated by the sea, one delightful, the other given over to evil spirits, seems to have read in advance the description of the purgatory of St. Patrick, which Giraldus Cambrensis was to give seven centuries later. It cannot be doubted for a moment, after the able researches of Messrs. Ozanam, Labitte, and Wright, that to the number of poetical themes which Europe owes to the genius of the Celts, is to be added the framework of the Divine Comedy.

One can understand how greatly this invincible attraction to fables must have discredited the Celtic race in the eyes of nationalities that believed themselves to be more serious. It is in truth a strange thing, that the whole of the mediæval epoch, whilst submitting to the influence of the Celtic imagination,

---

[27] A series of aphorisms under the form of triplets, which give us, with numerous interpolations, the ancient teaching of the bards, and that traditional wisdom which, according to the testimony of the ancients, was transmitted by means of mnemonic verses in the schools of the Druids.

and borrowing from Brittany and Ireland at least half of its poetical subjects, believed itself obliged, for the saving of its own honor, to slight and satirize the people to which it owed them. Even Chrétien de Troyes, for example, who passed his life in exploiting the Breton romances for his own purposes, originated the saying:

"*Les Gallois sont tous par nature
Plus sots que bêtes de pâture.*"

Some English chronicler, I know not who, imagined he was making a charming play upon words when he described those beautiful creations, the whole world of which deserved to live, as "the childish nonsense with which those brutes of Bretons amuse themselves." The Bollandists found it incumbent to exclude from their collection, as apocryphal extravagances, those admirable religious legends, with which no church has anything to compare. The decided leaning of the Celtic race towards the ideal, its sadness, its fidelity, its good faith, caused it to be regarded by its neighbors as dull, foolish, and superstitious. They could not understand its delicacy and refined manner of feeling. They mistook for awkwardness the embarrassment experienced by sincere and open natures in the presence of more artificial natures. The contrast between French frivolity and Breton stubbornness above all led, after the fourteenth century, to most deplorable conflicts, whence the Bretons ever emerged with a reputation for wrong-headedness.

It was still worse, when the nation that most prides itself on its practical good sense found confronting it the people that, to its own misfortune, is least provided with that gift. Poor Ireland, with her ancient mythology, with her purgatory of St. Patrick, and her fantastic travels of St. Brandan, was not destined to find grace in the eyes of English puritanism. One ought to observe the disdain of English critics for these fables, and their superb pity for the Church which dallies with paganism, so far as to keep up usages which are notoriously derived from it. Assuredly we have here a praiseworthy zeal, arising from natural goodness; and yet, even if these flights of imagination did no more than render a little more supportable many sufferings which are said to have no remedy, that after all would be something. Who shall dare to say where, here on earth, is the boundary between reason and dreaming? Which is worth more, the imaginative instinct of man, or the narrow orthodoxy that pretends to remain rational, when speaking of things divine? For my own part, I prefer the frank mythology, with all its vagaries, to a theology so paltry, so vulgar, and so colorless, that it would be wronging God to believe that, after having made the visible world so beautiful he should have made the invisible world so prosaically reasonable.

In presence of the ever-encroaching progress of a civilization which is of no country, and can receive no name, other than that of modern or European, it would be puerile to hope that the Celtic race is in the future to succeed in obtaining isolated expression of its originality. And yet we are far from believing that this race has said its last word. After having put in practice all chivalries, devout and worldly, gone with Peredur in quest of the Holy Grail and fair ladies, and dreamed with St. Brandan of mystical Atlantides, who knows what it would produce in the domain of intellect, if it hardened itself to an entrance into the world, and subjected its rich and profound nature to the conditions of modern thought? It appears to me that there would result from this combination, productions of high originality, a subtle and discreet manner of taking life, a singular union of strength and weakness, of rude simplicity and mildness. Few races have had so complete a poetic childhood as the Celtic; mythology, lyric poetry, epic, romantic imagination, religious enthusiasm—none of these failed them; why should reflection fail them? Germany, which commenced with science and criticism, has come to poetry; why should not the Celtic races, which began with poetry, finish with criticism? There is not so great a distance from one to the other as is supposed; the poetical races are the philosophic races, and at bottom philosophy is only a manner of poetry. When one considers how Germany, less than a century ago, had her genius revealed to her, how a multitude of national individualities, to all appearance effaced, have suddenly risen again in our own days, more instinct with life than ever, one feels persuaded that it is a rash thing to lay down any law on the intermittence and awakening of nations; and that modern civilization, which appeared to be made to absorb them, may perhaps be nothing more than their united fruition.

THE PLURALITY OF INHABITED WORLDS

—

BY

CAMILLE FLAMMARION

CAMILLE FLAMMARION

Camille Flammarion was born at Montigny-le-Roi in 1842. He received his early education at the public schools of Langres, a neighboring town, and at Paris. At the age of fourteen pecuniary difficulties in which his family became involved necessitated his looking for a means of livelihood, and he was apprenticed to an engraver, but in spite of all obstacles he continued his studies, and in 1858 entered the Observatory at Paris as a student of astronomy. Here he remained four years, and before leaving Paris published his first book, " The Plurality of Inhabited Worlds," a work that achieved instant success and gave its young author at once a brilliant reputation. It has been translated into many languages, and still remains one of the most widely read and greatly admired of all his works. At this time, when only twenty years old, Flammarion determined to devote himself to the work of popularizing the science of astronomy. By the time he was twenty-four, three notable books had followed one another in quick succession—" Les mondes imaginaires et les mondes reéls," " Les merveilles célestes," and " Dieu dans la nature."

Flammarion meantime had been one of the most active contributors to " Cosmos," and in 1866 he took charge of the scientific department of the " Siècle." The following year he began a series of popular lectures on astronomy which enhanced his already well established reputation. In 1868 he was nominated president of the scientific section of the Exposition at Havre, but with this exception he resigned from all his official duties and devoted himself henceforth entirely to his life-work. He was now in possession of a moderate income from his writings and lectures. This enabled him to establish a small observatory of his own, which was afterward greatly enlarged by gifts from some of his admirers.

In 1882 Flammarion founded the monthly " Journal d'Astronomie," of which he is still the editor, and in 1887 he founded the Astronomical Society of France, becoming its first president. A complete list of his later works would fill several pages, comprising, as they do, not only printed books, pamphlets, and monographs, but a great number of articles in magazines and even in weekly and daily newspapers, many of which are of great interest and importance. In 1893 Flammarion published a work on the planet Mars and its probable inhabitants, which gave rise to an extensive and animated popular discussion, and greatly increased the popular interest in astronomy.

Flammarion's style is light and graceful, vivid and fluent. As a master of the art of popular exposition of subjects naturally abstruse and difficult he has few equals in literature. Indeed, it is precisely because his work is so notably superior to that of compilers of textbooks and ordinary writers on scientific subjects that his name deserves a place among the masters of prose. He is by no means merely an interpreter of the discoveries of others, but an original investigator of no slight merit.

THE PLURALITY OF INHABITED WORLDS

THE astronomical truths which have been the subject of our conversation doubtless prove the high character of the human mind which aspires to them, and which, scrutinizing the organized laws of the universe, has been able to determine the causes which regulate the harmony of the cosmos and secure its perpetuity. No doubt, it is good for man, this spiritual atom inhabiting a material atom, to have penetrated the mysteries of creation, and to have been exalted to the knowledge of these sublime heights, the contemplation of which alone overwhelms and annihilates him. But if the universe remains to man only a great material mechanism, moved by physical forces, if nature is nothing in his eyes but a gigantic laboratory, where the elements are mingled blindly under the most various and casual forms; in a word, if this admirable and magnificent science of the heavens confines the efforts of the human mind eternally to the geometry of the heavenly bodies, the science would never attain its real end, and it would stop at the moment of reaping the fruit of its immense labors. It would remain supremely incomplete if the universe were never anything to it but an assemblage of inert bodies floating in space under the action of material forces.

The philosopher must go further. He must not confine himself to seeing under a more or less distinct form the great body of nature. But, stretching forth the hand, he must feel under the material envelope the life which circulates in great waves. God's empire is not the empire of death; it is the empire of life.

We live on a world which is no exception among the heavenly bodies, and which has not received the least privilege. It is the third of the planets which revolve round the sun and one of the smallest among them. Without going beyond our system, other planets are much more important than it; Jupiter, for instance, is 1,414 times greater, and Saturn 734 times. While it appears to us the most important of the universe, it is in reality lost in the immensity of the worlds which people the heavens, and the whole creation does not guess at its existence.

Of the planets of our own system there are only four, the inhabitants of which can know that the earth exists; these are, Mercury, Venus, Mars, and Jupiter; and even to this last one it is most of the time invisible in the solar aureola. Now, while the Earth is thus lost amid worlds more important than itself, the other worlds are in the same conditions of habitability as those that we observe on the Earth. On these planets, as on our own, the generous rays of the sun pour forth heat and light; on them, as here, years, months, and days succeed each other, drawing with them the seasons which, from time to time, support the conditions of existence; on them, as here, a transparent atmosphere envelops the inhabited surface with a protecting climate, gives rise to meteoric movements, and develops those ravishing beauties which celebrate sunrise and sunset. On them as here, vaporous clouds rise from the ocean with the deep waves, and spreading themselves under the heaven, carry dew to the parched-up regions. This great movement of life which circulates over the Earth is not confined to this little planet; the same causes develop elsewhere the same effects, and on many among these strange worlds, far from noticing the absence of the riches with which the Earth is endowed, an abundance of wealth of which our abode only possesses the first-fruits is observed. By the side of these bodies, the Earth is essentially an inferior world in many repects; from the unsatisfactory conditions of geological stability of which the terrestrial spheroid reminds us, its surface being only a thin pellicle, to the fatal laws which govern life on this Earth where death reigns supreme.

If, on the one hand, the other worlds have conditions of habitability quite as powerful, if not more so, as the terrestrial conditions, on the other hand, the Earth, considered in itself, appears to us like an overflowing cup whence life issues on all sides. It seems that to create is so necessary to the order of nature that the smallest piece of matter of suitable properties does not exist without serving as an abode of living beings.

THE PLURALITY OF INHABITED WORLDS 461

While the telescope discovered in the heavens fresh fields for creation, the microscope showed us below the range of visibility the field of invisible life, and that, not content with spreading life everywhere where there is matter to receive it, from the primitive period when this globe had scarcely left its fiery cradle, to our days, nature still heaps up existence, to the detriment of existence itself.

Leaves of plants are fields of microscopical flocks of which certain species, although invisible to the naked eye, are real elephants beside other beings, whose extreme diminutiveness has not prevented an admirable system of organization for the carrying on of their ephemeral life. Animals themselves serve as an abode to races of parasites which, in their turn, are themselves the abode of parasites still smaller. Under another aspect the infinity of life presents a correlative character in its diversity. Its force is so powerful that no element appears capable of struggling advantageously against it, and tending to spread itself in every place, nothing can stop its action. From the high regions of the air, where the winds carry the germs, to the oceanic depths, where they undergo a pressure equal to several hundred atmospheres, and where the most complete night extends its eternal sovereignty; from the burning climate of the equator and the hot sources of volcanic regions to the icy regions and the solid seas of the polar circle, life extends its empire like an immense network, surrounding the whole Earth, amusing itself with all obstacles, and passing over all abysses, so that there is not in the world any district which can pretend to be beyond its absolute sovereignty.

It is by studies founded on this double consideration, the insignificance of the Earth in creation, and the abundance of life on its surface, that we are able to raise ourselves to the first real principles on which the demonstration of the universal habitation of the heavenly bodies must be fixed. For a long time man could confine himself to the study of phenomena; for a long time he must still keep to the direct and simple observation of physical appearances, in order that science may acquire the precision which constitutes its value. But now this entrance of truth can be passed, and thought, outstripping matter, may rise to the idea of intellectual things. In the bosom of these distant worlds it sees universal life plunging its immense roots;

and at their surface it sees this life spreading itself, and intelligence establishing its throne.

Founded on the astronomical basis, the only possible foundation, researches made in the domain of the physical sciences, from celestial mechanism to biology, and in that of the philosophical science from ontology to morals, the old idea of the plurality of worlds has risen to the rank of a doctrine. The evidence of this truth has been revealed to the eyes of all those who are impartially and entirely given up to the study of nature. It does not come within the bounds of this discourse to enter fully on this philosophical aspect of creation; but if I consider it in itself as the logical conclusion of astronomical studies, I owe it to my readers at least to offer them as a modest conclusion of the narratives which they have followed up to this time, the principal results to which we have arrived on this great and beautiful question of the existence of life on the surface of the heavenly bodies.

In the first place, the following is the first consideration established on the astronomical character of the world and its history: If the reader follow the philosophical march of modern astronomy, he will discover that from the moment when the movement of the Earth and the volume of the sun were known astronomers and philosophers found it strange that a body so magnificent was solely employed to light up and warm a little imperceptible world, arranged in company with many others under a supreme rule. The absurdity of such an opinion was still more striking, when they found that Venus was a planet of the same dimensions as the Earth, with mountains and plains, seasons and years, days and nights, similar to our own; the analogy was extended to the conclusion that these two worlds, similar in their formation, were also similar in their rôle in the universe; if Venus was without population, the Earth ought to be equally so; and conversely, if the Earth was peopled Venus must be so also. But afterward, when the gigantic worlds of Jupiter and Saturn were observed, surrounded with their splendid retinues, they were compelled to refuse living beings to the preceding little planets, if they did not equally endow these, and moreover give to Jupiter and Saturn men much superior to those of Venus and the Earth. And indeed, is it not evident that the absurdity of the immovability of the Earth has been perpetuated a thousand times more extravagantly in this ill-conceived final causation, the object of which is to place our globe in the first rank of celestial bodies? Is it not evident that this world has been thrown without any distinction into the planetary cluster, and that it is not better adapted than the others to be the exclusive seat of life and intelligence? How little founded is the sentiment which animates us when we fancy that the universe is created for us, poor beings lost on a world, and that if we should disappear from the scene, this vast universe would be marred, like an assemblage of inert bodies, and deprived of light! If on the morrow not one of us was to awake, and if the night which, in each diurnal period enwraps the world, forever sealed the closed eyelids of all living beings, is it to be believed that henceforth the sun would no longer pour out its light and heat, and that the powers of nature would cease their eternal movements? No; these distant worlds that we have just reviewed would continue the cycle of their existence, rocked on the permanent forces of gravitation, and bathed in the luminous aureola that the orb of day produces round its brilliant focus. The Earth that we inhabit is only one of the smallest bodies grouped round this focus, and its degree of habitation has nothing which distinguishes it amid its companions. For an instant place yourself at a distance in space whence you can embrace the whole solar system, and suppose that the planet in which you saw light is unknown to you. For to give yourself freely to the present study you must no longer consider the Earth as your country, or prefer it to other abodes; and then contemplate without pretension and with an ultra-terrestrial eye the planetary worlds which circulate round the focus of our life! If you suspect the phenomena of existence, if you imagine that certain planets are inhabited, if you are taught that life has chosen certain worlds in which to spread the germs of its productions, do you intend to people this small globe of the Earth, before having established in superior worlds the wonders of living creation? Or if you have the intention of settling yourself on a body whence you can embrace the splendor of the heavens, and on which you can enjoy the benefits of a rich and fertile nature, shall you choose as an abode this mean Earth which is eclipsed by so many resplendent spheres? In reply, reader, and it is the least strong and most rigorous conclusion that we can draw from the preceding considerations, let us agree that " the Earth has no marked preëminence in the solar system to entitle it to be the only inhabited world, and that, astronomically speaking, the other planets are arranged as well as it is as abodes of life."

A second consideration, founded on the varieties of living beings on the surface of the terrestrial globe, on the infinite power of nature, that no obstacle has ever stopped, and on the eloquent spectacle of the infinity of life itself in the terrestrial world, conducts the argument into a new order of ideas: " Nature knows the secret of all things, puts into action the most feeble as well as the most powerful forces, renders all its creations answerable, and constitutes beings according to the worlds and ages, without the one or the other being able to place any obstacle in the way of the manifestation of its power. Hence it follows that the habitability and habitation of the planets are a necessary complement to their existence, and that of all the conditions enumerated, not one can stop the manifestation of life on each of these worlds. But let us add another observation which will complete the preceding; let us think for an instant of our forced ignorance in this little isle of the great archipelago where destiny has bound us, and of the difficulty we experience in searching into the secrets and power of nature. Let us prove that, on the one hand, we do not know all the causes which have been able to influence, and which still influence, the manifestation of life, its support and propagation on the surface of the Earth; and that, on the other hand, we are still far from knowing all the principles of existence which propagate in other worlds very dissimilar creations. Scarcely have we penetrated those which regulate the daily functions of life; scarcely have we been able to study the physical properties of the media, the action of light and electricity, the effects of heat and magnetism. There exist others which go on constantly under our eyes, and which have not yet been studied nor even discovered. How vain then would it be to wish to oppose to the possibility of planetary existences the superficial and narrow principles of what we call our sciences? What cause would be able to struggle with advantage against the effective power of nature, and to place obstacles to the existence of beings on all these magnificent globes which revolve round the sun! What extravagance to regard the little world where we first saw light as the only temple, or as the model of nature!"

Impressed with the value of the providential design of creation, these considerations become more imperious still. "That our planet was made to be lived in, is incontestable, not only because the beings which people it are here under our eyes, but again because the connection which exists between these beings and the regions in which they live brings the inevitable conclusion that the idea of habitation is immediately connected with the idea of habitability. Now this fact is an argument in our favor; for, unless we consider the creative power as illogical, or as inconsistent with its real manner of acting, it must be understood that the habitability of the planets imperiously demands their habitation. To what end have they received years, seasons, months, days; and why does not life come forth on the surface of these worlds which enjoy, like ours, the benefits of nature, and which receive, like ours, the rays of the same sun? Why these snows of Mars, which melt each spring, and descend to water its continents? Why these clouds of Jupiter, which spread shade and freshness over its immense plains? Why this atmosphere of Venus, which bathes its valleys and mountains? O splendid worlds, which float afar from us in the heavens! Would it be possible that cold sterility was ever the immutable sovereign of yonder desolate regions? Would it be possible that this magnificence, which seems to be your appanage, was given to solitary and bare worlds, where the lonely rocks eternally regard each other in sullen silence? Fearful spectacle in its immense immutability; and more incomprehensible than if Death had passed over the Earth in fury, and with a single stroke mowed down the living population which enlightens its surface, thus enveloping in one ruin all the children of life, and leaving it to roll in space like a corpse in an eternal tomb!"

Thus it is that, under whatever aspect we regard creation, the doctrine of the plurality of inhabited worlds is formed and presented as the only explanation of the final end—as the justification of the existence of material forms—as the crowning of astronomical truths. The summary conclusions which we have just quoted are established, logically and without difficulty, by observed facts; and when, having contemplated the universe under its different aspects, the mind is astonished at not having sooner conceived this striking truth, it feels within itself that the demonstration of such evidence is no longer necessary, and that it ought to accept it, even with no other reasons in its favor than the condition of the terrestrial atom compared with the rest of the immense universe. Humbled by this spectacle, one can but proclaim the luminous truth in a transport, disdaining all researches.

"Ah! if our sight was piercing enough to discover, where we only see brilliant points on the black background of the sky, resplendent suns which revolve in the expanse, and the inhabited worlds which follow them in their path, if it were given to us to embrace in a general *coup d'œil* these myriads of fire-based systems; and if, advancing with the velocity of light, we could traverse from century to century, this unlimited number of suns and spheres, without ever meeting any limit to this prodigious immensity where God brings forth worlds and beings: looking behind, but no longer knowing in what part of the infinite to find this grain of dust called the Earth, we should stop fascinated and confounded by such a spectacle, and uniting our voice to the concert of universal nature we should say from the depths of our soul: Almighty God! how senseless we were to believe that there was nothing beyond the Earth, and that our abode alone possessed the privilege of reflecting Thy greatness and power!"